GENEALOGY OF THE
BRUMBACH FAMILIES

INCLUDING THOSE USING THE FOLLOW-
ING VARIATIONS OF THE ORIGINAL
NAME, BRUMBAUGH, BRUMBACH, BRUM-
BACK, BROMBAUGH, BROWNBACK, *and*
MANY OTHER CONNECTED FAMILIES

BY

GAIUS MARCUS BRUMBAUGH, M. S., M. D.,

Member Pennsylvania German Society, Pennsylvania Historical Society, American Association
for Advancement of Science, American Medical Association,
Medical Society of D. C., etc.

VOLUME 1

SECTIONS A - D
PAGES 1 - 348

FREDERICK H. HITCHCOCK

GENEALOGICAL PUBLISHER

105 WEST FORTIETH STREET   NEW YORK

THE
BRUMBACH FAMILIES

One thousand copies of this
book have been printed from
type and the type distributed
This is copy Number

This Publication
is Affectionately Dedicated
to the
MEMORY OF THE MOTHERS AND FATHERS
of the within named Descendants
and especially to
MARIA BAER (FRANK) BRUMBAUGH
and
[E226] ANDREW BOELUS[5] BRUMBAUGH, M D.
Beloved Parents of the Author

CONTENTS

LIST OF ILLUSTRATIONS

PREFACE

" Biography is the only true history "—Emerson

" Biography is allowed on all hands to be one of the most attractive and profitable kinds of reading."—Archbishop Wheatley

" Every man is a bundle of his ancestors "—Emerson

Who and what were my ancestors? Such information is of vital importance if the present would improve upon the past, and yet honor the ancestry. In the subject matter of the above quotations, in the complexity of the general family lines under consideration, in the study of heredity problems, especially those of consanguineous marriages and their effects[a], in the desire to fashion a fitting monument to the ancestry, and to help and encourage both the present and future generations—in all such matters the reader will gather motives for the preparation of this volume   The definite purpose to ultimately undertake the project was formed while long ago listening to conversations between Father [E226] and Grandfather [E68], held upon the site of the original building at the " old homestead " in Penn Twp, Huntingdon Co, Pa.   I have very often regretted that my questions were then so superficial, and that we were unable to secure some important historical papers pertaining to [E2] Jacob[2] Brumbach

There was a great, cracked iron kettle at the old homestead which had been dropped from an old Conestoga wagon in making the difficult fording of the Susquehanna River, and recovered from it, as several of the ancestors were returning to " Woodcock Valley " from " the Gushehoppa " or " Gushehoppen region," " where some Brumbachs yet remained "   George[3] [E13] said the ancestors came from Germany and France, but he seemed not to have mentioned immigrants other than the lines " C " and " E "   They passed through eastern Pennsylvania into Maryland, and some went West and South, while others went into Cumberland Co, Pa   The latter made occasional trips to " Gushehoppa "   Some references to this general region are found upon pp 134-137

Early German and other colonists, especially in Pennsylvania, usually buried their dead on their farms in family or community plots   The graves were marked by field stones, or by slate slabs, using merely initials and rarely the dates of birth and death   Positive knowledge of the facts thus perished through death, loss of memory, and migrations   Family Bibles and other

---

[a] Those interested in the matter should write to Prof Charles B Davenport, Eugenics Record Office, Cold Spring Harbor, Long Island, N. Y   In connection with the Carnegie Institution, he is actively directing researches in experimental evolution, etc

records have been destroyed by fire, or lost. In one instance a Bible was sold in York Co, Pa., " to a man from Philadelphia for fifty cents," and it has never been located This actual occurrence, fortunately, is but illustrative, and did not happen in our families—but some of our valuable records have been destroyed because " *they were old* "

As a rule Brumbach-Brumbaugh and related families have not sought public office,[a] and this commonly fruitful source of information in public records has been closed Land records, however, have been of the greatest assistance. Will books but infrequently assisted, owing to the early and general practice of dividing property upon retiring from active business life, or of permitting the laws of descent to determine the division of property.

The military records ordinarily furnished extensive material for family history. Though loyal, the large majority of the families herein traced adhered to the non-resistent views, and military sources of information are therefore also of comparatively little assistance. In connection with the Friend, Mennonite, German Baptist and other church belief and practices, the following extract[b] is of interest:

" The Draft—Brethren who are drafted may pay $300 00 and be exempt, or be assigned to hospital duty, or to take charge of ' freedmen,' but will not be forced into the ranks "

The earlier data, gathered partly by Father, was taken up by me in 1889, and the search was pressed as opportunity permitted Later the writer learned that others were working upon our separate family histories, and finally learned that death had terminated their efforts. It was finally learned that Ephraim[5] Brumbaugh [E345], historian of the " Descendants of Conrad[3] Brumbaugh " [E9], preserved the material gathered by his late brother, Andrew[5] Brumbaugh [E344], in some fourteen years of persistent inquiry This material was secured and was found to deal largely with the descendants of Conrad[3] [E9], and of Margaret[3] (Brumbaugh) Fouse [E8]. About 1907, after a long search, the records of the late Edmund Green[4] Brumbaugh [G160][c] were secured from his widow. These records represented about nine years' search amongst the descendants of Hermanus Emanuel[1] Brumbach [G1], and without that assistance, and the later co-operation of Albert Jacob[4] Brumbach [G87],[d] Section G would scarcely have been included in this volume.

[a] Hon. Clement Laird[5] Brumbaugh [C203], now Deputy Superintendent of Insurance for Ohio, was elected a Member of Congress from Columbus, O, Nov 5, 1912, too late to note upon page 229. Others of the name have served in State Legislatures, but he is apparently the first to serve in the National body See Plate 61½
[b] *Christian Family Companion*, Vol. I, No. 2, p 11, Oct 4, 1864.
[c] Pl 197, p 785
[d] Page 778

The records of both Andrew Brumbaugh and Edmund Green Brumbaugh, and those of Father, preserved the results of personal interviews, letters, etc, from the oldest surviving persons both in the family lines and without them. The compiler carefully digested, collated, and made everything to assist in the completion of the present "progress report." Their basis work was most important, and the compiler profoundly regrets that they could not have survived to assist in completing this volume, which is evolved along wholly different plans. Their records included letters from numerous deceased ancestors, and a comprehensive plan should be formed for the union of the different Memorial Associations, or Reunions, and the permanent preservation of this data

The late Judge Jefferson[5] Brumback [D231][a] wrote of his investigations in Virginia tracing the descendants of The Widow[2] Brumbach [D2], and during his lifetime his assistance and interest in the project of the writer were most cordial. There were also found letters from Garrett Ellwood[5] Brownback [A132],[b] who was especially interested in the descendants of Gerhard[1] Brumbach [A1]. His co-operation with the compiler has been constant and most encouraging in the dark hours. He has preserved valuable records, at his own expense furnished many half tones for Section A, and has already loaned $200 to help the compiler to publish this volume. Orville Sanford[6] Brumback [D263][c] was also represented by letters to the late workers, has continued his enlarged interest in the undertaking, has furnished much information concerning his family lines, and has paid for many half tones in Section D. John Gainer[5] Fouse [E8-ix-6][d] and his brother, Adam Gainer[5] Fouse [E8-ix-8],[e] visited the late Andrew[5] Brumbaugh [E344] and encouraged and assisted him materially by securing facts concerning the Fouse families. That active interest and assistance has been continued to the compiler, and a volume, "Fouse Families in America," is planned by us for later publication

It has been very difficult to secure photographs, but an unusual number for a family history are reproduced in the belief that this expense will assure a more acceptable and valuable volume. A few composite or type photographs were planned, but this is reserved for the future. One old record and some facts were secured by one co-worker, who drove thirty miles through snow to secure them. Such assistance, together with that of Joseph Martin[5] Brumback [D256] and Frances Elizabeth[5] Brumback [D259]—see pp 270, 278, 330, Pls 67-70—have been intensely encouraging to the compiler.

[a] Page 323, Pl 78
[b] Plates 39-41, p 116
[c] Plate 81, p. 331.
[d] Plate 117, p 102
[e] Plate 118, p. 403

Dr Martin Grove[6] Brumbaugh [E682] took the necessary time from his busy life to read the page proofs for the volume and to kindly write the Introduction His continuous interest and decided commendation of the results secured, and his co-operation throughout the later stages of the project, are gratefully acknowledged

Mr Eugene Alleman, P M at Warsaw, Ind , kindly furnished information leading to a considerable number of hitherto unobtainable facts concerning Brumbaugh families in Kosciusko and Elkhart Counties, Ind

Mr. Luther R Kelker, Custodian of the Public Records, Harrisburg, Pa., rendered important help, and was instrumental in directing me to Mr Karl Brombach, Karlsruhe, Baden (see p 4), who has been of the greatest assistance in searching the foreign field for facts and illustrations Chalmers Sherfey[6] Brumbaugh [E756] also materially assisted in the study of the coats-of-arms (see pp 21-25, 616) Messrs Stephen Olop, Denver, Colo , Emory Alburtus[6] Zook [E231-n], and Michael Alvin Gruber, Washington, D C , very kindly assisted in making translations, etc.

The treasures of the Library of Congress were kindly placed at my disposal for reference and study (much is there yet ungleaned) , and the officials and attendants there, as also in other libraries, court houses, etc , etc , have been most helpful and courteous

Mr. Ernest Lindsley Crandall, Washington, D C , made the excellent photographs of most of the records herein produced, and deserves especial credit for the careful manner in which this often difficult work was done The half tones were made by Messrs Joyce & Co , Washington, D C., and Gatchell & Manning, Philadelphia, Pa The publication was produced under the direction of the publisher, Mr. Frederick H Hitchcock, of New York Their combined results speak for their workmanship, and the author hereby expresses his thanks for their continuous interest and zealous assistance.

[E105] Jesse K——[5] Brumbaugh, West Milton, O , and [E652] Noah Jay[6] Brumbaugh, and his wife, of Washington, D. C., [E348] Isaac[5] Brumbaugh, and others, at Hartville, O , [E1965] John Milton[5] Brumbaugh, Elkhart, Ind , [E2024] Melvin Washington[6] Brumbaugh, Maitland, Mo ; [E3054] Isaac[4] Brumbaugh, Huntington, Ind , O J D Haughtelin, Panora, Iowa, [C12] Jacob Brown (died Oct 11, 1912), Cumberland, Md , [C34] Rebecca (Clopper) Brumbaugh, Greencastle, Pa ; [C76] David Stuckey[4] Brumbaugh, Roaring Spring, Pa , and [D104] Lucy Gertrude (Lauck) Brumback, Stanley, Va , are a few of the many other active co-workers The number of the latter is so great as to render separate enumeration impractical.

The personal relations resulting from our work have become of much value, and it is with special gratitude that I return sincere thanks for all assistance extended to me Permit me to further ask a continuance of active help in securing extensive distribution of the completed book

The volume presents much authentic data hitherto inaccessible The great mass of facts has been built year by year, constantly verified and changed, through correspondence and visits to members of the families mentioned The comprehensive index gives numerous surnames only, to economize space, and it is one continuous whole carefully alphabeted It will enable searchers to quickly locate available information, and the general methods followed will doubtless be helpful The results are often fragmentary and incomplete. Sometimes differing dates have been given by members of the same family, and the rule has been to give preference to the oldest records, letters, etc., and such records at times have been found in far-distant places Over 10,000 envelopes containing letters and circulars of inquiry have been sent by the writer during the past four years In one instance 26 letters were sent to members of one family before the important replies were received, and the facts are condensed into three printed lines of the book Special thanks are extended to the faithful ones who lessened the labors, and encouraged, by speedily replying to troublesome inquiries These often involved trips through snow and ice-bound cemeteries, etc., etc.

Especial efforts have resulted in giving full given and middle names (a practice far too rare from the historian's and genealogist's standpoint), and to include the *female* ancestry *All ancestry is dualistic.* The marriages are italicized. Intermarriages in the direct line of descent were at first set in upper case letters, but in most instances these have been changed to italics The trouble, delay and expense involved in the change are the cause of the remaining exceptions to the italicizing rule Money has never been requested or received for the insertion of biographies, and some persons are yet unaware that extensive family details are here first published Completeness and authenticity have been the aim Owing to the wideness of the research, it is believed that a large majority of readers will find herein facts much in excess of personal knowledge, even in his or her own line Such has been the testimony of those who have seen portions of the work   .

CASH SUBSCRIBERS (BEFORE PUBLICATION)

ALASKA, *Fairbanks*—Raymond Brumbaugh [E2202]
CALIFORNIA, *Covina*—Mahlon Faulkender Brumbaugh [E779] (3 copies)
   Los Angeles—Lyman Brumbaugh Stookey [C77-11] (2 copies).

COLORADO, *Atchee*—Mary Elizabeth (Brumbaugh) Grimes [E3169].

    Colorado Springs—Newton N—. Brumback, M D [D241]

DISTRICT OF COLUMBIA, *Washington*—Noah Jay Brumbaugh [E652], Cora
    C Curry, Michael Alvin Gruber, Elizabeth P (Brumbaugh) La
    Grange [E596]

ILLINOIS, *Chicago*—Arthur Henry Brumback, M. D [D350], Roscoe Philip
    Brumbaugh [E1919], Saml. T Felmlee, M D [C107-n]

    Decatur—Joseph Marion Brownback [A150].

    Rockford—Elias Guilford Brumbaugh [C175].

INDIANA, *Elkhart*—John Milton Brumbaugh [E1965]

    Goshen—Mary Etta Bowser [E1753-vi].

    Huntington—Isaac Brumbaugh [E3054]

    Pendleton—Orlando W Brownback, M D [A84].

IOWA, *Glendon*—Lydia Nodle Ommen [E44-vi]

    Kingsley—Elizabeth (Faulkender) Nicodemus [E3013-v].

KANSAS, *Courtland*—Simon Jacob Snider, M. D [C3-iii]

MARYLAND, *Baltimore*—Chalmers Sherfey Brumbaugh [E756]

MISSOURI, *Easton*—Adam L Miller [E8-iii-3]

    Kansas City—Philip Shelley Brown [C3-ii], Hermann Brumback [D363].

    Maitland—Alwyn Leo [E2026], Melvin W [E2024] and Milton Clar-
    ence [E2025] Brumbaugh

    Rombauer—Arthur Wilson Zoll [E306-ii] (4 copies)

MONTANA, *Billings*—John E. Kurtz [E953]

    Butte—David John Brumbaugh [E1375]

NEBRASKA, *Omaha*—Mary Elizabeth (Brerbower) Klapp [A134-n]

NEW YORK, *New York*—Ernest de Mary Brumback, M. D [D370]

OHIO, *Akron*—Catherine J. (Brumbaugh) Fuedner [E721], Susie (Brum-
    baugh) Morter [E361]

    Atwater—Henry P Brumbaugh [E354]

    Canton—Emmet Clayton [E367] and Della [E366] Brumbaugh; Ange-
    line B (Brumbaugh) Summers [F933] (3 copies)

    Columbus—Clement Laird Brumbaugh [C203]

    Dayton—Granville W. Brumbaugh [E651]

    East Akron—Phoebe (Brumbaugh) Carver [E365]

    Forest—Isabella C. (Smith) Brumbaugh [G160]

    Granville—Arthur Marion Brumback [D369].

    Greenville—Abraham Brumbaugh [E307]

    Hartville—Daniel Lewis Brumbaugh [E368], Eli Brumbaugh [E356],
    Ephraim Brumbaugh [E345], Isaac Brumbaugh [E348], Jacob J

Brumbaugh [E720], Samuel Brumbaugh [E351], Nancy (Brumbaugh-Shafer) Harley [E346], Elizabeth (Brumbaugh) Swinehart [E349], John Chapman Whitacre [E210].

OHIO, *Kent*—Susan (Brumbaugh) Fox [E353].

Louisville—Elsie Pearl (Summers) Mock.

New Berlin—Ella Geidlinger [E362], Isaac Markley [E15-xi].

Seville—Wm. Grant Brumbaugh [E2152].

Suffield—Lydia (Brumbaugh) Steffy [E355].

Tallmadge—Allen Brumbaugh [E946]

Thornville—Rebecca Brumback [D238].

Tippecanoe City—Elmer Brumbaugh [E746]

Toledo—Orville Sanford Brumback [D263].

Union—John H. Rinehart [E64-vi].

Van Wert—Saida May (Brumback) Antrim [D266], David La Doyt Brumback [D264], Brumback Library, Estella (Brumback) Reed [D265].

West Milton—Jacob Henry Brumbaugh [E221], Jesse K—. Brumbaugh [E105].

PENNSYLVANIA, *Altoona*—Arthur St Clair Brumbaugh, M D [C207].

Clover Creek—Geo. Hoover Brumbaugh [E3071], Henry Dilling Brumbaugh [E183].

Defiance—Henry Holsinger Brumbaugh [E3141].

Greencastle—Rebecca (Clopper) Brumbaugh [C33], Eliza Jane (Brumbaugh) Hoke [C165], Mary Catherine Shrader [C160].

Henrietta—Mary Nicodemus (Brumbaugh) Hagey [E3095], Moses Robert Brumbaugh [E3168]

Huntingdon—Henry Boyer Brumbaugh [E276], Jacob H—. Brumbaugh [E232], John Boyer Brumbaugh [E278], Benj. Simonton Fouse [E8-viii-1], Juniata College Library, Emma A (Miller) Replogle, Emory Albertus Zook [E231-ii]

James Creek—Geo Boyer Brumbaugh [E225].

Juniata—Martin Pote Brumbaugh [C328]

Linfield—Garrett Ellwood Brownback [A132] (10 copies).

Martinsburg—Mary (Brumbaugh) Clapper [E215].

New Enterprise—Chas Ober Brumbaugh [C368], John Furry Brumbaugh [C320]

Philadelphia—Henry Lee Brumback [D382], Martin Grove Brumbaugh [E682] (3 copies), Adam Gainer Fouse [E8-ix-8] (3 copies), Levi Gainer Fouse [E8-ix-9] (2 copies), Historical Society of Pennsyl-

vania, Jesse Brownback Kimes [A29-iii], Mary Rosanna (Brownback) Sampson [A118], Flora B. Parks, Melvin B Summers [E933-i].

PENNSYLVANIA, *Pittsburgh*—Saml Longenecker Brumbaugh [C399], John Garner Fouse [E8-ix-6]

Reading—Albert Jacob Brumbach [G87] (8 copies)

Roaring Spring—David Stuckey Brumbaugh [C69], Horace Atlee Brumbaugh [C501]

Rochester—Mary Eshleman Gates [C101-i].

Royersford—Ulysses Sidney Grant Finkbiner [A123-iv].

Susquehanna—Geo Walton Brownback [A343]

Trappe—Edward Goodwin Brownback [A160]

Woodbury—J. C Stayer.

SOUTH DAKOTA, *Dunlap*—Geo. Washington Brumbaugh [E887]

TEXAS, *Denison*—David Irvin Brumbaugh [C367]

UTAH, *Salt Lake*—Lawrence McKinstry Brumbaugh [C386]

VIRGINIA, *Luray*—John Pendleton Grove [D41-iii].

Stanley—Lucy Gertrude (Lauck) Brumback [D104]

WASHINGTON, *Seattle*—Daniel Albert Brumbaugh [E2204] (2 copies)

Tacoma—Wm Henry Harrison Brumbaugh [E3120]

Wenatchee—Geo Washington Buntain [E569]

To the above subscribers who have advanced the cash, or half of same, for 150 copies, thus materially lessening my financial burden; to those who have also in advance ordered 106 copies, to be paid for upon delivery, to those who pledge themselves to assist in placing the remainder of the edition, and to all of the numerous co-workers in the United States and in parts of Europe, I take pleasure in extending greetings and in cordially thanking you

Errors doubtless exist. It will be considered a favor if attention be at once called to any such, and a separate pamphlet may be prepared to include such corrections and additions Your opinion of the results secured will also be appreciated. It is hoped that the volume may prove of much interest, stimulating in loyalty, unifying, and helpful in many other ways to those who may read its pages and look at the illustrations

Gaius Marcus Brumbaugh.

905 Massachusetts Ave., N W., Washington, D. C
November 12, 1912

INTRODUCTION

Biography is concrete history. The story of a life is the story of the race concreted The understanding of a life is in no unimportant way the understanding of an age The record of a family through successive generations is a large chapter in the history of the race To trace this record through the centuries and across the seas is a labor which only the trained spirit imbued with sacrificing love can adequately undertake

I have long wished that someone would gather the broken threads of my family and patiently and capably weave them into a connected and coherent whole. The difficulties in the way seemed to render the task prohibitive The family belonged to the Upper Palatine in Germany. It grew and wrought and worshipped along the historic Rhine and under the snow-clad Alps Its gradual increase and development contributed, I believe, no insignificant part in the history of the Fatherland. Just what it did and who the workers were no one knew.

Imbued with the spirit of religious freedom and wrought to protest against prevailing social and religious ideals, it broke away during the 18th century from its traditional moorings and came to America Here the family found itself a German-speaking group in an English colony Dispersed and denationalized, its records were lost and the task of the biographer made difficult to the point of despair. By bitter experience and by religious conviction much that had meaning for this world was lost in the holy enterprise of securing an assured entrance into the world to be Pious concern for the future rendered the family largely indifferent to the present.

All this complicated the work of the author Only those familiar with the task of writing personal history through the centuries and in different countries, with a forbidding sea between, can appreciate the gigantic task Dr Gaius Marcus Brumbaugh has here undertaken

And how splendidly has the work been done! With an industry and an intelligence worthy of the greatest commendation, he has for many years, with many discouragements and few encouragements, steadily traced the story and collated the records until at last and with almost inconceivable skill he has given us the record of the family, individual by individual, to the present time.

A service so signally well performed is worthy of all commendation, and merits the hearty appreciation and support of all those that love their family

and welcome the narrative of its development. There is in the volume abundant evidence to justify the conviction that our ancestors were God-fearing and God-serving people, who through the ages steadily walked honestly before men and humbly before God

There is also ample warrant for the claim that here in America, by rigid adherence to the homely virtues of honesty, frugality and industry, they have contributed only good to the country, and have left a record sacredly significant and worthy of unstinted praise and noble emulation.

By intermarriage the Brumbaugh family is closely identified with our worthy families, like the Groves, the Boyers, the Fouses, the Garners, the Hoovers, the Replogles, the Rineharts, the Studebakers, the Stutsmans, the Winelands, etc, etc. To trace these related lines of family life up and down the Piedmont Plateau, into the valleys between the Blue and the Allegheny Mountains, into Virginia, and out over the boundless plateaus of the West, and even along the Pacific coast, was an heroic effort and added to the task of the author additional difficulties These labors have been notably well done, and the result is most satisfactory. These groups, like the strictly "Brumbach" families here enumerated, are among the sturdy stock whose unflagging zeal and industry are alike commendable

It is worth much to be a member of any family whose achievements are so memorable It is worth more to add to the lustre of the family name by living under the more favored skies of today a life as ideally worthy as that of our fathers. To honor them best demands of us the same noble enterprise in all industrial, social, intellectual, and religious endeavor

A somewhat extended acquaintance with other family biographies leads me to say that the author of this volume has done his work exceptionally well It is a monumental effort I may be pardoned a personal reference The inherent strength and virility of the family I think is best shown by the leading part it took in the intellectual revival of the family at the close of the 19th century Around the story of the founding of religious papers, colleges, and professional careers, the family name rests like a halo. In that splendid galaxy, whose example has been guidance and inspiration to the writer, no one in the family is held in more reverent regard than the father of the author, my uncle, Dr. Andrew Boelus Brumbaugh [E226]. Others wrought with him and wrought splendidly, but "Uncle Doctor" was pioneer and inspiration to thousands. I humbly record my deep sense of obligation to him and to those who, with such great faith, wrought with him in the valley of the Juniata and with such phenomenal success.

The spirit of the father animates the son. It may well be that when God writes a full record it will be found that the loyalty of the author to his father will be set down as the animating and sustaining influence that sent the son with unflagging zeal into an enterprise of such significance to the family, and of such signal service to his kind.

Martin Grove Brumbaugh

(Superintendent of Schools.)

Philadelphia, Pa., October 24, 1912.

THE
BRUMBACH FAMILIES

ABBREVIATIONS AND EXPLANATIONS

To facilitate identification and description the reader will find preceding each proper name (rarely following) a capital letter and a number in a bracket, thus [A1] + Gerhard¹ Brumbach, or [C1] + Johann Jacob¹ Brumbaugh The Immigrant ancestors' are designated by capital letters, practically in the order of their arrival, and all in the same line of descent bear the same letter in bracket A cross, +, following the bracket, and preceding the name of the individual, indicates that at its numerical place further along in the volume additional details are given—omission of the cross means that details are unobtained The superior figure over the given, or Christian, name indicates the generation of the individual in America

In each series, [A], [B], [C], etc , the Immigrant is marked 1, the children are given consecutive numbers 2, 3, 4, etc , and in each succeeding generation the numbering is carried through the given series and generation taking all the children of the first *male* child, next all the children of the second male child, then of the third male child, etc In the case of female children, their descendants appear numbered in Roman characters, i, ii, iii, etc ; letters of the alphabet, a, b, c, etc , figures (1), (2), (3)

Special Note —The children of [E2] + JACOB² BRUMBAUGH are numbered throughout the generations, then the children of [E3] + CONRAD² BRUMBAUGH commence with [E1700],[b] the children of [E4] + JOHANNES² BRUMBAUGH commence with [E2900],[c] and the children of [E5] + GEORGE² BRUMBAUGH commence with [E3000].[d]

The *individual ancestry* is given at the commencement of each sketch in parenthesis, following the name, permitting quick and definite backward reference in the section, thus [E743] + Gaius Marcus⁶ Brumbaugh, M D , ([E226] Andrew Boelus⁵, M D , [E68] Jacob⁴, [E13] George³, [E2] Jacob², Johannes Heinrich¹) Only by such an arrangement is it possible to determine precise ancestry in our many families, having so many individuals of the same given names, and in some instances with change of the surname.

---

[a] See p 40. The foreign lines of descent are yet to be completed.
[b] See p 638
[c] See p. 701.
[d] See p. 703

To economize space, in addition to the usual abbreviations for States, months, etc., there have been used

admin —administration

admr.—administrator

admx —administratrix

atty.—attorney

b—born

bro.—brother

bur.—buried

Ch of Br.—Church of Brethren[*]

ch —church

Chr. Ch —Christian Church

C. H —court house

Dis Ch —Disciple Church

d or d—died, penny, pence

d y—died young

dau —daughter

dcd —deceased

Dea.—Deacon

dis —discharged

dys or ds—days

exr—executor

exx—executrix

F. A A M —Free, Ancient and Accepted Masons

G B. B Ch —German Baptist Brethren Church[*]

gs—grandson

gs r—gravestone record

gdn—guardian

grad—graduated

hist—history

intd—interred

int—interest

inv—inventory

J. P.—Justice of Peace

Luth Ch.—Lutheran Church

m—married

mds—merchandise

mfr—manufacturer

M.E Ch —Methodist Episcopal Church

mo—month

n ch—no children

n d s—no data supplied

priv—private

Ref Ch —Reformed Church in the U S

res—residence, resigned

s—son

S. S.—Sunday School

t r—town record

unm—unmarried

U. S —United States

w—wife

wid—widow

[*]June, 10, '08, name legally changed to Church of the Brethren

THE FOREIGN ORIGIN OF BRUMBACH FAMILIES, PRINCIPAL RECORDS THUS FAR DISCOVERED, COATS OF ARMS; ETC.

The name is of German origin, and is found in both German and Swiss records with "u" and "o" frequently interchangeably. There is a French branch of the old family, with altered colors in its coat of arms, but retaining the main features of the same. This investigation as to the French families is incomplete.

"Brum" is apparently a contraction of "Brummen," meaning noisy or roaring, sometimes humming, and "bach," a brook. The name in the first instance described an ancestor by locality, a common old method of designation. Owing to the general difficulty experienced by persons unfamiliar with German pronunciation, names ending in "bach" usually became "baugh" upon the landing of the immigrant, and in his deeds. The variations "Brumback," "Brownbaugh," "Brownback," etc., had local origin. Whether written with the more prevalent "ŭ" or "u," or "o," it was pronounced with the long German "oo" as in moon, or more rarely with the short "u" sound as in good.

"Brambach" and the older "Prampach" are mentioned elsewhere[a]—note especially the discussion based upon the cloister records at Brombach, etc.

Whenever the German speaking ancestor executed deeds, and other legal papers, we find that the English scribe in America usually wrote the name "Broombaugh," or "Brombaugh." In the case of [A1] Gerhard[1] Brumbach (who seems not to have written his name), the difficulties were greater, and the name in the third generation became "Brownback." [D2] Widow[1] Brombach easily became "Brumback." The descendants of [G1] Hermanus Emanuel[1] Brumbach in the main retain that spelling. An error once made in an important deed or other important paper, the ancestor sometimes simply made the small change in his name so as to conform to the erroneous writing of the name.[b]

A careful study of the reproduced immigrant lists, or ship papers, will show that the Brumbach-Brombach immigrants, whose signatures have been preserved, wrote good German script, even paying attention to the umlat, or distinction for ŭ—see [C1], [E1], etc. This fact gives value to the hope that somewhere in Germany and Switzerland we shall yet find that the ravages of

---

[a] See pp 6, 22, 23.
[b] This occurred with Ulysses S. Grant, and with thousands of soldiers in all the wars, etc.

the "Thirty Years' War" have spared early and historically valuable family records.

There evidently occurred a general dispersion of the various foreign branches of the Brumbach families Extended investigations have been made in various parts of Germany and Switzerland, and a portion of the results from this search is herein presented to form the basis for a more general investigation *

KARL[6] BROMBACH.

Especially painstaking and important assistance has been received from Mr. Karl[6] Brombach, Karlsruhe, Baden (late of Basel), Secretary to the General Management of the States Railroads of Baden   Karl[6] b Nov. 12, 1874, m Emma Trautmuller (1 ch.), is s Gottlieb[5], b April 25, 1842, and Rosina (Strittmatter) Brombach (3 ch), s Rudolf[4], b April 4, 1788, and Mechgunde (Forster) Brombach (7 ch); s Josef[3], b March, 1735, and Anna (Volz) Brombach (7 ch), s Josef[2], b 1705 at Minseln, Baden, and Anna (Klein) Brombach (7 ch), s Peter[1], b 1658, and Katharina (Umber) Brombach (6 ch).

EXTRACT FROM THE MIDDLE HIGH GERMAN NAME BOOK, COMPILED FROM UPPER RHINE SOURCES OF THE 12TH AND 13TH CENTURIES, BY ADOLF SOCIN, BASEL, 1903

CITIZENS WITH "DE"

Heinricus de Bianbach, pistor (baker)   (Records of death of the abbey of St Peter, 1289.)

dominus Johannes dictus de Branbach.   Ditto.

Ulricus de Brambach.   Ditto

Ulricus de Biambach   Ditto.

Wernherus advocatus dictus de Bianbach (Tithe register of the convent of Istein).

PLACE NAMES OR THEIR DERIVATIONS IN "ER" AS FAMILY NAMES

The mere name of a place, if used as a family name, has been shortened from "von." As soon as family names began to be extensively used, the incon-

---

*One celebrated author advised the compiler not to attempt anything beyond the landing of the immigrants. It is hoped that other discoveries may be forwarded to him by those interested in the definite tracing of the ancestral lines, and that a small supplemental volume may be the result   The foreign search is being continued

venience of the "von" in the structure of the sentence must have been felt, and it was simply omitted. Of this class is

dictus Brambach, 1265.

Heinricus dictus Branbach de Rotenlein, 1291.

The Brombachs of to-day correspond to the latter

On emigrating from the place Brombach (earlier Branbach, etc.) to Basel and vicinity, the people took the name of the place from which they came, which subsequently clung to them as the family name.

Herr Wernher der vogit von Branbach (Herr Wernher the governor of Branbach); Schultheiss (mayor) zur mirrum (?—illegible), Basel, 1207 (or 1287?), Johans der vogt von Brambach (Johans the governor of Brambach), 1299, dicta Vogtin de Brambach (called Governess of Brambach—governor's wife), (Basel), Willeburg Vogtin de Brambach (Willeburg, Governess of Brambach), belonging to the nobility, according to Socin.

(Beginning with the tenth century, the "von" is regarded as the mark of nobility.)

THE NAME VON BRUMBACH, BRUMBACH, BROMBACH

The names Brumbach, Brombach, are not mentioned in the other name books:

Forstemann· Altedeutches Namenbüch

Steub· Oberdeutsche Familiennamen

Villmar Namenbuchlem.

From Socin's statements and investigations it seems to be definitely established that an extensive family of the name "Brambach," "Brombach," "Brumbach" took their name from the ancient settlement in the Wiesenthal valley, called "Brombach " They adopted the name of the place.

"Brombach im Wiesenthal Ein Beitrag zur Heimatkunde von Pfarrer Mulrow in Altenheim, Lahr, 1905,"* is an interesting volume descriptive of the ancient town and castle The map herein reproduced shows the locality of Brombach, Bombach, Beuggen, Minseln, Basel, etc.

Native farmers of the name Brombach yet live near Beuggen, and persons of that name in Baden trace their ancestry to the vicinity of Basel, on both sides of the Rhine.

Basilar Brombach and others at Basel came from Rheinfelden, Minseln, Nordschwaben and Karsan—all about two hours' walking distance apart.

---

*Presented to the compiler by Mr Carl Brombach, Karlsruhe, Baden.

Those families remaining at Minseln,[a] Nordschwaben and Karsan remained Catholic in the Reformation period, while those at Rheinfelden became Protestants—under different governments.[b]

The inhabitants of Rheinfelden early left the Catholic religion, became Protestants, and later Altkatholiken (old Catholics, or reformers), which they remain. These inhabitants suffered greatly and were bitterly persecuted, causing most of the inhabitants to emigrate during the eighteenth century—the Brombachs-Brumbachs then emigrated

In Beuggen and in Rheinfelden, during the middle ages, there was a Deutsch-Ordens Commend or association which owned much property, and the records contain the name Brombach.

Hans Brombach, according to the records of Rheinfelden, served as Mayor, 1536-1543, and died 1545—three Mayors of the name Brombach are there mentioned in the records.

EXTRACTS FROM "BROMBACH IM WIESENTAL—PFARRER MULROW,"[c] (LAHR, 1905).

"For the identity of 'Prampahch' with the Brombach of to-day we had offered the records of the cloisters We could prove the same through the shifting of the consonant sounds (Grimm's Law) in the Old-Middle and New-High German In the record from the eighth century the place is called 'Prampahch,' in those of the twelfth century 'Brambach,' and in the sixteenth century 'Brombach' That is etymologically exactly according to the law of the language, and not one link is missing in the chain of sound shifting. And what does the name mean? There was a word in the time of Charlemagne which was spelled *prâma*, in the time of the Crusades *brâme*, and at the time of Luther *bram* and *brom*, and this means a 'long, pointed stalk' It appears with 'a' (bram) in North Germany yet in two forms· The top-most and thinnest part of a mast is called 'bram segel', and also the awlwort or broom they call there 'bram' + + The same etymologic relationship, only botanically applied, is our brombeer stranch (blackberry bush) Thus then Brombach has its name from that which we had conjectured at the first glance. from Bach (brook) along the pointed blackberry bushes.

"But in Karlsruhe the old as well as the new Council seal shows a spring, and Brombach had many fountains Is it not much more poetic to think of

---

[a]Father Kohler reports the church registers at this place all burned with the parish house during the XVII century
[b]Prussian Rhine provinces, Hessen, Nassau, Hanover and Westfalen, are yet to be searched
[c]Translated from the German by [E231—11] Emory Alburtus Zook, Huntingdon, Pa.

'Bronnenbach' (a brook of springs)? Its explanation would be very nice if Brombach were a newer place without old records. If its name came from the bubbling springs then it must have been called 'Brunnebach' in the Middle Ages, and in the old High-German 'Brunô-pach.' But that sounds different from 'prâm,' so we stay by the first explanation." [a]

"From the year 786 'till the year 1113 we do not find Brombach mentioned in the records. How in the meantime has the power of the Kaiser diminished, and that of the Pope increased! How much nearer has the influence of the cloister forced itself to the Wiesenthal in the 11th century, since the mighty house of God, St Blasien, was established by the Benedictines and its despotism and ban have spread out of the quiet Alb valley over the mountains and valleys 'till (it reached) the Rhine itself" [b]

". . . The ratifications . . . followed 44 yrs later, on June 8, 1157, through Pope Hadrian IV. On Apr. 26, 1173, Pope Calixt III ratified the contract for 71 places, Pope Alexander III the same on Mch 6, 1179, and Bishop Hermann on June 29, 1189. In all these writings the name of our village has been changed according to the rules of the shifting of the sounds. From the old High German *Prampahch* has come the middle High German *Brambach*, only once *Brambac* " [c]

"Kaiser Rudolph (von Hapsburg) was victorious. He captured and destroyed fortress Reichenstein and caused a terrible slaughter among the inhabitants. At that time, about 1270, the persecuted knights seem to have come over to Brombach and established a firm hold in a hiding place between the meadow and two streams running by. From the ruins and traditions one can learn that the castle was a real building about 45 meters long by 35 meters wide. On its four corners stood out great towers and the whole was surrounded with moats." [d]

". . . We have two entries in the church records·   .

"In the year 1676 this village of Brombach, during the French war, was burned and reduced to ashes till about 7 houses left, and further in a burial account a marginal note says 'Brombach burned and reduced to ashes except a very few houses'" [e] "On the 29th of June, 1678, the Rottler Castle went up in flames after the enemy had found the entrance by means of a traitor" [f]

"During the thirties and forties of the 18th century the Brombacher

[a] "Brombach im Wiesental," p 56, lines 14-23
[b] "Brombach im Wiesental," p 60, lines 20-28.
[c] "Brombach im Wiesental," p 71, lines 3-13.
[d] "Brombach im Wiesental," p 196, line 21, etc.
[e] "Brombach im Wiesental," p 127, lines 4-14.
[f] "Brombach im Wiesental," p 145

could not make progress because of the continuous dangers and demands of war, but in the second half of the century there was lasting peace It required, however, a long time until the living conditions were made better, and until the number of inhabitants was a little increased "[a]

The general locality of Brombach is interesting for other reasons   "In Warmbach, Heithen, Wyhlen, and Grenzach have also been found traces of former Roman culture,—on the other side of Dinkelberg they disappear almost entirely   Only at Minseln they found in 1898 fragments of a Roman two-handled urn which had a narrow neck " Glaciers repeatedly covered the region, coming from Norway and Sweden and from the Swiss Alps. In a cavern near Wunzingen skeletons of men were found with horn weapons made in the crudest manner.

From the 13th to the 17th century there were six large floods in the valley of the Wiese (Wiesenthal), as chronicled at Basel

KIRCH BROMBACH.

Scutter's map of 1740 and an unidentified map of about 1800 in the Library of Congress show "Kirch Brombach" in Hessen-Darmstadt, Germany, near "Konig N of Erbach, and S E of Darmstadt in Provinz Starkenberg, near a river emptying into the Main at Obenberg

KIRCHBROMBACH.

In the German Official R R. Guide on line No, 246 (Frankfort-Eberbach) 61 4 Km from Darmstadt, is "Mumling-Grumbach " On the same line 67 5 Km from Darmstadt is "Zell," the station nearest "Kirch-Brombach"—"Kirchbrombach," 1 Km distant—midway between Darmstadt and Heidelberg.

K. Gerhard, Pfarrei Evangelisches Pfarramt Kirch-Brombach, Gr Hessen, in June, '07, reported that the Kirchenbuch in existence contains no Brombach names

A few miles further E. near Werthein, there is another village named Brumbach

Tieffenau, hamlet in Baden, near Switzerland, where Franz Leopald lived, has copy of Brumbach coat of arms.

The church registers of Sinzheim and Kappel-Windeck will probably furnish interesting details   There are also three more communities carrying the name Brombach in Hessen and Hessen Nassau (Taunus).[b]

Section D—Melchior Brumbach came to Va. in 1714 "from the old prin-

[a]Brombach im Wiesental, p. 148.
[b]Mr. Karl Brombach, Karlsruhe, Baden.

cipality of Nassau-Siegen, Germany" ("Muesen")[a] and further search is to
be made in the old records there preserved

Lawyer Wernher "dictus de Branbach" (called von Branbach) at Basel
(1265) in certifying documents used the coat of arms of the city of Kleim
Basel, as shown by the document book of Basel (Rud, Wackernagel)

BROMBACH

"Ein Geschlecht in Stadt Basel, aus welchem Fridli, Schloss-Prediger auf
dem Schloss Varnsburg, und 1524 Decan des Varnsburger Capitul und Niclaus
Anno 1611, Pfarrer zu Prattelen und 1618 zu Ruemlingen, auch 1625 Decan
des Waldenberger-Capituls worden, und Anno 1662 gestorben." Schweizer-
isches Lexicon, Vol. IV, p. 316

BROMBACH

A family in the city Basel, of which Fridli became castle preacher at the
Castle Vainsburg, and 1524 Deacon of the Varnsburger Capital and Niclaus
in the year 1611, pastor at Prattelen and in 1618 at Ruemlingen, also in 1625
Deacon of the Waldenberger Capital, and died in the year 1662

BRUMBACH

'Ein Bachy welcher in der Pfarr Kilchdorf in dem Bernischen Land gericht
Seftingen sich mit denen Bachen Dampleton und Dwur vereiniget, und sich in
die Aren ergiesset." Same reference, p. 350.[b]

BRUMBACH.

A brook which in the parish of Kilchdorf in the Bernese judicial district
Seftingen unites with the brooks Dampleton and Dwur, and empties into the
Aren

CHRONIK OF THE PRIEST BROMBACH DEPOSITED IN LIBRARY OF UNIVERSITY AT BASEL, SWITZERLAND [c]

I, M. NICOLAUS BROMBACH, Ruemlingen, Pastor and Decanus of the
Waldenburg and Homburg Capitels (parish) was born at Basel in the house

---

[a] See p. 247.

[b] *References furnished by Hon Luther R Kelker, Custodian of Public Records, Harris-burg, Pa*

[c] Magister Nicolaus Brombach, pastor or priest at Basel, was a college graduate and a very learned man Brombach—Brumbach is evidently an old patrician family *Records copied by Mr Karl Brombach, and by him translated from the old into current German* This "chronic" also contains valuable details concerning the "Thirty years' war" then raging, and also says much shipping and migration transpired down the Rhine from Basel

"zum niedereu grunen Jager" (small or low green hunters) in the "Totenga Bleine," in the evening betw. 4 and 5 o'clock, according to the clocks of Basel, 1582 It was Elizabetha-day My parents were Johann Brombach, who was born at Rheinfelden but became citizen of Basc', and Justina Bischoff, the legal daughter of the celebrated Printer of Basel, Mr. Nicolai, Episcopii B and Elizabeth Peyerin, from Schaffhausen

Born: Hieronimus Brombach, the saddler at Rheinfelden, my near relative 5 July 1583.

Born Daniel, my dear Brother, Basel, 19 April 1588

1590 *Born.* Johannes, my dear Brother, on 28 February

1591 *Died.* Johann Brombach, my dear Father on 13 October.

1608 Hans Ulrich Brombach, my dear Brother married at Colmar (Elsass) 1 February.

1609 Johann Jacob Brombach, son of Conrad, the Council at Rheinfelden, who was married to F Maria Hugin, the secretary to the Council's daughter, 3 July

1611 *Born:* Johann Jacob Brombach, son of Johann Brombach, at Rheinfelden 2 September

1611 I, Nicholas Brombach, Pfarrer at Pratteln, married Anna Muller, right legal daughter of the Weissbacker in lower Basel, M Jacob Muller, on the 2 October.

1612 *Born.* Nicolaus, son of mine and my dear wife, Anna Muller, at Pratteln on 28 August (died 4/24 1659 in Handschuhstein, in Baden)

1615 *Born* Christoph my dear son in Baden

1648 *Born.* Nicolaus, son of Christoph Brombach, 20 August

1650 *Born:* Christoph, son of Christoph Brombach, 6 May

1654 *Born* Johannes, son of Christoph Brombach, ——.

"EXCERPT FROM THE MARRIAGE REGISTER OF RHEINFELDEN CONCERNING THE 'BROMBACHS'—from 1579.

1585   Conrad Brombach—Dorothea Kellerin

1589   Udalrikus Brombach—Ursula Ittingerin

1592   Conrad Brombach—Eva Wurtzlerin

1597   Hans Brombach—Veronika Schaferin

1602   Hans Jakob Brombach—Marina Huglin

1614   Hyeronimus Brombach—Elizabetha Mandacher

1678   23 Sept. Georg Udalricus Brombach Callebs—Ferivarius Margaretta Metzgerin.

From here on the name Brombach does not appear any more in the Marriage Register "

"EXCERPT FROM THE BAPTISM REGISTER AT RHEINFELDEN, OF THE FAMILY BROMBACH, COMMENCING 1581.

(1) 1585 27 Jan Maria of Ulricus Brombach and Magdalena Ittingerin.

(2) 1586 7 Aug Verena of Conradus Brombach and Dorothea Kollerin

(3) " 11 Nov Agnes of Ulrich Brombach and Magdalena Ittingerin.

(4) 1588 10 Aug Elsbeth of Ulrich Brombach and Magdalena Ittingerin

(5) " 30 Oct Hans Adelberg of Conradus Brombach and Dorothea Kollerin

(6) 1589 20 Sept Margaretha of Ulrich Brombach and Magdalena Ittingerin

(7) 1593 6 Sept Adeltritis of Ulrich Brombach and Magdalena Ittingerin.

(8) 1596 5 June Hans Ruodolff of Conrad Brombach and Eva Wurtzlerin

(9) " 17 Sept Ursula of Ulrich Brombach and Magdalena Ittingerin.

(10) 1597 25 Feb Maria Salome of Johannes Brombach and Veronika Schaferin

(11) 1598 22 Feb Margaretha of Geronimus Brombach and Adelheid Gebhardin.

(12) " 20 May Josef Georgius of Conrad Brombach and Eva Wurtzlerin

(13) 1602 22 Feb Maria of Conrad Brombach and Eva Wurtzlerin.

(14) 1606 29 Mch Anna of Conrad Brombach and Eva Wurtzlerin.

(15) " 2 July Maria of Hannss Brombach and Verena Schafferin.

(16) 1609 25 Nov Katharina of Conrad Brombach and Eva Wurtzlerin

(17) 1611 2 Sept Hans Jakob of Hans Jakob Brombach and Marina Hughn

(18) 1613 24 Oct Georgius Burckhard of Dominus Hans Jakob Brombach and Marina Hughn

(19) 1614 8 Nov Anna of Hyeronimus Brombach and Elsbeth Mandacher

(20) 1615 26 Sept Georgius Burkart of Hans Jakob Brombach and Maria Hughn.

(21) 1615 12 Dec Bartholomaeus of Hyeronimus Brombach and Elisab Mandacher

(22) 1620 28 Apr Susanna of Hyeronimus Brombach and Elisab. Mandacher.

(23) 1624 27 May Elisabeth of Hyeronimus Brombach and Elisab. Mandacher

(24) 1631 24 Nov Georg Burckardus of Hyeronimus Brombach and Elisab Mandacher

(25) 1636 10 Feb Georg Ulrich of Hyeronimus Brombach and Elisab. Mandacher.

(26) 1638 5 Aug Anna Barbara of Hyeronimus Brombach and Elisab Mandacher.

(27) " 25 Aug Johann Kaspar of Heinrich Biombach from Karsau and Anna (indistinct).

(28) 1646 29 July Hans Jakob of Hanss Brombach from Karsau and of Ursula Haumullerin.

(29) 1649) —— Maria Magdalena of Hanss Brombach and Ursula Magdalena.

(30) 1655 31 Aug Magdalena of Barthei Biombach and Anna Brannin

Nos. 27-29 evidently belong to family Brombach from Karsan which newly immigrated to here.

With 1635 the name Brombach disappears from the birth register

1536-1543 Mayor Hans Brombach is mentioned—died 1545 There are then 3 Mayors of name Brombach.

Rheinfelden, 26 Oct 1908

[Signed]   SEB. BURKHART, Priest"

Brombach disappears from the records of Rheinfelden in 1678, when they evidently emigrated.

"EXCERPT FROM THE DEATHBOOK OF RHEINFELDEN FROM YEAR 1585

1585 28 Nov Elisabeth Brombachin (Brombach)

1587 2 Jan Katherina Biombachin.

1589 1 Mch Ulrich Brombach, former Burgomaster (Mayor) of City Rheinfelden.

1590 16 Jan Dorothea Brombachin.

1601 20 Jan Conrad Biombach's daughter.

1603 —— Agnes Brombachin, legitimate daughter of Ungelter

1610 1 Nov Maria Brombachin

1612 5 Nov Hyeronimus Brombach.

1618 —— Johann Jakob Biombach

1622 29 Mch Conrad Brombach of the Council, Ungelter and Guildmaster.

1630 19 Feb Ulrich Brombach, 18 years Burgomaster (Mayor), died 75 years old

1632 —— a child of Hyeronimus was buried.

1639 2 Mch Hyeronimus Brombach of the Council, a saddler

From there the name Brombach does not appear in the death register."

EXCERPT FROM THE RECORDS OF BAPTISM (TAUFBUCHE) OF
THE PRIEST AT BEUGGEN.

(1)   Jacobus Brombach Oct 23, 1703 Jacob Brombach and Dorothea Wiech-
       serg?
(2)   Josephus Brombach, Feb 16, 1704, Sebastian Brombach and Margarita
       Livey
(3)   Johannes Georg Brombach, Aug 16, 1704, Bartolom. Brombach and
       Barbara Faggin
(4)   Antonius Brombach, Sept 2, 1705, Heinrich Brombach and Katharina
       Brombach
(5)   Maria Agatha Brombach, Aug 8, 1706, Jacob Brombach and Dorothea
       Wissmer
(6)   Elisabeth Brombach, Apr 10, 1707, Barthol Brombach and Barbara
       Faggin
(7)   Joseph Brombach, Sept 4, 1707, same as No 4
(8)   Marous Georgius Brombach, Apr 25, 1709, No. 3
(9)   Johannes Brombach, Dec 28, 1709, No. 4
(10)   Anna Maria Brombach, Sept 17, 1710, Antonius Brombach and Elisa-
       betha Stoerin
(11)   Caspar Brombach, Jan 6, 1711, No. 3
(12)   Maria Agatha Brombach, Feb. 5, 1711, No. 4
(13)   Catharina Brombach, Mch 2, 1712, No 10
(14)   Anna Catharina Brombach, Sept. 25, 1712, Anton Brombach and Anna
       M. Wissmer
(15)   Jacob Brombach, Feb 25, 1713, Bartholom Brombach and Barbara
       Sertin (3 ?)
(16)   Johannes Brombach, Sept 20, 1713, No. 4
(17)   Maria Agatha Brombach, June 3, 1714, Anton Brombach and Maria
       Wissmer
(18)   Anna Elisabeth Brombach, June 29, 1715, Anton Brombach and Elisab
       Stoerin
(19)   Caspar Brombach, Jan 27, 1716, No 4
(20)   Anna Maria Brombach, Apr 14, 1716, No. 3
(21)   Anton Brombach, Aug 11, 1716, No. 17
(22)   Johanna Brombach, Aug 11, 1716, No. 17
(23)   Thomas Jacob Brombach, Oct. 19, 1716, Johann Brombach and Eva
       Witzig
(24)   Peter Brombach, June 29, 1718, No. 17
(25)   Fridolin Brombach, July 15, 1718, No 4
(26)   Athanasius Brombach, May 3, 1719, No. 18

(27) Jacob Wendelin Brombach, Oct. 20, 1719, No. 23
(28) Franzisca Brombach, Jan. 22, 1720, No 17
(29) Karl Heinrich Brombach, Nov 3, 1820, No 4
(30) Catharina Brombach, July 31, 1721, No 17
(31) Anton Brombach, Jan 12, 1722, No. 23
(32) Blasius Brombach, Feb 2, 1722, No 4
(33) Maria Magdalena Brombach, July 20, 1722, Joseph Brombach and Maria ———
(34) Anna Maria Brombach, Nov. 20, 1722, No 10
(35) Anna Maria Brombach, Aug 17, 1723, No. 33
(36) Heinrich Brombach, Mch 12, 1724, No 4
(37) Elisabetha Brombach, Mch 16, 1724, No. 17
(38) Johannes Brombach, Dec 7, 1724, No 23
(39) Johannes Baptista Brombach, June 24, 1725, No 33
(40) Anna Elisabetha Brombach, Jan. 17, 1726, Jacob Brombach and Agatha Bruzzer
(41) Maria Katharine Brombach, Mch. 18, 1728, Jacob Brombach and Agatha Bruzzer
(42) Josephus Brombach, May 17, 1728, No 23
(43) Catharina Brombach, June 8, 1728, Joseph Brombach and Anna M. Baumgartner
(44) Johannes Brombach, Oct 6, 1728, No. 18
(45) Maria Anna Brombach, June 27, 1729, Fridolin Brombach and Urichin Kath
(46) Konrad Brombach, Nov. 26, 1729, Johannes Brombach and Anna Kath
(47) Agatha Brombach, Feb 22, 1730, Jacob Brombach and Anna M. Bruzzer
(48) Maria Anna Brombach, Sept 5, 1730, No. 43
(49) Antonius Martinus Brombach, Nov 10, 1730, No. 45
(50) Nicolaus Brombach, Dec. 6, 1730, No 40
(51) Anna Maria Brombach, Apr 22, 1731, Joseph Brombach and Eva Bannwartin
(52) Heinrich Brombach, July 16, 1731, No 23
(53) Antonius Brombach, Oct. 13, 1731, No 46
(54) Agatha Brombach, Jan. 1, 1732, No. 47
(55) Elisabetha Brombach, Apr 18, 1732, No 43
(56) Catharina Brombach, May 19, 1732, No 45
(57) Maria Anna Brombach, Nov. 2, 1732, No 51
(58) Michael Brombach, Sept. 27, 1733, No 45

(59) Michael Brombach, Nov 7, 1733, No. 47
(60) Josephus Brombach, Mch. 10, 1734, Anton Brombach and Anna Nann
(61) Anna Maria Brombach, Mch 18, 1734, Joseph Brombach and Elizab.
       Bannwartin
(62) Anna Maria Brombach, May 10, 1734, No. 43
(63) Johannes Jacob Brombach, July 23, 1734, No. 40
(64) Maria Elisabetha Brombach, Sept 29, 1734, No. 46
(65) Sebastian Brombach, Dec. 29, 1734, No. 45
(66) Fidelis Brombach, Oct 20, 1735, No 40
(67) Joseph Brombach, Nov. 8, 1735, No. 51
(68) Johannes Baptista Brombach, Nov 29, 1735, No 47
(69) Anna Maria Brombach, May 7, 1736, No. 43
(70) Anna Maria Brombach, Sept 16, 1736, Caspar Brombach and Elisa-
       betha Rietschle
(71) Johann Michael Brombach, Jan 17, 1737, Johannes Brombach and
       Anna Verichin
(72) Maria Azatha Brombach, Feb 20, 1737, No. 60
(73) Fridolin Brombach, Jan 27, 1738, No 45
(74) Bartholoma Brombach, Feb 1, 1738, No 70
(75) Josephus Brombach, Mch 10, 1738, No 40
(76) Maria Eva Ursula Brombach, Oct 21, 1738, No. 51
(77) Joseph Brombach, Nov. 8, 1738, No 43
(78) Franziscus Josephus Brombach, Oct. 4, 1739, No 70
(79) Maria Azatha Brombach, Apr 7, 1740, No. 60
(80) Johanna Brombach, May 12, 1740, No 45
(81) Joseph Fidelis Brombach, Aug 27, 1740, No 51
(82) Anna Maria Brombach, Jan. 7, 1741, Johann Brombach and Secunda
       Rohrer
(83) Maria Elisabetha Brombach, Feb 8, 1742, No 70
(84) Anna Maria Brombach, Feb 10, 1742, No. 43
(85) Anna Maria Brombach, Mch. 30, 1742, Caspar Brombach and Kath.
       Nann
(86) Maria Brombach, Aug. 12, 1742, Johann Brombach and Katharina
       Roser
(87) Anna Maria Brombach, Feb 14, 1743, No 60
(88) Fustina Brombach, Sept 27, 1743, No 70
(89) Michael Brombach, Oct. 9, 1744, No 43
(90) Erasmus Brombach, May 30, 1745, No 70
(91) Kunigunda Brombach, Sept 9, 1745, No 82

(92)   Theresia Brombach, Oct 13, 1745, No 85

(93)   Antonius Brombach, Oct 22, 1746, No 60

(94)   Joseph Brombach, Sept 4, 1747, No 85

(95)   Maria Ursula Brombach, Sept —, 1747, No. 70

(96)   Fridolin Brombach, Mch 2, 1749, No 60

(97)   Johannes Brombach, Dec 7, 1750, Joseph Brombach and Ursula Wagner (Wasmer)

(98)   Maria Katharina Brombach, Jan 1, 1752, No 85

(99)   Maria Brombach, Aug 28, 1752, No 97

(100) Simon Brombach, Oct. 29, 1752, No 60

(101) Josephus Brombach, Jan 2, 1753, Johann Brombach and Katharina Brombach

(102) Anna Brombach, July 24, 1753, Johann Brombach and Anna Maria Engler

(103) Maria Brombach, Nov. 21, 1753, Jacob Brombach and Katharina Bachmann

(104) Maria Elisabeth Brombach, Mch 17, 1754, Johann Brombach and Maria Bruzzer

(105) Caspar Brombach, Aug 21, 1754, No. 85

(106) Johannes Brombach, Jan 1, 1755, Nicolaus Brombach and Maria Anna Reuschin

(107) Joseph Brombach, Feb 26, 1755, No 103

(108) Maria Rosa Brombach, Feb 26, 1755, No 103

(109) Maria Theresa Brombach, Mch. 8, 1756, Jacob Brombach and Gertrud Muller

(110) Catharina Brombach, July 3, 1756, No. 97

(111) Johannes Wolfzang Brombach, Oct 30, 1756, No 104

(112) Maria Anna Brombach, Mch 22, 1757, No 106

(113) Johannes Baptista Brombach, June 19, 1758, No 109

(114) Maria Catharina Brombach, Sept 12, 1758, No. 97

(115) Nicolaus Brombach, Dec 5, 1758, No 106

(116) Johanna Brombach, Aug 7, 1760, Heinrich Brombach and Katharina ———

(117) Jacobus Brombach, July 25, 1761, Johann Brombach and Maria Engler

     Beuggen*, May 29, 1909

                    FR BUSAM PFARRER (Priest) "

_____

*Beuggen parish includes Karsan.

LITERAL EXTRACT FROM THE OBERBADISCHEN GESCHLECH-TERBUCH BY JULIUS KINDLER VON KNOBLOCH.

VON BRUMBACH.

Brombach, village in the Bezirksamt Loerrach   Matthias Reich, Knight, sold the castle, which was destroyed by earthquake on the 18th day of the 10th month, 1356, to the Bishop of Basel in 1294 and received it from him as a "lehen" (feud under feudal law)   Heinrich von Brombach was in 1113 witness to a Document of the Bishop of Basel for St. Blasien   Marquardus de Brumbach, 1164, was witness to a Document of Emperor Friedrich I for the Church of St Thomas in Strassburg   Count Heinrich, Herr zu Veldeuz (Squire of Veldeuz), documented in 1292 that Ulrich ——— von Brunebach and Kunteh, his brother, have sold to the Johanniter in Freiberg 1289 a piece of property in Kenzingen   Cunrad von Brunnebach, witness in 1299   Jungfrau (maid) Grede von Brunnebach in year 1356   Ulrich von Buernebach 1380. Junker (young nobleman) Barthel von Buernebach 1430   Ursula von Brünnebach, widow of the Hans Brenner von Winterbach 1446   Hans von Brumbach had 1424 a quarrel over his "Lehen" located in the valleys of Arnsbach and Brinsbach, of which "Lehen" he should renounce per verdict by a "Mannengericht" (feudal court) for an indemnification of 240 florins subject to interests of 12 florins from the hundred, another agreement was reached regarding this "Lehen" in 1466. Those von Brumbach were "Lehensleute" (feudal dependants) of the House Austria | Kolzennos | of the Markgraf von Baden, Graf (Count) von Moers-Saarweden, Graf von Fuerstenberg, of the Herren von Geroldseck (: Stonehouse and estate with garden in Oberwila 1476-1679 .) of Schwassburg, etc   To Strassburg they came by marriage

A certain Maria von Brumbach was, according to genealogical tables, wife of Hans Jacob von Muellenheim-Reichenberg

HARTMANN[1] von BRUMBACH, feudal dependant at Geroldseck, died 1434, married ———

Johann[2] von Brumbach lived 1434-1493 at Oberweir, where he held a stone house and an estate in Dependence at Geroldseck, 1457 in Dependence at Furstenberg, 1470 in Dependence of Geroldseck (as his brothers-in-law are mentioned in 1457 Friedrich Widergruen von Staufenberg, and Matthias Bock von Staufenberg) married to Ursula (alias Anna) von Digesheim 1467

Children (3)

Jacob[3], 1486-1528, member of the Knighthood of Mortenau 1491, feudal dependant of Moers-Saarweden, in 1528 feudal dependant of the margrave of Baden, married Susanna Jungzorn, 1486-1515.

Ursula[3], nun at Gunthersthal, 1467-1510

Jacob[3], contentual in Geugenbach, 1523

(The remainder of this interesting genealogy is reserved for a later volume.)

COATS OF ARMS· In silver a red ornamented green double eagle with red ornamentation in the wings. *Helmet·* Two red ornamented green eagle (or swan) necks and heads one behind the other. *Helmet Covers.* Green silver (.Wappen-Codex Reiber, fol 26—Code of Coat of Arms by Reiber, vol 26).

A Franz Leopold Brumbach von Tiefenau was "belehut"* and his wife appears in 1764, 1773?, Catharina, Ursula born Datt (Adels und Lehns—Archiv Karlsruhe; in K. and K. Adels—Archiv in Vienna it was impossible to obtain any information regarding this family which was probably nobled). His seal shows in the shield a springing Deer and on a crowned Helmet the same rising. Perhaps these belonged to this family: Johannes Brombach, 1615 citizen of Rheinfelden (about 1 hour from Minseln, Kaisan or Nordschwaben) and the "nobilis et doctissimus dominus Jacobus Ferdinandus Brombach," whose widow, Anna Maria Pistorin, 1682, 26 of 7th month, was married to Johann Ferdinand Ignaz Sax in Gengenbach.

Quirinus Conradus Henricus a Brumbach, canonicus capitularis ecclesiae Moguntinae, 1629, mentioned in the preface of Wuerdtwein's Nova Subsidia Diplomatica, XII, could have hardly belonged to the family mentioned above

Hans von Burnebach, also named von Einsiedeln, named himself after Brombach a Zinken (portion?) of the community Kappel-Windeck, Bezirksamt Buhl, Feudal dependant of the Herr von Windeck and twelfth man of the Court at Buhl 1336-1346 he is mentioned repeatedly in documents of the monastery Frauenalb pertaining to the estate Einsiedeln, he carried and used no seal of his own His sons were Johann, Peter and Bastian Katharina, Hans Brumbach's widow, donated a "Jahrzeit" for her husband in 1360 in the church at Kappel

VOGT VON BROMBACH.

(: Brombach in Bezirksamt Loerrach :)

Johannes the Vogt von Brombach, citizen of Klein Basel belehut* the Heinrich von Bethcon at Wile (: Wyhlen .) in 1323 the estates which he

---

*"Belehut" means given the right to care for but not possess an estate or property under the feudal law

owned and had given up previously His three-cornered seal (also 1326) shows in the shield an inclined lobster (See illustration)

KREBS VON BROMBACH, Konrad K , 1366, 1370, and after him (probably his son) Friedrich K , 1394-1406, were "markgrafliche Vogte" at Brombach, Bezirksamt Loerrach The last died between 1413, 11th of 9th month, and 1425, 25th of 6th month (See illustration)

"All except Brumbach (deer or stag) were drawn by expert in Basel from Gr Adels und Lehnsarchiv in Karlsruhe (Baden). Brumbach was drawn from a literal description.

Stein says "Springender Hirsch im Schilde auf gekrontem in demselben wachsend"—(Franz Leopold Brumbach).

"Stag salient in the shield and on crowned helmet growing the same "

"NOBLES AND PATRICIANS AT BASEL FROM THE 13TH TO THE 15TH CENTURY."[*]

At the meeting of the Historians' and Antiquarians' Society at Basel, February 3, Dr August Burckhardt delivered a discourse on "Nobles and Patricians at Basel from the 13th to the 15th century " The questions of descent and of displacements of families were illustrated by striking examples, which at the same time prove how little agreement there is between tradition and history The original nobility was of high and low degree Among the former were the Counts of Honberg, whom we meet with at an early date as governors of our city A peculiar process is observed in the Von Falkenstein family One line of it renounced the title of count, Count Rudolf, marrying below his rank, caused his line to be deprived of knighthood, afterward that line regained its insignia and belonged once more to the high nobility A similar renunciation occurred in the family to which Bishop Heinrich belonged, whose administration extended from 1262 to 1274 Neuenburg was the name of the family, and one of its lines, too, renounced the title of count, but assumed it again later on In the beginning of the 13th century we meet with the free lords Von Ramstein Here, too, we find two lines, one of which rises higher and higher until it becomes extinguished, bishops and mayors are to be found in its ranks The other line, through marriages with subordinate officials, descends to the ranks of the lower nobility, so that members of the same House are to be found in the most diverse circumstances The most distinguished of all were the Lords of Eptingen Their original possessions were Eptingen and Diegten, and they managed to acquire one lordship after the other As early as 1262 we find an Eptingen as governor of Basel, and other shortly after as mayor.

While the rural nobility, such as the lords Von Eptingen, Von Biedertal, Von Lorrach, Von Rothberg, etc , transferred their residence to the city, the urban nobility moved to the country, lost the consciousness of their urban origin, and called themselves after their new residence In this way, born city knights became new country knights Such was the case with the Von Hertenberg, Von Neuenstein, Von Barenfels families The history of the Von Barenfels family can be traced Its ancestor was Ludwig the Mercer, citizen of Basel, and a member of the Council The development of his family shows what was then possible in the social line The family begins with the Mercer and rises steadily. Ludwig's son Konrad, rising through his wealth and ability, is found more and more frequently in the higher ranks, till he acquires the knightly fief of Hertenberg, and calls himself Noble Knight Konrad

*This digest of an interesting discourse by Dr August Burckhardt Feb 3, 1910, a prominent European authority upon genealogical matters, is given because of its bearing upon the numerous families von Brombach

uses the seal which was afterward used by his descendants However, his new acquisition estranged him from his home The development cannot be traced everywhere with the same accuracy The Von Neuenstein family in the Jura, for example, are already knights at their first appearance—in the chronicles of Matthias Von Neuenburg To this family belonged a major by the name of Rudolf, whose daughter became the ancestors of the Von Reinach family

Johann Von Barenfels is for us the first of his line He filled the important office of Episcopal procurator His son Konrad occupied the same position The family is found in possession of the highest offices, so that we are probably dealing with a line of early prominence—originally from Klein Basel Their ancestors are probably to be sought in the Governors Von Brombach, and there may have been some kinship with the Lords of Lorrach It is true that the seal of the Von Brombach family shows a crawfish (Krebs), and this seems to contradict that hypothesis However, even the men continued to use the old seal of their family, so that in this case (zem) Krebs would be the old name of the Von Brombach and the Von Barenfels families

Among the knights we find the ministerial (official) families, who were in the service of the bishop and performed the functions of chamberlain, treasurer, butler, equerry, master of the kitchen, holding them by hereditary right They took their names from their offices The consciousness of this origin remained alive, as shown by the struggle between the Psitticher and Sterner On the one side we find the Monch and Schaler families, the most distinguished of the official nobility, their adherents are the Marschalk, Kammerer, Reich and other families, called by the name of their office or by their original surname, or by the name of their original home Reich von Reichenstein—"Reich" is here a mere supernumerary name—Steinlin and Vorgassen are originally related All three have the same image on their seals Vorgassen is the old name The separation of the three lines must have taken place at an early date Heinrich Steinlein, an official patrician, owning estates at Blotzheim, who had not resided long in Basel, is confirmed as first mayor of Basel His successor is a Reich The line of the Steinlin became extinct at an early date.

Beside the knights who were incumbents of the offices of the episcopal court and of the city offices, we find the Achtburger, the real patricians. They rose from the ranks of the merchants, their development began with Krämer and Wechsler (mercers and brokers) There is a remarkably rapid change in the lines of descent; marriages between the Achtburgers and the knights effaced the barriers Few were derived from the ancient craftsman's class Usually they belong to the four lordly guilds of housemates, merchants, wine dealers and mercers The Zum Luft family were originally saddlers, the Offenburg family were originally druggists The change of constitution in 1515 put an end to this development

A peculiar state of affairs is presented by the Zschekkenburlin family They were active business men, controlling a degree of wealth unusual for those days They were unwilling to join the Achtburgers by giving up their trade and thus becoming idlers without occupation They also abstained from entering on a kind of development resembling that of the Fuggers The Offenburg family pursued the opposite course The first of them to become a citizen of Basel was the son of Albrecht, Heninan Offenburg (born in 1379) He became Councilor of the Saffron Guild to which he belonged as druggist He held the office of chief Guild Master and passed a large part of his life in travel, both in the course of business and of office His diplomatic intelligence was esteemed far beyond the confines of the city In 1423 he gave up his trade and his guild right and entered the high chamber at Achtburger Sigismund conferred knighthood on him As early as 1396 (when not yet 17 years old) he married Anna Kupfernagel, and thus did not marry within his rank

The further development of the lines of descent is influenced by the intermarriage between nobility and burghers in the 15th century While the nobles were attracted by the wealth of the burghers, social ambition acted as a stimulus on the other side, inducing marriages which in most cases ended unhappily

WAPPEN

"Bist edlen Blutes du, vergiss es nicht
Und handle recht, wie deine Ahnen thaten,
Dass nicht von dir die Nachwelt einstens spricht·
'Der Stamm war gut, die Frucht nur ist missrathen' "

"Art thou of noble blood, forget it not
And live aright, as thy forbears have done,
That posterity may never say of thee·
'The tree was good, the fruit alone was bad.' "[a]

COAT OF ARMS[b]

I. BRUMBACH—*Alsace.* D'argent à l'aigle éployé de sinople, becqué d'or, membré de gueules. *Cimier:* deux cols de cygne d'argent, becqué de gueules *Lambrequins* d'argent et de sinople
BRUMBACH—*Alsace.* Argent, an eagle displayed vert, beaked or, membered gules *Crest.* Two swan's heads argent beaked gules *Lambrequin* Argent and vert
(From Armorial Général, par J B. Rietstap. Vol I, 1884, p. 317)

II. BRUMBACH—*France* D'argent à l'aigle éployé de sable.
BRUMBACH—*France* Argent, an eagle displayed sable.
(From Armorial Général par Rietstap. P. 192. Gouda, 1861.)

III BRUMBACH—d'argent, à l'aigle éployé de sable.
BRUMBACH—argent, an eagle displayed sable
(From Armorial Général des Familles Nobles de France. Vol. V, p 433 Paris, 1873.)

IV. BRUMBACH—d'argent, à l'aigle éployé de sable.
BRUMBACH—argent, an eagle displayed sable
(From Dictionaire de la Noblesse, par De la Chenaye-Desbois et Badier. Vol IV, p 378 Paris, 1864)

V. BRUMBACH—D'argent à l'aigle à deux têtes de sable

---

[a]"Wappenbuch des Westfälischen Adels" Herausgeben von Max von Speiken, Gorlitz, 1901-03
[b][E756] Chalmers Sherfy Brumbaugh repeatedly assisted in the study of the various coats of arms and especial thanks are due to him. See also pp. 18-20.

BRUMBACH—Argent, a double-headed eagle sable.

> (From Armoïal Universel, par M. Jouffray D'Escha-
> vannes   Vol. I, p 101   Paris, 1844.)

VI   BRUMBACH—Schweizer Familie, aus dem Baslischen   Heinrich von
Brumbach kommt schon 1113 urkundlich vor—   Spater gehorten
sie zum Elsasser Adel und zum Strasburger Patriziat, wo sie seit
1572 mehrfach Stattemeister waren   (+ Ende 17 saec)

Wappen· In Silber ein rothgewaffter grun Adler.   (Hattstein II,
> 378)·   *Auf dem Helme* hintereinander zwei rothgeschnabelte
> silbern Schwanrumpfe   *Dechen*   grun silbern.

> BRUMBACH—A Swiss family which hailed originally from
> Basel.   Heinrich von Brumbach, it seems, according to
> record, came without doubt in the year 1113   The family
> later belonged to the nobility of Alsace and to the pa-
> triciate of the city of Strasburg, where since 1572 they
> were time and again Stattemeister
> *Coat of Arms:* Argent, an eagle vert armed gules.
> *Crest:* two swan's heads and necks, one behind the
> other argent beaked gules.   *Lambrequin·* vert and
> argent
>> (From Siebmacher Wappenbuch 11-9-11, Nurn-
>> berg, 1871.   Der Adel des Elsass, p 5, Taf 6)

VII   von BRUMBACH—Argent, a double-headed eagle displayed vert
armed gules.   *Crest* two eagle's (or swan's) heads vert beaked
gules   *Lambrequin* vert and argent.
> (Wappen Codex, Riebel, fol 26)

VIII.   BROMBACH—*Bâle*   De gueules à un tertre de trois coupeaux d'or,
surmonte d'un meuble en forme de sautoir alésé du même, les ex-
trémités supérieures réunies par une traverse   *Cimier*   un buste
d'homme barbu, habillé de gueules, au rabat d'or.

> BROMBACH—*Basle.* Gules, mount with three coupeaux or, sur-
> mounted by a saltire couped of the same, the upper extremi-
> ties joined by a bar   *Crest:* the bust of a bearded man hab-
> ited gules, with the turnback of the collar or.
>> (From Armorial Général, par J B Rietstap, Vol I,
>> p 308. 1884) ·

IX.   von BRAMBACH—Deutsches Adels Lexicon 2, Kneschke, p 7, and
Siebmacher Wappenbuch, Vol VI, 7 Abgestorbner Nassaudischer

Adel, p 17, Taf 22 contain recently discovered references which are of interest, especially the former   Not only the resemblance in name, the use of the double eagle in the shield as in "von Brumbach," but also the fact that the old family of the Rheinland aristocracy (Bernard von Piampach, who died in 1314 as Prince— Bishop of Passau") had Mansfield, who was Justice in Siegen, etc., etc , whence came Milcaid Brumbach in April, 1714 (see Germanna —Germantown, Va.'), make all this a matter for further investigation.

THE COAT OF ARMS

von BRUMBACH—D'argent à l'aigle éployé à deux têtes de sinople, becqué d'or, membié de gueules   *Cimier*   deux cols de cygne d'argent, becqué de gueules   *Lambiequins*   d'argent et de sinople.

Or, in technical (?) English, as follows

von BRUMBACH—Argent, a double-headed eagle displayed vert, beaked or, membered gules   *Crest:* two swan's heads argent, beaked gules.   *Lambrequin*   argent and vert

Comparing with Siebmacher's drawings, the arms are, in detail, as follows·

In the shield, which is silver, the charge is a green double-headed eagle displayed, the beak colored gold, and the talons colored red   The two heads look away from each other   The eagle is the old *German* heraldic conventionalized form.   *Crest*   two silver swan's heads and necks, one behind the other, with red bills, both heads facing in the same direction, to the right (i.e , to the left of the drawing)   They are of the conventionalized heraldic form, with protruding tongues.   The necks are settled solidly upon a three-barred helmet, either profile or affronté (hard to determine, but most probably affronté; cf. Siebmacher)   It may be that upon the helmet there is a marquis' coronet (i e., a coronet with three strawberry leaves and two pearls showing), from which in turn emerge the two swan's heads.   *Lambrequin:* silver and green. From the drawing in Siebmacher, it is perhaps somewhat florid

The fact that the family in France has a black instead of a green eagle, and also possibly a single-headed one (at least according to sources dated later than 1884—cf V, also II, III, and IV), may be due to a change, voluntary or involuntary, adopted by the family, or the French branch of it, when it went to France; or at least when it became a part of the French nobility.   The later omission of mention of two heads, as well as other details (as the gold beak,

---

*Pages 8, 239-243   See also pp. 3, 6, 22, for discussion as to names

etc.), is probably explained on the basis of careless oversight on the part of the compilers when copying the descriptions

In view of the probability that the family was early connected with Basle and Alsace, at least during the centuries within which all noble families assumed arms, there is reason to believe that the above description, carefully arrived at by constructive criticism, is to be relied upon as probably authentic.

THE EAGLE.—The bird of Heraldry before all others is the eagle. Its earliest and chief popularity was in Germany, where it was adopted by the empire and by many of the principal sovereign princes. Its earliest appearance *as an heraldic charge* was in 1136 From about this time it was borne not only by the emperor and king of the Romans, but also by the princes who, as vicars of the empire, were charged with the government or defense of the empire's provinces Under Frederick I, Barbarossa, 1152-1189, the eagle had become the recognised standard of the Holy Roman Empire. The empire had double incentive for adopting this charge. For the eagle, the Bird of Jove, was not only the imperial emblem of the old Romans, and hence a natural adoption of the later Roman empire; but it was also, by tradition, the symbol of the fourth evangelist, imparting spiritual significance to its use by the Holy Roman emperors Thus as affecting the Empire and its princes, the eagle lent force to their claims to an ancient succession of both temporal and spiritual imperial power The origin of the double-headed eagle is mooted. But a probable explanation seems to be (cf. Nisbet), that, upon decline of the Roman empire in the East, the emperors of the Western empire joined the two eagles together with their heads separate, to indicate a double sovereignty probably claimed by them

"The most usual method of differencing in Germany was by alteration of the *tinctures* (colors), or alteration of the *charges* (the *figures* represented on the shield)
"The Eagle was a very popular charge in early Germany armoury
"In Germany, a change in the crest is often the only mark of distinction between different branches of the same family, and in Siebmacher's 'Wappenbuch' 31 different branches of the *Zorn* family have as many different crests, which are the sole marks of difference in the achievements
"The German idea of the crest is that it has not the *personal* character of the arms, but is rather attached to, or an appanage of, the territorial fief or lordship German arms are often accompanied by a number of crests over one shield Practically all changes of crests are due to inheritance (through heiresses or ancestresses) of an alternative crest"a
                                                                         A B DENT

RANK OF THE FAMILY —In all countries and at all times the condition of society has been one of inequality Upon this fact, in brief, is Heraldry

*The above quotations are from "Art of Heraldry," by A C Fox-Davies The work is compiled from all the older heraldic authorities The Articles on German Heraldry are mainly from Herr N G Strohl's "Heraldischer Atlas"

founded   In times of medieval armor bearing, nobles bore shields that were blazoned, because they were worthy of notice. The peasant or plebean bore his shild without blazon, being considered unworthy of notice. There were many earmarks about heraldic devices by which the rank of the bearer was indicated   Probably, however, especially on the continent, the rules were as often honored by the breach as by the observance   So if any significance attaches to the coronet used in the BRUMBACH arms charged with a springing deer, the family von BRUMBACH was of the rank of marquis   The same is indicated by the *barred* helmet. The barred helmet (even though in profile) indicates a very high rank—a rank anywhere above that of knight. Marquis —originally the title of the princes who, as lords of the *marches*, were charged with the defense of the imperial provinces—is a title of honor next in dignity to that of duke   The title given a marquis in the style of the heralds is "most noble and potent prince"

MOTTO —In continental heraldry the motto is seldom or never found Accordingly no motto is likely to be found with the BRUMBACH arms

THE PREFIX *von* —When a German is ennobled or made a gentleman of coat armor, he acquires the right to use the *territorial* prefix *von*. (At the same time, the Dutch *van* means practically nothing) *Von* is used in the sense of "of" or "from," to be followed by the name of the estate or territory over which the possessor is lord. Thus the early HEINRICH von BRUM- BACH. of 1113 (or his predecessors or successors), was lord of an estate, district, or territory by the name of BRUMBACH. Beginning with the tenth century "von" is regarded as the mark of nobility

REUNIONS

"But the home we first knew on this beautiful earth,
The friends of our childhood, the place of our birth,
In the heart's inner chambers sung always will be,
As the shell ever sings of its home in the sea "

Dana

"To live in the hearts we leave behind is not to die "

"These are Deeds that shall not pass away
And Names that must not wither."

Bayard Taylor

Throughout the nation there is a commendable fostering of "Home Coming," "Old Home" and "Reunion" days   They are beneficial to all concerned   Brief accounts are herewith given of the first and last meetings of the Reunion by Descendants of [E9] Conrad[3] Brumbaugh in Ohio, the Brumbaugh-Rinehart Reunion in Ohio, the Gerhard Brumbach Memorial Association in Pennsylvania, and of the Brumbaugh Reunion also in Pennsylvania.   There are numerous other organizations amongst the closely allied families, but lack of space prevents mention of them

BRUMBAUGH REUNION—DESCENDANTS OF [E9] CONRAD[3] ● BRUMBAUGH.

This Reunion has occurred annually since 1894 upon the third Saturday of August   "It was urged by a few of my sisters, and intended for brothers and sisters and their families, but was at once enlarged to include all the Brumbaughs and their friends "[a]   At the first meeting the late [E344] + Andrew[5] Brumbaugh was selected president, but declined, as he desired to give an address upon the family history, and also to devote all his time to gathering needed facts from those in attendance.   Franklin Dulebahn was the first president and Samuel Brumbaugh the first secretary-treasurer.   [E344] Andrew[5] Brumbaugh served as historian during his lifetime

The officers for 1911-12 are ·

President, Monroe[6] Brumbaugh [E768], East Akron, O

Vice-president, Emmet Clayton[5] Brumbaugh [E367], Canton, O

---

*Letter from [E345] Ephraim[4] Brumbaugh, second president, who has attended each meeting and is the historian.

·

26

2d Vice-president, Clayton C.[6] Schoner [E317-v], Hartville, O.
Chorister, Eva Aultman, Tallmadge, O
Historian, Ephraim[5] Brumbaugh [E345], Hartville, O
Executive Committee, Jacob C.[7] Luneman [E352-ii], Tallmadge, O.;
Edward Shanafelt, E Akron, O ; L. O. Brittan, E. Akron, O
  The next place of meeting will be in the grove of [E345] Ephraim[5] Brumbaugh, near Hartville, O , on the third Saturday in August, and the program is left for the secretary to arrange

BRUMBAUGH-RINEHART REUNION   MINUTES OF THE FIRST MEETING, SEPT 5, 1903 *

  About two hundred and fifty were present at the basket dinner, which was served at 11 30 o'clock, on tables under the trees   During dinner and immediately afterwards photographs of the company were made.
  The exercises of the afternoon were held under a large tent   After a brief address of welcome by Noah Webster Rinehart [E64-x], and the devotional exercises which consisted of the reading of the First Psalm and prayer by Elder Andrew[5] Brumbaugh [E344], the following program was rendered·
Devotional Exercises
Early Settlements of the Brumbaugh Family in Ohio.
Jacob Henry[5] Brumbaugh [E221]
Early Settlements of the Rineharts in Ohio   Dr Henry D.[5] Rinehart [E64-ix]
Singing
The Relationship of the Brumbaugh and Rinehart Families   Sarah Rinehart
Public Worship of the First Settlers .   ... John Christian
Singing
How Farming Was Done in the Early Days .... .Henry Baker
Housekeeping Among Our Grandmothers ..   . .   Martha Brumbaugh
Singing.
  Letters of greeting were read from J. W Christian and family, Payette, Idaho; Dr. J. S Rinehart, Camden, Arkansas, Rev Levi Winklebleck, Hartford City, Indiana, and Stell and Sarah Smith, Logansport, Indiana   .
  At the close of the program a business session was held   A report of the expenses of the meeting showed that $26 79 had been paid out.   A general collection was taken, and $27 01 received.
  On a motion by Dr Henry D.[5] Rinehart [E64-ix], seconded by Jacob Henry[5] Brumbaugh [E221], it was voted that the annual reunion of the

─────

*Held in the woods on the farm of David[4] Heekman [E 219], near Union, O   See illustration

Brumbaugh and Rinehart families shall be held on the first Saturday of September.

A committee consisting of Granville Webster[6] Brumbaugh [E651], Henry Baker and Minnie Rinehart was appointed by the chair to report nominations for the Executive Committee for 1904 The report of this committee, which was unanimously accepted, was as follows

> Dr. Henry D[5] Rinehart [E64-ix], Chairman
> Samuel Leroy[6] Brumbaugh [E623], Vice-Chairman.
> Samuel B[6] Heckman [E219-vi], Secretary and Treasurer.

The meeting was closed by singing "Blest Be the Tie that Binds," and prayer by Elder Jesse K—[5] Brumbaugh [E105]

Only an approximate account of those present can be given, as many failed to leave their names.

Members and Descendants of the [E16] Samuel[3] Brumbaugh Family.	59
[E13] George[3] Brumbaugh Family. .	8
[E10] Jacob[3] Brumbaugh Family (not represented).	
[E59] Catharine[4] (Brumbaugh) Baker Family	20
[E61] Susanna[4] (Brumbaugh) Beam Family.. .	5
[E65] Nancy[4] (Brumbaugh) Winklebleck Family	2
Elizabeth (Brumbaugh) Hoover Family	8
[E66] Mary[4] (Brumbaugh) Christian Family	17
Daniel Rinehart Family.	31
Enoch Rinehart Family	8
John Rinehart Family (not represented).	
Jacob Rinehart Family .	3
Susan (Rinehart) Barnhart Family ..	7
Mary (Rinehart) Yost Family.....	8
Daniel Brumbaugh Family	10
Jacob Brumbaugh Family..	7
Henry Rinehart Family	4
Other related families .	26
Friends .	60
Total .	273

Executive Committee

> NOAH WEBSTER[5] RINEHART [E64-x], Chairman.
> SAMUEL B—[6] HECKMAN [E219-vi], Secretary.
> JACOB HENRY[5] BRUMBAUGH [E221]

CONSTITUTION AND BY-LAWS OF THE BRUMBAUGH-RINEHART REUNION ASSOCIATION *

The Brumbaugh and Rinehart families, with those families related to either, or both of said families, in order to gain the knowledge of the past family history; to keep record of present whereabouts of said families, to trace better the out-going branches by birth and marriage, and to increase fellowship and the family love for one another, do organize themselves into this the "Brumbaugh-Rinehart Reunion Association"

This Association is the result of the "Brumbaugh-Rinehart Reunion," established in 1902, by the children of Samuel Brumbaugh, born 1806, whose wife was Elizabeth Rinehart, born 1808, and Daniel Rinehart, born 1812, whose wife was Esther Brumbaugh, born 1817 (Esther Brumbaugh-Rinehart was present at the adoption of this constitution)

CONSTITUTION.

Section 1 The name of this organization shall be The Brumbaugh-Rinehart Reunion Association

Sec. 2 The officers of this Association shall consist of a Chairman, Vice-Chairman, Secretary, Assistant Secretary and Treasurer.

Sec. 3 The Chairman shall preside at all meetings of the Association and the Executive Committee He shall have the power to call meetings of Executive Committee whenever necessary, and shall have interest in every department of the Association

Sec 4 The Vice-Chairman shall assist the Chairman in the work, and assume full duties of the Chairman in the latter's absence

Sec. 5. The Secretary shall make and keep the minutes of all meetings of the Association, and of the Executive Committee. He shall report same annually in printed form within twenty days after the annual reunion He shall receive all money and pay same to the Treasurer, taking receipt for same each time. Receipts of all money shall be reported in the annual report He shall perform all other duties belonging to said office, and call the Executive Committee when business demands attention

Sec. 6 The Assistant Secretary shall have charge of all general correspondence, such as mailing notices, mailing of annual minutes, and all other duties belonging to said office He shall be assistant to the Secretary, and in the absence of the Secretary, or vacancy of this office, he shall assume full duty of both Secretary and Assistant Secretary until such vacancy is filled

---

*Fourth Ann Rept Brumbaugh-Rhinehart Reunion Association, adopted at the Eaton, O, meeting, 1906, which was its fourth annual reunion

Sec. 7. The Treasurer shall receive the money from the Secretary and give receipt for same   He shall pay out money only upon the written order of the Secretary   He shall make a written report to the "Annual Reunion" each year.

Sec. 8   The Executive Committee shall consist of the five officers—Chairman, Vice-Chairman, Secretary, Assistant Secretary and Treasurer   It is the duty of this Committee to supervise the work and interests of the Association, to arrange for all Reunions, select location, make the program, appoint the committees, etc

Sec. 9   All persons by the name of Brumbaugh or Rinehart, and all persons related to them by blood or marriage may become regular members of this Brumbaugh-Rinehart Reunion Association, and shall be so considered after complying with conditions of this instrument   Other persons tracing no relation may become honorary members

BY-LAWS

Section 1.   The officers of this Association shall be elected by ballot; each regular member of the Association, fifteen or more years of age, may write one name for each office on one ticket   Ballots shall be dropped into a receptacle provided for such purpose   The one who receives the plurality of votes cast for an office shall be declared elected to such respective office by the Chairman.   A committee shall be appointed by the Chairman to count the ballots and report to him in writing   In case only one name is before the Annual Association for election to either office, this law may be suspended, and Secretary instructed to cast the ballot for said candidate.

Sec. 2.   The time of holding the Annual Reunion shall be the first or second Saturday of September each year   The exercises of the meeting shall consist of social greetings, introductions, business sessions, dinner, invocation, short addresses, music, etc

Sec. 3.   It being the purpose of this Association to trace and record the history of these families, a committee on "family history" shall be appointed by Chairman which shall report at each reunion   It is furthermore the purpose of this Association to make and keep on record a history of these families, to this end a committee on "current history" shall be appointed by Chairman, which shall report at each Reunion   To aid the aforesaid Committee in its work, it shall be the duty of each member of this Association to report to these Committees any death, birth, sickness, marriage, accident, great achievement of any member of this Association, and such other things as might be considered of value to such record

Sec 4 The expenses, such as postage, printing, etc , of the Association or Executive Committee and all other committees, also all persons called upon to perform duty for this Association shall be borne by the Association

Sec 5 It shall be the duty of each member of the Association to attend the Annual Reunions and give hearty assistance in every way to make them successful, to encourage both the older and the younger of these family branches to meet as one family each year at the "Reunion Meeting "

NINTH ANNUAL REUNION OF THE BRUMBAUGH-RINEHART FAMILIES

This was again held at the Darke Co Fair Grounds, Greenville, O., Sept. 2, 1911. The program contained.

"Come early with a soul full of joy and good fellowship and baskets prepared to care for the most perfect appetites "

A number of the members of the reunion having expressed a desire to devote the major portion of the meeting to renewing old friendships, making new ones, and having visits with those from a distance, a program was not prepared.

OFFICERS 1911

Chairman—Dr. Charles Baker, Palestine, Ohio

Vice-Chairman—Franklin[6] Bookwalter [E59-vi-4], Versailles, Ohio

Secretary—Adah Baker

Treasurer—Levi Brumbaugh, West Milton, Ohio.

Chairman of Committee on Introductions—Henry D—[5] Rinehart, M D. [E64-ix]

Chairman of Committee on Arrangements for Dinner—Mrs Lesta E. Wright

THE GERHARD BRUMBACH (BROWNBACK) MEMORIAL
ASSOCIATION.

This association has held five annual meetings in Chester County, Pennsylvania, and they have been extensively attended The Application for Incorporation herewith presented is practically as it was recorded, and one of its certificates of membership is also reproduced. The first invitation is reproduced, and also the program for the fifth reunion:

"Yourself and family are invited to attend the
BROWNBACK FAMILY REUNION
At Bonnie Brae Park,
SATURDAY, JUNE 8, 1907
To be given in honor of Dr Orlando Walker⁵ Brownback [A84], of Pendleton, Indiana
JAMES⁵ BROWNBACK [A80], Linfield, Pa
LEVI J ⁵ BROWNBACK [A83], Birchrunville, Pa
WM. H ⁶ MOSTELLER, M D [A78-h], Phoenixville, Pa.
Each family furnish such refreshments as will be suitable for a family dinner "

APPLICATION FOR INCORPORATION OF "THE GERHARD BRUM-
BACH (BROWNBACK) MEMORIAL ASSOCIATION "
In the Court of Common Pleas of Chester County, Pennsylvania   Term 1909,
No ——
To the Honorable the Judges of said Court.
The undersigned, all of whom are citizens of the Commonwealth of Pennsylvania, having associated themselves together for the purpose of organizing and establishing "The Gerhard Brumbach (Brownback) Memorial Association" and being desirous of becoming incorporated agreeable to the provisions of the Act of Assembly entitled, "An Act to provide for the incorporation and regulation of certain corporations," approved the 29th day of April, A. D. 1874, and the Supplements thereto, do hereby certify:
1. The name of the proposed corporation is   The Gerhard Brumbach
   (Brownback) Memorial Association
2. The corporation is formed for the purpose of forming and continuing
   a Genealogical Tree of the Brumbach-Brownbaugh (Brownback)
   blood kindred, to collect the historical incidents and relics of the

32

said Gerhard Brumbach-Brownbaugh and his descendants, to compile a history of the said Gerhard Brumbach-Brownbaugh and his descendants; and to cultivate, teach, develop, instruct and bring forth genius, talent and general scientific knowledge in the coming generations.

3 This Association shall transact business in the County of Chester and state of Pennsylvania

4. The said Corporation shall exist perpetually.

5. To have power to institute, maintain and defend judicial proceedings; to enter into any obligation necessary for the transaction of its ordinary business

6. To make and use a common seal and alter the same at pleasure.

7. To hold, purchase and transfer such real and personal property as the purposes of the said corporation require, not exceeding the amount limited by the laws of this Commonwealth

8. To make by-laws not inconsistent with the laws of this Commonwealth for the management of its property and the regulation of its affairs, to appoint and remove such subordinate officers and agents as the business of the Association requires and to allow them a suitable compensation for services performed

9. The names and residences of the subscribers are as follows· Dr. William H [6] Mosteller [A78-11], Phoenixville, Pa ; U. S. G. Finkbiner, Royersford, Pa , Harry I Hiestand, Royersford, Pa , Garret Ellwood[5] Brownback [A132], Linfield, Pa ; Edward Goodwin[6] Brownback [A160], Trappe, Pa

10 The said corporation is to be managed by a Board of Directors, consisting of twenty-five members, and the names and residences of those chosen as such for the first year are:
Garret Ellwood Brownback, Linfield, Pa
U. S G. Finkbiner, Royersford, Pa.
Edward G Brownback, Trappe, Pa
John Mock, Pawlings, Pa.
Stephen S Brownback, Philadelphia, Pa.
Jesse Keims, Philadelphia, Pa.
Harry I Hiestand, Royersford, Pa
W. H. Mosteller, M D , Phoenixville, Pa
John Bingaman, Altoona, Pa.
Max A Kaiser, Philadelphia, Pa.
Rev. Oscar D Brownback, Parker Ford, Pa.

Orlando W. Brownback, M D , Pendleton, Ind
Rev. James Sampson, Philadelphia, Pa
Webster P Brownback, Pughtown, Pa
W. M Stauffer, Reading, Pa
Dr. Wm. Campbell Posey, Philadelphia, Pa
J. D. Landis, Philadelphia, Pa
J Harry Francis, East Coventry Township, Chester Co.
Lewis C Brownback, East Vincent Township, Chester Co
Levi Brownback, West Vincent Township, Chester Co
George Keim, West Pikeland Township, Chester Co
Ellwood Detwiler, Charlestown Township, Chester Co
James Bingaman, South Coventry Township, Chester Co
Harmon Prizer, East Coventry Township, Chester Co
Amos Hiestand, East Vincent Township, Chester Co

FIFTH ANNUAL REUNION OF THE BROWNBACK FAMILY HELD IN BONNIE BRAE PARK, EAST PIKELAND TOWNSHIP, JUNE 17, 1911.

Mother's Day—"A perfect woman, nobly planned,
To warm, to comfort and command "
—*Wordsworth.*

PROGRAMME

9 30 a m —Greeting of friends and relatives under large pavilion
10:00—Music by Orchestra.
10 30—Literary Exercises.
Welcome...   . . . .By President of B M A
Invocation   . . . .   Rev. Chas Slinghoff
          Pastor Brownback's Reformed Church, East Coventry, Pa
Address· "Mary Papen, the Mother of the Brownbacks"
                    W. H. Mosteller, M D. [A78-ii], Phoenixville, Pa.
                              Music
Address· "The Hand That Rocks the Cradle Rules the Nation"
                                        Rev F L. Kerr
          Pastor of St John's Reformed Church, Phoenixville, Pa
Singing . . . ."A Hundred Years to Come"
                         "In Memoriam."
                              Recess
12 00 noon—The Annual Brownback Banquet, to which every one is invited
          "Come, let us feast in honor of our Mother "

2.00 p. m.—Music . . . . Brownback Quartette, Philadelphia

Address· "A Mother's Meditation" Rev Oscar Davis[6] Brownback [A229]
       Pastor of the First Presbyterian Church, Port Alleghany, Pa

Music . . . . .Brownback Quartette

Address "The Queen of the Home". Rev Abner J Irey, D D
       Pastor of Danville Baptist Church—A Papen descendant.

Address .. .. Prof Martin Grove[6] Brumbaugh [E682]
       Supt. Public Education, Philadelphia.

       Family Conference.

Subject .. .."The Domestic Hearth"
       "Where we love is home—
       Home that our feet may leave
       But not our hearts."

Singing. . . . ."Home, Sweet Home"

OFFICERS:

[A78-ii] William H—[6] Mosteller, M D , President, Phoenixville, Pa.

[A160] Edward Goodwin[6] Brownback, Vice-President, Trappe, Pa.

[A123] U. S G Finkbiner, Secretary, Royersford, Pa.

[A132] Garrett Ellwood[5] Brownback, Treasurer, Linfield, Pa.

FIRST BRUMBAUGH REUNION, SNYDER'S GROVE, MARTINS BURG, BLAIR CO, PA, JUNE 22, 1906

This "Reunion" embraces mainly the counties of Bedford, Blair, and Huntingdon, although in the estimated two thousand persons who attended this first reunion many sections of Pennsylvania and adjoining States were represented* "The day was everything one could wish for No cloud appeared to mar the pleasures of the day The park itself was a place of beauty, and the cool inviting air of Martinsburg had much to do with the enjoyment of every one

"The meeting was called to order by the chairman, Moses Roberts Brumbaugh [E 3168], of Henrietta 'All Hail the Power of Jesus Name' was sung by the audience Rev, Henry Boyers Brumbaugh [E 276], of Juniata College, Huntingdon, conducted the devotional exercises, reading from the 21st chapter of Revelations

"A quartette, composed of Messrs Martin Potes Brumbaugh [C 328], Lloyd Replogle, Emmert Replogle and Samuel Nicodemus⁵ Brumbaugh [E 3100], sang 'We Must Answer to Our Names,' which was much appreciated by the audience

"The address of welcome was made by Elder George Wineland⁴ Brumbaugh [E 3016], of Fredericksburg, Pa He said in part·

"'Mr Chairman, fellow-kinsmen, neighbors and friends It is with a high appreciation of the honors you have conferred upon me that I appear before you to extend a hearty welcome to all who have assembled here on this happy occasion And while there are many here who, if called upon, could have performed the part better than myself, I am sure there is no one among you who is prouder of his ancestry than I am We have come here to-day as a happy, united family

"'The family is a divine institution In the morning of time, when the all-wise Creator crowned His work by giving to one of His creatures the attributes of intelligence, He at once found that the work was incomplete and uttered the general truth, that it was not good for man to be alone Woman was created and given to man, the sharer of his joys and sorrows, trials and triumphs, to keep watch with him in all the experiences of life They were made social creatures There was put into each heart a yearning for the companionship of the other And when two hearts are thus united, the sweetest and happiest joys of life are attained Thus the benevolent Creator not only instituted marriage, but He Himself presided at the first marriage altar Hence we have the family, a divine institution It is the first as well as the greatest institution on earth Father, mother, son, daughter, brother and sister are names that speak to the heart and call forth the highest and best impulses of which humanity is capable

"'Keep the family pure and virtuous and the nation and church are filled with good, strong men and women Corrupt the family and the church is gone and the world is filled with beings of a lower rank

"'Much of the future is with you We hope your coming here will increase your faith and hope and zeal, and make your life better and more useful because you have been here We welcome our young men and women We refer to you with pride as examples of virtue and sobriety. We welcome your coming here to mingle with your kindred, to light your torches at their altars so that you may go out better equipped to help keep the world better because you have lived in it

"'We welcome the children, God bless them, the future is theirs

"'We welcome the strangers that are within our gates We appreciate the honor you have done us by coming here Our ancestors were people of large hospitality Their hearts and altars were free to strangers. The noble grace still lives in the hearts of their children and let us hope will continue to live as long as human hearts need sympathy and love, and If your being with us will afford you as much joy as it gives us to have you here, it will certainly make a day of pleasant memories to all

"'We want this to be a day of joy to all And as we go out to face the scenes of the unknown and untried future, we know not what is awaiting us, what is written on the scroll

*From *Martinsburg Herald*, June 29, '06

36

of fate Though we may not draw the veil aside that hides the mysterious future and see the joys or sorrows that await us, we can say with the poet

  " ' "Let fate do her worst, there are relics of joy,
   Bright dreams of the past which it cannot destroy,
   Which come in the night time of sorrow and care,
   And bring back the features that joy used to wear

   Long, long be my heart with such memories filled,
   Like the vase in which roses have once been distilled,
   You may break, you may shatter the vase if you will,
   But the scent of the roses clings 'round it still " '

"The response to this address was given by David Stuckey⁴ Brumbaugh [C76], of Roaring Spring He said in part

" 'I am glad to respond to the elegant address of welcome We must make this day the best one of our lives by clasping again the hands of old friends and those of new ones. The objects of these reunions are to know each other and renew the family ties Almost every State in the Union has our representatives and we are not ashamed of our name, since it is a great one

"He also gave much history concerning the early Brumbaugh settlers, which was much enjoyed

"The meeting was then adjourned until 2 30 p m

"Dinner, a most important as well as enjoyable feature of the day, now occupied the attention of every one It was indeed a pretty sight to look over the park and see the tables laden with their weight of good things, which the ladies of the Brumbaugh family know how to prepare

"The afternoon session was called to order by Vice-president Levi Brumbaugh⁶ Stoudnour [E3105-11] 'O Think of a Home Over There' was sung by the audience, after which the following officers were elected for the coming year:

"President, Dr Martin Grove⁶ Brumbaugh [E 682], superintendent of public schools of Philadelphia, vice-president, Martin Pote⁵ Brumbaugh [C328], of Altoona; secretary, Miss Lula May⁶ Brumbaugh [E 3107], of Clover Creek, treasurer, Samuel Nicodemus⁵ Brumbaugh [E3100], of Altoona, music director, Henry Holsinger⁵ Brumbaugh [E3141], of Defiance This was followed by a quartette, 'Far Out on the Seas.'

"Dr Andrew Boelus⁵ Brumbaugh [E226], of Huntingdon, next favored the audience with an address in which he gave very good information concerning the Brumbaugh family He explained the origin of the Brumbaugh name, which means humming brook. Brum— humming, baugh—brook

"This address was followed by a much appreciated solo by Mrs Carrie Elizabeth⁶ (Hagey) Endsley [L3095-1], of New York City, entitled 'Nobody at All '

"Short addresses were made by Charles Ober⁵ Brumbaugh [C368], of New Enterprise, Levi Hoover⁸ Brumbaugh [E181], of New York City, Dr F. A Rupley, of Martinsburg, and Rev Geo Boyer⁵ Brumbaugh [E225], of James Creek

"Elder Geo W Brumbaugh, of Fredericksburg, and son S N, of Altoona, then sang a duet entitled 'The Old Ship Zion,' which was much appreciated by the audience

"The committee on resolutions gave the following report. We, the committee appointed by the chairman of the Brumbaugh reunion, present the following resolutions First—We hereby express our appreciation for the very efficient manner in which the various committees rendered their services Second—To the committee on music for its elaborate and well prepared music Third—To the organist and owner of the organ, and also to Mrs Endsley for the pleasing rendition of a solo Fourth—To the owners of the Snyder park for the use of the grove we extend our thanks Fifth—To the friends of the organization for helping to make the reunion a success Rev Henry Boyer Brumbaugh, L B Stoudner [F3105-11], Prof Horace Atlee⁶ Brumbaugh, S N Brumbaugh [C501], Miss Lula May⁴ Brumbaugh [E3107], committee

"The following committees were appointed for the ensuing year

"History Committee—Dr Gaius Marcus⁶ Brumbaugh [E743], Washington, D C, Dr Martin Grove Brumbaugh, Philadelphia Dr Andrew Boelus Brumbaugh [E226], Huntingdon, Rev Geo W Brumbaugh, Clover Creek, Nicholas Brumbaugh, Huntingdon; David Stuckey⁴ Brumbaugh [C76], Roaring Springs; H H. Brumbaugh, Defiance Committee on Place of Meeting—H B Brumbaugh [E276], Huntingdon; Charles Ober⁴ Brumbaugh [C638], New Enterprise; L B Stoudner [F3105-11], Roaring Spring

"Miss Lula May⁶ Brumbaugh [E 3107], secretary of the association, kindly furnished

the foregoing report of the exercises It was the greatest day in the history of the local
Brumbaughs About a year ago Miss Bertha Brumbaugh first became interested in holding
a reunion, and among others, mentioned the matter to M R Brumbaugh, of Henrietta, who
at once took up the matter, and by their advocating a reunion, L. B Stoudnour joined in
the movement, which terminated in probably the largest reunion ever held in the Cove, and
the forming of a permanent organization

   *   *   *   *   *   *   *   *   *

"The Brumbaugh connection is one of the largest relationships in this part of the United
States With each succeeding generation they are becoming more and more distinguished
Among them are educators, lawyers, doctors, teachers, farmers, merchants, clerks, tradesmen,
and are represented in nearly all the walks of life Dr Martin Groves Brumbaugh [E 682],
who recently succeeded Dr Edward Brooks to the superintendency of the schools of Philadelphia, is one of the most distinguished educators east of the Alleghenv mountains The
founding of Juniata College at Huntingdon and the success and growth of that institution
are largely due to the energy of the Brumbaughs connected with the school."

REUNIONS OF BEDFORD, BLAIR AND HUNTINGDON COUNTIES, PENNSYLVANIA

Fifth Brumbaugh Reunion, held Thursday, June 22, 1911, in Snyder's
Grove, Martinsburg, Blair County, Pa

OFFICERS.

Horace Atlee[6] Brumbaugh [C501], Roaring Spring, Pa .. ..President
Charles Ober[5] Brumbaugh [C368], New Enterprise, Pa ....Vice-President
Lula May[6] Brumbaugh [E3107], Eldorado, Pa . ..Secretary
John Elvin[8] Brumbaugh [E530], Altoona, Pa . .. . .Treasurer
David Hoover C[5] Brumbaugh [E3112], Martinsburg, Pa Musical Director
Moses Robert[5] Brumbaugh [E3168], Henrietta, Pa .. .General Manager
Gaius Marcus[6] Brumbaugh, M D. [E743], Washington, D C ... Historian

PROGRAM.
Forenoon Session.

Music . ... Audience
Devotional Exercises .. Henry Boyer[5] Brumbaugh [E276], Huntingdon
Address of Welcome
        David Stuckey[4] Brumbaugh [C76], Esq., Roaring Spring
Response... . . . . Samuel H Replogle, Altoona, Pa.
Quartette
Reading of Minutes . ... By Secretary
Address.. . . . Dr C. I. Brown, President Findlay College, Findlay, Ohio
Solo . ....Carrie Elizabeth[6] (Hagey) Endsley [E3095-1], New York City
Reading ... .Frank Nicodemus[5] Brumbaugh [E3104], Reading, Pa.
Address .... Hon. John M Reynolds, Bedford, Pa.
Quartette.

"The Work of the Historian".   ... . John Elvin[6] Brumbaugh [E530]
Reading   . .. .Samuel Nicodemus[5] Brumbaugh [E3100], Altoona, Pa.

Afternoon Session.

Music
Report of Committees.
Short Addresses and Music
Adjournment.

(This organization has not adopted a Constitution and By-Laws.)

BRUMBACH-BROMBACH IMMIGRANTS *

[A1]   *Gerhard[1] Brumbach* arrived at Germantown, Pa , probably on the sailing vessel *Concord*, Oct 6, 1683, when there was but one house in Germantown.   Descendants spell the name *Brownback* [b]

[B1]   *Georg[1] Bombach* arrived at Philadelphia, Pa , on the ship *Samuel*, Capt. Percy, Dec 3, 1740, from Rotterdam—"natives and late inhabitants of the Palatinate upon the Rhine and places adjacent."

[C1]   *Johann Jacob[1] Brumbach* arrived at Philadelphia, Pa , on the ship *Nancy*, Capt. Thomas Coatam, Aug 31, 1750, from Rotterdam, and last from Cowes.

[D1]   *Johan Melchior[1] Brombach* arrived at Philadelphia, Pa , on the ship *Halifax*, Capt. Thomas Coatam, Sept. 22, 1752, from Rotterdam, and last from Cowes.

[D2]   *Widow[1] Brombach* passed from Pa. to Va about 1760; descendants spell the name *Brumback*.   The presumptive evidence is that she was probably the widow of [D1] *Johan Melchior[1]*.

"*Milcard* [*Melchior*] *Brumbach*—came into this country (Va) to dwell in the year 1714"—lived at Germanna, Va.   (Recently discovered facts are in Section D)

[F2]   *Peter Brombach* landed at Jamestown, Va , about 1770   His descendants together with those of his brothers [F3] *Charles*, [F4] *Paul*, [F5] *William*, and [F6] *John*, landing the same year at *Jamestown, Va.*, are numerous throughout Va., and especially throughout Ky.—they spell the name *Brombach*, or *Brumback*.

[E1]   *Johannes Henrich[1] Brumbach* arrived at Philadelphia, Pa , on the ship *Neptune*, Capt. Waire, Sept 30, 1754, from Rotterdam, and last from Cowes.

[E3]   *Conrad[1] Brombach* and [E4] *Johannes[1] Brombach* arrived at Philadelphia, Pa , on the ship *Countess of Sussex*, Capt Thomas Gray, Oct 7, 1765, sailing from Rotterdam

[G1]   *Hermanus Emanuel[1] Brumbach* arrived probably through Baltimore about 1770.   Descendants retain the spelling, except that one branch (Va) spells the name *Brumback* and another (Ohio) spells it *Brumbaugh* (the late Rev Edmund Green Brumbaugh belonged to the latter family).

---

*Chronologically arranged, except for "Milcard" and the "Widow Brombach," and [F2] Peter Brombach et seq   Photographic copies of the *Original Immigrant Lists* in half tones are reproduced in the various sections through the cooperation of Mr Luther R Kelker, Custodian of the Public Records, Harrisburg, Pa

[b]Origin and History of the Rittenhouse Family—Cassel, Vol I, p 109 et seq, 1893.

40

GERMAN IMMIGRANTS

"To the German immigrants from Pennsylvania and the Palatinate, however, must be ascribed the largest share of honor in that wonderful development of the fertile plains and valleys of Western Maryland which has added so much to the general growth and prosperity of the State As in other portions of the country, so in Western Maryland, the German element has played an important part from the earliest period of colonial history, and at the present day, woven in by time with the general prosperity and progress, forms one of the chief constituents of the industrial, agricultural, moral, and intellectual well-being of Western Maryland, as well as of other portions of the State. Even before Penn and his followers made their settlement upon the Delaware, certain German Protestants, in quest of a refuge from religious oppression, had come into the province and had been hospitably received."[a]

"To the sturdy German stock that came to the Colony of Pennsylvania (Md., Va , etc —G M B) in the first half of the eighteenth century we are indebted for more of the initial influences that have made for the progress and prestige of our American civilization than many historians record or know "[b]

"When they left the Fatherland which, with all its tender associations, had grown to be cruel, and came to dwell under strange skies in a wilderness with the wolf and savage they brought with them their Bibles."—*Pennypacker*

CONESTOGA WAGON.

"Next to barn and dwelling-house the most important architectural product of the Pennsylvania Germans is the great Conestoga wagon, which Rush called the 'ship of inland commerce.' Before the advent of railroads these were the chief means of transport between the farms and towns of Pennsylvania. In them the wheat, vegetables, fruit, and, alas, whiskey—which often formed a side industry of many a farmer—were carried for miles to Philadelphia. Says Rush 'In this wagon, drawn by four or five horses of a peculiar breed, they convey to market, over the roughest roads, 2000 and 3000 pounds' weight of the produce of their farms In the months of September and October it is no uncommon thing on the Lancaster and Reading roads to meet in one day fifty or one hundred of these wagons on their way to Philadelphia, most of which belong to German farmers ' These teams were stately objects in those times; owner and driver alike took pride in them and kept them neat and trim. They consisted of five or six heavy horses, well fed and cur-

---

[a]*"Western Maryland"*—*J T Scharf, Vols I-II, Vol I, p 59*
[b]*Life and Works of Christopher Dock*—Martin Groves Brumbaugh [E682], p 11.

ried, wearing good harness, and sometimes adorned with bows of bells, fitted
so as to form an arch above the collar   These bells were carefully selected to
harmonize or chime, from the small treble of the leaders to the larger bass
upon the wheel-horses   The wagon body was necessarily built stanch and
strong, but by no means clumsy   Upon them the wheelwright and blacksmith
expended their utmost skill and good taste, and oftentimes produced master-
pieces of work, both in shape and durability   The running gear was invariably
painted red, and the body blue   (This did not apply amongst the G B. B ,
Mennonites, etc —G M B)   The cover was of stout white linen or hempen
material, drawn tightly over, shapely, fitted to the body, lower near the middle
and projecting like a bonnet in front and at the back, the whole having a
graceful and sightly outline '"'

The wagon shown in Plate 15 is said to have been built by a Brumbaugh in Frederick County, Md , a descendant of Johann Jacob[1] Brumbaugh
[C1], but authentic information has not been secured on this point. Mr. B.
W. T. Phreaner, Hagerstown, Md , copyrighted the photograph   The
"schooner" is in service in Washington Co , Md , and illustrates the general
class of "prairie schooners" familiar throughout the west before the advent of
railroads   Our ancestors unquestionably used them in their overland migrations

----

[1]German and Swiss Settlements of Penna , p 98, and Ellis and Evans' History Lancaster Co , Pa , p 350

CENSUS, TAX AND OTHER RECORDS

The records reproduced upon pages 46 to 68 are of widespread interest and importance The assessments are of extensive and general genealogical importance.

HEADS OF FAMILIES AT THE FIRST CENSUS, 1790; MARYLAND, PENNSYLVANIA AND VIRGINIA

	Free white males of 16 yrs & upward, including heads of families	Free white males under 16 years	Free white females, including heads of families.	All other free persons	Slaves
*Md —Washington Co.**					
Angle, Henry [See C1]	3	2	5		
Brumbach, Jacob [E2]	3	4	4		
Brumbagh, Jacob [C1]	1	4	2		
Brumbagh, John [C4]	1		4		
Pa.—Bedford Co.					
Boyer, Micall	1	2	5		
Broombough, Conrod [E3]	1	6	4		
Ulery, Samuel [See C3]	1	1	5		
Ulery, David	1	5	2		
Coventry Twp , Chester Co					
Bromback, Edward [A11]	2		1		
Bromback, John [A10]	1	3	3	1	
Vincent Twp , Chester Co.					
Bromback, Henry [A6]	4		2		
Bromback, Henry Jr [A9]	2		1		
Dauphin Co —Harrisburgh Town.					
Bumbaugh, Conrad [B2]	2	1	3		

*Corrections certified by the enumerators who "Made oath on the Holy Evangills of Almighty God "

HEADS OF FAMILIES AT THE FIRST CENSUS, 1790; MARYLAND, PENNSYL-
VANIA AND VIRGINIA —*Continued.*

	Free white males of 16 yrs & upward, including heads of families.	Free white males under 16 years.	Free white females, including heads of families	All other free persons.	Slaves.
Franklin Co.					
Broombough, Conrad	2		1		
Broombough, Hans	2	1	5		
Huntingdon Co					
Brumbough, Jacob [L2]	3	4	4		
Brumbough, George	1		6		
Brumbough, John	1		1		
Fouss, Nicholas	1	2	1		
Garner, Michle	2	3	3		
Gochanour, David	1	2	4		
Hover, Christian	1	3	3		
Hover, Jacob	1	1	1		
Metzker, Philip	2	2	5		
Miller, Abraham	2	2	4		
Cocalico Twp , Lancaster Co.					
Brombach, Frantz	1	3	5		
York Co.•					
Bumbaugh, John	1	2	1		
Va.—Fairfax Co.					
Bromback, John	9	1	3		

ORGANIZATION OF COUNTIES

In connection with the foregoing extracts from the first U. S Census,
and because the information will help clear up questions to arise later in this
volume, and in searches through land and other records, certain facts are here
given concerning the said counties ·

Maryland—*Washington Co* was formed from part of Frederick Co in
1776

___

•Berwick, Cumberland, Franklin, Germany, Hamilton, Heidelberg, Mt Pleasant, Mount-
joy and Strable Townships

Pennsylvania—Bedford Co was organized March 9, 1771, from part of Cumberland Co.

"*Blair Co.* was formed from parts of Huntingdon and Bedford by an Act of Assembly, approved the 26th day of Feb, 1846 The act declares that on and after the fourth Mon of July, 1846, the territory within the townships of North Woodberry and Greenfield in the Co. of Bedford + + + and of Allegheny, Antis, Snyder, Tyrone, Frankstown, Blair, Huston, Woodberry, and a portion of Morris, in the county of Huntingdon, should constitute a new county, to be known as Blair Co " [a]

"*Chester Co.* is one of the three original counties (Phila, Bucks and Chester) established by Wm Penn in 1682 + + within two months after the arrival of Penn." + + + "The western boundary of Chester Co. was established by the erection of Lancaster Co. in 1729, and the northern and northwestern by the erection of Berks Co. in 1752. Philadelphia Co. formed the northeastern and eastern boundary, until the establishment of Montgomery in 1784." [b]

Cumberland Co was formed Jan. 27, 1750, from part of Lancaster Co., and its immense area included "+ northward and westward with the line of the Provinces, eastward partly with the Susquehanna and partly with said county of York, and southward, in part by the line dividing said province from that of Maryland "

Dauphin Co. was formed March 4, 1785

Franklin Co was formed from Cumberland Sept , 1784, largely upon the petition of the "dwellers on the Conococheague" or the S W. portion of the county.

Huntingdon Co. was formed Sept 20, 1787, from part of Bedford Co., and from its immense territory Centre Co was taken Feb. 13, 1800; Clearfield and Cambria Cos March 26, 1804, Blair Co., Feb. 26, 1846

Montgomery Co was formed Sept 10, 1784, from part of Philadelphia Co

York Co. was formed from part of Lancaster Aug. 19, 1749.

Virginia—Fairfax Co formed from Prince William in 1742; Spottsylvania formed in 1721, Orange in 1734, Frederick in 1738, etc. See Sec. D.

The map of Bedford Co., Pa., is from a special photograph of the earliest map in the office of the Sec of Int. Affairs (Pa.); and the map of Huntingdon and Blair Cos is from the map (1883) prepared by J. Murray Africa, Huntingdon, Pa., and was published in History of Huntingdon and Blair Counties, Pa , by J. Simpson Africa. NOTE: These maps have been omitted from the vol., because of their size.

[a] History of Pa —Egle, 1883, p. 397
[b] History of Pa.—Egle, 1883, pp. 517-518

NORTH WOODBERRY TOWNSHIP, PENNSYLVANIA

"This township is the S E division of Blair Co   From the extinguishment of the Indian title to lands in this region in 1758 to the time of the formation of Bedford Co in 1771, this bit of the vast domain of the commonwealth was included within the boundaries of Cumberland, and from the latter year until the erection of Blair in 1846 it formed part of Bedford + +   With Tussey's Mountain on the east, it embraces a portion of the beautiful and fertile region known as the Great or Morrison's Cove   Martinsburgh Borough is situated in the northwest part   About 3 miles east of Martinsburg, near Clover Creek, is the small village of Fredericksburg, otherwise known as Clover Creek post office, southward from the latter place the hamlet known as Millerstown, and in the southeastern part of the twp. is Henrietta, also a post office, and the terminus of the Morrison's Cove branch of P. R R " + + +

"About 1755 a colony of Dunkards, otherwise known as German Baptists (G B. B), began to settle in the southern portion of the Cove, they gradually worked their way northward, until many of them became residents of the present twp. of North Woodberry, Taylor and Huston, and numbers of their descendants hold possession to this day

Early History —It is an historical fact that the Great Cove, changed to Morrison's Cove as early as 1770, which commences at Pattonsville, in Bedford Co., and ends at Williamsburg, on the Frankstown Branch of the Juniata, bounded by Dunning's and Lock Mts on the west, and Tussey's Mt. on the east, was settled by Scotch-Irish as early as 1749, but these lands were yet owned by the Indians, and in answer to their prayers the bold squatters were expelled by officials representing the Penn family   Nothing daunted, however, many of them returned soon after and continued their improvements   Yet the northern, or Blair Co portion of the Cove, was almost unexplored until the Penns made the new purchase in 1754."

"During the Indian wars of 1762 quite a number of murders were committed in the Cove, and many captives taken. + + + During the Great Cove massacre, among others carried off was the family of John Martin (See p. 47) This incursion was indeed a most formidable one, led by the Kings, Shingas and Beaver in person   How many were killed there is no living witness to tell, neither can we conjecture the number of persons taken   The following petition was sent to Council:

"August 13, 1762

"The Humble Petition of Your Most Obedient Servant Sheweth, Sir, may it pleas Your Excellency, Hearing me in Your Clemancy a few words   I, One

of the Bereaved of my Wife and five Children by Savage War at the Captivity of the Great Cove, after Many & Long Journeys, I Lately went to an Indian Town, viz, Tuskaroways, 150 miles Beyond Fort Pitt, & Entrested in Col Bucquits & Col Croghan's favor, So far as to bear their Letters to King Beaver & Capt. Shingas Desiring them to Give up One of my Daughters, if Alive, Among them, and after Seeing my Daughter with Shingas he refused to Give her up, and after some Expostulating with him, but all in vain, he promised to Deliver her up with the Other Captives to yr Excellency.

Sir, Yr Excellency's Most Humble Servt, Humbly & Passionately Beseeches Yr Beninger Compassion to Interpose Yr Excellencies Beneficent in favor of Yr Excellencies Most Obedient & Dutiful Servt.

John Martin."

"In May, 1781, a band of marauding savages entered the cove and murdered a man, woman, and two children, and took one man prisoner within a mile of the fort of John Piper, who was then colonel of the county At another time several other prisoners were taken. It has also been related to us that during one of these Indian forays a man named Houser and his son were killed, and two children of the same family carried away into captivity The two first mentioned were buried on the farm of David Rice, in the present township of Taylor."

"Soon after the close of the Revolutionary war, and the consequent cessation of Indian depredations, *bona fide* settlers swarmed into the cove, and it is presumed that prior to 1790 all desirable lands had passed to individual ownership. + +,+ We are quite certain that among those who were here prior to the beginning of the century now passing, or very soon thereafter, were the Albrights, Allenbaughs, Blakes, Burkets, Bridenthals, Bowers, Brumbaughs, Benners, Bulgers, Camerers, Conrads, Cowans, Deeters, Dillingers, Emricks, Eversoles, Faulkners, Flenners, Gensingers, Grabills, Hoovers, Holsingers, Knees. Lowers, Looses, Longeneckers, Martins, Metzkers, Myerses, Moores, Nicodemuses, Nisewangers, Oungsts, Puderbaughs, Rhodes, Roemers, Strayers, Shoenfelts, Stoners, Skyleses, Stoufflers, Stoudenours, Smiths, Shifflers, Stonerooks, Tetwillers,[a] Winelands, and Zooks, besides many others + + +"[b]

---

[a] "A remarkable early resident of the cove is John Detwiller, who lives just northeast of Martinsburg He was born in Lancaster Co, Pa, Sept 25, 1789 His father finally removed to Franklin Co, Pa, from whence John came to the cove in 1811 He was a shoemaker, as was usual in those days, worked at his trade from "house to house" He tired of shoemaking, he tells us, and became a cooper, at which he was quite successful, earning enough money in a few years to buy a small farm After various changes in location by selling and buying farms, he located on the premises now occupied in 1868 He has been a successful hunter He killed 7 bears on Tussey's Mountain, and deer and turkeys without number He m Elizabeth Snowburger in 1815, and of 6 ch b to them 4 survive Samuel, his youngest son, is a grandfather The name is written variously as Tetwiller and Detwiller."

[b] History of Blair Co, Pa—North Woodberry Twp.—Africa, 1883, pp. 183-185

"Among those who were settlers" (of Huston Twp, formed 1842, then part of Woodberry Twp., Bedford Co, Pa) "prior to the beginning of the Revolution were Jacob and Conrad Brumbaugh, Harmonus, John, Jacob and Henry Clapper, David Coughenour, Isaac Hutson, Christopher Hoover, Paul and Jacob Rhodes, Philip Metzker, Jacob Smith and his son Jacob, Jr; James Spencer (who lived on the premises now occupied by a Mr Obenour), William and Jno Shirley, Christopher Shrom, Henry Wesour or Wisour, and doubtless a number of others."

"During the years intervening between the close of the first struggle with Great Britain and the year 1800, many other families had taken up their abode in this portion of the Cove Among those who were residents in 1800 we find mentioned Christian, Leonard and John Acker, George, Jacob, John, John, Jr., and Conrad Brumbaugh, Emanuel Ludwig, David Coughenour, Abraham Ditch (the latter two operating a grist- and saw-mill on Clover Creek), Caspar Dillinger (who owned a saw-mill), John and George Everhart, Nicholas Fouse [E8], John, Matthew and Richard Hutson, Christian Hoover (who owned an oil mill on Piney Creek), Abraham Longenecker, Philip Metzker, Samuel Mobley, Harmon Obenour, Paul, Jacob and Christian Rhodes, James Spencer, Jacob Sheets, Stoephel Shrom, Jacob Smith, Adam Sorrick (who then owned a grist mill), Henry Solliday, Henry Wisour, and Jacob Wilhelm

Among additional residents mentioned in 1810 were Joseph Everhart, Geo Foutz, Saml, Jno., Fredk, Wm, Jonathan, Martin and Jacob Hoover, Andrew Metzker and Daniel Wiltrout " + +

(History of Blair Co, Pa, Huston Twp.—Africa, 1883, p 122)

"*Early Residents* —When the Bedford Co pioneers, chiefly Germans, pushed out their settlements to the northward and westward during the years immediately succeeding the close of the French and Indian war of 1756-63, some of them located within the present limits of Taylor Twp (Bedford Co, Pa.*). Thus we find that prior to 1775 Jacob Neff, the Dunkard miller + +, the brothers Martin and Jacob Houser, Christian Hoover, and probably a few others, were already here "

"After peace and quietness had been restored, other families located in this part of the 'Cove,' and before the organization of Huntingdon Co, in 1787, John Brumbach, Daniel Ellrich, Christopher Markle, Abraham and Jacob Plummer, Peter Hoover, who built the old log house near Jacob Shoenfelt's present residence nearly 100 years ago, and Philip and Peter Stoner, who

---

*Until 1842 the territory now embraced by Taylor Twp. was partly in Woodberry, Huntingdon Co, and partly in North Woodberry, Bedford Co, Pa

lived at the 'Mineral Spring,' were also counted as residents. After them, but before the year 1800, came Jacob Shoenfelt, Sr., John Ullery, the miller (Neff's successor at Roaring Spring), Edward Cowen, the Neterers, John and Adam Lower, Fredk Hartle, John Morgan, and Tobias Shiffler, who operated a tannery prior to the year mentioned "

"The Shoenfelts (or Shanefelds, as the name was written a century ago) are of German origin, and their ancestors of that name were among the first settlers of Washington Co , Md + + Jacob Shoenfelt was b near the banks of the Antietam Creek, 3 miles distant from Hagerstown, Md , Sept 9, 1792 His father's name was Jacob also, and in 1795 he (Jacob, Sr) removed with his family from Md. to the locality now known as Sharpsburg, and settled upon premises formerly occupied by John Brombach. The tract contained 400 a, and it had been purchased of Brombach previously by Henry Shanefeld for his son Jacob + +"

"Jacob Shoenfelt, Sr , completed the stone house in Sharpsburg in 1802, the log house adjoining it, still standing, having been erected by John Brombach about 20 yrs. before The venerable Jacob Shoenfelt, now 90 yrs. of age, who never used glasses, and now reads fine print quite readily, still further informs us that at the time his father came here from Md. and for some yrs. after the only grist mills in the 'Cove' were those of John Snyder's at Pattonsville and John Ullery's at Roaring Spring An old log mill, however, stood where the Lower Maria Forge was afterward built A man named Tracy had owned it at an early day, afterwards one by the name of Stephens or Stephenson was its proprietor. Myers owned the Gap mill before George McKee bought it."

"At the same time, too, i e , about 1800, there was not a store in Morrison's Cove. Wm Davis was the justice of the peace The early teaching was all done in German, indeed, Mr Shoenfelt remarks that although he was a very good reader and writer in German, he was 20 yrs of age before he could count in English The Dunkards (G B B.) and Lutherans were the only religious denominations The former met for worship in their dwellings, the latter built an early church near Replogle's Mill, in Bedford Co The German Reformed people came next, after them the Methodists. Christy Myers built the first house in Sharpsburg."

(*History of Blair Co., Pa , Taylor Twp —Africa, 1883, p 220)*

"The first permanent white settlers of Blair County, coming into the southern end of Morrison's Cove about 1760 or earlier, are Tunkers, and that was probably the first religious denomination to obtain a foothold in Blair

County territory   A Presbyterian minister by the name of Beatty preached
a sermon one Sunday at Beaver Dams, now called McCann's Mills, in 1756,
but it is likely that the Tunkers, who resided here, as above stated, held
religious services at a still earlier date, and that the congregation consisted of
residents of the Cove." *

I further glean from this history that about the year 1765 Jacob Neff, who
was a Tunker, built a mill where Roaring Spring is situated. His mill was
burned by the Indians, and rebuilt by him prior to the Revolution   Later, but
still long, long ago, it was owned by John Ullery He had a brother named
Samuel, who was the first Tunker minister in the Cove, a great-grandfather,
on the mother's side, of the writer of this article He preached in the Yellow
Creek congregation, southeast end of the Cove, in the vicinity of New Enterprise So far as I remember, his successors in office were Martin Miller, John
Holsinger, David Brumbaugh, Jacob Miller, John Eshelman, Leonard Furry
and Daniel Snowberger

According to the Biographical Cyclopædia of Blair County, "Jacob Neff
killed two Indians who attacked him at his mill at Roaring Springs in November, 1777, and then fled, after which the entire war party came up and burned
his mill " This statement must be wrong, he killed only one Indian The facts,
as I gather them from the early settlers, are these While in his mill, two
Indians suddenly came upon him He hid in the water-wheel He remained
there until everything was quiet, for a good while. Then he emerged with his
gun, and ran up the hill in the direction of East Sharpsburg As he glanced
back he saw one of the Indians close upon him, gaining on him, when he suddenly turned and fired The Indian fell dead, and Neff escaped. But he was
afterwards disciplined by the church Some said he was expelled I do not
vouch for the truth of the last statement

S. B. FURRY "^b

"ASSESSMENT OF WOODBERRY TOWNSHIP, BEDFORD COUNTY, PA.—1789" (COMPLETE) ^c

	a	h	c	£	s	d	s	d
Adam, Peter, State tax, 5s 8d, County tax, 2s 11d								
Adam, William	100	2	2		5	1	2	7
Bare, John	230	3	1		8	3	4	2

*Semi-Centennial History of Blair County—Charles B Clark
^bHistory of the Tunkers and the Brethren Church—Holsinger, p. 182.
^cOwing to the widespread interest in the early Bedford and Huntingdon County records,
and their historical and genealogical importance, these assessments have been carefully
copied by the compiler from the originals

"ASSESSMENT OF WOODBERRY TOWNSHIP, BEDFORD COUNTY, PA—1789"
(COMPLETE)—*Continued*

		a	h	c	£	s	d	s	d
Bowman, John		230	2	3		8	3	4	2
Bowman, George			1				6		3
Beaman, Wm		278	2	2		16	4	8	2
Brown, Henry		100	3	2		4	7	2	4
Burkhard, Adam		210	2	3		10	10	5	5
Baird, Jacob		100	2	2		7	7	3	10
Batticote, Nicholas			1	2		7	5	3	9
Brinnen, John		100	2	2		7	8	3	10
Brumbaugh, George		130	3	4		7	7	3	10
Belser, Peter			1				3		2
Bowser, John			3	2		7	9	3	11
Creveston, Jacob			1				6		3
Creveston, Nicholas		279	3	3		16	10	8	5
Cow, Ludwick		50	3	3		2	1	1	1
Cowins, William		352	2	2		18	6	9	3
Cowins, Edward		209	2	2		7	4	3	8
Crul, John		251	2	1		4	8	2	4
Caller, Joseph		200	3	4		15	3	7	8
Drish, Christian		50	2	2		2	4	1	2
Dilts, William		200	2	2		10	2	5	1
Dill, George			1	1		1	1		7
Dilts, John		100	2	3		7	0	3	6
Dible, Jacob		175	1	1		8	5	4	3
Dick, Harman		150	2	2		7	8	3	10
Ditsch, Abraham	1 mill	150	3	3		13	11	6	6
Doil, Henry		60		1		2	0	1	0
Dillinger, Caspor			2	3		1	4		8
Easton, Felty		262	3	4		15	2	7	8
Embler, Peter				1			3		2
Engel, John		600	2	3	1	2	2	11	1
Erlebough, Henry		200	2	2		7	2	3	8
Forckeson, John			4	4		2	5	1	3
Falkner, John		100	2	3		8	8	4	4
Folck, Peter		200	2	2		6	7	3	4
Fenlow, William		50	2	2		2	4	1	2
Good, Jacob		150	3	4		10	3	5	2

"ASSESSMENT OF WOODBERRY TOWNSHIP, BEDFORD COUNTY, PA —1789"
(COMPLETE)—*Continued.*

	a	h	c	£	s	d	s	d
Ginsinger, Abraham	180	2	2		5	4	2	8
Galson, William	100	1	2		5	3	2	8
Hiple, John	419	2	2		11	4	5	8
Hay, Simon	50	1	1		1	9		11
Hay, Michael ·	100	2	2		3	11	2	0
Hart, John		1	2		1	4		8
Hart, William	150	4	3		6	4	3	2
Henry, John		1				6		3
Jordy, William		1	2		1	10		11
King, George	100	1	2		5	2	2	8
Knort, James	100	2	1		2	6	1	3
Knee, Phillip	100	2	3		5	11	3	0
Kline, Leonard	272	2	1		10	6	5	3
Loy, Martin	241	2	2		9	3	4	8
Lier, Jacob	215	3	2		13	7	6	10
Leedy, Abraham	100	3	3		4	8	2	4
Long, Joseph 300 and	750	2	2	2	0	0	1£	1
Lower, John	100				2	7	1	4
Lingefalter, Abraham	175	1	1		8	5	4	3
Lingefalter, George		1	1			3		2
Mecksel, Phillip	300	2	4	1	1	5	10	11
Morgin, Gabriel		2	2		16	3	7	0
Miller, Daniel	214	3	4		13	11	7	0
Miller, David	474	2	3		14	4	7	2
Magan, Daniel		1			9	3	4	8
Martin, John	449	4	4	1	0	3	10	2
Magraw, Edward	100	1	1		5	1	2	7
Matzgar, John	200	3	6		11	5	5	9
Nicholas, William	50	2	2		2	4	1	2
Nave, Jacob	400	4	4		18	9	9	5
Newkomer, Briston	175	1	1		8	5	4	3
Newswanger, Abraham		2	2		5	11	3	0
Necodamus, Conrod	100	1	1		6	2	3	1
Oberholser, Abraham 1 mill	220	3	3		15	10	7	11
Oberholser, John	80	2	1		3	0	1	6
Oil, Thomas		1	1		1	1		7

"ASSESSMENT OF WOODBERRY TOWNSHIP, BEDFORD COUNTY, PA —1789"
(COMPLETE)—*Continued.*

	a	h	c	£	s	d	s	d
Prisler, George		2	2		2	3	1	9
Puterbaugh, Jacob	75	3	3		3	3	1	9
Ditto for Landlord	210				10	8	5	4
Pote, Michael	327	2	3		16	1	8	1
Rapelogel, Rinehard	476	1	2		16	1	8	0
Rapelogel, Rinehard, Junr.	100	2	2		9	1	4	7
Ray, James	100		2		4	9	2	5
Ragmer, Peter		2	3		2	11	1	6
Rote, George	100	3	2		6	2	3	1
Sensebaugh, Peter	100	3	2		7	2	3	7
Satorius, William	1 still 100	2	2		9	10	4	11
Snider, John	950	3	8	1	19	10	19	11
Shoman, Peter	100	1	2		3	5	1	10
Smith, Jacob	tanyard	2	3		8	9	4	5
Stoll, Nicholas	200	1	1		6	11	3	6
Shirley, John	150	2	2		9	6	4	9
Stall, John	300	1	3		9	0	4	6
Stutsman, Jacob	148	3	4		11	9	5	11
Teator, Abraham	327	3	5		15	3	7	9
Teator, John	250	3	6		18	3	9	2
Ulerick, Stephen	148	3	5		11	10	5	11
Ulerick, David	148	3	4		14	3	7	2
Ulerick, Samuel	200	2	2		6	6	3	3
Ulerick, Daniel	150	2	3		15	9	7	11
Warner, Henry	50	2	2		2	10	1	5
Wyent, Jacob		1	1		11	0	5	6
Wesinger, Ludwick	100	3	2		6	6	3	3
Wetston, Christian		2	1		14	5	7	3
Whick, Christopher	50	4	2		3	3	1	8

SINGEL FREEMEN.

Flicher, John, State tax, 10s; Co. tax, 5s; Boner, Wm, do, Boner, George, do, Cronik, Isaac, 10s 5d and 5s 3d; Jones, Thomas, do, Kramer, John, do, Hayng, Geo., do, Snider, Simon, 12s 1d and 6s; Stutsman, David, 10s 5d and 5s, Rapelogel, Adam, 10s 5d and 5s 3d; Hutson, John, 10s and 5s,

Hay, Fetty, do, Stall, Daniel, 11s 4d and 5s 8d: Ulerick, John, 16s and 8s,
Welss, John, £1 2s 6d and 11s 2d and also 10s and 5s

Nonresidentors.	*Acres*	*State Tax*			*Co Tax*	
		£	s	d	s	d
Wallis, Samuel	—		13	3	7	9
Brumbaugh, Jacob	897	1	18	9	19	6
Brumbaugh, John	200		7	3	3	8
Bemperton, Isral	190		12	4	6	2
Dickson, Andrew	272		11	10	5	11
Huffman, Henry	84		2	0	1	0
Houser, Martin	76		7	7	3	10
Morrison, Jacob	250		6	8	3	4
McKune, Thomas	800		1	9		11
Puderbaugh, George	225		3	1	1	7
Puderbaugh, John	103		3	3	1	9
Sellar, John	200		12	4	6	2
Stutsman, David	60		4	0	2	0
Weetmer, Peter	—		16	5	8	3
Vickroy, Thomas	464		11	0	5	6
Kronekleton, Joseph	100		2	2	1	1
Adams, John	100		3	1	1	7
Stevans, Jacob	200		4	5	2	3
Vanbell, Richard	219		8	10	4	5
More, John	503	1	7	7	13	10
Rush, George	369		15	11	8	0
Gerregas, William	237		8	10	4	5
Dorsey, Benedick	232		8	10	4	5
Loosley, Robert	298		11	0	5	6
Patterson, Moses	315		12	0	6	0
Richard, Samuel	367		15	5	7	8
Walker, Thomas	398		15	11	8	0
Robison, Abraham	475		17	8	8	10
Horvel, Isaac	355		13	3	6	9
Stapleton, Thomas	295		11	0	5	6
Boquet, Col Henry	388		15	5	7	9
Cook, Joseph	321		13	3	6	9
Cook, Thomas	304		12	2	6	1
St. Clair, Arthur	317		13	3	6	9
Smith, Timothy	281		12	2	6	1

NONRESIDENTORS.—*Continued*

Nonresidentors	Acres.	State Tax.		Co Tax.	
		£ s	d	s	d
Logston, Edward	56	2	5	1	3
Gardner, Allex, and Hundel, Jam	252	13	3	6	9
Starling, James	364	18	2	9	1
Potter, Matthew	390	17	4	8	8
Keneday, William	356 ·	15	8	7	10
Evans, Edward	453	19	9	9	11
Leab, George	586	1 6	0	13	0
Smith, William, Do	390	17	3	8	8
Ditto	559	1 4	9	12	5
Low, James	213	9	2	4	7
Palmer, John	413	18	3	9	2
Davis, George	254	11	2	5	7
Hunt, Abraham	351	15	6	7	9
Connoly, Roger	210	9	3	4	8
Miller, Jacob	311	19	9	6	11
Cline, John	305	13	7	6	10
Lasher, John	301	13	4	6	8
Brown, William & Comp	—	— —		—	—
Penrose, Thomas	403	17	8	8	10
Hollowell, Israel	412	18	1	9	1
Lockyer, Benjamin	428	18	11	9	6
Brown, Mary	436	19	3	9	8
Martin, Christopher	383	16	9	8	5
Edward, Enock	423	18	8	9	4
Hawkins, John	432	19	1	9	7
Tully, Ferrel	404	17	10	8	11
Leech, Samuel	391	17	3	8	7
Taylor, John	403	17	10	8	11
Laming, Thomas	440	19	6	9	9
Mordock, John	428	18	11	9	6
Smith, Robert	428	18	9	9	5
Roney, James	434	19	2	9	7
Chandler, John	250	11	0	5	6

118 Inhabitants—Joseph Long, Collector. State, £99 7s 3d, County, £52 7s 0d.

ASSESSMENT OF WOODBERRY TOWNSHIP, BEDFORD CO , PA.— 1795 (PARTIAL).

Burger, Adam	10s	6d	Burger, Abraham	8s	9d
Brumbough, John	11s		Brown, Joseph	8s	9d
Brombough, Conrod, now Shanefield's				16s	6d
Boyar, Henry, now Abraham Hollinger				9s	
Clapper, Henry	11s	3d	Deeter, Abraham	£1 4s	4d
Deeter, Susannah	£1 10=				
Brombough, Jacob & Ditto for Moon				16s	10d
Kinsinger, Abraham	9s	6d	Martin. John	£1 5s	6d
Metzker, John	10s	6d	Miller, David	13s	7d
Miller, Andrew	2s		Miller, Daniel	2s	6d
Martin, Conrad	3s	6d	Ditto for L L	6s	7d
Neff, Jacob, now *Jac.* & *John Brombough*				£1 6s	7d
Nichodamus. Conrod	7s	1d	Overholser, Jacob	12s	
Overholser, John, now John Empfield				3s	9d
Puterbough. Jacob	13s	9d	Puterbough, Jacob for Jo	3s	9d
Rhoad. George	5s	9d	Rhoad, Daniel	15s	9d
Ripleogal. Rinehart	2s	9d	Snider. John	£2 11s	
Repleogal, Jacob, L L, now Budger				£1 9s	1d
.Snider, Joseph	15s	6d	Stutzman, David	4s	10d
Ullerick, Daniel	17s	3d	Zook, John	7s	7d
Ullericke. John	14s	10d	*Brumbough, Jacob*	£1 5s	
Ulerick, Samuel	11s	3d			

RETURN OF PROPERTY. WOODBERRY TWP., HUNTINGDON CO., PA , 1790.

Persons.	Acres.	Horses	Cattle.	Mills.	Valuation.
Jacob Brumbaugh	337	4	5	1	271
Conrad Brumbaugh	250	4	5		147
Single Freemen.					
Wm. Brumbaugh.					
John Brumbaugh.					
Non Residents.					
Jacob Brumbaugh, 650 acres Piney Creek, 1791					356

		Rates	Horned			Valua-
	A. Rates on Land	Cattle	Mills	H.		tion.
John Brumbaugh		3				9- 0-9
George Brumbaugh	130	0-7-6	3		3	1000	96-15-0
Jacob Brumbaugh. *saw mill*	300	0-7-6	5	1	2	600	171-10-0
Single Freemen.						
Wm. Brumbaugh	0-15-0					

RETURN OF PROPERTY, WOODBERRY TWP, HUNTINGDON CO, PA.,
1790.—*Continued.*

Non Residents	A. of Land	Rates of Land.	Valuation
Jacob Brumbaugh, Pine Run	3 5 0	0 10 0	175 0 0
John Canan & Co	3 0 0	0 7 6	112 10 0

State and Co Tax—Total of Woodberry Twp.: State, 16-18-4; Co.,
25-12-0.

Duplicate—Woodberry Twp., Hu Co., 1791.

Assessment.	State Tax.	Co. Tax.
John Brombaugh	— 6	— 9
Geo. Brombaugh	4 1	6 3
Jacob Brombaugh	7 10	11 9
Single Freemen		
Wm Brumbaugh	15	
Non Residents		
Jacob Brumbaugh	8 3	12 7

Amt. of duplicate for Co. Tax, Twp, 26-9-6. Wm. Phillips, Jr., Collector, not a freeholder. Board appts. Danl. B Paulus Collector for present
year.

Patrick Cassidy, —— Biddle, John Cadwallader, Commrs

A RETURN OF WOODBERRY TWP., 1792.

	A	Rates of Land	Horned Cattle	Mills	Rates H. on H.	Valuation. £	s.
Jacob Brumbaugh	194	0-7-6	5	1		141	
	(Co. Tax, 11s 3d)						
Wm Brumbaugh	.139	0-5-0				34	15
	(Co. Tax, 2s 10d)						
John Brumbaugh			2	1		12	
George Brumbaugh	140	0-7-6	5	3	£6	85	10
Non Residents.					Acres.	Rate	
Jacob Brumbaugh					400	10s	

Jacob Brumbaugh, Co. Tax, 15s 3d.

Collector, Frederick Herring for insuing year, 1792.

"Duplicate sent by Mr. Brumbaugh on 27 March, 1792"

endorsed by Herring

Return of Property made for Woodberry Twp —Anthony Bever, in 1793 George Brumbaugh, Collector for 1794, Philip Walker, Assessor [*]

	Acres	Horned Cattle	Saw Mills.	Horses.	Valuation	Tax
Jacob Brumbaugh	350	4	1	1		12s 6d
	(250)	(3)	(1)	(1)	(94 10)	(8s 3d)
Wm. Brumbaugh	130	1		1		4s 6d
	(100)	(2)		(1)	(£40)	(3s 6d)
John Brumbaugh	(200)	(2)		(1)	(£65)	(5s 8d)
Geo Brumbaugh	149	3		2	74.5	6s 6d
	(142)	(5)		(1)		(7s 10d)

Non Residents

Jacob Brumbaugh, 400 Piney Run   14s 4d
John Cannon, 300 adj Sinenier

Non Residents, 1794.

Jacob Brumbaugh, Junr   250 Acres   Rate 4   Val 75   6 6
Daniel Brumbaugh   200 Acres   Rate   Val. 75   6 6
John Patton Esq   100 Acres on Pine Run,—part of Jacob
   Brumbaugh's.   •

Return of Property, Woodberry Twp , 1795-(1796).

	A.	Rates	Horned H.	Cattle.	Saw Mill.	Val.	Tax.
Jacob Brumbaugh Sen.	300	0-5-0	1	6	1	107	0-12-2
	(380)	(0-3-9)	(2)	(7)	(1)	D 290, 33c	1-62
Jacob Brumbaugh Jr.	200	0-5-0		1		53	5-6
George Brumbaugh	242	0-5-0	2	7	.	97 10	10-10
							D. c.
	(130)	(0-3-9)	(1)	(7)		(134D , 33c)	(0-85)
John Broombaugh	150	0-5-0	2	2		55.10	6-0
							D. c
(John Brumbaugh)	(—)		(—)	(2)		(16D)	(0-12)

Non Residents.

John Brumbaugh	60	adj Erhbaugh		007/10	0/1/3
	(60)	adj Eilibaugh		(80D.)	
Daniel Brumbaugh	400	adj Sidoner		100	/10/0
	(400)				($106 66)

(1796) *Freemens Names*
   Conrath Brumbaugh

---

[*]1793 return is first given That of 1794 is beneath in parenthesis; and the same applies to (1796), (1798), (1800)

Return of Property, Woodberry Twp , 1797-(1798)

	Valuation	*Tax.*
Jacob Brumbaugh	$290 33c	
	($307	$2 46)
George Brumbaugh	$134 33	
	($149 50	$1 20)
John Brumbaugh	$16	
	($99 75)	(.80c)
(John 2d, 1798	$10)	(9c)
1798 *Non Residents*	*Valuation.*	*Tax.*
Daniel Brumbaugh 400 acres adj Sudner	$106 66	$1 50
John Brumbaugh adj Erlbough	$8.	12c
	($12)	(10c)

Single Freemen

  Conroth Brumbaugh 50c

(1799) Conrod Brumbaugh 40c

Return of Property, Woodberry Twp , 1799-(1800).

	Acres.			*Cattle*	*Horned H*	*H.*	*C.*	*Val* *Val.*	*Val.*	*Tax.*
Jacob Brumbaugh	— .			1	1	$6				3c
				(1)		($11)				
George Brumbaugh	130	$650		1		30	6	$36	$716	
	(130)			(1)					($710)	($1 94)
John Brumbaugh C C.	115	$575		1		20	2	$12	$607	
	(115)			(1)			(2)		($492)	($1 33)
John Brumbaugh P.							5	$30	$30	
John Brumbaugh (P C.)							(5) ·		($30)	(8c)
Non Residents.										
Daniel Brumbaugh			400	$100						
John Brumbaugh			60	$ 15						

No of lots as they stand in town of Williamsburg·

Jacob Brumbaugh No 59 Valuation $5

Conrad Brumbaugh 100 acres 2 cows Value $112   30c

Unseated Lands	*Acres*	*Val.*	*Tax.*
Daniel Brumbaugh	400	$100	27c
John Brumbaugh	60	$15	5c

"WOODBURY TOWNSHIP, HUNTINGDON CO , PA , RETURN, 1788; JACOB SERVER, £9815—COMPLETE.

	Horses	Cows	Lands		Sants	
Boyer, David	2	2			28	
Boren, John	1					
Beal, Benjamin	2	3	100		132	
Berry, John	2	2	200		178	
Brombaugh, Conrod	3	5	250		237	10
Clapper, Harmonis	2	2	020		38	
Coakenour, David	1	1			14	
Clapper, Henry	2	3	150		144	10
Chapman, Joseph	3	2	200	1	188	
Cullins, Edward	3	4	100		146	
Davis, Reasin	2	1	100		74	
Hutson, Isaac	2	1	050		49	
Herren, Frederick	2	2	100		128	
Houser, Marten	2	4	200		236	
Houser, Jacob	1	1	100		114	
Hoover, Christian	2	2	150		178	
Johnston, Thomas	2	2	200		178	
Medsker, Philip	1	3	200		172	
Marcle, Christopher	2	3	140		137	
Painter, Henry	2	3	100		107	
Powel, Daniel	3	4	150		158	10
Phillips, William	3	2	400		338	
Porter, Margaret	1	1	100		64	
Rench, Peter	2	2	125		121	15
Rhodes, Jacob	2	2			28	
Rhodes, Powl	5	2	500		558	
Smith, Jacob, Junr.	2	3			32	
					3779	5
Shipley, Michael	2	3			32	
Sarver, Philip	2	1			24	
Scholes, John	2	2	060		73	
Spencer, James	2	2	200		178	
Shirley, John	1	1	070		49	
Shirley, William	1	1	150		126	10
Shane, George	2	1	050		74	

"WOODBURY TOWNSHIP, HUNTINGDON CO, PA , RETURN, 1788,
JACOB SERVER, £9815—COMPLETE—*Continued.*

	Horses	Cows	Lands	Sants	
Shrom, Christopher		2	100	58	
Stoll, John	2	1	150	124	10
Smith, Jacob, Senr.	3	2	150	150	10
Tuder, Benjamin	1	1	030	29	
Ulerick, Daniel	3	4	150	98	
Wineland, Christian	—	1		4	
Walker, Philip	2	1	200	174	
Wineland, Peter	4	4	240	174	
Wesower, Henry	2	2	150	140	10
Wesinger, Ludwick (?)	2	2		28	

1535

			Lands	
Albaugh, Peter	300	1	300	adjoining *Jacob Brumbaugh*
Brumbaugh, Jacob	487	10	650	adjoining Henry Clapper
Barrick, William	150		200	Clover Creek
Ball, William	600		600	adjoining Jacob Sarver
Cryder, Michael	750		200	adjoining Philip Walker
Do	——		800	adjoining Joseph Chapman
Clapper, John, the younger	44		088	adjoining Sd Chapman
Clapper, John, the older	28		056	adjoining Sd Chapman
Davis, John	65		130	adjoining Henry Wesower
Eliot, Benjamin and Co.	80		080	big spring frankstown branch
Gamil, Elisabeth, Widow	600		600	adjoining William Ball
Hoover, Jacob	75		100	adjoining Henry Clapper
Miller, John	150		200	adjoining Daniel Powl
Plummer, Abraham	220		300	adjoining Willm Phillips
Porter, Thomas	55		055	at the mouth of Clover Creek
Stoner, Philip and Co.	120		160	adjoining Jacob Smith
Smith, William, D D.	400		400	at the mouth of Pine Creek
Swift, John	800		800	on Frankstown branch
Stewart, David	75		100	
Shirley, William	——		200	Hopewell Township
Walles, Samuel	300		550	Frankstown gap
Wickery, Thomas	150		200	Sinking Spring
Watson, William	75		100	adjoining David Stewart

"WOODBERRY TOWNSHIP, HUNTINGDON CO, PA, RETURN, 1788;
JACOB SERVER, £9815—COMPLETE—*Continued*

Worrel, Isaac	150	200	adjoining Barrick	
George Reynolds, Jr John Canan, Esq. }	120	270	Big Spring	

		Horses	Cows	Lands.
Single Freemen				
Jacob Sarver, Junr.	313	2	1	289

ASSESSMENT WOODBERRY TOWNSHIP, HUNTINGDON CO, PA., 1788; JACOB SERVER, COMPLETE

	State Tax.			Co. Tax.		
	£	s	d	£	s	d
Boyer, David	0	1	11	0	1	0
Boal, Benjamin		9	1		4	8
Berry, John		12	3		6	2
Brombaugh, Conrod		18	3		8	2
Clapper, Harmones		2	8		1	4
Cookenour, David			11			5
Clapper, Henry		9	10		4	11
Chapman, Joseph		12	1		6	6
Cullins, Edward		9	11		4	6
Davis, Reasin		5	1		2	7
Hutson, Isaac		3	4		1	8
Herron, Frederick		8	10		4	5
Huser, Marten		16	2		8	1
Huser, Jacob		7	9		3	10
Huver, Christian		12	3		6	2
Johnston, Thomas		12	3		6	2
Medsker, Philip		11	10		5	11
Marcle, Christopher		9	5		4	9
Painter, Henry		7	4		3	8
Powel, Dainel		10	10		5	5
Phillips, William	1	3	2		11	7
Porter, Margaret		4	4		2	2
Rench, Peter		8	4		4	2
Rhoads, Jacob		2	0		1	0
Rhoads, Powel	1	18	2		9	1

ASSESSMENT WOODBERRY TOWNSHIP, HUNTINGDON CO , PA , 1788,
JACOB SERVER—COMPLETE—*Continued*

	State Tax.			Co Tax		
	£	s	d	£	s	d
Smith, Jacob, Junr.		2	3		1	2
	12,	18	2	6	9	6
Shiple, Mickel		2	3		1	2
Saor, Philip		1	8		0	10
Scholse, John		5	0		2	6
Spencer, James		12	3		6	2
Shirly, John		3	4		1	8
Shirly, William		8	8		4	4
Shane, Genge		5	2		2	7
Shrom, Christopher		4			2	
Stoll, John		8	6		4	3
Smith, Jacob, Senr.		10	3		5	2
Tuder, Benjamin		2			1	
Ulerick, Dainel		6	8		3	4
Wineland, Christian	0	0	3		0	2
Winiland, Peter		11	11		6	0
Walker, Philip		11	11		6	0
Wesour, Henry		9	7		4	10
Wisinger, Lodvick		2			1	0
	5	5	5	2	13	0
Nonresidents						
Albaugh, Peter	1	0	6	0	10	3
Brombaugh, Jacob	1	13	4		16	8
Ball, William	2	1	0	1	1	0
Barrick, William		10	3		5	2
Cryder, Michel	2	11	3	1	5	8
Clapper, John, the younger		3	0		1	6
Clapper, John, older		2	0		1	0
Davis, John		4	5		2	3
Elet, Benjamin		5	6		2	9
Gamil, Elisabeth, widow John Hains	2	1	0	1	1	0
Hoover, Jacob		5	2		2	7
Miller, John		10	3		5	2

ASSESSMENT WOODBERRY TOWNSHIP, HUNTINGDON CO., PA, 1788;
JACOB SERVER—COMPLETE—*Continued*

	State Tax.			Co. Tax		
	£	s	d	£	s	d
Plummer, Abraham		15	1		7	7
Porter, Thomas		3	9		1	11
Renolds, Geo , and John Canan, Esq.		5	1		2	7
Stoner, Philip		8	3		4	2
Smith, William, D D.	1	7	4		13	8
Swift, John	2	14	8	1	7	4
Stewart, David		5	2		2	7
Walles, Sameull	1	0	6		10	3
Wikery, Thomas		10	3		5	2
Watson, William		5	2		2	7
Warrel, Isaac		10	3		5	2
	19	8	1	9	15	5
Single Freemen						
Jacob Sarver	1	1	5		10	9
		7			3	
	1	8	5		14	3

Note.—Enquire which of the Smiths, Stoners land lies near.

"WOODBERRY TOWNSHIP, 1788" (COMPLETE).

Persons' Names	State			Persons' Names.	State.		
Berry, John	0	9	0	Smith, Jacob	0	10	0
Brombagh, Conrod	0	8	2	Stoll, Nicholas	0	5	3
Beal, Benj.	0	7	8	Shane, George	0	3	3
Chapman, Joseph	0	11	3	Shiom, Christopher	0	2	6
Clapper, Henry	0	7	3	Server, Philip	0	0	6
Cullens, Edward	0	7	8	Tuder, Benjamin	0	1	3
Davis, Reason	0	1	3	Ullery, Daniel	0	7	8
Hutson, Isaac	0	3	2	Walker, Phillip	0	8	9
Houser, Martin	1	4	1	Wineland, Peter	1	2	2
Houser, Jacob	0	5	9	Weesour, Henry	0	11	6
Hoover, Christian	0	8	11	*Single Men.*			
Heron, Fredrick	0	5	10	Hou ? durf, John	0	11	0

"WOODBERRY TOWNSHIP, 1788" (COMPLETE) —*Continued*

Persons' Names	State			Persons' Names	State.		
Johnston, Thomas	0	9	5	Server, Jacob	0	16	8
Midicer, Phillip	0	9	4	Stall, John	0	7	2
Phillip, William, Esq	1	1	9	Wineland, Christley	0	11	6
Porter, Margaret	0	4	5	*Nonresident.*			
Powl, Daniel	0	5	4	Bower, George	0	11	0
Painter, Henery	0	5	4	*Brombagh, Jacob*	1	10	0
Rhodes, Pawl	1	15	10	Barrick, William	0	7	6
Rench, Peter	0	6	2	*Brombagh, Jacob*	0	4	0
Scoles, John	0	2	11	Cryder, Michael	0	10	0
Sherley, John	0	2	6	Clapper, John, Jr.	0	3	0
Spencer, James	0	1	5	Clapper, John	0	1	3
Sherly, William	0	6	11	Canan, John & Co.	0	7	6
Shipley, Michal	0	1	5	Elbott, Benjamin	0	2	7
	—	—	—	Gamble, Widdow	1	10	0
	10	12	9	Miller, John	0	7	6
				Porter, Thomas	0	5	0
				Plumer, Abraham	0	11	3
				Swift, John	1	11	3
					—	—	—
					14	1	0
				Smith, William, D D	0	15	0
				Watson, William, and David			
				Stewart	0	7	6
				Worrel, Isaac	0	6	3
					—	—	—
					1	8	9
					14	1	0
				The amt in the paper	10	12	9
					—	—	—
					26	2	6

"ASSESSMENT OF WOODBERRY TOWNSHIP, HUNTINGDON CO., PA , 1789; ABRAHAM PLUMMER, COLLECTOR "

Persons' Names.	State Tax			Co. Tax.			H.	C	Lds.	Ms.		
Boren, Henry	0	7	1	0	3	2	1	0	185	143	14	6
Berry, John	0	8	6	0	4	9	2	2	200	178	0	0

"ASSESSMENT OF WOODBERRY TOWNSHIP, HUNTINGDON CO, PA, 1789, ABRAHAM PLUMMER, COLLECTOR "—*Continued*

Persons' Names	State Tax.			Co. Tax			H	C	Lds.		Ms.		
Brumbaugh, Jacob—sawmill	0	12	10	0	7	4	4	5	337	1	290	12	6
Bower, Peter	0	3	7	0	2	2	2	2	100		103	0	0
Brumbaugh, Conrod		12	9		7	4	4	5	250		147	10	0
Boyer, David	0	1	3	0	0	9	2	2			0	28	0
Beal, Benjamin	0	5	4	0	3	2	2	2	100		103	0	0
Clapper, Jacob	0	0	4	0	0	3	0	2			080	0	0
Clapper, John	0	3	7	0	2	2	2	2	100		065	10	0
Clapper, Aimonas	0	1	3	0	0	9	2	2			028	0	0
Clapper, Henry	0	6	6	0	3	9	2	2	150		140	10	0
Cullens, Edmond	0	6	7	0	3	10	3	3	100		154	10	0
Christopher Srim (?)	0	3	7	0	2	2							
Chapman, Joseph—*grist mill*	0	12	0	0	6	11	2	2	250	1	148	0	0
Davis, Rezin	0	2	2	0	1	4	1	1	60		040	0	0
Herrin ("Herron") Fred'k	0	10	11	0	5	8	4	5	200		210	0	0
Houser, Marten	0	8	7	0	5	0	3	4	150		156	10	0
Hoover, Christian	0	10	0	0	5	10	2	2	250		140	10	0
Hutson, Isaac	0	1	4	0	1	1	1	1	50		032	15	0
Houser, Jacob	0	4	11	0	2	10	1	2	100		130	10	0
Johnson, Thomas	0	11	11	0	6	10	2	2	400		178	10	0
	6	11	5	3	15	10							
Markle, Christopher	0	5	10	0	3	5	3	2	100		150	0	0
Medsker, Philip	0	7	10	0	4	5	1	2	250		111	15	0
Phillips, Wm, Sr	0	12	6	0	7	2	3	3	300		267	0	0
Phillips, Wm, Junr	0	4	6	0	2	7	2	1	100		94	0	0
Porter, Margaret	0	9	7	0	0	4	1	1			014	0	0
Prawley, Samuel	0	3	1	0	1	9	2	1	88		77	0	0
Prough, Peter	0	0	5	0	0	3	1				10	0	0
Painther, Henry	0	5	6	0	3	2	3	3	100		170	0	0
Plummer, Abraham	0	9	5	0	5	4	1	1	250		170	15	0
Powel, Daniel	0	6	6	0	2	7	2	5	150		196	5	0
Rench, Peter	0	5	4	0	3	2	2	2	125		169	2	0
Rhodes, Jacob	0	1	5	0	0	11	2	3			32	0	0
Rhodes, Paul	1	15	8	1	0	2	4	4	800		806	0	0
Shane, George	0	4	3	0	2	6	3		100		67	10	0
Stall, John	0	12	1	0	6	11	2	3	400		182	0	0

"ASSESSMENT OF WOODBERRY TOWNSHIP, HUNTINGDON CO, PA, 1789, ABRAHAM PLUMMER, COLLECTOR "—*Continued*

Persons' Names	State Tax			Co Tax			H.	C.	Lds	Ms		
Smith, Jacob, Sr	0	7	8	0	4	9	3	3	150	98	5	0
Smith, Jacob, Jr.	0	2	4	0	1	5	2	2	30	50	10	0
Shirley, John	0	3	4	0	2	1	2	0	70	36	5	0
	6	0	3	3	12	11						
Spencer, James	0	1	6	0	0	11	2	2	200	178	0	0
Scholes, John	0	2	9	0	1	8	2	2	60	50	10	0
Server, Jacob, Senr	0	12	9	0	7	3	2	1	289	207	7	6
Shipley, Michael	0	1	5	0	0	11	2	3		32	0	0
Shaner, Henry	0	0	8	0	0	5	1	1		14	0	0
Tuder, Benjamin	0	4	8	0	2	8	1	2	160	78	0	0
Varner, Nicholas	0	2	6	0	1	5	0	1	100	41	10	0
Wineland, Peter	0	7	5	0	4	3	2	4	242	124	15	0
Walker, Philip	0	8	9	0	5	1	3	2	200	188	0	0
Wineland, Christian	0	2	6	0	1	5	2	2	50	46	15	0
	2	11	11	1	9	10						

Non Residents	State Tax			Co Tax			Lands			
Albaugh, Peter, Piney Creek	0	14	4	0	8	1	300	225	0	0
Brumbaugh, Jacob, on Do Creek	1	2	10	0	15	2	650	356	5	0
Ball, Wm, adj Widow Gamble	1	1	3	0	17	0	600	450	0	0
Barrick, Wm, adjoining Hutson	0	6	10	0	3	4	200	75	0	0
Crider, Michael, Piney Creek	1	4	0	0	14	0	700	412	10	0
Canan, John, Esq, Big spring	0	5	10	0	3	4	300	112	10	0
Eliott, Benjamin, Esq.	0	1	8	0	1	2	75	28	2	6
Gamble, Elisabeth, adj Server	1	1	3	0	17	0	600	450	0	0
Hoover, Jacob, Piney Creek	0	5	5	0	3	4	100	75	0	0
Porter, Thomas, adj. Server	0	1	10	0	1	6	55	41	5	0
Stoner, Philip, adj Jacob Smith	0	9	1	0	4	0	300	225	0	0
Smith, Wm, D D, Frankstown Br.	0	14	2	0	8	0	300	225	0	0
Swift, John, Frankstown Branch	1	13	0	0	18	8	700	525	0	0
Stewart, David	0	2	5	0	1	4	100	37	10	0
Worrel, Isaac	0	7	1	0	4	0	200	75	0	0
Watson, William	0	2	5	0	1	4	100	37	10	0
Drinker, James and Henry	0	12	0	0	7	0				
Neff, Jacob, Stevens gap							300	225	0	0

"ASSESSMENT OF WOODBERRY TOWNSHIP, HUNTINGDON CO, PA, 1789,
ABRAHAM PLUMMER, COLLECTOR."—*Continued*

Vickroy, Thomas, Sinken Spring	0	5	11	0	3	6	250	93 3	0
Ulerick, Daniel	0	6	5	0	3	6	150	168 15	0

Single Freemen. (1789)	*State Tax.*			*Co. Tax*			*Still*		
Brumbaugh, William	0	14	6						
Brumbaugh, John	0	14	.6						
Doyl, John	0	14	6						
Fogle, Michael	0	14	6						
Server, Jacob	0	14	6						
Stall, Daniel—*still*, 60 gal.	0	14	6	0	0	11	1	12 0	0
	4	7	0	0	0	11			
Clapper, John	0	2	2						

WARRANTIES OF LAND—CO OF BEDFORD, PA.—1771-1893.

Broombach, Jas	60	March 14, 1785, p. 457
Broombach, Jas	150	March 14, 1785, p 457
Broombach, John	300	March 14, 1785, p. 457
Broombach, Conrad	200	March 14, 1785, p. 457
Broombach, Jacob and others	400	April 25, 1785, p. 457
Broombaugh, Conrad	40	June 14, 1785; p 457
Broombaugh, Jacob	200	May 6, 1786, p 458
Broombaugh, John	100	Sept. 12, 1786, p 458
Broombaugh, John	60	Nov 25, 1786; p. 458
Broombaugh, Jacob	75	Feb. 15, 1787; p. 458
Broombaugh, George	300	May 6, 1796; p 469
Brombaugh, Conrad	300	Aug 30, 1810, p 687
Brombough, John	268½	May 12, 1812, p. 470
Brombough, John	304½	May 12, 1812, p. 470
(Brumsbough, John and Thos.	20	April 27, 1836; p 472)
Brumbaugh, Geo S and J. S.	40	Jan. 24, 1859, p 474
(Pa Archives, 3d Series, Vol. XXV.)		

WARRANTIES OF LAND—CO OF HUNTINGDON, PA.—1787-1889.

		Surveyed
Brombaugh, Jacob, Jr.	150	Jan. 15, 1788; p 679
Broombaugh, Jacob	13	Oct 19, 1792; p. 680

Broombaugh, John   100   Oct 19, 1792; p. 680
Brumbaugh, Jacob   200   Jan 4, 1797; p 687
Brombaugh, Conrad   300   Aug 30, 1810, p 687
Broombaugh, John   20   March 1, 1820; p 688
Brumbach, Geo , Jr   13   Dec. 29, 1823, p. 688
Brumbach, Geo and others in trust 40 Jan. 24, 1824; p 688
Brumbaugh, Daniel   300   Jan. 5, 1831; p 688
Brumbaugh, Daniel   70   March 20, 1837; p 689
Brumbaugh, Jacob   101 129   June 29, 1854; p. 689
Brumbaugh, Isaac   200 4½   Aug 4, 1857, p 689
Brumbaugh, John   163.94   Aug 13, 1863, p. 690

(Pa Archives, 3d Series, Vol XXV)

LEDGER B (P 70), HUNTINGDON, PA , "CONTAINING TAXES ASSESSED UPON NON RESIDENT LAND IN HUNTINGDON COUNTY," PENNSYLVANIA

Dr. *Jacob Brombaugh—Woodberry Twp.*[*]

100 A 1791 350 A on Pine run		12	7
Sold			
7-10-0 1792 To tax on do		15	3
adv To Costs		3	2
Residented 1793 To tax on do		14	4
by Frederick		6	10
	2	12	2
Sidner 1794 To tax on do		6	6
	2	18	8

Cr.

Sept. 24, 1793 By Cash in pt per John Patton Esq	2	12	2
Dec. 22, 1794 By Cash per hand *George Brombough*		6	6
	2	18	8

*The arrangement given is exact copy of the entries.

LEDGER B (P 159), HUNTINGDON, PA , "CONTAINING TAXES AS-
SESSED UPON NON RESIDENT LAND IN
HUNTINGDON CO ," PA

Daniel Brombaugh, Dr

1794	To tax on 200 a of Land in Woodbury Townp.	£	6	6
1795	To tax on 400 a of Land in Woodbury Townp		11	
			17	6

Per Contra Credt (159)

1794	By Cash per the hand *George Brombough*	6	6
1797	June 1st By Cash per the hand of		
	Danl Brombough	11	
		17	6

LEDGER B (P 175), HUNTINGDON, PA , "CONTAINING TAXES AS-
SESSED UPON NON RESIDENT LAND IN
HUNTINGDON CO ," PA.

John Brumbaugh, Dr

1795	To Tax on 60 a in Woodberry Township	1	3
	Contra Cr.		
	By Balance Carried to Book C 126*	1	3

*Book C could not be found at Huntingdon, Pa Accounts were also noted in B, p 73,
for 1792, with *Jacob Hoover*, and on the same p for 1793 with *John Clapper*

SECTION A
GERHARD[1] BRUMBACH AND DESCENDANTS.

AGREEMENT FOR PURCHASE OF HORSES FOR THE COLONIAL GOVERNMENT, AUGUST 25, 1780.

The Agreement of The Inhabitants of Vincent the Eastern Side of French crick Met & Agreed to this 25th Day of August 1780 at the house of Peter Cypher in sd District in Vincent Township Chester County

Viz to Appoint Two Sponsible free holders in sd. District or Company to purchase or provide three horses for the present press & in case of future Presses for horses to provide them & prevent any Individual person from Suffering more than his proportion Agreeable to this agreement *Edward Parker & Henry Brownback* Were Regularly Chosen by vote at the sd Meeting by us Whose names are under Written—

Viz it is further & Mutually Agreed at sd Meeting & by sd Company to advertise another meeting to Choose Two Sponsible men to Cess & Levy a Publick Tax in sd District to Defray the Expense & pay for sd 3 Horses to be Provided by sd men above named—

Simon Schunck	Joseph Basler (Baster?)
Abraham Turner	Michael H———
Johannes Hosz (Hass)	William Rogers
Rudolph Essick	Peter Miller
Casper Schneider	Edward Parker
Görg Jager (Yeager)	Henry Brownbach [A6]
John Rotes (Rhoads)	Thos. Evans
John Myer	John Loyd
Peter Botts	Hazael Thomas
Henry Acker	Henry Christman [A20]
Isaac Turner	

The above important historical paper is preserved by [A132] Garrett Ellwood Brownback, who also furnishes the plate of the Rittenhouse coat-of-arms, etc. The German translations of the signatures have been made by Prof. Michael Alvin Gruber, who also compared the names with the U S Census of 1790, for Vincent Twp, Chester Co., Pa, p 72 See p. 79 and the Almsbook Record for "Henry Brombach," as signed on Aug. 28, 1774.

SECTION A.

GERHARD[1] BRUMBACH AND DESCENDANTS

[A1] GERHARD[1] BRUMBACH was *b* in 1662*, probably in Saxony, near "Wittenberg," Germany His name is found spelled also BROMBACH, BRUMBACK and BROWNBAUGH, as, signing by mark, he was dependent upon the spelling often of English-writing colonists who could not understand his German speech He *d* Sept, 1757 A history of Vincent township (deposited in the Pennsylvania Historical Society, Philadelphia, in manuscript form), written in 1846 by Frederick Sheeder, says: "He came from Germany and settled at Germantown when there was but one house there." The first houses were built in Germantown in 1683 by a colony of forty-one Germans who landed in Philadelphia in October, and who came chiefly from Creisheim and Creyfelt These settlers were mostly linen weavers, intelligent and industrious, as well as devout Christian people, Mennonites, who came to America to avoid oppressions at home Tradition says that Gerhard Brumbach lived among these Germantown settlers and helped build the first houses erected there; that he came from the Palatinate of the Rhine, and that he landed in Philadelphia from the ship *Concord*[b], Oct. 6, 1683.

In 1716 or 1718 Gerhard[1] *m Mary Rittenhouse Papen*, *b* about 1695, daughter of *Heivert* and *Elizabeth* (*Rittenhouse*) *Papen* Mary was a woman of many virtues and of excellent character Her father, Heivert,[c] a Mennonite, came from Muhlheim, Germany, in 1685. In 1698 he erected the house herein reproduced (torn down in 1883). It was on the "side lot appurtenant to town lot toward Schuylkill—No 8 in the first drawing of

<hr/>

*Extracts made from "The Gerhard Brumbach Family," *Pennsylvania German* Vol XI, No. 3, March, 1910, by [A112] *Garrett Ellwood[5] Brownback* and [A229] *Rev Oscar Davis[5] Brownback* The illustrations from that article, together with others furnished for this section by the former, are but a recent expression of his interest and investigations The constant assistance in gathering information rendered by [A112] Garrett Ellwood[5] Brownback and by his dau [A247] Caroline Evans[6] (Brownback) Fell, in the face of the marked difficulties encountered in gathering the facts for this section, has made possible the publication of much here given pertaining to [A 1] Gerhard[1] Brumbach and his descendants.

Dr. Wm. H[6] Mosteller [A78-ii] has also assisted in gathering information, partly revised the manuscript for Section A, and shown especial co-operation in advancing this work

[b]The published American lists for the ship *Concord* do not contain his name The effort to secure a complete list from the Holland archives is being made through the U S State Department The assertion has been made that [A 1] Gerhard Brumbach's name appears in a fuller Holland list—this and his birthplace are yet to be verified

[c]Thirty Thousand Names of Immigrants—Rupp (Reprint), p 432—"Hufert Papen," same—p 430, for Nich Rittenhouse

lots." That lot and the side lot were conveyed by Abraham Op de Graff to Jacob Schumacher March 4, 1685, the latter conveyed both lots in 1693 to Heivert Papen, and in 1705 the latter conveyed the side lot and appurtenances to Samuel Richardson, Richard Townsend, Thomas Potts, Sr , and Samuel Cort, trustees for the Quaker meeting   During the battle of Germantown two cannon were placed in front of this house and aimed at the "chew house" opposite

In 1701 Heivert Papen "declined to serve as burgess of said town (Germantown) through consciencious scruples."   About 1690 he m *Elizabeth Rittenhouse*, only daughter of *Wilhelm Rittinghausen* — the sons were Nicholas and Gerhard   Wilhelm was b in 1644 also near Muhlheim, Germany, later resided in Holland, whence he came to America in 1688, and about 1690 erected the first paper mill in the colonies, near Germantown.   He d in 1708, aged 64 years, and was buried in the Mennonite churchyard in Germantown, which church he founded—the first preacher and later the first Bishop of that denomination   The Rittenhouse forefathers long carried on the manufacture of paper at Arnheim, Holland   Nicholas inherited the paper mill at Germantown from his father William, and was the father of Matthias Rittenhouse   The latter was father of David Rittenhouse, the greatest astronomical and mathematical genius of his age.

Heivert Papen owned extensive real estate, largely farms, and d in 1707. His family consisted of five daughters, of whom Mary in 1713 m [A1] GERHARD[1] BRUMBACH   He settled the estate and his name is that of the first subscribing heir in a receipt dated March 17, 1719, mentioning certain sums of money received by each from the said estate.   His name in the same was written (in German letters) "Brombach" and "Brumbach," but as he did not write the scribes of those early days have handed down to us a variety of spellings.   Especial attention is directed to the photographic copy of the signature of his son [A6] "Henrich Brombach" (see Plate 22)   Brambach, Brumback, Bromback, Brownbagh, Brownbaugh (see Plates 25, 26, 27), Broomback and Brownback are other spellings often found   His descendants spell the name "Brownback," commencing with the third generation—the second generation usually spelled the name "Brumback."

Gerhard[1] was one of the pioneers and opened up a large farm in the wilderness, settling in Vincent Township with his family some time between the years 1721 and 1724   In a Deed Poll of "Gerhard Brownback to Leonard Streeper," dated Dec 28, 1721-2, he is said to be "of the County of Philadelphia in the Province of Pennsylvania "   In 1724 he was one of the taxables

of Vincent Twp , Chester Co., paying a tax of 2 S 4 d. He must have moved to Vincent some time between these two dates

He first took up 600 acres of land in Vincent Twp   Vincent Twp then included both East and West Vincent, and consisted of about 20,000 acres, half of which belonged to the heirs of Major Robert Thompson, of Newington Green, England, and the other half to the West New Jersey Society, excluding probably some small tracts which were actually sold to settlers. Vincent Twp. was then leased by farmers and settlers with the reserved right of purchase Because of this the land was developed rather slowly—the settlers built inferior houses, and were indifferent about improvements, until they became actual owners of the land, which did not become possible until the last part of the century, about 1790   Gerhard's 600-acre tract was a part of the Major Thompson 10,000 acres, and lay in the northern part of what later was called East Vincent, about the head waters of Stony Run.

He also took up a large tract in Coventry Twp , adjoining his property in Vincent.   June 23, 1736, the Proprietaries conveyed to him by warrant the privilege of taking up 350 acres of land in Coventry Twp , for which he agreed to pay at the rate of 15 £, 10 S for 100 acres, and a yearly Quit Rent of ½ d for each and every acre thereof   The certificate of conveyance states that Gerhard was settled on this land before 1732, and in it his name is spelled "Garret Brownbagh "   He was naturalized as "From Chester Co , 1734 to 1735—Gerhart Braunbeck "*

These two tracts together equalled 950 acres. But it was customary in those days to add 6 per cent to the land transferred for roads, etc , and so the entire tract that Gerhard controlled must have been about 1007 acres

This land was then new and uncultivated   Thick forests covered the rich soil, and Indians wandered about the neighborhood   A village of about 300 souls of these Delawares nestled about a quarter of a mile from where Gerhard built his first house   It lay at the corner of the crossroads where Bethel M E Church now stands (Chester Co , Pa)   Gerhard[1] made friends of them and engaged them to work for him, giving provisions in return.   They were fond of potatoes, turnips, and especially of milk   The tradition is that they smoked the pipe of peace with him, that he took part in their wrestling matches, and that they always remained friends   He was called by them "*Minquon*," meaning never violent or wrong in dealings.

Gerhard[1] improved his land, erected buildings, and prospered in his work. He built the first house and barn of logs in 1723   It is said that the door of the

---

*Votes of Assembly III, p 131, and Rupp's Thirty Thousand Names of Immigrants (Reprint), p 436

house was large enough to drag logs through it with a horse, into the great fireplace. The buildings stood on the bank of the little creek in the extreme southern end of Coventry Twp It was about ten miles from there to the Valley Forge, and Gerhard was accustomed to carry his plough-irons on horseback to the latter place to get them sharpened. (See accounts, pages 83-86.)

The farms herein illustrated belonged to Gerhard[1] until 1757, to [A6] Henry[2] Brownback until 1804, to [A14] Peter[3] Brownback until 1834. The upper farm until 1899 belonged to [A41] Jesse[4] Brownback, and the lower until 1899 to [A14] Peter[3] Brownback—both farms belong to [A132] Garrett Ellwood[5] Brownback and have never been owned outside the family since the original grant from Penn

Gerhard was a leading and popular settler in his community He is described as "a merry German who accumulated considerable means " He lived along a much-traveled highway called Nutt's Road, and was often beset by travelers for meals and lodging   Therefore, May 25, 1736, he sent a petition to His Majesty's Justices for the privilege of conducting a "Public House" on the ground that he was frequently oppressed by travelers whom he was obliged to entertain," and that there was "no Public House within twenty miles below, nor thirty miles above his house, on the Great Road which leads from Philadelphia to the Iron Works, and from thence to Conestoga " This Petition was dated May 25, 1736, and was signed by "Garret B Brumbbough" (his mark) and twenty-six of his neighbors and friends, who testified that Gerhard was "a man of good-repute, and was best qualified for such an Employment." This was the first public house in Coventry Twp , and was among the first in the county,—the first was established at Downingtown in 1717.

He conducted this inn until his death in 1757, and was succeeded by his eldest son [A5] Benjamin[2], who continued in business for nearly 30 years, he, in after years, erected a larger house at the junction of the Lancaster and Ridge roads, now called Hiestands Corner*, and the latter is yet standing

Sept 4, 1777, and for several days thereafter, both Generals Washington and Lafayette were entertained at the Brownback Inn, while pressed by Howe of the British army—[A5] Benjamin[2] Brownback, then proprietor, held a commission as Lieut in the Continental army (dated Aug 21, 1776).   Lafayette was wounded at Warren Tavern, and retreated to join Washington's army on its way from Parkersford to Lancaster, to ford the Schuylkill at Parkerford on his way to Germantown

Besides conducting an Inn, Gerhard engaged in other enterprises.   He

*See pp 255, 275

built the first grist-mill in Vincent, and owned a half interest thereof He also built and operated the first saw-mill in the same township. The most enduring monument to his memory, however, was the part he took in the founding of a German Reformed Church, which bears his name.

Brownback's Ref Ch. was the first Ref Ch in Chester Co, Pa, and was organized May 19, 1743. Philip Breitenstein and 33 other men, including [A1] Gerhard[1] Brumbach, on May 19, 1743, issued a call for Rev Jacob Lischey to become their pastor * The same day the Discipline was signed and it is hereafter reproduced There was no church building.

DISCIPLINE OF BROWNBACK'S CHURCH, AS ADOPTED BY SAID CONGREGATION 19TH MAY, 1743.[b]

"There shall be four Elders, nominated by the Minister and elected by a majority of voters who are of respectable standing and among the whole congregation of good report
"Their office and duty is
"(1) Carefully to watch over the whole congregation and to have strict oversight over each member in particular
"(2) They must make known without respect to person everything evil and unbecoming which they see and discover in the one or the other member, this they are to do in this manner First, they are to make it known to the Minister alone; Secondly, to the Minister and the other Elders, Thirdly, to the whole congregation, if the first and second admonitions prove fruitless, that there may be no impenitent sinners tolerated in the church, and that through through them no weak members may be offended
(3) They must see that there be good order and management together with sound and pure doctrine be preserved
"Wherefore they shall in the (4) place frequently consult and confer with the ministers, particularly as anything occurs in the congregation, meet with him to consider impending subjects, in order to seek and to promote the welfare of the congregation
"(5) The Elders and the Ministers shall hold consistorial meeting among themselves everytime before the administration of the Lord's supper, in which they must bear according to their conscience and their knowledge of each member who proposes to commune, when each one according to the best judgment of the Minister and his Elders may be admitted or rejected, inasmuch as the consistory has power not only to keep from the Lord's table all sinners who give offense to the congregation, but also to cast them out of the church (or excommunicate) until they show amendment of life
"It is therefore necessary that each one who intends to commune will give in the name after sermon one Sabbath before the administering of the Lord's supper, that there may be time to consult in regard to the case of each member; inasmuch as by reason of our discipline not any one without exception, as has been our custom, can be admitted to the Lord's table, but only those who have a just conception of the important fundamentals of religion, as well as a true hunger and thirst after Christ—that there may not openly known wicked and hardened sinners enter with the communicants, and thus, through their impenitence, bring the wrath of God upon themselves and upon the whole congregation Wherefore particularly young people as much as possible be taught and instructed—wherefore it shall be the duty of all parents and heads of families in our church to see that their children and those under their care be diligently trained up to this, and suffer no opportunity to be lost by which they may grow in the knowledge and increase in the love of the Lord, and to build upon the most holy foundation to which the Elders shall see, and shall take the lead in the congregation with a good example
"To the preservation of the church, the things required in it as bread and wine in the ministering of the Lord's supper, &c, there shall every time at the end of divine service be

*Translated from the German
[b]A History of the Reformed Churches in Chester County—J. Lewis Fluck, 1892, p 19.

a regular collection taken, when each member can contribute voluntarily and according to circumstances Further, the youngest of the Elders shall each take care of it for one year, while another of the Elders shall keep a regular account of what was contributed, so that settlement may be made semi-annually before the congregation Nothing shall be paid out without the knowledge and consent of the whole congregation

"Given in Philadelphia May 19, A 1743

"This discipline was adopted and signed by the following persons

"Philip Breitenstein, Eld	John Carl
"Henry Steger, Elder	John Hubel
"John Schohholz, Eld	Conrad Seibert
"Nicholas Korper, Eld	Adam Stein
"John Schoder	Henry Boer
"John Fry	Rudolph Boer
"Christian Strohm	Frederick Funck
"Valentine Scheidecker	Jacob Fryman
"Conrad Ression	John Paul
"Michael Shany	Heinry Freis
"Simon Schunck	Melchior Koch
"Jacob Cone	Samuel Ash
"John Neidig	John Clowen
"Casper Beener	Albert Ehrewein
"Conrad Walter	Frederick Miller
"Henry Miller	Adam Schott
"GERHART BRUMBACH	William Adam
"Henry Boener	Lorentz Poffenbach

"June 11, 1837 the Constitution of the Church was Alterd "

The plot of ground upon which the church stood, including the cemetery, was donated to the congregation by Gerhard about 1741. He gave it "for a burial place for his family, his descendents, and his neighbors " Because of this donation, and because of the active part which Gerhard took in helping to found the church, it was called "Brumback's Church," later "Brownback's Reformed Church of East Coventry "

An extract from directions of General George Washington contains this reference. "The Ridge road leading to Brumbach's Church," etc.

Frederick Sheeder, in his history, says the first log church was built "about 1750." But Jesse Brownback (1807-1899), son of Peter (Sr), said that it was built in 1741 His statement is more in keeping with a fragment of the old church record, which says: "Frederick Miller was the third preacher in the old log church, 18th day of February, 1753 " If the church was built in 1750, it would be very improbable that they had three different pastors within three years—especially in those days Therefore it is more in accord with the evidence at hand to say that the first log church was built in 1741

It was built close to the little log school-house in the southeast extremity of Coventry township on a plot of ground owned by Gerhard[1] Brumbach Frederick Sheeder saw this venerable old building in 1793 and describes it as follows· "It was a structure of hewn logs one and a half stories high, with gallery and broken roof Two four-light windows were made at each gable end, and two of the same size in either side of the roof to light the pulpit and

gallery The lower story had twelve light windows The graveyard, then small, was fenced close to the church by pales, and part with posts and rails " This ancient building stood where Daniel Benners' family vault now is until the year 1800, when it was taken down and replaced with a stone structure. The stone structure was erected outside of the graveyard, and stood where the present building stands

BROWNBACK CHURCH RECORDS.

The Almsbook Record of "Biumbach's Church," Vincent Twp , Chester Co , Pa., 1773 and 1774, herewith reproduced, concludes with

"On the 28th of August, 1774, church reckoning was held and there was a balance given in custody of Henrich Krob to the amount of 6—0—2

HENRICH BROMBACH [A6]
CONRATH SHRINER
HENRICH KROB" [Elders]

During the time of the old log church a number of different ministers served the congregation, but their names and dates are not all known, because the first church records have been lost There is one old record* of this church wherein we find:

"Frederick Miller was the third preacher in the old log church, 18th day of February, 1753 Gerhard Brumbach brought his children to be baptized. His wife's name Mary Papen 1 his son Benjamin, 22 yr. , 2 Henry, 20; Mary, 24 , Catharine, 18 "

"Richard Custard and his children were baptized" in Brownback's Ref. Ch. "Sept 14, 1740, by Rev Lennard Snell

Richard Custard 28 yrs.

ELIZABETH CUSTARD 30 yrs "—[A2]*

From time to time improvements were made, and several times the church was rebuilt Jesse⁴ Brownback [A41] left the following private record "The first German Reformed Church of Coventry, known by the name of Brownback's Church, was built in 1741 of logs, rebuilt in 1800 of stone, rebuilt in 1846, and in 1878 the members of the church called a meeting to rebuild and enlarge it, and appointed Jesse Brownback, Frederick Sheeder, Lewis C. Brownback, Henry Miller, William Davis and Daniel Benner the building committee to rebuild it " The last improvement was made in 1907, when a tower and Sunday School room were added to the main building. It is one of the largest and most beautiful country churches in the county, and is supported

---

*Recently lost, or accidentally destroyed

by a membership of nearly three hundred members   Many of Gerhard Brumbach's descendants worship here at the present time, and the family has always
been well represented   The pastor officiating is Rev. Charles H. Slinghoff,
who has served the congregation for the last nine years in a very commendable
manner.

The cemetery connected with the church has been much enlarged and is
an interesting place to visit, because of its many old graves and its beautiful
location.   It occupies an elevated position and commands fine views of the
surrounding country.   Some of the oldest graves are marked with sandstones
without dates, while a few have no stones   The oldest grave marked with an
inscribed stone is that of Christian Benner, who *d* in 1767.   Other old graves
marked with inscribed stones are those of Jacob Mason, who *d* in 1776, Sebastian Kelley, who *d* in 1777, and John Young, who *d* in 1780   Many of the
descendants of [A1] Gerhard[1] Brumbach have been buried here   His own
grave is near the center of the older portion of the yard, and is marked with
a sandstone without date.   He *d* Sept., 1757, aged about 95 years, and his
wife, Mary Rittenhouse (Papen) Brumbach, *d* in the same year, aged 62 yrs.
—12 yrs old when her father *d*, and 18 when married   Her remains were laid
beside those of Gerhard[1]   A beautiful monument of gray granite, 7 feet high
and 5 feet broad, and weighing about 7 tons, was erected by [A132] Garrett
Ellwood[5] Brownback over their graves in 1908   It is polished and lettered
on both sides, and contains the names of Gerhard[1] and one hundred and sixty-
five of his descendants

The dedication occurred Oct. 10, 1908 (225th anniversary of Oct 6,
1683)

PROGRAM OF THE DAY

10.30 A M —Hymn: "All Hail the Power of Jesus' Name," Choir and
. Audience
Invocation   Rev Charles Slinghoff (Pastor Brownback Ch)
Scriptural Reading
Address by the Chairman of the Executive Committee of the
Brownback Memorial Association, Mr E. G Brownback, of
Trappe, Pa
Solo   "Father, I bend to Thee," J O K. Robarts

11 00 A. M —Historical Memoirs   Wm H—[6] Mosteller, M D [A73-ii],
Phoenixville, President of the Memorial Association

12.00 M. —Presentation of Memorial Stone to the Brownback lineage by
Garrett Ellwood[5] Brownback [A132], Linfield, Pa.

Procession to Memorial Stone, singing· "My Country, 'Tis of
Thee," during which the memorial stone will be unveiled
Invocation.
Responsive Reading
Singing· "Rock of Ages "
Consecration
Prayer and Benediction.
1·00 P M —Dinner.
2:15 P. M.—Addresses
Family Conference.

CONSECRATION.

In the name of the Father, the Son, and the Holy Ghost.

Beloved and descendants of our father, Gerhard Brownbaugh: Animated
by the pious example and worthy lives of those who have gone before us, and
still sustained by their loving grace, we, their kindred, in filial love, do hereby
set apart, consecrate, this memorial stone to their noble lives, whose virtues in
the beginnings of this great land of promise were founded upon the solid rocks.
Freedom, Immortality, and God, the triad of moral truths which formed their
belief in the age that gave this land religious freedom and civil liberty   For to
know Thee, O God, is perfect righteousness: yea, to know Thy power is this
not of immortality?

The memory of the just is blessed, but the name of the wicked shall rot.
Moreover, the nations in their wicked conspiracy being confounded, found
out the righteous and preserved them blameless unto God.   They shall receive
a glorious kingdom, and a beautiful crown from the Lord's hand.   For the
memorial thereof is immortal, because it is known with God and with men.   And
some thereby which have no memorial, who are perished as though they had
never been, and are become as though they had never been born, and their
children after them

But to-day we come with praise unto the Father that begot us   For
through His mercy unto the original owners of this land, He established a
righteousness that hath not been forgotten   This act of mercy shall continuously remain a good inheritance to all his children within the covenant.   And
their glory shall not be blotted out, but their name liveth forever.

PRAYER AND BENEDICTION

O God of our fathers and Lord of mercy, who hast made all things with
Thy word, we bless Thee that Thou hast enabled us to fulfil the desires of our

heaits in erecting this memonial stone to the honoi and good name of our worthy paients, for in all things, O Loid, Thou didst magnify Thy people and glorify them. Neither didst Thou lightly iegard them, but didst assist them in every time and place. We thank Thee, our heavenly Father, for this eveilasting covenant and the fulfilment of Thy piomises, unto his seed that has come forth to bless this nation and to exalt it to the utmost paits of this great land.

O Lord, hear the prayers of these, Thy servants, sanctify and consecrate this place unto him, whose good name we inherit. And grant that Thy praise may be honorable from generation to generation. And that nobility of character shall be exalted unto Him that is all glory, as it was in the beginning, is now, and ever shall be, woild without end.   Amen.

POTTS' MANUSCRIPT, VOL. XLII.

"This most interesting volume is the first book of accounts of the Valley Forge, or Mount Joy Forge, under the ownership of the Potts family   John Potts of Potts Grove bought the property Mch 12, 1757, and the first entry here is dated Mch 18, 1757   There were 200 a of land in Chester Co (Pa) and 175 a in Phila. Co , on the latter on the south side of the creek were a forge and a saw mill   Potts immediately built a grist mill, a blacksmith shop, a cooper shop, and started a store   Daniel Watkins, the blacksmith, was paid £30 a year   Persons as far away as Moses Coates, living where is now Phoenixville, bought their shoes and other supplies at the store   There were a boat and a canoe on the Schuylkill, and logs were floated down the river to the saw mill. The iron was piled up in the store to at least the amount of four tons, and was hauled by wagons to Phila. The supplies, even the shingles and the Indian corn, were hauled from that city. Cows were driven there to be sold Deer ran wild in the woods   During the troubles with the Indians wagons were sent to Raystown and Ohio   There was a library maintained by a company in Providence Twp , Phila Co , to which the annual subscription was 5 s   The fuel for the Forge was wood cut and coaled in the forest   The labor was in part that of negro slaves and two servants, Thos Connor and Henry Selig, men who were bought for £30   Teamsters were paid £20 per annum.

Saml W Pennypacker, May 18, 1907 "

The above quotation is a copy of the memorandum made by Hon. Samuel W. Pennypacker, whose splendid and unique library contains the *Potts Mss.*, an invaluable historical collection, which he kindly placed at the writer's disposal and from which the following entries were copied by the author:

GARROTT BROWNBACK DR *

1727 From B. foll 17	00	00	00
Aug ye 26 To Bar iron for ye Road A Dutchman 14	00	05	0
To ye Cash pd	02	05	0
	—	—	—
1727 P Contra Cr	£02	10	0
Mar 21 By Peter Millman acct	02	10	0
1727			
Oct ye 19 To Cash	00	00	00

*From *Potts Mss* B I—*Coventry*, 1726, p 41

Nov 21, 1727

		£	s	d
Jan ye 26	To 2 half Barrels at 3/0	00	06	0
	To One hank of mohair	00	00	5
	To Silk	00	00	7
Apr ye 25	To 26 lb of Iron		9	6
June 25	To 1 ——			1
		£00	17	4

Sept 9/1728

1730

		£	s	d
June 11	To 1 5 G 6 pott 36½ lb at 11		11	6
15	To one 15 G 6 pott wt 97 lb at 11	1	12	4
	To 3 lbs of Sole Leather at 9c		2	3
Septm ye 1, 1730 fr 100		£ 3	3	5
Septm ye 17	To James Sqodory Acct for Bleeding his man			9
	To ½ Gallon of molasses		1	3
	To Rum No 7 3			1½
		£3	5	6½

CR.

		£	s	d
1730	By Sum pd for a warrant for Robt Stephens			9
June 8	By Saml Savage acct for overplus payment		1	0
11	By Wm Shnell acct		10	0
	By 33 lb and ½ of butter wd at 6c		16	9
15	By Tho felton for 7 and ¾ of butter at 6		3	10
	By Wm Ridge acct for 20 lb of butter		10	2
		2	2	6½
	By Mordcai Lincon acct		15	6
		2	18	½

Dr £3   s5   d6½
Cr £2   18   0½

Balance—See B C for 131   £0   7   6
(From B Potts Mss II, Coventry 1728.)

The iron works in Comp *Cr*

GARRAT BROWNBACK Acct

p   8 By Bar iron w 0 0 26   £9   6   p 41

p 248 By Bar non   0 1   4 of Iron at 37   0   10   7 p 75
p 100 By one   5 G⁶ pott w 34 @ 4c   0   11   6 p 41
　　　By one 15 G⁶ pott 97 @ 4c   1   12   4
　　　By 3 lb of Sole Leather   0   2   3
　　　　　　　　　　　　　　　　　　　　　　 —— —— ——
　　　　　　　　　　　　　　　　　　　　　　 2   6   1
p 143 By one Little pott p 131   4
p 162 By 1 lb of Nails   1

(From B Potts Mss IV p 75)

GARROT BROWNBACK Dr

1733 To one Quart of Rum No 11 p 60   1   8
Mar 5/69/To 1 Quart of mallos   0   8
　　29/87/To 4 Quarts of fine Salt   8
　　6　　To 2 Barrels omitted by I Bottridge
Octr 22/149 To Daniel Longanacre Cr   15   0
　　　　　　　　　　　　　　　　　　　　　　 —— —— ——
　　　　　Cr   £0 18   0
　　　　　By Ball brot from B C fs 131   12 1½
　　　　　　　　　　　　　　　　　　　　　　 —— —— ——
　　　　　　　　　　　　　　　　　　　　　£0   5 10½
feb 28 To 2 Ca? qt 1—4 @ 38   10 10½
　　　To ballance Due   £   16   9

(From B Potts Mss, VII Coventry 1736 p 103)

BROWNBACK GARRET

John Goncher Dr
　　To pd Garret Brownbacks Acct   0   2   4

(Potts Mss XLVII p 219)

MARTIN BROOMBACK Woodcutter Dr To Cash   £1
—Mount Joy or Valley Forge Feb 22, 1759.
　　(The next entry is:)
James Hockley Cr By Cash paid Mr Broomback   £1
(B XIII p 114) This was repaid May 10, 1759 By Thomas Potts & Co   Also
a/c same vol p 9, p 18
　　Dec 12, 1759 he recd cash   £1   15   0 (XLVII p 89)
　　July 30, 1760 he recd cash   15   0 XLVII p 155
(Same vol p 302)
　　Dr to 150 lbs of Beef at 2¾   1   14 4½
　　to 2 grs Strip Stuff   7   6

Nov 21, 1761 (p 310) Sundries to Smith Work Dr as per Smith
    Book   3

Nov 28, 1761 (p 311) Dr to a pare Buck Bra	1	10	0
(p 315) paid him	8		
19 Jan 1762 (p 325) Cr by 14½ Bushel of Wheat @ 5/2 wt 58	3	14	11
25 Jan 1762 (p 328) Dr to 1 lb of Coffae			
1 lb of Sugar			8
29 Jan 1762 (p 330) paid him	3	0	0
(p 339) Cr by 9½ Wood at Ridenois at 2/	0	19	0
(p 342) Dr to 1 gr of Strip Stuff		2	9
(p 345) Dr to 2 grs of Strip Stuff		5	6
(p 348) Dr to 1 lb of Sugar			9

MARTIN BROOMBACK

(p 353) Dr to 2 grs Middling		7	6
(p 354) Dr to Phillip Dewces paid for him with the Boat		1	6

(Feb 1761 p 367)

    Paid by Saml Potts to MARTIN BROMBACK for 11 Days
        work @ mine @ 2/6 Pickering Mine   1   6

Apr 6, 1761 p 368

    paid Jacob Bear for 7 days work of P Sailor at the mines   14   0
                      (Potts Mss LVII p 30)

Sept 11, 1765 Saml Potts Cr By MARTIN BROOMBACKS
.   acct   33   20   9   6
                      (Potts Mss LVII, p 52)

[A5] BENJAMIN BROOMBACK Dr

1765 Sept 10 To Thos. Rutters accd from (29)	7	2	0
Dec 21 To Cash paid him by Thos Hockley (40)		5	6
1765 Sept 10 Cr			
By 2 Cattle Bot (29)	7	7	6

WILL OF [A1] GARRETT[1] BROWNBAUGH

    Aug 4, 1757, at age 95, and a few weeks before his death, Garrett[1]
(Gerhard) executed his will, herewith reproduced, and the same was proven at
Philadelphia, Pa , Sept 23, 1757

    "In the name of God Amen, ye 4th day of August Anno Domo 1757 I GARRETT
BROWNBAUGH of vincent in the County of Chester yeoman being Sick & weak in body
but of perfect Sound mind & Memmory thanks be to God do make this my last will & Testament in maner & form following viz

    "first I bequeath my Soul to Almighty God & my body to be buried in a decent manner
at the discretion of my Exrs and as touching ye disposition of my Real& personal Estate
I dispose of the Same as folloewth first I will that all my just debts shall be truly paid.
It(em) I give & bequeath to my beloved wife MARY BROWNBAUGH all my right being

one halfe of ye grist mill in Vincent for her use during her widowhood I also give Unto her the little house ye other Side of ye Road to live in during her widowhood and one good Cow to give her Milk & ye sd cow my Son BENJAMIN² [A5] is to keep as he keeps his own, during her widowhood likewise my wife is to have ye Servant girl HANNA MILLER for her use till She Comes of age, and my Son Benjamin Must put the sd house in good Repair with a stove in it And my Son Benjamin must give his Mother Sixty weight of pork annually during her widowhood allso Its my will that my wife shall have her bed & beding & two Iron potts one pott about 1½ sh price ye other pott about 8 price & one big pewter dish & one little pewter Do, and Six pewter plates & her Chest,——Item I bequeath to my son HENLRY² [A6] all that Tract of land now layd out Joyning to Henery Acres land Containing 200 Acres to him & his heirs & Assigns for Ever My Said Son HENERY his heirs & assigns paying the owner of the sd 200 acres It being his full Dividend for his portion together with what he has already Recd Item I give & bequeath to my son in law RICHARD CUSTAR [A2] & to his heirs & assigns forever one hundred & thirty acres of land as Its now layd out Joining to my Son Henery land he my sd Son in law Richd Custar paying ye owner of Said land for the same It being his full Dividend for his portion —— Item I give & bequeath to my soninlaw FREDERICK BINGIMAN [A3] all my right of the saw mill in vincent afforesd, to be his full Dividend & portion besides ye Sum of Twelve pounds wch he owed me I forgive him allso——Item I give & bequeath to my son in law PAUL BENNER [A4] one Shilling Sterg for his full portion & Dividend Item I give & bequeath to my daughter KATHEREN [A7] one good feather bed & furniture & also one chaff bed & bedding & three pounds worth of pewter—one chest of drawers or five pounds in lieu thereof also the young mare that goes in her Name & three Cows & Six Sheep & allso that my Son Benjamin Shall give her a good Spinning wheel & ye Sum of thirty pounds in Manner following that is to Say he shall pay unto her ye Sum of ten pounds in one Year after my decease & ye Sum of ten pounds annually till ye sd Sum of Thirty pounds be paid wch Shall be her full portion & Dividend It being my will that my Son Benjamin Shall Supply his Mother in firewood to be left at her door or convenient to ye sd little house Item I give & bequeath to my Son Benjamin Brombaugh all the Remainder & Residue of the plantation whereon I now live with the improvements thereon to him & his heirs & assigns for Ever he paying the owner of sd land & allso I give & bequeath unto him all debts due unto me or that Shall become due & allso all the Residue of my personal Estate of what kind Soever now belonging to me on the Said premises and after my wifes decease her dowery Must descend to my Son Benjamin & his hrs allso Its my will that as I paid for about 700 Rails—making on my Son Henerys land that my Son Benjamin Shall have sd Rails with liberty to Hawl sd Rails away at his leisure without let or hindrance and I do allso Nominate Constitute & appointe my Son Benjamin & my beloved wife Mary Brownbaugh my true & faithfull Exrs of this my last will & Testament & do utterly Revoke & disanul & make void all former wills & bequests by me heretofore made & do declare this my last will & Testament

"Garrett Brownbaugh X his mark"

(See photographic copy)

AN INVENTORY.

Or bill of appraisement taken and made Ye Twenty-first day of September Anno Domini One thousand seven hundred and fifty seven of the Personal Estate of Garrett Brownbaugh, late of Vincent, in the County of Chester, Yeoman, Deceased, per us the subscribers according to the best of our knowledge viz —Imprimis,

	£.	s	d.
To wearing apparel	10	0	0
a Riding horse Saddle and Bridle	10	0	0
four horse kind	26	0	0
13 head of horned Cattle	40	0	0
11 Swine	06	0	0

	£	s	d
10 Sheep	02	10	0
Wagon and Gears	12	0	0
Ploughs Harrows and cart	02	0	0
Pewter	04	0	0
Brass	01	0	0
Dressing ware	0	6	0
3 Tables	1	10	0
Sundry Chears	1	4	0
Iron pots and pans	2	10	0
Wooden ware and Stillyard	1	0	0
Spinning Wheel	0	15	0
Iron ware and sider mill	1	10	0
Sundry beds and bedding	15	0	0
a windmill	2	0	0
5 Stacks of Corn	50	0	0
a cutting box	0	15	0
Sundry Implements of husbandry	0	15	0
Sundry Stacks of hay	10	0	0
Sundry Notes	13	14	8
Book debts to profit and loss	20	0	0
600 Acres of land taken up by warrant	150	0	0
the Improvement on said 600 acres	300	0	0
a Grist Mill and land belonging	100	0	0
lumber Goods	3	0	0
Total	787	9	8

Errors excepted

Sheeders' manuscript History, before mentioned, gives the following inscription on a tombstone in Brownback Ch cemetery· "Wm Posey son in law of Garret Brumbach died aged 62 years," also that he owned a small farm of 33 acres, died intestate, leaving a w named Susanna and six ch John, William, Peter, Susanna, Edward and Sarah (there were 8 ch in all).

According to the tombstone records at Brownback Ch . William Posey was *b* 1759 and *d* Mch. 9, 1821, Susanna was *b* 1758 and *d* Dec. 6, 1840 She was *b* in 1758 and [A1] Gerhard *d* in 1757, aged 95, therefore this Susanna cannot be a daughter of Gerhard, and is not included amongst his children

"There are more than a thousand descendants of this one man living to-day, and many of them hold important and lucrative positions in business,

in politics, and in the various professions   Not a few have served their country during the Civil War, and on the whole they have all shown themselves to be patriotic and worthy citizens.   The family is strong, energetic, and religious, and promises to maintain its virtue and industry for many generations "[a]

Children (6)

[A 2] + Elizabeth[2], b 1716, d Nov 12, 1823
[A 3] + Mary Magdalena[2], d 1776.
[A 4] + Anna Mary[2].
[A 5] + Benjamin[2], b 1731; d 1786
[A 6] + Henry[2], b Feb 18, 1733, d Aug. 1, 1804
[A 7] + Catharine[2], b 1735

[A2] ELIZABETH[2] BRUMBACH ([A1] Gerhard[1]) b at Germantown, 1716; m "Richard Custard" (Custer?).[b] Gerhard[1] willed to his son-in-law, Richard Custer, 130 acres of land   Elizabeth d Nov 12, 1823   They had 3 ch: Anna, Susann and Richard, and perhaps another son

[A3] MARY MAGDALENA[2] BRUMBACH ([A1] Gerhard[1])[c] b in E. Coventry Twp, Chester Co, Pa, 1829, d 1776, m Frederick Bingaman, "the German of Coventry," came from Germany about 1740; commenced their married life upon a tract first taken up by his father-in-law [A1] Gerhard[1] at the mouth of Birchrun Creek[d] on the W. side of French Creek Frederick was a mill-wright and erected the first saw mill in that neighborhood, adding a grist mill in a few years   Frederick Sheeder says that in 1794 "There was nothing to be seen but part of the hole where the buildings stood.   The head and tail races were more visible "   'The land on the left side up this stream toward the source, or where two streams met, was chiefly timber land, and on the right side cleared and cultivated, studded with many buildings In the course of two miles there were four grist mills, four saw mills, one oil mill, one tilt and the best seat for a mill vacant, that of John Shuler's, formerly that of Frederic Bingaman   The greater part of this timber land belonged to the Grunds and Casper Himes   That Grund and Michael Kolb had a difficult law suit about 1805 concerning the water, where the oil and saw mill is now the property of Owen Grates, and in the direction of where the two branches of the Birchrun meet.   At this point the first school house was in the township of West Vincent, after the division of Vincent   In it the elections

[a]Pennsylvania German, Vol XI, No. 3, Mch, 1910
[b]See record of baptism, p. 79
[c]From data furnished by Dr. Wm H[4] Mosteller [A78-11].
[d]Named by the Indians because of the numerous birch trees.

were held. Nearly all the land on the right side of said run was taken up by the Jenkins family as the first settlers," etc.

The Bingamans were a strongly religious people, and "Mary Magdaline was destined to be the star of religious life in the northern end of Chester Co."

"Their descendants are numerous to-day, and they have spread into several States. Most of them are occupied in business pursuits and in farming Some have entered professional life Gerhard[1] willed to his son-in-law, Frederick Bingaman the saw mill in Vincent township " *

They were also patriotic. Two sons, Frederick[3] and Garrett[3], served in the Continental Army Frederick served in a rifle company, wearing trimmings which were colored with maple bark juice. Garrett[3] served a term of military service, was again drafted, and his brother Frederick[3] took his place in the service

> *Children* (4)

i *John[3] Bingaman b* May 4, 1787, Feb 21, 1809 *m* ——— dau Judge *John Ralston*, they lived in Coventryville, where he *d* Dec 4, 1825 His wid later *m Henry R—*, and lived to be almost one hundred years old.

John owned the "Cold Spring Farm," and its magnificent grove of giant oaks and hickories for years served as noted Methodist camp meeting grounds These fine trees were felled some years ago and a new growth of timber is taking their place

There were 8 ch· Joshua[4], Eliza[4], John[4], Ralston[4], Frederick[4], Robert[4], William[4] and Levi[4], *b* Oct 21, 1824, in the former "Rising Sun Inn "

ii *Frederick[3] Bingaman; m Elizabeth*, dau *Casimer Missimer* of Montgomery Co , Pa , and they lived there for some years, Revolutionary soldier; he *d* 1832 and she about 1833 , both bur in Brownback Ch cemetery. There were two ch· John[4], *b* Sept. 23, 1783, Mary[4], who *m Jacob Eman*

"RISING SUN INN "

Frederick Bingaman, Jr , established in Coventryville an inn which for many years was a noted hostelry. The building stands to the left of the Ridge road as you go toward the falls of French Creek The inn was conducted by Frederick and his s John until Sept 11, 1817 Upon that night the former attended a religious meeting, became converted, returned home, cut down his sign, and closed the public house, which had antedated the Revolution.

iii *Garrett[3] Bingaman* (Rev. soldier).

iv *Mary[3] Bingaman*

---

*Pennsylvania German, Vol XI, No 3, Mch, 1910

[A4] ANNA MARY² BRUMBACH ([A1] Gerhard¹) *m Paul Benner*, and to this union were born three sons and one daughter: Abraham, Jacob, ———, ———. Their descendants are not so numerous, but they represent a worthy and industrious branch of the family Gerhard¹ willed to his son-in-law Paul Benner only one shilling because he said that Benner owned more land than he himself possessed

Children (4), surname Benner·

i Abraham³, *b* Aug. 18, 1764, in Vincent Twp., *d* Feb. 10, 1859, in Chester Co, Pa ; *m Catherine Hause b* Nov 29, 1767, in Vincent Twp , *d* Dec. 2, 1837, and bur E Vincent Ref. Ch. cemetery.

Children:

(1) Mary⁴, *b* about 1800, *d* 1850 in Chester Co , Pa , *m Benjamin Hartman*

Children (9), surname Hartman

(a) Mary⁵, *b* June 4, 1824; *d* June 4, 1892; *m Reuben Bierbower, b* May 18, 1819 Latter's s PENROSE WILEY⁶ *m* [A134] MARTHA EVANS⁵ BROWNBACK

(2) Jacob⁴, unm

(3) George ⁴, *m Anna M Sturges*

(4) Susanna⁴, *m Jacob Hipple*

(5) Elizabeth⁴, *m Henry Busch*

(6) Hannah⁴, *m William Wagoner.*

(7) Sarah⁴, *m William Pugh.*

(8) Rebecca⁴, *m Christian Renyken*

ii Jacob³.

iii John³.

iv "Mrs. Allen Hamer "

[A5] BENJAMIN² BRUMBACH—BRUMBACK ([A1] Gerhard¹) *b* 1731; *m* (1) *Elizabeth (or Mary ?) Paul,* dau *John Paul;* she died young and was the mother of three children June 9, 1773, Benjamin² *m* (2) *Rachel Parker, b* 1752, dau *Edward Parker,* and probably sister of *Capt Edward Parker* of 2d Battn , Chester Co Militia Rachel was murdered by persons unknown during the night of April 15, 1837 Benjamin² was a great jumper, and gave some Indians a bear skin because he beat them in several jumping matches near the old Indian village elsewhere mentioned. He became Executor of Gerhard's¹ will and received the largest portion of the estate—the Inn and over 600 acres of land which lay in Vincent and Coventry Twps , Chester Co , Pa The descendants are numerous and mostly remain in Eastern Pa.

REVOLUTIONARY WAR SERVICE

"BENJAMIN BRUMBACK" appears as having been commissioned First Lieut Aug 5, 1776, of Capt. Edward Parker's Co of 2d Battn. of Chester Co. Militia, commanded by Col. Thos Hockly, Capt of the 8th Battalion of Chester Co Militia, commanded by Lieut Col Joseph Spear, 1779, and Capt. of the 4th Co of 2d Battalion of Chester Co. Militia, commanded by Lieut. Col. Thomas Bull, July 3, 1780 *

ASSESSMENTS.

Chester Co Rates—1765.

	Acres	Horses	Cattle	Sheep	Servants
Brownback Henry [A6]	200	3	4	4	
Benj'n [A5]	140	2	5	8	2

Coventry Rate.

Brownback Benj'n [A5]   250

(*Pa. Archives*, 3d Ser., Vol. XI, p 59—p 89 of same *Broombach Benjn* is assessed for 110 a)

Vincent Rate—1766.

Broomback Benj'n, tavern, is assessed for 179 a, 3 h, 5 c, 6 sh, 1 serv.

(*Pa. Arch*, 3d Ser., Vol XI, p 207):

1767 he is assessed 170 a, 3 h, 5 c, 8 sh, 1 serv.

(*Same, p 371*):

1768 he is assessed 170 a, 4 h, 5 c, 10 sh, 1 serv., and the name is "Brumback, Benj'n, tavern."

(*Pa. Arch., 3d Ser., Vol XII, p 502*):

1769 he is assessed, same locality and same spelling, 170 a, 3 h, 4 c, 6 sh, 1 serv ; and Henry is assessed 180 a, 2 h, 3 c, 0 sh, 0 serv.

(*Same, p. 621*) ·

Broomback, Henry, same locality, 1766 (same reference p. 207), is assessed 200 a, 2 h, 3 c.

Broomback, Henry, same locality (same ref , p. 371), in 1767 is assessed 150 a, 3 h, 4 c, 6 sh

Brumback, Henry, same Twp , 1768, assessed 180 a, 3 h, 4 c, 6 sh, 0 serv

(*Same ref., p 502*) ·

Bromback, Henry, 1771, same locality (same ref , p. 770), is assessed 170 a, 2 h, 3 c.

---

*Penna Archives, 2d Ser , Edn 1888, Vol XIV, pp 67, 117, 119 P. 67 also gives his bro. "Henery" [A6] as Ensign Aug 5, 1776, in the company of which Benj was 1st Lieut

Chester Co Rates—Coventry Twp —1774.

Bromback, Benja tavern, 150 a, 4 h, 4 c, 10 sh, 0 serv.

Bromback, Henry 150 a, 2 h, 2 c, 6 sh, 0 serv.

(*Pa. Arch , 3d Ser , Vol. XII, p. 92.*)

Chester Co Rate—Vincent Twp.—1780.

Brumback, Benjn. 180 a, 4 h, 7 c, 0 sh, 0 serv

Brumbock, Henry· 250 a, 3 h, 6 c, 0 sh, 0 serv

(*Same, p. 297*)

Coventry Return—Chester Co.—1781.

Brumback, Benj'n 100 a   Tax   3£   10s   3d

Brumback, Henry   Tax   2£   11s   6d

(*Pa. Arch., 3d Ser., Vol XII, pp 493 and 613.*)

Vincent Rate—1781.

Brumback, Benjn   160 a, 3 h, 6 c, 0 sh, 0 serv—Tax,   £9   1s   4d

Brumback Henry   160 a, 3 h, 5 c, 0 sh, 0 serv—Tax,   £8   13s   6d

(*Same ref , pp 432 and 545*)

Brumback, John[3] (of Benjamin)—"Inmates," is assessed £1. (*Same ref , pp 435 and 548*)

Vincent Twp Rates—1785

Brombach Benjn [A5]   £2   13s   10d

Brombach Henry [A6]   £3   0s   7d

Bromback John [A10]   .   10s   0d

(*Same ref., pp 809 and 813*)

Chester Co. Rates—Coventry Twp —1785.

Brombach, Benjm [A5]   £1   17sh   6d

Bromback, Henry [A6]   £1   0sh   0d

Bromback, John [A10]   £1   9sh   10d

(*Same ref , p 703*)

CENSUS OF 1790—CHESTER COUNTY, PA.

In *Vincent Twp* [A6] "HENRY[2] BROMBACK" is enumerated as having three sons over 16 years, and two females, including his wife; also HENRY[3] BROMBACK, JUNR [A9], is enumerated as having one son over 16, and his wife.

In *Coventry Twp.* we find enumerated. JOHN[3] BROMBACH [A10] as having three sons under 16 years, three females (including wife), and one other white person; also EDWARD[3] BROMBACK [A11] as having a son over 16 years and his wife. At that time Chester Co. contained 27, 937 souls.

AGREEMENT OF [A5] BENJAMIN² BRUMBACK—"BROWNBACK"—
APRIL 22, 1786

Know all men by these presents that I Benjamin Brownback of Vincent Township in the County of Chester am held and firmly bound unto George Gilbert of New Hanover Township in Philada Co in the Sum of Thirty Pounds in Gold & Silver Coin lawful money of Pennsylvania to be paid unto the Said George Gilbert or to his Certain attorneys, Exetrs Admitors or Assigns   To the which payment well & truly to be made I do hereby bind myself, my heirs, Lxecutors, Admtors and every of them firmly by these presents Sealed with my seal dated this fourth day of September, 1784

The Condition of this obligation is Such that Whereas Peter Paul & others the Heirs and Representatives of John Paul late of Vincent Township aforesaid deceased August last past, for the Consideration therein mentioned did grant release and Confirm unto the above named George Gilbert his heirs & Assigns, All their respective shares of in and to certain forty three lots of ground Situate in Pottstown marked and numbered in the general plan of Pottstown as in the Said Indenture Specified   And whereas Edward Brownback (son of the Said Benjamin Brownback) being a minor under the age of twenty one years, and incapable at present to sign and execute a sufficient conveyance for his Share therein— know ye that if the Said Edward Brownback his heirs and assigns Shall at the request of the Said George Gilbert his heirs or Assigns Sign Seal & Execute a Sufficient Deed of Conveyance for his Said Share of and in and to the above recited forty three lots of ground and every part thereof unto the Said George Gilbert his heirs and Assigns, then this present obligation to be void and of none effect or else to be and remain in full force & virtue

his
Benjamin B Brownback
mark

Sealed and delivered }
in the presence of us }
   Henry Misimer }

When Edward Brownbach became of age, he refused to sign the above document, which fact affects title to the valuable real estate mentioned therein The original document is in the possession of Garrett Ellwood⁵ Brownback [A112]

AGREEMENT AS TO DIVISION OF [A5] BENJAMIN'S² REAL ESTATE—APRIL 22, 1786

(1)   "Plantation known as 'Swan' and 40 acres lower down the Roade joining Jacob Stogeis, Samuel Rees, and Others, all in the Twp of Coventry to be one Division."

(2)   "Track known by the name of 'Tavern' in Vincent Twp as far up as a Line run by Francis Hopson Dividing it from his Other Lands, some in Vincent aforesaid and some in Coventry Twp "

(3)   "All the Remainder of this Land Some in Vincent and some in Coventry to the Said Line run by P. Hopson "

"And we do further Report as Our Judgment in Order to make the Sd Division Equal that the Son that takes the first Devision or Swan track and the 40 a shall pay the sum of £133 Six Shillings and 8d in hand to the Son

that takes the (3) Dev. and also pay unto the Son that takes the Tavern Track in Vincent, or Second Dev the Sum of £3, 6s, 8d, the above Sums to be paid Imediately upon the taking of the Swan track etc "

John Ralston

Henry Acker

[A6] HENRY × BRUMBACK

Apr 22, 1786

[A10] John³ took division (1)

[A 9] Henry³ took division (2)

[A11] Edward³ took division (3)

Children by 1st m (3):

[A 9] + Henry³

[A10] + John³.

[A11] + Edward³, *b* 1766

[A6] HENRY² BRUMBACH—BRUMBACK ([A1] Gerhard¹) *b* Feb 18, 1733, *d* July 30, 1804, *m Mary Magdalin* Paul*, *b* Feb 23, 1739, *d* Aug 23, 1784, dau *John* (*d* 1766) and *Mary Paul.*

This branch of the family consists of a larger number of descendants than any of the others, and they have spread into ten different States, viz : Pennsylvania, Ohio, Indiana, Illinois, Kansas, Nebraska, Oklahoma, Montana, Idaho and California They have been engaged in various occupations, chiefly in business and in farming, but a goodly number are found in professional life Gerhard¹ willed to Henry² 200 acres of land, and by dint of perseverance and good management the latter increased his property to the extent of more than 600 acres. He was collector of the "County Rate" for Vincent Twp in 1795.[b]

Henry² was an Elder in the Brownback Church, and his signature appears in the Church Book for 1773, written both "Henry Brombach" and "Henry Brambach."[c]

REVOLUTIONARY WAR SERVICE

"Henry Brumback commissioned Ensign Aug 5, 1776, in Capt Edwd Parker's Co , 2d Battn., Chester Co Militia, Thos. Hockley, Col "[d]

Henry Brumback also appears as a Private on a "Return of the names and number of the Volunteer Militia Light Horse for the County of Chester, with a State of their equipment and the Battalions to which they respectively be-

---

[a]Spelling from tombstone of [A6] Henry¹

[b]Garrett Ellwood³ Brownback [A132] has his original tax book and his certificate of appointment as collector

[c]See Plate 22.

[d]*Pa Archives, 5th Series, Vol. V,* p 509.

long, 1780-1781 "   "He belonged to the Second Battalion under the Command of Colonel Thomas Bull."[a]

Henry's[2] silver knee buckles and other articles used by him in the Revolutionary War are preserved by his grandson, Garrett Ellwood[5] Brownback [A132].

WILL OF [A6] HENRY[2] BRUMBACK, MAY 20, 1804.[b]

'In the name of God Amen, the twentieth day of May in the year of our *Lprd* one thousand eight hundred & four I, Henry Brunback of the Township of Vincent in the County of Chester & State of Pennsylvania being weak in body but of sound mind & memory thanks be to God therefore calling to mind the mortality of my body and that it is appointed for all men once to die do make this my last will & Testament I do order that all my just debts & funeral charges be first paid & discharged by my executors herein after named Imprimas it is my will and I do order that *John Titlow William Posey & John Ralston* shall immediately after my decease divide my Plantation where I now live part in Vincent Township & part in Coventry Township which I hold by three deeds & a warrant in two parts or divisions as they may think proper or most advantageous and set or put a Valuation on each part and I do order and direct that my son Benjamin [A15] shall have the first choice and may take it at the Valuation and my son Peter [A14] shall have the refusal of the other division or part at the Valuation and in case that my son Benjamin and Peter or either of them should decline or refuse to take them or either of the said divisions it is my will that my son John [A13] shall have the refusal of the land so divided or either part that is declined to be taken by either of my sons Benjamin or Peter and I do order that if my sons or either of them should take my land or any part after it is divided and Valued as aforesaid the Valuation shall be divided in five equal payments to be paid unto my Executors annually and if none will take my land at the Valuation immediately after the said Valuation is made I order and direct that my Execu's shall sell the same or such part that is not taken by my sons and I impower them or the survivor of them to Convey to the purchaser or purchasers by Deed in fee the same Item it is my will and I order and direct that immediately after my decease my executors sell by public vandue all my personall property excepting my wearing apparel which I order to be equally divided between my five children namely John [A13] Peter [A14] Benjamin [A15] Hannah [A12] and Susannah [A16] but they would not wish to have my wearing apparel so divided between them then I order that my Executors to give my wearing apparel to such poor persons as they may think proper and it is my will and I order and direct that the amount of the Valuation and sales of my estate both real and and personal also what my said children hath received from me but no interest shall be demanded from them for what they have received from me I shall be divided in the following manner it is my will and I order that my son John [A13] shall have or receive the sum of forty Pounds my son Peter [A14] shall receive the sum of one hundred pounds the above sum to be paid them immediately after the sales of my estate and the remainder of my estate or the amount thereof to be equally divided between my five children namely John Brunback Peter Brunback Benjamin Brunback Hannah Snyder [A12] and Susannah Prizor [A16] share and share alike to them and their heirs forever to be paid unto them in equal shares as it comes in to my Executors hands by my executors and I do hereby constitute make and ordain my three sons John Brunback Peter Brunback and Benjamin Brunback Executors of this my last will and testament and I do hereby revoke and disanul all former will and wills Legacy or legacies ratifying and confirming this and no other to be my last will and testament In witness whereof I have hereunto set my hand and seal the day and year first above written

his
Henry ✕ Brunback [Seal]
mark

Signed sealed published pronounced and declared by the said Henry Brunback as his last will and testament in the presence of us the sunscribers John Titlow Roger Davis John Ralston   West Chester, August 24th, 1804

---

[a] *Pa. Archives, 2d Series Vol XIV*, p 126—p 67 also gives "HENERY BRUMBACK" as Ensign, Aug 5, 1776, in the 2d Battan, and his brother BENJAMIN [A5] as First Lieut of same

[b] Recorded in Book II, p 33, Chester Co, Pa. Certified copy furnished by [A132] + Garrett Ellwood[5] Brownback

Children (5):

[A12] + Hannah[3], *b* Jan 3, 1759, *d* Nov 5, 1811
[A13] + John[3], *b* Aug 8, 1761; *d* Dec. 16, 1838
[A14] + Peter[3], *b* Apr. 3, 1764, *d* July 9, 1834
[A15] + Benjamin[3], *b* May 7, 1768, *d* March 20, 1837.
[A16] + Susanna[3], *b* July 5, 1772, *d* May 7, 1856

[A7] CATHARINE[2] BRUMBACH—BRUMBACK ([A1] Gerhard[1]) after her father's death *m Jacob Munshower*, and to this union were born three sons, and perhaps two daughters The descendants of their branch of the family are numerous, and they live mostly about the old homestead in the Schuylkill valley. They are engaged in farming, in various trades and business pursuits Jacob Munshower owned a large farm which occupied the present site of Spring City Gerhard[1] willed to his daughter Catharine some household goods, a horse and several cows, and thirty pounds sterling in cash.

[A9] HENRY[3] BROWNBACK ([A5] Benjamin[2], Gerhard[1]) *m Elizabeth Shaner.*
    Children (2).
[A17] Henry[4]
[A18] John [4]

[A10] JOHN[3] BROWNBACK ([5] Benjamin[2], Gerhard[1]) *m Ella Parker;* they lived on the ridge, or "Tavern tract"
    Children (6):
[A31] Henry[4].
[A32] Mary[4] ("Polly"), *b* Dec 31, 1781, *d* 1859, unm
[A33] John[4], *b* May 7, 1783, *d* Dec 7, 1878, *m Eleanor* ——.
[A34] Rebecca[4], *b* 1792; *d* May 11, 1865, unm
[A35] + Elizabeth[4], *d* 1847, *m John S Messimer.*
[A36] + Edward[4], *b* Dec 19, 1799, *d* April (Sept ?) 16, 1845

[A11] EDWARD[3] BROWNBACK ([A5] Benjamin[2], Gerhard[1]) *b* 1766, *m Susanna De Frain, b* July 5, 1765, and *d* Dec 12, 1853, dau *Peter* and *Eve De Frain, b* Aug 5, 1733, and *d* March 23, 1782, latter buried at Lower Hill Ref Church Peter De Frain served as "private in Capt. Edward Parker's Co , 2d Battn , Chester Co. Mil , Aug. 5, 1776, Thos. Hockley, Col." [*]

---

[*] Vol. V, Pa Arch , 5th Series See also [A14] for further services

Edward³ *d* Nov 17, 1799, and was bur at Brownback's Ch. His widow later *m* [A14] PETER³ BROWNBACK

> *One son*

[A42] + Edward⁴, *b* June 10, 1798; *d* Dec 15, 1858

[A12] HANNAH³ BROWNBACK ([A6] Henry², Gerhard¹) *b* Jan. 3, 1759; *d* Nov. 5, 1811; *m Casper Snyder* They are buried at the Lower Hill Ref. Ch, located on Ridge Road above ·Phoenixville, Chester Co, Pa — an old church which was used as a hospital for wounded Revolutionary soldiers

> *Children* (6), *surname Snyder*

- i   Henry⁴.
- ii Mary⁴, *m Jones Pennypacker.*
- iii Benjamin, d y
- iv Thomas⁴, *m Elizabeth Shipley*
- v   Elizabeth⁴, *m John Trinly*
- vi Susanna⁴, *m Casper Francis*

[A13] JOHN³ BROWNBACK ([A6] Henry², Gerhard¹) *b* Aug 8, 1761, in West Vincent Twp., Chester Co, Pa, *d* Dec 16, 1838, *m Margaret De Frain*, *b* Nov 26, 1763, *d* March 12, 1828; dau of *Peter* and *Eve De Frain*; sister of *Susanna* who *m* (1) EDWARD³ BROWNBACK [A11], and (2) PETER³ BROWNBACK [A14]

John³ served as a Col of Militia in the War of 1812, and both himself and w were bur at Brownback's Ch

> *Children* (10)

[A20] + Elizabeth⁴, *b* Jan 5, 1795, *d* March 19, 1870
[A21] + John⁴, *b* May 29, 1800, *d* Oct. 12, 1821
[A22] + Henry⁴, *b* June 13, 1802, *d* June 18, 1893
[A23] + Rebecca⁴, *b* July 19, 1804, *d* April 28, 1885.
[A24] + William⁴, *b* Sept 19, 1806
[A25] + Jesse⁴, *d* June 30, 1898.
[A26] + Mary⁴
[A27] + Hannah⁴
[A28] + Sarah⁴
[A29] + Catharine⁴.

[A14] PETER³ BROWNBACK ([A6] Henry², Gerhard¹) *b* April 3, 1764, *d* July 9, 1834; *m* (1) ——; *m* (2) *Susanna De Frain*, *b* July 5, 1765; dau *Peter* and *Eve De Frain*, and widow of [A11] EDWARD³

BROWNBACK, she *d* Dec. 12, 1853, aged 88 yrs., and was bur. at Brown-back's Ch

Peter[3] Brownback's daily journal* of the period covering Sept, 1794, gives the events of the march from home to Downingtown, Harrisburgh, etc, during the "Whiskey insurrection" He was Adj Gen. and commanded the battalion He also sawed out and made gun stocks* for the Government in the old log shop which stood in the vineyard upon the old farm

When the Revolutionary troops marched from Valley Forge they stopped at the home of Peter De Frain on the "Ridge road" and Susanna helped her mother, Eve De Frain, to bake bread for the troops. The British followed them; the Revolutionary troops left De Frain's at midnight, crossing the Schuylkill river at Parker's Ford and going on to Germantown, where the battle was fought.

AGREEMENT BETWEEN PETER BROWNBACK [A14] AND FREDERICK SMITH, JAN. 1, 1805 [b]

Articles of agreement made and Concluded on the first Day of January in the year of Our Lord one Thousand Eight Hundred and five; By and Between PETER BRUMBACK of Vincent Township Chester County and state of Pennsylvania of the one part and FREDERICK SMITH of Coventry Township County and State aforesaid of the other part + + + PETER BRUMBACK + + Term of one year to commence from the first Day of April Next all that Plantation farm and Tavern House now in his Tenure receiving as is hereinafter received first the said PETER BRUMBACK doth receive Two front Rooms in the said House one on the lower floor and one on the upper floor both next to the Road at the North West corner of the said house + + he also receives a piece of meadow, from a watering ditch running to the land of the late HENRY BRUMBACK Deceased [A6], Extending from the same along the Bushes to the lot of GEORGE HALL'S Next adjoining the afforesaid lands or the so called INDIAN FIELD, he also receives the Water right which is received by a former Contract to the estate of HENRY[3] BRUMBACK JUNR Deceased [A9]

The said Frederick Smith + + + agree to pay to the said Peter Brumback + + the sum of Eighty Dollars Exclusive of the covenants hereinafter mentioned first the said Frederick Smith is to pay all the Taxes Assessed + + + to clear the Bushes out of the meadow + + + to repair and make the fence of a New from the Ground round the meadow to the field now in tenure of BENJAMIN[3] BRUMBACK [A15] and half the middle fence between that field and the meadow and repair the other fences where necessary he is to deliver to RACHEL BRUMBACK[c] half a tun of Bank hay and hall the third Part of her firewood during said term + + + he is not to cut or destroy any green Timber for fuel while there is dead Timber to supply the same or if the case requires Green timber to be cut the said Peter Brumback is to Show and direct the same + + +

Peter Brownback [Seal]
Frederick Smith [Seal]

Witnesses·
Anthony Shaffer
Abrm Fertig

Children (3) ·

[A39] + Peter[4], *b* May 22, 1802, *d* April 20, 1882.

---

*Both preserved by [A132] Garrett Ellwood[3] Brownback See also [A13]
[b]Preserved by [A132] Garrett Ellwood[3] Brownback Notice 'Brumback" in body of agreement and "Brownback" in signature—also the careful preservation or "conservation" of the trees
[c]First w of [A14] Peter[4] Brownback

[A40] John⁴, *b* Sept 20, 1804, *d* Sept. 27, 1813, unm.
[A41] + Jesse⁴, *b* March 18, 1807, *d* Aug. 3, 1899.

[A15] BENJAMIN³ BROWNBACK ([A6] Henry², Gerhard¹) *b* May 7, 1768, *m Elizabeth Grubb, b* Dec 19, 1767, dau *Nicholas* and *Catharine (Harwick) Grubb*. They lived in Vincent Twp, Chester Co, Pa., on the [A6] Henry² farm. (See [A6] for Benjamin's³ signature, etc.) The latter *d* March 20, 1837, and was bur in Brownback Cem, Elizabeth *d* July 2, 1862, and was bur at E Ringold, O See Plate 28—Washington's Headquarters

Children (8):

[A43] + Catharine⁴, *b* Oct. 11, 1791
[A44] Benjamin⁴, *b* Nov 19, ——, *d* Nov 20, 1837; unm.
[A45] + David⁴, *b* Aug 18, 1800.
[A46] Mary⁴, *b* Jan 15, 1803
[A47] + Henry⁴, *b* Oct 12, 1805
[A48] + William⁴, *b* Jan. 21, 1808
[A49] Samuel⁴, *b* Dec 14, 1810
[A50] Elizabeth⁴, *b* Dec 14, 1813

[A16] SUSANNA³ BROWNBACK ([A6] Henry², Gerhard¹) *b* July 5, 1772; *m Frederick Prizer, b* Dec 9, 1768; lived on a farm in Coventry Twp, Chester Co, Pa Frederick was a member Lutheran Church and *d* Jan 27, 1823; Susanna³ *d* April 7, 1856, aged 83 years 27 days; both bur in cemetery adjoining Brownback Ch.

Children (3), *surname Prizer:*

i Hannah⁴, *b* May 9, 1796, *m John Diffendafer, b* 1794 and *d* Oct. 30, 1862; Hannah⁴ *d* July 10, 1875, both bur. in cemetery of Brownback Ch.

Children (1 *s and* 7 *dau*), *surname Diffendafer.*

(1) Mary Ann⁵, *b* March 1, 1817, *d* July 1, 1887; *m Peter Brower, d* May 9, 1901 (5 s and 4 dau).
(2) Susanna⁵, *b* April 2, 1819, *d* age 80 yrs. 6 mo 25 ds, *m* [A39] PETER⁴ BROWNBACK (3 s and 1 dau.)
(3) Julian⁵, *b* July 18, 1827; *m John Kulp, b* 1817, and *d* April 29, 1890 (2s and 1 dau).
(4) Lafayette⁵, *b* Sept 22, 1831; *d* April 1, 1837
(5) Eliza Ann⁵, *b* May 13, 1833; *d* Sept. 10, 1836
(6) Sarah E⁵, *b* Aug 30, 1837, Oct. 28, 1855 *m Jacob Y. Reifsnyder* (12 ch).

(7) Hannah Lovina[5], *b* July 8, 1840, *m Daniel Fry* (3 ch)

ii John[4], *b* May 29, 1800; *d* Oct 12, 1821; *m Elizabeth* —— (10 ch)

iii Henry[4], *b* June 13, 1802; *d* June 18, 1893 (91 y 5 ds) ; March 13, 1826, *m Elizabeth Diffendafcr*, *b* Sept. 17, 1803; *d* Aug 6, 1881 (77 10 19).

    Children (6), *surname Prizer*

(1) Sarah[5], *b* Aug 15, 1827, *d* 1849, *m* [See A114] URIAH SEBASTIAN ROOT[5] BROWNBACK, *b* June, 1822; *d* Feb , 1878 (2 ch).

(2) Elizabeth[5], *b* March 20, 1829, *m John Prizer* (10 ch.)

(3) Leah[5], *b* Jan. 10, 1831, *m Joseph C Green*, who *d* March 10, 1906, she lives at Pughtown, Chester Co , Pa. (No ch)

(4) Hannah[5], *b* Nov 5, 1832, *m Mary A Berger Wanger* (10 ch)

(5) Susan[5], *b* April 21, 1835, *m William M. Staufer* (1 ch).

(6) Esalinda[6], *b* Jan 20, 1838, *d* Nov 13, 1901

[A20] ELIZABETH[4] BROWNBACK ([A13] John[3], [A6] Henry[2], Gerhard[1]) *b* Jan 5, 1795, in W. Vincent Twp , Chester Co , Pa ; Jan. 14, 1814, *m George Christman*, *b* May 9, 1793, in E Vincent Township, same county; son *Henry* and *Susan Keeley Christman* George *d* June 17, 1866, aet. 72-8-8 ds, and Elizabeth[4] *d* March 19, 1870, aet 75-2-14, both bur. at Zion's Lutheran Church, E Pikeland Twp , Chester Co , Pa George was a farmer, Dem , and member Luth. Ch.

"Henry Christman private Capt Hallman's Co., 2d Battn., Chester Co Mil., Aug. 12, 1780 " [*]

    Children (8), *surname Christman*

i Joshua[5], *b* July 2, 1815, *d* Sept. 9, 1887.

ii Sophia[5], *b* July 29, 1817, *d* July 25, 1838

iii Susannah[5], *b* Feb 12, 1820, *d* July 29, 1820.

iv Margaret[5], *b* Oct 25, 1822, unm.; living

v Isabella[5], *b* March 3, 1825, *d* Oct. 19, 1849

vi Elizabeth[5], *b* April 3, 1827, *d* Oct 23, 1908.

vii John[5], *b* Feb 16, 1830; *d* Dec. 3, 1905

viii Hannah[5], *b* Feb. 16, 1830, unm; living

[A21] JOHN[4] BROWNBACK ([A13] John[3], [A6] Henry[2], Gerhard[1]) *b* May 29, 1800, *d* Oct 12, 1821, *m Hannah Keeley*, *b* May 9, 1796 (It is re-

———
[*] Vol V, Pa Arch , 5th Series.

ported that Hannah *m* (2) *John Diffendarfer*—see [A16-1]—but there is some uncertainty about it.)

Children (5) ·

[A66] + Oliver Davis[5], *b* Nov. 4, 1822; *d* Feb 10, 1906.

[A67] + Holland Keeley[5], *b* Sept , 1827

[A68] Mary Magdalene[5], unm

[A69] + Rebecca Keeley[5], *b* Sept 18, 1833

[A70] Malinda, *m Jacob Acker.*

[A22] HENRY[4] BROWNBACK ([A13] John[3], [A6] Henry[2], Gerhard[1]) *b* June 13, 1802, *d* June 18, 1893; *m Catharine Shuler.*

Children (4):

[A56] + Lydia[5].

[A57] + Margaret[5].

[A58] + William[5], *b* July 22, 1822, *d* May 18, 1910

[A59] + Sophia[5], *b* 1824; *d* Dec 20, 1910

[A23] REBECCA[4] BROWNBACK ([A13] John[3], [A6] Henry[2], Gerhard[1]) *b* in W. Vincent Twp., Chester Co, Pa , July 19, 1804, Feb 24, 1831, *m Samuel Stauffer, b* July 13, 1803, in the same township, Samuel *d* July 16, 1865, and his w *d* April 28, 1885, both bur. at St Matthew's Ref Ch

Children (6), *surname Stauffer*

i Mary C.[5], *b* Aug. 26, 1833, *m Joseph Friday*

ii Abraham B [5], *b* March 2, 1835, Dec. 26, 1867, *m* (1) *Ella E Shantz, b* May 17, 1844, *d* Nov 6, 1869, dau *Isaac* and *Catherine (Christman) Shantz*, Sept 9, 1875, Abraham *m* (2) *Mary Ada Stauffer, b* Aug 8, 1854, dau. *John M.* and *Sophia (Pennypacker) Stauffer* (2 ch)

iii Sarah A [5], *b* June 10, 1838, *d* Oct 7, 1890.

iv John B [5], *b* Nov 11, 1840, *m Olivia W. Wynne*, ad Chester Springs, Pa , R R 2. Ch J. Harwin[6], S Lillian[6]; William W.[6], *d*, S. La Roy[6], *d*, Elsie[6], *d*.

v Samuel Brownback[5], *b* Dec 1, 1844; *m* CLEMENTINE[5] BROWNBACK [A131]+

vi William Brownback[5], *b* Feb 21, 1847; Sept 2, 1886, *m Clara B. Danman, b* May 30, 1857, dau *John* and *Jane (Barford) Danman*; merchant, Proh , memb Pres Ch , ad 346 E. Lancaster Ave , E Downingtown, Pa. Ch (6) · Edith Jane[6], Mabel Rebecca[6]; Samuel Earle[6]; William Danman[6], Mary Emma[6]; Clara Mildred[6].

[A24] WILLIAM⁴ BROWNBACK ([A13] John³, [A6] Henry², Gerhard¹) *b* in W Vincent Twp., Chester Co., Pa , Sept. 19, 1806; *d* July 28, 1890 He *m* (1) *Eliza Wilson, b* 1808, *d* 1840, dau *John* and *Mary* (*Whiteside*) *Wilson;* and *m* (2) *Frances M Burgoin, b* Aug 16, 1812, at North East, Cecil Co , Md ; dau *John* and *Hannah* (*Reed*) *Burgoin.* William⁴ was a prominent, highly esteemed, and successful farmer; lifelong member Ref. Ch.

  Children by 1st m (5).
[A78] + Mary⁵, *b* Feb 24, 1829
[A79] John C. G ⁵, *b* Aug 13, 1830; *d* May 21, 1881, unm.
[A80] + James⁵, *b* March 4, 1833.
[A81] Wilson⁵, *b* Nov 6, 1836, *d* March 7, 1837
[A82] Lewis⁵, *b* Nov. 12, 1839, *d* Nov 12, 1851
  Children by 2d m (4).
[A83] + Levi J.⁵, *b* Oct. 14, 1843
[A84] + Orlando Walker⁵, M D., *b* March 23, 1846.
[A85] William Henry⁵, *b* Dec 10, 1848, *d* Aug 16, 1858
[A86] Galena Frances⁵, *b* Sept 25, 1851, *d* July 21, 1853

  [A25] JESSE⁴ BROWNBACK ([A13] John³, [A6] Henry², Gerhard¹) *m Sarah Keeley, b* Nov. 13, 1815; *d* June 30, 1898. He was called "Pale Jesse," to distinguish him from the other Jesse⁴ [A41].
  Children (7)·
[A93] Martha⁵, *b* Dec 4, 1840, living.
[A94] Sophia⁵, *b* 1843, *d*
[A95] Morris⁵, *b* Aug 5, 1845.
[A96] George⁵, *b* Oct. 25, 1851, *d*
[A97] Davis⁵, *b* 1853, living
[A98] Hannah⁵, *b* 1855, living.
[A99] Clara⁵, *b* March 19, 1858; living.

  [A26] MARY⁴ BROWNBACK ([A13] John³, [A6] Henry², Gerhard¹) *m Wayne Emery*
  Children (2), *surname Emery:*
 i Abner⁵; ii Augustus⁵.

  [A27] HANNAH⁴ BROWNBACK ([A13] John³, [A6] Henry², Gerhard¹) *m George Ralston.*
  Children (3), *surname Ralston*
 i Delilah⁵, ii John⁵, iii Sarah⁵

[A28] SARAH[4] BROWNBACK ([A13] John[3], [A6] Henry[2], Gerhard[1]) *m Henry Emery*

Children (2), *surname Emery*

i Davis[5], ii Elizabeth[5].

[A29] CATHARINE[4] BROWNBACK ([A13] John[3], [A6] Henry[2], Gerhard[1]) *m Samuel Kimes*, *b* Jan 4, 1802, in W. Pikeland Twp, Chester Co, Pa. Catharine[4] *d* Aug 22, 1885, and Samuel April 30, 1888; both bur at St. Matthew's Ch, Chester Co, Pa

Children (4), *surname Kimes*

i John[5], *b* March 10, 1830, *d* Aug 24, 1894

ii Elizabeth A[5], *b* Jan 5, 1832, Dec 30, 1869, *m* JACOB CHRISTMAN[5] BROWNBACK [see A128].

iii Jesse Brownback[5], *b* Sept. 26, 1834; *m Evaline Graham*, *b* May 31, 1840, at Coatesville, Chester Co, Pa ; dau. *Hamilton* and *Mary* (*Kurtz*) *Graham*; slate miner, Repn.; memb. Pres. Ch., ad 4823 Walton Ave., Phila, Pa

At the commencement of the Civil War *Jesse Brownback Kimes* resided at Charlottesville, Va., was imprisoned (by order of the Confederate States Government for refusing to take oath of allegiance to said Government) in the military prisons at Richmond, Va, and Salisbury Garrison, N. C, for over nine months

After being released from prison in 1863, he was given a Captain's commission in U. S Vol, and assigned to duty, Co F, 109th U S Colored Infantry. 3d Brig, 1st Div, Mil. Dist of Eastern Kentucky. Sept, 1864, transferred with regiment to 18th Army Corps, Army of the James, Virginia. Dec., 1864, was detailed Act Asst. Adj Gen of 1st Brig, 2d Div., 25th Army Corps. Army of the James, then engaged in sieges of Richmond and Petersburg, Va

On the campaign to Appomattox, ending with surrender of General Lee's Army, April 9, 1865, his Division was transferred to the Sixth Corps, Army of the Potomac His regiment was transferred May, 1865, to Dist of Rio Grande, Texas, Army of Observation; detailed Asst Insp Gen on Staff of Brev, Brig Gen Shaw, Indianola, Texas Oct, 1865, was detailed Act. Asst. Q M in charge Q M. depot, Matagorda Bay, Texas Mustered out of service with regiment at Port Lavacca, Texas, Feb 6, 1866

Children (2):

(1) Horace[6], *b* Feb 27, 1869

(2) Jessie Evalyn[6], *b* Jan 24, 1872; *m Dr. Emery Marvel*, ad 811 Pacific Ave., Atlantic City, N. J.

iv George Christman[5] Kimes, *b* Jan. 12, 1838; *m Maria Peterman, b* Aug. 8, 1853 (2 ch).

[A35] ELIZABETH[4] BROWNBACK ([A10] John[3], [A5] Benjamin[2], Gerhard[1]) *d* 1847, *m John S Missimer;* farmer; resided in Limerick Twp *Children* (9), *surname Missimer*

i Susanna[5], *b* 1803; *d* 1883, *m John Koons*

ii Matthias[5], *b* 1805, *d* 1894, unm

iii Josiah Brownback[5], *b* April, 1808, *d* 1870; *m Catharine Christman, b* Jan., 1814, dau *John* and *Susanna (Schwenk) Christman*—8 ch., of whom Rebecca[6], *b* Feb, 1838, *m Robert Brooke Evans*, a bro of *Emma (Evans) Brownback* [see A132]

iv Manoah[5], *b* Nov 10, 1810, *d* March 31, 1844, *m Hannah Fegley*

v Eleanor[5], *b* 1812, *d* 1891, *m Isaac S Christman*

vi John B [5], *b* 1814, *d* 1878, *m Cornelia Clemmens*

vii Jacob B.[5], *b* 1816, *d* 1885, *m Harriet Reese*

viii Elizabeth[5], *b* 1822, *d* 1890, *m Peter Fry*

ix Mary Louisa[5], *b* 1822, *d* 1824

[A36] EDWARD[4] BROWNBACK ([A10] John[3], [A5] Benjmain[2], Gerhard[1]) *b* Dec 19, 1799, *m Elizabeth Geist*, lived and *d* in Chester Co, Pa., former *d* April 16, 1845, and both were bur adjoining Brownback's Ch., of which they were members

Children (7) ·

[A101] John[5].

[A102] Mark[6].

[A103] Benjamin[5].

[A104] + Edward[5].

[A105] Harriet[5]; unm

[A106] Catherine[6], *m Peter Emory.*

[A107] Infant, d y

[A39] PETER[4] BROWNBACK ([A14] Peter[3], [A6] Henry[2], Gerhard[1]) *b* May 22, 1802, Dec 13, 1838, *m Susanna Diefendeifer, b* April 2, 1819, dau *John* and *Hannah (Prizer) Diefendeifer* [A16-i] Peter[4] was a farmer and merchant, Repn, member Ger. Ref. Ch., lived at Brownback's Corner, E. Coventry Twp, Chester Co, Pa, where he *d* April 20, 1882, and where Susanna *d* Oct. 27, 1899.

Children (4) ·

[A109] Madison[6], *b* June 24, 1840, *d* March 10, 1864, unm.

[A110] + Franklin⁵, *b* March 8, 1843, *d* May 15, 1907.
[A111] + Irvin⁵, *b* Sept 2, 1846
[A112] + Almiranda⁵, *b* Dec 14, 1853

[A41] JESSE⁴ BROWNBACK ([A14] Peter³, [A6] Henry², Gerhard¹) *b* March 18, 1807, at Bethel, Chester Co, Pa , *m* Dec. 27, 1832, *Elizabeth Christman, b* Oct 18 1812, in Vincent Twp , dau *Jacob* and *Margaret* (*Evans*) *Christman* Elizabeth *d* June 21, 1853, and Jesse⁴ *d* Aug 3, 1899 Jesse⁴ was a practical and successful farmer and cabinet maker, Repn ; member Ref Ch , and one of the first directors of the Natl. Bk of Pottstown, Pa.

Col Jacob Christman, father of Elizabeth, was an extensive land owner* and a prominent citizen of Chester Co , Pa During the days of general musters he was prominent in military affairs (Col of Militia). He was a member of Luth. Ch. , ch were Jacob, Henry, Susan, and Elizabeth

Children (11)
[A125] + Edith⁵, *b* Oct 18, 1833, *d* May 18, 1908
[A126] + Margaret⁵, *b* Sept 9, 1835, *d* Sept. 18, 1895.
[A127] + Lewis Christman⁵, *b* Jan 29, 1837
[A128] + Jacob Christman⁵, *b* April 3, 1840 [See A29-ii].
[A129]   Theodore⁵, *b* Oct 29, 1841, *d* Dec 7, 1842.
[A130] + Penrose Wiley⁵, *b* Oct 17, 1843
[A131] + Clementine⁵, *b* Aug 15, 1845
[A132] + Garrett Ellwood⁵, *b* Dec 27, 1846
[A133] + Annie Evans⁵, *b* March 25, 1848
[A134] + Martha Evans⁵, *b* May 18, 1850
[A135] + Frederick W ⁵, *b* June 3, 1853.

[A42] EDWARD⁴ BROWNBACK ([A11] Edward³, [A5] Benjamin², Gerhard¹) *b* June 10, 1798, *m Margaret Root,* dau *Sebastian Root, b* Dec 1, 1800 Edward⁴ *d* Dec 15, 1858, and Margaret *d* Aug 16, 1885, both were buried at Bethel Methodist Church

Children (12) ·
[A113] + Edward⁵, *b* July 10, 1820
[A114] + Uriah Sebastian Root⁵, *b* June, 1822, *d* 1879
[A115]   Rachel Luretta³, *b* Aug 1, 1824, *d* Dec 9, 1897
[A116]   Susanna⁵, *m* (1) *James Setzler,* (2) *John Garber.*
[A117]   Enos Marshall⁵, *b* 1828, *d* 1829

*Assessment of Frederick Twp for 1776 shows Jacob Christman was there taxed for 160 a , 3 horses, 4 cows.—The Perkiomen Region, Vol I, p 69

[A118] Mary Rosanna[5], *b* Aug 17, 1830; *m* (1) *William B. Walton;* (2) *James Sampson*

[A119] + Lewis Washington[5], *b* Jan 12, 1831.

[A120] Edith Matilda[5], *b* Nov, 183—; *d* Jan. 5, 1897; *m* (1) *Joseph Vanler;* (2) *Stephen Wright*

[A121] Noah[5].

[A122] Stephen Sylvester[5], unm.

[A123] Margaret Sophia[5], *b* March 17, 1840; *m David Finkbiner*

[A124] + Malinda Sabina[5], *b* June 4, 1843.

[A43] CATHARINE[4] BROWNBACK ([A15] Benjamin[3], [A6] Henry[2], Gerhard[1]) *b* Oct 11, 1791, *m Abraham Weiant.*

   Children[a] (7), *surname Weiant ·*

   i David[5], ii Elizabeth[5], iii Enos[5], iv Josiah[5].

   v William[5] ·

      (1) S B [6] Weiant, Assumption, Ill.

      (2) and (3) Daughters in Ohio.

   vi Rebecca[5], vii Sarah[5].

[A45] DAVID[4] BROWNBACK ([A15] Benjamin[3], [A6] Henry[2], Gerhard[1]) *b* Aug 18, 1800, in E. Vincent Twp, Chester Co, Pa ; Jan. 15, 1829, *m Elizabeth Rhoads, b* Oct 27, 1797, dau *Daniel Rhoads.* David[4] *d* May 6, 1861, and his w June 19, 1881 ; both bur. at Brownback's Ch.

   Children (4):

[A136] Sarah[5], *b* July 16, 1831; *d* May 18, 1864, *m George Cadwalader.*

[A137] Lavina[5], *b* Aug. 26, 1834; *d* April 1, 1906, *m Jonas Dehaven*

[A138] + William[5], *b* Oct 19, 1836

[A139] Catharine[5].

[A47] HENRY[4] BROWNBACK ([A15] Benjamin[3], [A6] Henry[2], Gerhard[1]) *b* Oct 12, 1805; *d* April 17, 1892; *m Rebecca Zepp, b* Oct. 6, 1811, in Pa.; *d* and bur. at Tower Hill, Shelby Co, Ill Henry[4] was a farmer, Dem, member Ref. Ch. in Pa., but in the absence of such in new home united with U. B Ch

   Children (8).

[A143] + Edwin[6], *b* May 12, 1837.

[A144] + Elizabeth[5], *b* March 25, 1839, *d* Sept., 1900, *m David Jester.*

*[A155] Saml H[4] Brownback of Assumption, Ill, says that William[4] (V) was the only one to marry

[A145] + John Benjamin⁵, *b* April 8, 1842, *d* Nov. 19, 1904
[A146]   Sophia⁵, *b* Oct. 18, 1843, *d* Oct 16, 1853
[A147] + William Henry⁵, *b* April 22, 1845
[A148] + David Alexander⁵, *b* March 27, 1847
[A149] + Jacob Malin⁵, *b* Oct 26, 1849
[A150] + Joseph Marien⁵, *b* Oct. 16, 1853.

[A48] WILLIAM⁴ BROWNBACK ([A15] Benjamin³, [A6] Henry²,
Gerhard¹) *b* Jan 21, 1808; *m Sarah Shutt*, *b* July 11, 1867, dau *John
Shutt*. William⁴ *d* June 22, 1848, at Pickway, O , and his w *d* July 11,
1867; both bur at E Ringgold, Pickway Co , O., carpenter, Dem ; member
Ref. Ch.
        Children (6—2 *inf*) ·
[A152] + Malinda⁵, *b* July 20, 1834 ; *d* May 2, 1862.
[A153]   Eliza⁵, *b* Jan 20, 1836; *d* April 6, 1859, *m John Brentigam.*
              (No ch)
[A154]   Sarah Alice⁵, *b* Oct. 22, 1839, *d* April 15, 1860. (No ch).
[A155] + Samuel H ⁵, *b* Jan 21, 1843

[A56] LYDIA⁵ BROWNBACK ([A22] Henry⁴, [A13] John³, [A6]
Henry², Gerhard¹) *m Nathan Pennypacker;* residence, Lincoln, Placer Co , Cal
        Children (2), *surname Pennypacker:*
        i Emma⁶, ii Pierce⁶.

[A57] MARGARET⁵ BROWNBACK ([A22] Henry⁴, same ancestry
as [A56]) *m Dr. Arnold Yarnal,* residence, Lincoln, Cal
        Children (2), *surname Yarnal.*
        i Janet A Cole⁶, ii Granville⁶, *d*

[A58] WILLIAM⁵ BRUMBACK⁴ ([A22] Henry⁴, [A13] John³, [A6]
Henry², Gerhard¹) *b* in Chester Co , Pa , July 22, 1832; *m Rebecca Ridge,*
dau of *Elizabeth (Wood) Ridge* of Va   Rebecca *d* April, 1884, at Piper City,
Ford Co , Ill , and was bur near Chatsworth, Ill . William⁵ *d* May 18, 1910,
at Lincoln, Placer Co , Cal   He had lived at Arlington and Piper City, Ill ;
Herington, Kans , and near Corning, Cal

"VETERAN MASON DIES ᵇ

After a lingering illness, William Brumback died at his home in Lincoln May 18th, 1910.

────────

*His wife came from Va , where "Brumbach" became "Brumback," which latter spelling
he adopted upon his removal to Ill in 1855
ᵇThe News of Lincoln, Placer Co , Cal

Mr Brumback was born in Chester county, Pennsylvania, July 22, 1832 Deceased was a widower, his wife having died twenty-eight years ago. He was the father of eight children, three of whom survive Mrs Elizabeth Fowler, of Lincoln, Mrs H W Hyde, of Brookings, S Dak, and Miss Cora Brumback, also of Lincoln He had been a farmer, also a merchant, and was a man of sterling integrity and generous to a fault Mr Brumback was a man of great industry and successful in business until sickness compelled him to give up his labors, since which time his two faithful daughters have devotedly cared for him Deceased had been a member of the Masonic order for twenty-five years He has left a legacy of well doing to cheer the hearts of his sorrowing daughters The funeral was held at his home Thursday afternoon, Rev C C Cragin officiating At the grave the Masons took charge and tenderly laid to rest all that was mortal of another brother who has gone before Mrs Walter Jansen, Mrs M W Hogle and Mrs. Frank L Sanders rendered appropriate hymns"

Children (8)·

[A175]   Luselle Ridge⁶, *b* 1817, *d* 1870, *m William F. Lyons*

[A176]   Sophia⁶, d y

[A177]   Elizabeth Ridge⁶; *m* —— *Fowler*, Lincoln, Cal.

[A178]   Jane⁶, d y.

[A179] + Anna Ridge⁶, *b* Dec 5, 1853.

[A180]   Iva Van Fossen⁶, *d*, *m John Mitchell*; (5 ch).

[A181]   Cora May⁶, unm; Lincoln, Cal

[A182]   Horace Lincoln, *d* at Arlington, Ill.

[A59] SOPHIA⁵ BROWNBACK ([A22] Henry⁴, same ancestry as [A56]) *b* 1824, *d* Dec 20, 1910, *m David Buckwalter*, lived at Lincoln, Cal
Children (3), *surname Buckwalter*.
i Elwood⁶, *d*, ii Anna B ⁶, *d*, iii Addie⁶, Phoenixville, Pa

[A66] OLIVER DAVIS⁵ BROWNBACK ([A21] John⁴, [A13] John³. [A6] Henry², Gerhard¹(*b* in Upper Uwchland Twp, Chester Co, Pa., Nov. 4, 1822; *d* Feb. 10, 1906, and bur at Ivy Hill Cem, Mt. Airy, Phila, Pa.; *m Hannah Leggett*, *b* May 26, 1823, in Marsh Twp., Chester Co, Pa., *d* Nov. 17, 1903, dau *John* and *Sophia (Kurtz) Leggett*. Oliver⁵ was a retired mill owner, Dem, memb Pres Ch
Children (3):
[A163] Anna⁶, *b* Dec. 19, 1855; *d* Feb 20, ——.
[A164] Ella Louise⁶, *b* Sept 24, 1858.
[A165] + Evalyn⁶, *b* Aug 31, 1861

[A67] HOLLAND KEELEY⁵ BROWNBACK ([A21] John⁴, same ancestry as [A66]) *b* Sept., 1827, in Chester Co, Pa., *d* May 13, 1899, at Downingtown, Pa, Dec 6, 1854, *m Margaret Fetters*, *b* June 30, 1827, and *d* July 17, 1906, bur. St Matthew's Luth. Cem ; dau *John* and *Mary (Sloyer) Fetters*, farmer; member Luth. Ch

Children (3) ·

[A166] + George Francis⁶, *b* Nov. 12, 1855
[A167] + John H ⁶
[A168] + Hannah Mary⁶, *b* June 14, 1862.

[A69] REBECCA KEELEY⁵ BROWNBACK ([A21] John⁴, same ancestry as [A66]) *b* Sept 18, 1833, Dec. 25, 1866, *m Abram Fetters, b* Sept 17, 1828, at Lionville, Chester Co., Pa , *d* Aug. 23, 1893, and bur. St Matthew's Ref. Ch., s *Samuel* and *Mary (Acker) Fetters;* farmer; member Ref. Ch.

   Children (2), surname Fetters:
   i John⁶, *b* Oct. 19, 1867, *d* Sept 10, 1885.
   ii Horace⁶, *b* Nov. 1, 1871.

[A78] MARY⁵ BROWNBACK ([A24] William⁴, [A13] John³, [A6] Henry², Gerhard¹) *b* Feb 24, 1829, Jan 15, 1851, *m John Mosteller, b* Feb 24, 1824; both *b* in West Vincent Twp , Chester Co., Pa , s *Henry* and *Margaret (Sheneman) Mosteller,* John *d* March 31, 1907, and was bur. at St Matthew's Ref. Ch , St Vincent, Pa., farmer, Dem., memb. Ref. Ch.

   Children (3), surname Mosteller
   i Clinton Knipe⁶, *b* July 19, 1853; *m Elizabeth Lumis,* res West Chester, Pa.
        Children (2):
        (1) Iva May⁷.
        (2) Mary⁷.
   ii William H— ⁶, M D , *b* March 21, 1859, *m Mary Detwiler Custer, b* Sept. 13, 1864, in Worcester Township, Montgomery Co , Pa , daughter *David* and *Margaret (Detwiler) Custer* He attended the public schools, Ursinus College (1873-74), Edgefield Institute, Pickering Institute (1879-80), and graduated (M D) in Class of '84 from Med. Dept of Univ. of Pa. He located in Phoenixville, Chester Co., Pa , Oct. 1, 1884, where he is actively engaged in the general practice of medicine Member of Chester Co Med Soc for a number of years: Burgess of Phoenixville, 1893, Pres. Phoenixville Bd of Health. In politics he is Dem and was Pres of Dem Club for 8 yrs , candidate for Pa Leg and Sen , 1896-1900, and for Rec of Deeds (Independent ticket) in 1906 Lecturer Ursinus College on "Hygiene and Sociology " He has always been much interested in S S work, and for over 18 yrs has been Supt of the Ref. Ch. S S. (Phoenixville) ; S S. teacher for over 27 yrs.

Pres and Historian of "The Gerhard Brumbach (Brownback) Memorial Association," and one of its active incorporators and workers The author acknowledges extensive assistance received from him in the preparation of this section of the work (Illustration)

Children (2)

(1) Margaret Custer[7], *b* March 22, 1896

(2) William David[7], *b* June 13, 1899.

iii James Brownback[6], *b* Aug 9, 1868; *m Melinda Dewees;* farmer, lives in West Vincent Twp, Chester Co , Pa

Children (4) .

(1) Dewees[7].

(2) Sarah Dewees[7].

(3) Clinton[7].

(4) James Paul[7]

[A80] JAMES[5] BROWNBACK ([A 24] William[4], same ancestry as [A78]) *b* March 4, 1833, at Birchrunville, W. Vincent Twp., Chester Co , Pa ; Dec. 12, 1857, *m Eleanor S. March,* *b* Sept 6, 1838, at Lawrenceville (Parkerford), Chester Co , Pa.; dau *Michael* and *Susanna* (*Christman*) *March* After obtaining a common school education, he followed agricultural pursuits for eight years, taught five years in the public schools of his county, and in 1865 engaged in the foundry business The firm of "March-Sisler Co ," with which he was connected, moved across the river to Linfield and built at the latter point in 1866, 1868 he purchased the interest of Henry C. March in "March & Church", 1889 the "March-Brownback Stove Co " of Pottstown, Pa., was incorporated, and he became its first president, thus continuing until 1896, when he resigned, continued as director until 1908, when he was succeeded in the directorate by his s [A188] William Michael[6] Brownback

In company with William March and J Keeley, in 1872, he purchased the Dauphin Co , Pa , furnace, which they owned and operated for two years James[5] was a director in several other companies; for a number of years he served as trustee of Ursinus College, and also as school director He retired from active business and lived in Linfield, Pa , where he *d* from heart disease Jan. 4, 1909

James[5] has been described as "always an active man of affairs, he was widely known and highly esteemed " He was an ardent religious worker, being a member of the Ref Ch , Repn ; member of Masonic Lodge, Commandery and Chapter, of Phoenixville, Pa.

Children (3)

[A186] + Ada Eliza[6], *b* March 6, 1859.

[A187] + Henry March", *b* Dec. 17, 1860.
[A188] + William Michael⁶, *b* Oct. 3, 1863

[A83] LEVI J ⁵ BROWNBACK ([A24] William⁴, same male ancestry as [A78]) *b* Oct 14, 1843, near Birchrunville, Chester Co , Pa , which continues to be his address, and near which he resides upon a farm, member Ref. Ch ; 1866 *m Priscilla E. Murray*, b in Chester Co., dau *Levi* and *Eliza* (*Shingle*) *Murray*

    Children (8) .
[A189] Galena F.⁶, *m George Swinehart*
[A190] Margaret L ⁶, *m Charles Hughes*
[A191] William⁶, *d*, *m* —— *Drake*
[A192] Eliza M ⁶, *m Allie Reis.*
[A193] Mary E ⁶, *m John Guilfor.*
[A194] Hannah L ⁶, *m Norman Roland*
[A195] Anna R ⁶, *m Herold Kaleton*
[A196] Jennie⁶

[A84] ORLANDO WALKER⁵ BROWNBACK, M D ([A24] William⁴, same male ancestors as [A78]) *b* at Birchrunville, Chester Co., Pa , March 23, 1846, Sept 15, 1869, *m Kate King Baird*, *b* Nov 2, 1846, at Philadelphia, Pa ; dau *Alexander* and *Mary Ann* (*King*) *Baird.* Dr. Brownback spent his early days on his father's farm, attending the public school about a mile distant, attended Oakdale Seminary, Pughtown, Pa , and a two years' course at Franklin and Marshall College, graduated M D from Univ of Pa March 14, 1867 The following September he located in Pendleton, Madison Co , Ind., where he has since continued in active and successful practice of his profession, attaining high rank therein and in the confidence of the community. He is a public-spirited and progressive citizen, has served several years as school trustee, and since 1887 has been gen mgr and secy of a local natural gas company

    Dr. Brownback⁵ was made a Mason in Madison Lodge, No 44, F. & A M , at Pendleton, Ind , Feb 13, 1874, and advanced step by step until May 28, 1901, he became Grand Master of Masons in Indiana He became 32 deg A A. S R in Dec , 1897 In politics he is Repn The picture herewith reproduced was taken in 1901

    Children (3) ·
[A198] Frances", *b* Aug 14, 1870 , *m Walter Hays*, Loogootee, Ind
[A199] Baird", *b* Dec 23, 1872; *d* Dec 18, 1887.
[A200] Katharine⁶, *b* April 29, 1877.

[A5] Benjamın², Geihard¹) *b* July 10, 1820, in Chester Co , Pa.; *d* Nov. 12, 1871; Sept 15, 1842, *m* *Hannah Peterman*, *b* Oct 27, 1824, ın Montgomery Co , Pa., dau *John* and *Susanna (Garber) Peterman*   Hannah *d* Feb 17, 1904, and was bur at Phoenıxville, Pa

> *One son*

[A258] + Stephen Sylvester⁶, *b* Dec 5, 1845

[A114] URIAH SEBASTIAN ROOT⁵ BROWNBACK ([A42] Edward⁴, same ancestry as [A113]) *b* June, 1822, *d* Feb, 1878, bur at Bethel Ch ; Aug 25, 1846, *m* (1) *Sarah Przzer*, *b* Aug. 15, 1827; dau [A16-ııı] *Henry* and *Ehzabeth (Dıffendafer) Przzer*. Dec 18, 1849, he *m* (2) *Mary Keesey*, *b* Norristown, Pa , Sept. 12, 1822 (yet lıvıng), dau *Jessie* and *Jane (Griffie) Keesey*

> *Children by 1st m* (2) ·

[A259] + Webster Przzer⁶, *b* Feb. 2, 1847.
[A260]   Lovın Pıızer⁶, *b* Feb 8, 1849, *m* *Elmira Wamshıre*; (1 ch d y).
> *Chıldı en by 2d m* (5) :
[A261]   Ellıngton⁶, *b* Jan 6, 1851.
[A262] + Walton⁶, *b* July 17, 1852
[A263] + Doremus⁶, *b* Aug. 20, 1855
[A264]   Clarinda⁶, *b* Aug , 1854, *d* Dec. 21, 1856
[A265] + Hıckman⁶, *b* Oct 14, 1858
[A266] + Laura Vırgınıa⁶, *b* Feb 17, 1860.

[A119] LEWIS WASHINGTON⁵ BROWNBACK ([A42] Edward⁴, same ancestry as [A113]) *b* Jan 12, 1831; *d* Dec. 31, 1871; *m* *Maria Ashman*; dau *Peter* and *Dorothy (Huhn) Ashman* of Philadelphia.   Lewis⁵ was a produce salesman , Repn , member Meth Ch

> *One daughter:*

[A267] + Eudora Vırgınıa⁶, *b* Oct. 3, 1861.

[A124] MALINDA SABINA⁵ BROWNBACK ([A42] Edward⁴, same ancestry as [A113]) *b* June 4, 1843, in E. Coventry Twp., Chester Co , Pa , Sept. 5, 1865, *m* *Wıllıam M Swindells*, *b* Nov. 29, 1843, at Maple, Cheshıre Co., England, and *d* Sept. 9, 1896, at Ocean Grove. N. J , bur. Mt. Zıon Cem , Pottstown, Pa ; *s* *James* and *Margaret (Howe) Swindells*. Rev Wıllıam Swindells came from England in 1853, began preachıng in 1860; first charge was at Churchtown, Pa , and was minister in M. E Ch for thirty-six yrs.; editor of *Philadelphıa Methodıst* for two yıs., D D. was conferred upon him

by Dickinson College in 1887   Malinda[5] lives at 3423 N 17th St , Philadelphia, Pa

    Children (4), *surname Swindells:*

i Florence May[6], *b* July 16, 1866; *m*

ii Rosanna Bunting[6], *b* Oct 25, 1868.

iii William Milton[6], *b* Nov. 13 ,1870 , *d* Aug. 31, 1871.

iv Edward James[6], *b* Nov 18, 1872; *m*

v Walton Creadick[6], *b* Dec. 20, 1876.

    [A125] EDITH[5] BROWNBACK ([A41] Jesse[4], [A14] Peter[3], [A6] Henry[2], Gerhard[1]) *b* Oct 18, 1833, *d* May 18, 1908; *m Nathan P Yeager.*

    Children (7), *surname Yeager*

i Oscar[6].

ii David[6]

iii Ida[6], *m* —— *Potter*

iv John Brumback[6], *b* June 9, 1862, *m Emma A. Miller* (7 ch).

v Elizabeth[6].

vi Della[6].

vii Jesse[6].

    [A126] MARGARET[5] BROWNBACK ([A41] Jesse[4], same ancestry as [A125]) *b* Sept 9, 1835, *m Washington F. Setzler*   Margaret[5] stepped upon a nail, and *d* from lockjaw Sept 18, 1895

    Children (3), *surname Setzler*

i Hart[6]. d y.

ii Adaline[6], d y.

iii Horace[6], *m*

    [A127] LEWIS CHRISTMAN[5] BROWNBACK ([A41] Jesse[4], same ancestry as [A125]) *b* in E Coventry Twp , Chester Co., Pa , Jan 29, 1837; April 30, 1867, *m Elmira Grubb, b* Feb 13, 1843, dau *George* and *Mariah Grubb* of Frederick Twp , same Co ; educated in the public schools , assisted upon his father's farm, working upon shares for six years; May 12, 1874, removed to the farm of George Grubb in E Vincent Twp , which highly cultivated farm of 81 a became the property of his w upon Mr. Grubb's *d,* Aug 31, 1874 , Repn , member Ref Ch , address Spring City, Pa.

    Children (4):

[A231] George Grubb[6], *b* July 23, 1872.

[A232] Jennie Manola[6], *b* Aug 26, 1874, *d* Feb 6, 1875.

[A233] Emma E.⁶, *b* Nov 6, 1876, unm.
[A234] Louis Marion⁶, *b* Jan 6, 1880

[A128] JACOB CHRISTMAN⁵ BROWNBACK ([A41] Jesse⁴, same ancestry as [A125]) *b* April 3, 1840, Dec. 30, 1869, *m* ELIZABETH A⁵ KIMES [A29-ii], *b* Jan 5, 1852; dau SAMUEL and CATHARINE⁴ (BROWNBACK) KIMES [A29]

Aug 5, 1862, Jacob⁵ enlisted in Co I, 6th Pa. Cav.; he was a faithful soldier, and *d* in the Union service at Cloud Mill, Va., June, 1865

In 1873 the family purchased a farm of 140 a in West Pikeland Twp, Chester Co, ad, Anselma, Chester Co, Pa.

Children (4)
[A236] Catharine Kimes⁶, *b* Oct 1, 1870, *m* Edwin J. Moses
[A237] George Roland⁶, *b* May 2, 1873; *m* Susan March
[A238] Jesse Kimes⁶
[A239] Maurice Fussel⁶, *b* Nov 23, 1877, *m* Stella Davis.

[A130] PENROSE WILEY⁵ BROWNBACK ([A41] Jesse⁴, same ancestry as [A125]) *b* Oct 17, 1843; *m* Catherine Stroud, *b* Nov. 26, 1844, dau *Edward* and *Susan (Hettrick) Stroud*. Edward was a brick manufacturer and also engaged in the draying business in Reading, Pa, where he *d* 1878, and where his w *d* Aug 12, 1907

In early life Penrose⁵ was a carpenter and an excellent mechanic, he was director of Spring City (Pa) National Bank for many years; and for about 40 years he conducted a general merchandise store at Linfield, Pa, part of the time being associated with his brother, [A132] Garrett Ellwood⁵ Brownback   Owing to paralysis he retired from active business in 1908   During his active life he was much interested and active in church and S S work; member Ger. Ref Ch, ad, Linfield, Pa

Children (2):
[A241] Elsie Eugenia⁶, *b* Jan 8, 1882
[A242] Maud Stroud⁶, *b* Sept. 16, 1884.

[A131] CLEMENTINE⁵ BROWNBACK ([A41] Jesse⁴, same ancestry as [A125]) *b* Aug. 18, 1845, Dec 1, 1868, at Chester Springs, Pa, *m* Samuel Brownbach⁵ Stauffer [A23-v], *b* Aug. 15, 1845; farmer, memb Ger. Ref. Ch, res. Birchrunville, Chester Co., Pa. (No ch.)

[A132] GARRETT ELLWOOD⁵ BROWNBACK ([A41] Jesse⁴, same ancestry as [A125]) *b* Dec 27, 1846, at East Coventry, Chester Co, Pa, on

the original tract bought by [A1] Gerhard[1] in Vincent Twp , reared upon
the farm, while extensively interested in other enterprises, he has gradually
extended his landed interests and owns seven fine farms, containing 600 acres;
he takes pleasure in retaining as part of his tracts 220 a. in Chester Co , to
which there has never been a deed excepting the original patent* from Penn,
Proprietor of Pennsylvania   He attended the local public schools, the Guldin
Sch (Pughtown), and briefly at Millersville State Nor. Sch , and his practical
belief in education is shown in the thorough educational and business training
given to all his children

   In 1867 he left the farm and entered into a partnership with his brother,
[A130] Penrose Wiley[5] Brownback, and they conducted a general merchandise
store at Linfield, Pa.   In 1870 he there built a block for store purposes, where
his brother continued in business until his retirement in 1908   In 1876 Garrett[5]
took over the general store and conducted it alone until 1887, when he sold it
to [A130] Penrose[5], and began his present extensive creamery business.   He
mastered the details of the latter business, erected a fine creamery in 1887 at
Linfield, and gradually enlarged the business until he owns and operates 12
creameries at various points in Eastern Pa   These are equipped with the best
machinery and have a daily output of 4,000 lbs of "Golden butter "   This and
other dairy products he sells through wholesale and retail trade at Ridge Ave
Market, Phila, Pa., Atlantic City and Cape May, N J., and in New York
Reliability of products, absolute personal integrity, a pleasing personal address, and close application to business have resulted in his extensive business
success and diversified interests

   Mr. Brownback is Secy -Treas Linfield Cold Storage & Ice Co ; Treas.
Linfield Elec Light Co , V.-P Royersford Trust Co ; director Girard Ave.
Title & Trust Co , and director Ridge Ave. Market Co , both in Phila   He is
Treas Gerhard Brumbach (Brownback) Memorial Assn ; one of its incorpor-
ators, and a moving spirit in its activities   See footnote p. 73.

   Jan. 20, 1874, Garrett[5] m Emma Evans, b Aug 30, 1848, dau Maj.
Thomas Brook and Mary A (Schwenk) Evans.   Mrs Brownback is a graduate of Pennsylvania Female College, and has been an active "help-mate" in all of
her husband's many activities

   In 1897 Mr Brownback erected his fine stone residence in Linfield, Pa ,
and. because of its fine architecture and the happy home life which therein
exists to his personal knowledge, the author has caused two good views of the
said building to be reproduced herein

   The family have all united with the Ger Ref Ch (Mrs Brownback,

*See Plate 19.

however, is member Luth Ch), and mostly attend services at the old Brownback Church[a], elsewhere described, of which the subject of this sketch is an
elder. Politically the family are Repn , Mr. Brownback is a member of the
various Masonic bodies (32 deg), and member of Penna. Hist. Soc , ad. Linfield, Pa

          Children (9) :
[A244] + Mary Elizabeth[6], *b* April 15, 1875
[A245]   Harold[6], d y
[A246]   Garrett Ellwood[6], d y
[A247] + Caroline Evans[6], *b* May 16, 1879
[A248] + Charlotte Evans[6], *b* Jan. 7, 1881.
[A249] + Garrett Arthur[6], *b* April 30, 1882.
[A250] + Jesse Evans[6], *b* July 19, 1883.
[A251]   Thomas Alden[6], d y.
[A252] + John Kenneth[6], *b* Oct 3, 1890

    [A133] ANNIE EVANS[5] BROWNBACK ([A41] Jesse[4], same ancestry
as [A125]) *b* March 25, 1848, *m J Franklin Stauffer*, *b* Nov. 20, 1845; s
John M. and *Sophia (Pennypacker) Stauffer* [See A23-ii] , farmer; member
Luth. Ch ; ad Spring City, Pa , R.R. 2
    One son, surname Stauffer
    i Harry C [6], *b* Oct 27, 1884

    [A134] MARTHA EVANS[5] BROWNBACK ([A41] Jesse[4], same an-
cestry as [A125]) *b* in Chester Co , Pa , May 18, 1850, Nov. 28, 1872, m
PENROSE WILLY[6] BIERBOWER. *b* Dec 12, 1849, also in Chester Co ; s
REUBEN and MARY (HARTMAN) BIERBOWER [A4-i-(1)] , latter a
great-grand-daughter of [A4] ANNA MARY[2] (BROWNBACK) BENNER,
real estate dealer, Repn , member Ger. Ref Ch , address, 2003 Burt St ,
Omaha, Neb

    Children (3), *surname Bierbower.*
    i Harry Claud[6] (M D.), *b* May 10, 1874; in active service U. S A. about
        10 yrs.; *m Hilda Altimus*, ad (1910), Fort Robinson, Neb
    ii Mary Elizabeth[6], *b* Aug. 23, 1876, at Phoenixville, Pa , Dec 22, 1900,
        m Orrin Edgar Klapp, b June 1, 1874, at St Paris, O ; s *Jeremiah*
        and *Eliza (Knode) Klapp*, occupation, real estate and investments;
        res, 833 S 30th St , Omaha, Neb.
    iii Reuben Franklin[6], *b* Feb 8, 1890

────────────
*See pp. 77-79, and Plates 22-24.

[A135] FREDERICK W⁵ BROWNBACK ([A41] Jesse⁴, same ancestry as [A125]) *b* June 3, 1853, 1876 *m Elizabeth Barkley, b* 1855   He is the owner of a large ranch near Pony, Madison Co., Mont., where he is an extensive dealer in cattle

  Children (4):

[A253] Frederick W⁶, *b* 1882, *m Elizabeth Lyon.*

[A254] J Eugene⁶, *b* March 10, 1885.

[A255] Jesse C⁶, *b* July 18, 1887.

[A256] Flora⁶, *b* Oct. 22, 1892.

[A138] WILLIAM⁵ BROWNBACK ([A45] David⁴, [A15] Benjamin³, [A6] Henry², Gerhard¹) *b* Oct 19, 1836, in E Vincent Twp., Chester Co., Pa.; Nov 4, 1862, *m Mary R Bickhart, b* Dec 6, 1840, at Pughtown, Chester Co., Pa., dau *Christian* and *Mary (Boughter) Bickhart,* carpenter; ad Spring City, Chester Co., Pa

  Children (7)

[A271]   Emma Jane⁶, *b* March 28, 1865, *m Charles Heiter.*

[A272]   Mary Ella⁶, *b* Oct 6, 1866; *m Thomas A Harbison.*

[A273] + Franklin⁶, *b* March 23, 1869

[A274]   Harvey⁶, *b* July 24, 1871, *m Eva Light.*

[A275]   Catharine⁶, *b* May 9, 1874; *m Horace Mowrey*

[A276]   Clara E⁶, *b* April 19, 1877; *m Luther Mauger.*

[A277]   Arthur⁶, *b* Aug 15, 1880; *m Loie Oberholtzer*

[A143] EDWARD A⁵ BROWNBACK ([A47] Henry⁴, [A15] Benjamin³, [A6] Henry², Gerhard¹) *b* May 12, 1837; Sept 22, 1860, *m Eliza Ann Liston,* dau *Oliver Perry* and *Mary Ann (Riley) Liston,* res. Pleasant Plains, Sangamon Co., Ill

  Children (7) ·

[A278] Rebecca Elnora⁶, *b* Aug 5, 1861, *d* July 20, 1868

[A279] Henry Oliver⁶, *b* Jan. 24, 1862, ad. Ashland, Ill.

[A280] James Carey⁶, *b* Nov. 5, 1865; ad Pleasant Plains, Ill.

[A281] Inf s, *b* May 10, 1867, *d* May 22, 1867

[A282] + Mary Alta⁶, *b* May 12, 1869; *m R A Irwin,* Pleasant Plains, Ill.

[A283] Charles Edward⁶, *b* April 7, 1873, ad 520 S 4th St., Springfield, Ill

[A284] Eda Amanda⁶, *b* Jan. 27, 1875; ad Pleasant Plains, Ill.

[A144] ELIZABETH⁵ BROWNBACK ([A47] Henry⁴, same ancestry as [A143]) *b* March 25, 1839; *d* Sept., 1900; *m David Jester, b* about 1837;

6 *Stephen* and *Ann Elizabeth (McDonald) Jester,* farmer; both members Bap
Ch ; ad of the family, Tower Hill, Shelby Co , Ill

> *Children* (7), *surname Jester:*

   i   John Henry[6], *b* April, 1860
   ii   Melissa[6], *b* Jan , 1862; *m Douglas Higgins;* (Cal)
   iii   William[6], *b* April, 1864.
   iv   Ida Ellen[6], *b* May, 1866; *m Joseph Parr;* (Missouri).
   v   Eliza[6], *b* March, 1868; *m Bert Hemphill.*
   vi   Charles[6], *b* March, 1868, unm.
   vii   Otis[6], *b* April, 1871 , unm.

[A145] JOHN BENJAMIN[5] BROWNBACK ([A47] Henry[4], same ancestry as [A143]) *b* April 8, 1842, *d* Nov. 19, 1904, Sept 12, 1863, *m Nancy
Ellen Liston, b* Aug. 1, 1845 at Terra Haute, Ind ; sister of *Eliza Liston,* who
m [A143]

> *Children* (8) .

[A285] Oliver Perry[6], *b* 1868; Corbin, Kans.
[A286] William Carey[6], *b* 1870, Anadarko, Okla.
[A287] Florence[6], *b* 1872, *m E D. Duncan,* Anadarko, Okla.
[A288] Charles Alexander[6], *b* 1874; Anadarko, Okla
[A289] Effie[6], *b* 1877, *m Reece Mudd,* Walters, Okla.
[A290] Bertha[6], *m De Witt Crosby,* Ft. Scott, Kans.
[A291] Jessie[6]; *m Carl Douglass,* Anadarko, Okla.
[A292] Henrietta[6].

[A147] WILLIAM HENRY[5] BROWNBACK ([A47] Henry[4], same
ancestry as [A143], *b* April 22, 1845, near Ringgold, Ohio; 1870 *m Lizzie
Decourcy, b* in Ky.; dau *Miles Decourcy,* stock dealer; Repn., for about
twenty years lived at Edinburg, Christian Co , Ill

[A148] DAVID ALEXANDER[5] BROWNBACK ([A47] Henry[4], same
ancestry as [A143]) *b* March 27, 1847. in Fairfield Co , O , June 25, 1878,
m (1) *Mary Alice Settles, b* April 23, 1880, bur Bethany Cem , Shelby Co ,
Ill David[5] *m* (2) *Celesta Foor,* dau *William* and *Mary Ward Foor,* stock
raiser; Dem , member M E. Ch.; ad. Tower Hill, Shelby Co , Ill.

> *Child 1st w*

[A293] + Ora[6], *b* April 10, 1879.

> *Children 2d w* (3) :

[A294]   Mary[6], *b* March 1, 1890.

.[A295]   Helen[6], *b* June 5, 1892
[A296]   Robert[6], *b* Sept 20, 1894.

[A149] JACOB MALIN[5] BROWNBACK ([A47] Henry[4], same ancestry as [A143]) *b* Oct 26, 1849; *m* *Mary Mellin;* dau *Thomas* and *Margaret (Warren) Mellin;* members U. B. Ch.

[A150] JOSEPH MARIEN[5] BROWNBACK ([A47] Henry[4], same ancestry as [A143]) *b* Oct 16, 1853, at Shelbyville, Shelby Co , Ill , left home at age sixteen, *m* *Mary Vandeveer, b* Taylorville, Christian Co , Ill , dau *James II* and *Elizabeth (Beeson) Vandeveer;* w *d* 1904; cashier Milliken National Bank, Decatur, Ill
        Children (2)
[A299] Alcienn Vandeveer[6], *b* Aug 4, 1888
[A300] Eloise Vandeveer[6], *b* May 21, 1892

[A152] MALINDA[5] BROWNBACK ([A48] William[4], [A15] Benjamin[3], [A6] Henry[2], Gerhard[1]) *b* July 20, 1834, *d* May 2, 1862, *m* *Abner Settles*
        Children (4), *surname Settles*
    i Eliza[6], *m* *Oliver Carmany,* Canal Winchester, Franklin Co , Ohio.
    ii Mary A [6], *d*
    iii Emaline[6], *d*
    iv William[6], *d*

[A155] SAMUEL H [5] BROWNBACK ([A48] William[4], same ancestry as [A152]) *b* Jan. 21, 1843, in E. Ringold Twp., Pickaway Co , O.; April 3, 1870 *m* (1) *Mary D Smith, d* and bur at Henton, Ill. He *m* (2) *Elizabeth A. Cochrane,* dau *Robert* and *Mary Ray Cochrane;* farmer; Dem.; member Chr. Ch ; ad Assumption, Ill
        Children (2) ·
[A303] + George D [6], *b* Dec. 21, 1872
[A304] + Mary E [6], *b* April 11, 1876

[A160] EDWARD GOODWIN[6] BROWNBACK ([A104] Edward[5], [A36] Edward[4], [A10] John[3], [A5] Benjamin[2], Gerhard[1]) *b* Trappe, Pa., March 3, 1868, educated in pub sch , Washington Hall, bus. col in Phila ; before *m* taught sch. during winter months and worked upon the home farm in summer, 1895 he bought the general merchandise store of his father-in-law, Jno. K Beaver, who retired, which store he yet conducts at Trappe, director

of Spring City Natl Bk , Dem , and served as P M in the Cleveland admn ;
Feb , 1903, was elected burgess of Trappe, in which position he gave much
satisfaction, elder in Luth. Ch and Supt of S S. for many years; 1895 *m*
Mary V. Beaver, *b* Trappe, 1866, dau *John K.* and *Mary* (*Shellenberger*)
Beaver.

    Children (2)

[A311] John H [7], *b* Sept 19, 1897.
[A312] Oliver S [7], *b* March 23, 1899

[A165] EVALYN[6] BROWNBACK ([A66] Oliver Davis[5], [A21] John[4],
[A13] John[3] [A6] Henry[2] Gerhard[1]) *b* Aug. 31, 1861, in Upper Uwchland
Twp , Chester Co , Pa ; April 10, 1884, *m* *Samuel Thomas Roberts, Jr* , *b* Nov
17, 1857; s *Samuel Thomas* and *Isophena* (*Ivins*) *Roberts,* res 304 E. Walnut
Lane, Germantown, Pa

    Children (4), *surname Roberts ·*
i Howard Shreve[7], *b* Dec 12, 1890.
ii Louise Brownback[7], *b* July 9, 1893
iii Evalyn[7], *b* July 1, 1898.
iv Edith[7], *b* May 20, 1902.

[A166] GEORGE FRANCIS[6] BROWNBACK ([A67] Holland Kee-
ley[5], [A21] John[4], [A13] John[3] [A6] Henry[2], Gerhard[1]) *b* Nov 12, 1855,
March 21, 1889, *m Mary L Taylor*, *b* June 23, 1860, in West Goshen Twp ,
Chester Co., Pa., dau *Jesse J.* and *Annie M* (*Entriken*) *Taylor;* farmer;
Dem ; ad Font, Chester Co , Pa

    Children (2).

[A315] Jessie Taylor[7], *b* Jan 27, 1890.
[A316] Margaret Fetters[7], *b* May 25, 1893.

[A167] JOHN H [6] BROWNBACK ([A67] Holland Keeley[5], same ancestry as [A166]) *m Mary V. Fisher;* res 235 Windemere Ave , Wayne, Pa.

    Children (2).

[A317] Valeria R[7].
[A318] John H[7].

[A168] HANNAH MARY[6] BROWNBACK ([A67] Holland Keeley[5].
same ancestry as [A166]) *b* June 14, 1862, at Font, Chester Co , Pa . June 9,
1886, she there *m Harvey H. Slusser*, *b* June 25, 1862, at Louisville, Stark Co ,
O.; s *Daniel M* and *Lydia* (*Holwick*) *Slusser,* memb Ref. Ch ; res Canton, O

Children (2), *surname Slusser:*
i   Holland B [7], *b* April 10, 1887
ii Ruth M [7], *b* Nov 13, 1888

[A179] ANNA RIDGE[6] BRUMBACK ([A58] William[5], [A22] Henry[4], [A13] John[3], [A6] Henry[2], Gerhard[1]) *b* Dec 5, 1853, at Pt Pleasant, Bucks Co , Pa , July 25, 1882, at Piper City, Ford Co , Ill , *m Alfred William Hyde,* M.D., *b* April 20, 1854, at Birmingham, Eng., s *George W* and *Sarah* (*Owen*) *Hyde;* physician and surgeon; Proh ; member M E. Ch , ad Brookings, S. Dak.

Children (6), *surname Hyde.*
i   Winifred Rebecca[7], *b* July 6, 1884
ii   Hallie Walker[7], *b* Jan 1, 1886.
iii Owen Rockwell[7], *b* Nov 25, 1887.
iv   Lloyd Garrison B [7], *b* Feb. 6, 1890
v   Greeley W [7], *b* Jan 16, 1896.
vi   Hara[7].

[A186] ADA ELIZA[6] BROWNBACK ([A80] James[5], [A24] William[4], [A13] John[3], [A6] Henry[2], Gerhard[1]) *b* March 6, 1859, *d* Nov. 13, 1899, April 9, 1888, *m Henry G Kulp* of Pottstown, Pa., s *Jacob* and *Maria* (*Geist*) *Kulp.* Ada Eliza[6] survived her husband, and was his second wife. (No ch.)

[A187] HENRY MARCH[6] BROWNBACK ([A80] James[5], same ancestry as [A186]) *b* Dec. 17, 1860, in W Vincent Twp., Chester Co , Pa ; in 1867 his parents moved to Linfield, Montgomery Co , Pa , where he attended school; he later attended Ivy Institute, Phoenixville, Pa , and Ursinus College, Collegeville, Pa., 1878 began reading law with Franklin March, father-in-law; admitted to the bar Dec 4, 1882, he at once began the practice of his profession, later formed a partnership with his former preceptor under the firm name of March & Brownback, and this continued until Jan 1, 1893, when it was dissolved by mutual consent

"He became the nominee of the Repn party for the position of district attorney in 1889, and was elected   .   serving the term of three years with credit to himself, and with fidelity to the interests of the public He has filled the position of solicitor for several county officials from time to time, and has achieved exceptional success as a lawyer."

Early in July, 1899, Mr Brownback was appointed postmaster at Norristown, and has been reappointed, now serving his fourth term in that position. "Mr. Brownback has been faithful, energetic and progressive, always desiring

to promote in every possible way the convenience and accommodation of the public   Under his supervision free rural delivery has been established   .   .   During his administration, also, the movement for a public building in Norristown was carried to a successful conclusion.   Courteous, obliging and faithful in the discharge of his duties, he is a model official "[*]   Res 823 W Main St, Norristown, Pa , resident of that town since 1890

July 2, 1890, Mr Brownback *m Augustine Marguerite Lowe*, dau Prof. *Thaddeus Sobiecki Constantine* and *Leontine Augustine* (*Gochon*) *Lowe*
Children (2)
[A323] Henry Lowe[7], *b* June 13, 1891.
[A324] Russel James[7], *b* Oct 1, 1893

[A188] WILLIAM MICHAEL[6] BROWNBACK ([A80] James[5], same ancestry as [A186]) *b* Oct. 3, 1863, at Kimberton, Chester Co , Pa.   In 1867 the family moved to Limerick Sta , now Linfield, Montgomery Co , Pa., where his father [A80] James[5] purchased a fourth interest in the March, Brownback Stove Co.   He was educated at private school and Ursinus College; at 18 became connected with March, Brownback Stove Co., and remained with the same until 1893, when he resigned and became manager of the Richmond Co. of Norwich, Conn   He continued in this position until the company disposed of its interests, when he resigned and became division manager located in Phila., Pa., for the Yale and Towne Mfg. Co. of New York and Stamford; 1909 resigned after meritorious service, and became vice-pres. of the Oakland Co of America, with a fourth interest in the said company—his company sells Oakland pleasure cars and commercial trucks and is one of the largest of such companies in Phila , Pa

Jan. 26, 1889, at Bryn Mawr, Pa , Mr Brownback *m. Annie Crawford Yocum, b* July 31, 1865, at Bryn Mawr, Pa , dau *Jacob Hagy* and *Hannah Emily (Crawford) Yocum*   Immediately after marriage he moved to Bryn Mawr, Montgomery Co., Pa , which beautiful place has continued to be the family residence, business ad , 506-508 North Broad St., Phila, Pa.

Children (2):
[A325] Emily Yocum[7], *b* Jan 21, 1890
[A326] Helen Estelle[7], *b* Dec. 4, 1891

[A229] OSCAR DAVIS[6] BROWNBACK ([A111] Irvin[5], [A39] Peter[4], [A14] Peter[3] [A6] Henry[2], Gerhard[1]) *b* Jan 27, 1878, in E Coventry Twp , Chester Co., Pa , educated in the public schools, Ursinus College, graduating

---
[*]Biographical Annals of Montgomery Co , Pa—Vol I, p 25, 1904

(A B.) 1904, Princeton Univ (M A) and Princeton Theological Seminary, 1907; Leipzig Univ (Germany), 1908-09 He worked upon the farm, was agent for three commercial firms, taught two years (Parkerford, Pa, '97-'99), filled various pulpits as a supply and became pastor of First Pres Ch of Port Allegany, McKean Co, Pa, Jan, 1910, ordained April 28, 1910

[A239] LOTTIE EMMA⁶ BROWNBACK ([A111] Irvin⁵, same ancestry as [E229] Oscar Davis⁶) b Oct. 18, 1880; m John David Mayor Heck, b Jan 10, 1876

One son ·
i Oscar Davis Brownback⁷ Heck.

[A244] MARY ELIZABETH⁶ BROWNBACK ([A132] Garrett Ellwood⁵, [A41] Jesse⁴, [A14] Peter³, [A6] Henry², Gerhard¹) b at Linfield, Pa, April 15, 1875; ed in the local pub. schs, Linden Hall Sem., Lititz, Pa. (4 yrs.), graduating therefrom, and also taking post graduate work there in '89, '92, '93; has also taken special courses in china decoration

Mary Elizabeth⁶ Nov 1, 1905, m *William Steele*, M D., s *William* and *Ellen Ann (Blair) Steele*, attended Brown Preparatory and graduated M D 1903 from Hahneman Med Col Dr. Steele is actively engaged in the practice of his profession, ad. 2340 N 13th St., Philadelphia, Pa.

Children (3), surname Steele
i Mary Elizabeth⁷, b Nov. 13, 1906, d July 8, 1908.
ii William⁷, b May 16, 1909
iii Margaret Ellen⁷, b Feb, 1911.

[A247] CAROLINE EVANS⁶ BROWNBACK ([A132] Garrett Ellwood⁵, same ancestry as [A244]) b May 16, 1879, educated in the pub schs of Linfield, Pa, Linden Hall Sem, Lititz, Pa ('91-'95), graduating therefrom in '94, and she also spent one year at Hollidaysburg (Pa) Sem Mrs Fell has shown much interest in this publication, and has been of material assistance to her father and to the compiler in their efforts to complete Section A of the same.

Caroline⁶ m *Percy Jacob Fell*, b April 7, 1875, s *Jacob Frederic* (b Dec. 25, 1823) and *Mary Jane Custer* (b Dec 21, 1840), gs *Christian Jacob Fell* (b Aug 16, 1795) and *Christiana (Kinsler) Fell* (b March 8, 1797) These grandparents were both born in Germany, but early in life came to America Both the grandfather and the father were highly successful farmers near Philadelphia, and the former was pres of the Board of Trustees of the old historical Luth Ch. near 4th and Arch Sts, Philadelphia

Percy J. Fell is engaged in the brokerage business, and is much inter-
ested in social, musical and religious circles, member Hist. Soc. of Montgomery
Co., Pa , Colonial Soc of Pa , and of the various Masonic orders, ad 333
Dekalb St , Norristown, Pa.

Daughter, surname Fell ·

i Virginia Burrough[7], *b* July 11, 1908

[A248] CHARLOTTE EVANS[6] BROWNBACK ([A132] Garrett Ell-
wood[5], same ancestry as [A244]) *b* Jan. 7, 1881: unm., educated in pub schs
Linfield, Pa ; graduated from Linden Hall Sem , Lititz, Pa , attended Wilson
College, Chambersburg, Pa., '98-'01, receiving degree of B. of Mus   June 15,
1911, Charlotte[6] *m Charles Hinkley Van Kirk*, s *Charles Beebe* and *Margaret
(Towne) Van Kirk*, gs *David* and *Sarah (Beebe) Van Kirk*   Charles Hinkley
Van Kirk was ed at the Hill Sch , Pottstown, Pa., received the degree C E
from Sheffield Scientific, Yale, spent four yrs in practical engineering work
upon the Santa Fe R R , and during the past year has successfully engaged
in the general advertising business; ad 1363 E. 50th St , Chicago, Ill.

[A249] GARRETT ARTHUR[6] BROWNBACK ([A132] Garrett Ell-
wood[5], same ancestry as [A244]) *b* April 30, 1882; educated in the pub. schs
of Linfield, Pa.; entered The Hill Sch (Pottstown), 1896, graduating therefrom in 1900, entered Yale Univ. in Fall 1900. graduating (A B.) 1904;
worked for his father one yr., studied law and entered the Law Sch Univ of
Pa., 1905, graduating (LL.B.) therefrom 1908; held a fellowship at Univ. of
Pa. for two yrs , admitted to the bar of Philadelphia Co. Sept , '08, and of
Montgomery Co. (Pa.) Dec., '08, actively engaged in his profession at 609
West End Trust Bldg., Phila., Pa., associated with Owen J. Roberts. He is also
lecturer on doctrines in equity, etc , at Law Sch , Univ of Pa.; Repn ; member
and Secy. Ger. Ref. Ch., Linfield, Pa , unm , member Phi Beta Kappa Soc

[A250] JESSE EVANS[6] BROWNBACK ([A132] Garrett Ellwood[5],
same ancestry as [A244]) *b* July 19, 1883, ed. in pub. schs. of Linfield, Pa.,
Hill School, Pottstown, Pa (3 yrs), graduating therefrom 1904, entered
Sheffield Scientific, Yale, graduating 1907 in electrical engineering   Oct 14,
1911, he *m Elizabeth Stroh Marshall*, dau *Robert Louis* and *Elizabeth Butcher
(Johnston) Marshall*. Ad Linfield, Montgomery Co , Pa.

[A252] JOHN KENNETH[6] BROWNBACK ([A132] Garrett Ell-
wood[5], same ancestry as [A244]) *b* Oct 3, 1890; educated in pub schs. of

Linfield. Pa., Hill School, Pottstown, Pa , Nazareth Mil Acad , graduating, tutored for college at Blake County School; now student at State College

[A258] STEPHEN SYLVESTER⁶ BROWNBACK ([A113] Edward⁵, [A42] Edward⁴, [A11] Edward³, [A5] Benjamin², Gerhard¹) b Dec. 5, 1845, in E. Vincent Twp , Chester Co , Pa , m Anme Turner Keim, b April 24, 1840, in N. Coventry Twp , Chester Co , Pa , dau David and Sarah (Turner) Keim; both members Geiger Mem Breth Ch and S S , 26th and W. Lehigh Ave , Phila , Pa , of which he has been deacon, Supt. of S. S and janitor for a number of yrs. , produce dealer, Repn ; ad 2517 W Somerset St , Phila , Pa
          Children (2) .
[A331] David Keim⁷, b Nov 4, 1865, d March 31, 1885.
[A332] Clinton Sylvester⁷, b April 27, 1870

[A259] WEBSTER PRIZER⁶ BROWNBACK ([A114] Uriah Sebastian Root⁵, [A42] Edward⁴, [A11] Edward³, [A5] Benjamin², Gerhard¹) b July 2, 1847, m Isabella Swinehart, res Pughtown, Chester Co , Pa.
          Children (7) ·
[A333] + Emma Rosella⁷, b March 29, 1872.
[A334]   Mervin A—⁷, b Sept. 27, 1873, unm.
[A335]   William Morris, d y.
[A336]   Susanna⁷, b Jan 21, 1878, m William Mowrer (1 ch)
[A337]   Mary E—⁷, b Aug. 25, 1881, m M Wilnner Rosen (1 ch).
[A338]   Harry Levin⁷, b March 6, 1884
[A339]   Rosanna W—⁷, b March 18, 1887

 ·   [A262] WALTON⁶ BROWNBACK ([A114] Uriah Sebastian Root⁵, same male ancestry as [A259]) b July 17, 1852, m (1) Mary Saylor, dau George F. and Eva Magdalene (Herzog) Saylor, m (2) ———, dealer in stoves at West Chester, Pa
          Son from 1st m
[A343] + George Walton, b May 24, 1873
          Children from 2d m (4) :
[A344]   Mary Rosanna⁷.
[A345]   Walter Lee⁷
[A346]   Elida⁷, d y.
[A347]   Infant⁷, d y

[A263] DOREMUS⁶ BROWNBACK ([A114] Uriah Sebastian Root⁵, same male ancestry as [A259]) b Aug. 20, 1855, m Ella Bisbing, res 141 N. 18th St , Philadelphia, Pa.

Children (2):

[A348] Laura Virginia⁷.

[A349] Maurice⁷

[A265] HICKMAN⁶ BROWNBACK ([A114] Uriah Sebastian Root⁵, same male ancestry as [A259]) *m Annie L. Bisbing*, who survives him and lives at Royersford, Pa

Children (5):

[A350] John⁷.

[A351] Sumner⁷.

[A352] Walton⁷

[A353] William Alison⁷, unm

[A354] Beulah Bertha⁷.

[A266] LAURA VIRGINIA⁶ BROWNBACK ([A114] Uriah Sebastian Root⁵, same male ancestry as [A259]) *b* Feb 17, 1860; Nov. 29, 1883, at Philadelphia, Pa *m* (1) *Samuel H. Smith, b* May, 1854, and *d* May 22, 1885, s *Houston Smith*. Laura⁶ Oct. 9, 1888, *m* (2) *William A Bunting, b* April 19, 1844, at Reading, Pa , s *Horatio Bunting* of Oxford, Pa (no ch)

[A267] EUDORA VIRGINIA⁶ BROWNBACK ([A119] Lewis Washington⁵, [A42] Edward⁴, [A11] Edward³, [A5] Benjamin², Gerhard¹) *b* Oct. 3, 1861, in West Phila , Pa., Jan 19, 1882, *m Henry Brook Moore, b* May 8, 1858, at Media, Delaware Co , Pa ; s *John P* and *Rebecca (Barr) Moore,* res 2018 N Woodstock St , Philadelphia, Pa

    Children (4), *surname Moore*

i   Elsie Amanda⁷, *b* Dec 12, 1882, *d* Dec 19, 1902

ii   Robert M—⁷, *b* April 29, 1884.

iii   Henry Brook⁷, *b* May 31, 1887.

iv   Lillian Boyer⁷, *b* April 22, 1891

[A273] FRANKLIN⁶ BROWNBACK ([A138] William⁵, [A45] David⁴ [A15] Benjamin³, [A6] Henry², Gerhard¹) *b* March 23, 1869, Nov. 6, 1897 *m Elizabeth Reifsnyder, b* July 6, ——, dau *Ira* and *Mary A (Gallegar) Reifsnyder,* pattern fitter; res Parkerford, Pa.

    Children (2).

[A360] Mary Ella⁷, *b* Nov. 26, 1898

[A361] Edna Pearl⁷, *b* April 2, 1901

[A282] MARY ALTA⁶ BROWNBACK ([A143] Edwin⁵, [A47] Hen-

ry⁴, [A15] Benjamin³, [A6] Henry², Gerhard¹) b May 12, 1869; educated in the public schools of Sangamon Co , Ill , June 9, 1887, m *Robert Alexander Irwin*, b near Pleasant Plains, Ill , March 22, 1863, s *Amos Dick* and *Rebecca Jane (Plunkett) Irwin* Mr Irwin was tax collector 1896-1897, Twp. treasurer 1910-1911, and has been an elder in Pres Ch. since 1892; ad Pleasant Plains, Sangamon Co , Ill.

Children (7), *surname Irwin*

i Lecta Gertrude⁷, b April 7, 1888; d Aug 10, 1889
ii Leslie Alexander⁷, b May 1, 1890, d July 15, 1890.
iii Liston Brownback⁷, b June, 1892, d Aug., 1892.
iv Homer Oliver⁷, b Sept 6, 1894.
v Eda Laura⁷, b Dec. 17, 1896
vi Charles Adolphus⁷, b July 27, 1902
vii Mary Viola⁷, b June 7, 1905

[A293] ORA⁶ BROWNBACK ([A147] William⁵, [A47] Henry⁴, [A15] Benjamin³, [A6] Henry², Gerhard¹) b April 10, 1879, Oct. 29, 1898, m *Hollis Price;* res Tower Hill, Shelby Co , Ill.

Children (3):

[A367] Nelson Price⁷, b June 1, 1900
[A368] Catharine Price⁷, b Jan 27, 1902 *
[A369] Harold Price⁷, b July 19, 1904 ᵇ

[A303] GEORGE D—⁶ BROWNBACK ([A155] Samuel H—⁵, [A48] William⁴, [A15] Benjamin³, [A6] Henry², Gerhard¹) b Dec. 21, 1872, m *Hettie Reed*

One son:

[A370] Glen⁷.

[A304] MARY E—⁶ BROWNBACK ([A155] Samuel H—⁵, same ancestry as [A303]) b April 11, 1876; m *Sidney G. Potter*

Children (3), *surname Potter*

i Alice Madge⁷
ii Leota Maud⁷.
iii Grace Marie⁷.

[A332] CLINTON SYLVESTER⁷ BROWNBACK ([A258] Stephen Sylvester⁶, [A113] Edward⁵, [A42] Edward⁴, [A11] Edward³, [A5] Benja-

ᵃ and ᵇ b in Louisville, Ky.

min², Gerhard¹) *b* April 27, 1870; member Geiger Memorial Brethren Ch and
S. S., *m Henrietta Jane Reynolds, b* Apr. 22, 1879; ad. 2517 W. Somerset
St., Philadelphia, Pa.
    Children (2).
[A372] Elizabeth Frances⁸, *b* Sept 7, 1895
[A373] William Sylvester⁸, *b* April 10, 1906

    [A333] EMMA ROSELLA⁷ BROWNBACK ([A259] Webster Pixer⁶,
[A114] Uriah Sebastian Root⁵, [A42] Edward⁴, [A11] Edward ³, [A5] Benjamin², Gerhard¹) *b* March 22, 1872, *m George W Moyer.*
    Children (4), *surname Moyer.*
  i Daniel W ⁸, ii Levin B ⁸, iii George W ⁸, iv Lawrence H ⁸, d y.

    [A343] GEORGE WALTON⁷ BROWNBACK ([A262] Walton⁶,
[A114] Uriah Sebastian Root⁵, [A42] Edward⁴, [A11] Edward³, [A5] Ben-
jamin², Gerhard¹) *b* May 24, 1873, at Reading, Berks Co , Pa.; April 29, 1904,
at Newark, Essex Co., N. J., *m Blanche De Cou, b* March 4, 1879, at Mt.
Holly, N. J ; dau *John* and *Cordelia (Rue) De Cou,* ordained to Cong. min-
istry at Reading, Pa., June 18, 1899, was pastor of Cong Ch at Athens,
Mich., First Cong. Ch of Saugatuck, Mich , and now of First Cong Ch of
Susquehanna, Pa (1911)
    One dau
[A375] Cordelia Rue⁸, *b* July 14, 1907, *d* Feb 29, 1908

EAST VINCENT TOWNSHIP, CHESTER COUNTY, PA , BY FRED-ERICK SHEEDER, FEBRUARY 18, 1846

    This remarkable manuscript history was presented to the Pennsylvania
Historical Society and was published in the Pennsylvania Magazine of History and Biography, Vol XXXIV, Nos 1, 2, 3, from which the following
extracts have been taken since the balance of this section was put in type
The manuscript begins.
    "To the Historical Society of Pennsylvania: With due Respect."
    An Introduction by Hon Samuel W. Pennypacker concludes
    "It has been thought best that the history should be printed in the quaint
phraseology and orthography in which it was written, believing that it loses
nothing in strength or value because of the fact that the author was without
education and expressing his thoughts in an unfamiliar tongue "
    * * * "Since now the place of John Shuler [See A22] at the mouth
of Birch run, birch run derived its name as the chief of the Timber growing
along the same was birdch this place was first taken up and Settled by garrit
Brumback [A1] of whom i shall treat more largely in its turn Frederick Bing-

aman [See A3]. The father of the late old Frederick Bingaman a mill wright by trade erected the first saw mill that was erected in this neighborhood and in his time added a grist mill to but at this time nothing to be seen as part of the hole were the building stood but head and tale ranes more visible this is at the mouth of birdch run in the year 1794" (Pp 85-86).

* * * "Next place is Jacob Christman's the Second Son of Henry [See A20] deceased which place was first Settled by one Philip Thomas this place joins mine and the lands of garrit Brumback's in whose behalf I have to treat largely in its turn. P Thomas and g Brumback been two of the first settlers in that part of the Township Thomas a Seven day baptist and Brumback a calvinist." (P 96)

* * * "and now begin the different places till part Brumback Church [See A1] on the left of the Ridge road when i come to treat of the churches I shall give the particulars in detail now crossing the road a distance above the church * * * Edward Brumback's [See A11] place The great grandfather of Said Edward was the first Settler here garrit Brumback [A1] came from germany when but one house Stood where germantown now stands he tarried a wile there and came up here took up 1000 acres and erected buildings and the first house was of logs all split with the wip saw and about four years past Edward [A11] tore it away and erected a Stone house in the place and now lives in, garrit as soon as he had erected builting he capt Tavern in and there was then an Indian village about 50 or 60 perches where the roads now crosses, Pottsgrove and Schullkill roads (and a new meeting house now Stands) of 300 Souls and garrit got them under his commant they helpet him to work and got provition in return, gearhard to had to Set down with them and Smoke a pipe of tobacco and rassel with them this pleased them much and they then Sang war Songs for him his time he had to go to the Valley forge 10 miles to git his plough irons Sharpened and carried one on each Side of his horse, this was the first public house kept in these parts that he kept   The indians had been verry fond of potatoes Turnips and especially milk i could mention the lines of this tract, but takes too much time." (Pp 97-98.)

"Garrit had other farms that he in his will willed to Son in law's of his, but these 1000 acres he willed cheafly to his Sons, as his Sons came to man hood he placed them on certain tracts, for his oldes son he erected the tavern on the Ridge road and put him their, his house that he had erected is from that on the Pottsgrove road, Benjamin [A5] his oldest son, for him he erected this to keep tavern in and did so, has of late been Wm Whitbys, Served a tour in the revolution, the widdow he left was murdered and robbet one knight 10

years since, they murderer never discovered. This tract, the before mentioned 1000 acres, are now devited and contain 13 farms with the necessary buildings, 21 lots with buildings thereon of from 5 to 30 acres, the church lot and grave-yard and the new meeting house lot and the cheafest part of owned by grand and greatgrand children   I consider it wast time to give a description of all these places and persons residing and had from time to time past of the above described property is in Coventry and part in East Vincent   Garrit has no grave Stone to See when he died or when born, but the date of his will is 1757 say he been 60 years old when deceased and 23 years old when came to live here and alow him to died in 1759 will be on 90 years that he Settled here now i proceed down the Ridge road—then are several farms that been owned by the old Millers and old Ackers they been considered to had been the first settlers thereon likewise the old Sniders place, now i will proceed up Schilkill road and River—widdow Francis place i scipt in my cours here was g Wash-ington's first nights loging when he left the Springs. *Peter De fracine* [See A11 and 14] the first Settler, after him the Millers place, for many years old *Nicholas Snider's*   Zions church stands near to the line * * * [See A12]. (Pp 194-195)

"Now Reinards factories, *Ulery Reinhard*' the great and great grant father of the present Reinhards Uhley R when came from germany he re-mained about the neighborhood of germantown when but one house stood their then came to Coventry and took up a large tract of land on both Sides of Pitchen creek and erected buildings first a hous which is at this time in good repair george a grand Son of Uhley had previously erected his first house about the Shulkill road * * * It was John the son of uhley that erected the mill with the assistance of his father and saw-mill a Son of John Daniel erected the woollen factory about 1810 he however died in the year 1816 and Samuel the younges Son of John is the present owner and occupant an older brother had the grist and Sawmill and some of the land he however Sold out and moved back george Hoffman purchased of him but died within a year George Reinhard is the owner of the old mansion and part of the place They been of the german baptist persuation their meeting house this Side that used to been the Swan tavern till of late George and Samuel took with the Battle ant, All these places when first taken up run from the Schulkill up towards the Ridge to the line of gerritt Brumback [A1], 1000 acres that he took up and settled, This track is part in Coventry and part in Vincent about 1 mile up from the Tavern of Brumbach's is the Church called Brumback's of the german reformed persuation, the first log church built here about 1750 or 5,

---

*Does this appertain to the ancestry of [E64] Esther and Daniel Rinehart?

the writer of this been in the same in the window of 1793 and 4 was of hewn logs one and a half Story with gallery broken roof two 4 light windows at each gable end and two of the Same Sise in the roof at each side these been for to light the gallery and pulpit the lower story had 12 light windows and the grave yard then but Small and fanced close at the church with pail and the rest with posten fance The Rev Minicus was the first preacher after him the Rev J Philip Leydick and in 1784 the Rev Frederick Daelhker (Dallıker) In 1800 this present Ediffice been erected outsid the grave yard to enlargen the Same, and J Longecker gave the Congregation more ground and they surrounted all in one graveyard and the church yard impailed after this new church was built and at the consecration The Rev Frederick Harman came to officiate til 1821 The Rev John C. guldin Son in law of the former the later of late years, done not to the Satisfaction to all or exhilaration to all of which more when comming to treat of the hill church below, after guldin, their been Several preaching but of Short duration the last one the Rev. Folk, but left, There is a School house here and School kept I have coppied Some names of the grave Stones as follows *John young* born 1744 died 1780 age 37 *George young* son of the former and father and grandfather to the *John young* at Coventry living yet born 1773 died 1821 *Nicholas Keller* born 1759 died 1822 age 69 years. *Philip Miller* born 1750 died 1809 age 59 years *Frederick Priser* [A16] born 1768 died 1823 age 55 years *William Shuler* [See A22] born 1773 died 1835 age 62 years *Henry Hooch* born 1760 died 1835 age 69 years *Henry Brumbach* [A6] a son of garrit born 1733 died 1804 Age 71 years he was born in this country 113 years ago *Jacob Mason* born 1712 died 1776 age 64 years *Frederick Bingeman* [A3-ii] the Son of *F Bingeman* [A3] of the Son in law of garrit Brumback that is made mention of in the description of the places born 1765 died 1832 age 75 years *Peter Kline* born 1755 died 1824 age 68 years *Theadore Miller* born 1758 died 1838 age 80 years *Peter Fertig* born 1765 died 1842 age 75 years *Sebastian Root* [A42] a member of Zion church born 1761 died 1843 age 82 years he been born near Pottstown *John Fertig* born 1736 died 1833 age 94 years came to America 1754 *Jacob Fertig* born 1778 died 1823 age 45 years *John Hiester* son of *general Hiester* born 1774 died 1822 age 48 years *Henry Titlow* born 1719 died 1793 age 74 years *John Titlow* born 1757 died 1827 age 68 years *a son of the former Henry Brumback* [probably A17 of A9] born 1791 died 1829 age 36 years *Sebastian Killy* born 1734 died 1777 age 43 years *Peter Brumback* [A14] was an officer in the Westren expedition born 1764 died 1834 age 69 garrit been his grandfather *Wm Posey* a son in law of garrit Brumback [A1]* born 1759 age 62 *Peter Paul* born 1742 died 1802 age 60 years *Chris-*

*See refutation of this statement, p 88.

tian Benner [See A4] died 1767 the oldest and the first enterred here have no grave Stones   This church Stands at the, or near the line of Covantry Township and in Vincent Township. *Sebastian Root* [A42] above mentioned of his father *Sebastian Root* came to this country and picked berries on the ground where the first marked house in the City Phila afterwards was erected and Settled himself afterwards in the neighborhood of Pottsgrove now, then he was a young man with no family * * * (Pp 202-204

* * * "The time I been with *Jesse Brumback* [A25] and when he hanted me the Coppy of his great grandfather's will, he the same time tould me that he would let me have his fathers Journall That he had kept when out in the westren expedition, I refused excepting of it by telling him that i allways had considered that A disgrace to the State and the less observation would be made of The better * * * That good democrats Should to never from that time out Tasted a trop of whisky; I been the first church man in these parts of the country That refused giving liquors to workmen as i could persive no good derive from giving it and never made it a custom to use it out in the field in haymaking and harvesting but the paid the hands 12½ cts more wages to buy it themselves But i never followed that custom when i quit I did quit. * * * And if anything in this report is represented reprehensive, then draw a black line over the Same and if anything lacking as to intelligibly if you inform me of I will try to rectify the Same.

Respectfully yours, &c.,

FREDERICK SHEEDER

East Vincent, at Sheeders industry, February 18the 1846 "   (Pages 379-380.)

GOSHENHOPPEN.

The general locality wherein live the descendants of [A1] Gerhard[1] Brumbach, and which includes part of the "Goshenhoppen Region," is likewise interesting to the descendants of [E1] Johannes Henrich[1] Brumbach, because of the tradition[a] in the "Woodcock Valley," Huntingdon Co., Pa., that their ancestors passed through the "Goshehoppa," were identified with it, and in earlier days traded there. It is not thought that there was any relationship between [A1] and [E1], and no traces of land ownership there by [E1], or the children, have yet been discovered.[b]

---

[a] See Preface
[b] The compiler will be grateful to any persons in Eastern Pa who will assist in carefully searching the old land and church records for anything pertaining to the earlier representatives of any of the families, and then communicate with him

"THE LEGEND OF GOSHENHOPPEN—REV. C. Z. WEISER "[a]

"Notes   The origin and significance of Goshenhoppen is still a puzzle. It is a name given to a region of country extending from North Wales to Macungie, north and south. and from the Falcondr to the Great Swamp, east and West   Its orthography is variously written, but preference is of late inclining to *Goshenhoppen*   It is doubtless a derivation and degeneration from some Indian name—perhaps a mixture of several names   The nearest approach to the term, as now written, is offered in the Titles of such Chiefs as Shak-a-happa, Guch-i-a-thion and En-shock-hippo   These stand broad and plainly written in the Early Vols of the "Colonial Records" and "Penna Arch."   From a comparison of a number of Indian Deeds to William Penn, given during 1683-5, we incline to the opinion that Shack-a-hop-pa was the Chief over the Region   His signature or "Mark," as we would say, was a Big Smoke Pipe.

Onas, which means a pen, was the name under which the Indians knew Wm. Penn.

Pat-ke-ho-ma is the Original of Perkio-men.   Mough-ough-sin had been the Indian Proprietor of that District which is now called Macungie "

"FEW NOTES RELATING TO GOSHENHOPPEN AND ITS CHURCHES."[b]

"I have an old deed of a Tract within the bounds of Goshenhoppen of 1733 which reads 'There was surveyed unto George Cowhill of the county of Philadelphia a certain Tract of Land situate in old Cowissippin in the said County, etc.

Gordon's Gazatteer of Penna. under New Hanover says the W. branch of the Perkiomen passes through the N W angle of the Township of Swamp Creek centrally and the population is German and have two churches upon opposite sides of a branch of Swamp Creek, one of which is called the Swamp Church

New Goshenhoppen is not on the list of P O any more—it is changed to New Hanover "

"ADDITIONS MADE FEB 28, 1879, FOR PA. HIST. SOC "

"I would further say in regard to Goshenhoppen that Mr. Weiser is wrong in saying 'It is a name given to a region of country extending from North Wales to Macungie,' etc   It never embraced so large an extent, for a part of it

---

[a] Page 231, Manuscript Penna Hist Soc, Phila, Pa.—prior to 1879.
[b] Manuscripts Penna Hist Soc., p 231

was embraced in what was then known as Methachey which now forms a part of Yoomencing, Worcester and Skippack Townships

It appears these names were originally applied to certain localities *without special boundaries*, before Counties and Townships were surveyed   Skippack' was also such a General name which embraced the present Perkiomen and Lower Salford Townships, without any special limits eastward   It comprehended about the middle district between Methachey and Goshenhoppen to Perkasie, while Goshenhoppen extended to Macungie, which is another such a locality whose original boundaries cannot be defined, besides many others especially in Western Penna

I have nothing reliable concerning *Schwartzwalde* but think Mr. Super or Rev. Mr Weiser could give the desired information if applied to. Their address is Pennsburg, Montgomery Co , Pa.

ABM. H CASSEL "

"Old Goshenhoppen distant 6 miles. New Goshenhoppen Reformed Church (Hornerly ? P. O.) is now Hanover P O   Reformed Lutheran Church is near by 'The New Goshenhoppen Ref Ch' is ¼ mile from the Perkiomen opposite Pennsburg, which was originally called 'Heiligsville' The first building was used by the Reformed Lutherans and Mennonites and was built as early as 1716   The second church building was put up in 1796 The first regularly organized church dates to 1731   It is said that John Henry Sprogle from Holland arrived in Phila in 1705, owned altogether about 13,000 acres in Montgomery and Berks   He gave 6 acres for a burial place for Mennonites, Lutherans and Reformed, though they had no lawful title before 1796 —they had titles of their own in 1749, but no legal patent

He further says 'In 1741 Father Theodore Schneider, a Jesuit priest, founded the Mission at (New) Goshenhoppen, where he lived in the utmost self-denial and poverty, ministering to the wants of the people over 20 years He built a church in 1743 where the present Catholic church in Washington Township, Berks Co , now stands; a part of the building is still attached to the present building' The Mennonites and Herrnhutters helped him to build his church out of Respect   Father Schneider established the first school (in that locality) which was attended by Mennonites and other children   The church owned 500 acres of the best land in Penna—a farm of 110 acres still

---

*The Life and Works of Christopher Dock, America's Pioneer Writer on Education— by Martin Grove' Brumbaugh [1682], Phila , 1908   Introduction by Samuel W Pennypacker   "Twenty-five years ago the name of Christopher Dock, the pious schoolmaster on the *Skippack*, was unknown to the reading world, and the light of local fame, extending from Germantown to *Goshenhoppen* which in the eighteenth century gave a general glow to his life, had faded into an almost imperceptible ember,' etc

belongs to it This church is also called the Goshenhoppen, besides another one on the North side of Pennsburg known as the Six Angular church is also called the New Goshenhoppen, and as they are not far apart Mr. Mulenberg no doubt frequently visited each of them " •

"GOSHENHOPPEN , The region lying partly in Berks, Montgomery and Bucks counties, that is in the angle formed by the three named districts, together with a strip of Lehigh, has been ycleped 'Goshenhoppen' for a full century In 1728 it is first written in the public prints Its orthography was framed by every writer after his own choice Cowissa-hoppen, Queso-hoppen, Coss-he-hoppen, Cosh-enhoppen, Coshahopin, Coache hoppe and Goshenhoppen, and, it may be, still other specimens may be found

The German settlers derived it of German origin, but, like Tulpehocken or Conshohocken, it came from Indian source We are all the more ready to believe this *herkunft*, from the fact that two Indian chiefs contributed to its patronymic, who owned contiguous tracts of land in its lattitude. Their names were severally 'Enschockhoppa' and 'Shakahoppa ' Their marks were Smoke Pipe, which they invariably attached opposite their names Until we are better informed, we are disposed to hold fast to this dusky origin. It embraces a tract extending from Treichlerville to Sumneytown, north and south, and from the Bucks county line to the Perkiomen, east and west. It covers a region rather than a township or country The only part which retains a part of the old name is Hoppenville."

The above quotation is from "Folk-Names of Places," by C Z Weiser, D D , in "The Perkiomen Region," Vol I, No 4, p 64. The latter, in Vol I, pp 88-90, contains an excellent sketch by Wm J. Buck, and illustration, of the "Old Goshenhoppen Church," erected in 1732 and used by both German Reformed and Lutheran congregations "The Perkiomen Region," Vol. III, p 76 et seq , contains a reprint of the "oldest Congregational Record" in the Ref. Ch., 1731-1761, and the pastor of that church informs the compiler that the later records are also in good preservation An examination of the latter is yet to be made for possible traces of our families—"Schippach, Alt Coschenhoppen, Neu Coschenhoppen, Schwam, Sacen, Aegipten, Macedonia, Missilem, Oh, Bernet Dolpenhacen" are included in these old records

---

*Mr Martin I J Griflin in *Penna -German*, Vol XII, No 9, p 571, says the Catholic Goshenhoppen Ch records are found in the Amer Cath Hist Soc of Phila, Vols 2, 3, 8, 11—1741 to 1810

SECTION B

GEORG¹ BOMBACH AND DESCENDANTS.

[B1] GEORG¹ BOMBACH arrived at Germantown, Pa., Dec. 3, 1740, on the ship *Samuel*, Captain Percy—"natives and late Inhabitants of the Palatinate upon the Rhine and places adjacent."

"The same name appears among the list of Surveys for Land in Lancaster Co., Pa., Dec 21, 1750. again on a Tax List of the Town of York, 1779. In the latter year the same name is found on a Tax List of Allen Twp., Cumberland Co., Pa."[1]

Georg's¹ name appears as the 18th signature in the first column (see arrow in accompanying illustration) of "Captain Percy's Passengers, 1740." The fifth name above his signature is that of *Daniel Furry*, and the second beneath his signature is that of *Poulus Züg* (*Zook*), both of which are of interest to certain families included in this work. In this connection those interested in this ship's immigrants should notice that the list as given in Rupp's Thirty Thousand Immigrants, 2d Edn., 1898, p. 144, is wholly different from the photographic copy of the ship's papers herewith reproduced

[B2] CONRAD² BOMBACH ([B1] Georg¹) *b* at Middletown, Pa., about 1750, millwright, and established the first mill at Standing Stone, now Huntingdon, Pa.; located at Highspire, and in 1794 is chief burgess of Harrisburgh, Pa., where he welcomed General George Washington in connection with the latter's activities in the "Whiskey Rebellion", served in the Continental Army, *m* Catherine Zell, *d* April, 1821

"Conrad Bombaugh"—"A Muster Roll of the Revolution" "A true return of Capt Samuel Cochran's company of the 4th Battn., Col Robert Elder, as it stood at Middletown Aug 12, 1777, in the march to Phila." (Notes & Queries, Egle, 1897, p 55.)

"Conrad Bomback" took oath (or affirmation) of allegiance to Pennsylvania at Lancaster May 1, 1779

CONRAD BOMBACH RELEASES TO PETER EICHER—AUG 20, 1793 [b]

"At the request of Peter Eicher the following release was recorded 20th Aug., 1793.

[a]Luther R Kelker, Custodian of the Public Records, Harrisburg, Pa
[b]There is some uncertainty as to the identity of this Conrad

138

Know all men by these presents that I *Conrad Bumbaugh* of Harrisburgh in the County of Dauphin in the State of Pennsylvania one of the Heirs and Roproportations of Anthony Sell late of Huntingdon County and State of Pennsylvania afore said yeoman deceased for and in consideration of the sum of five shillings lawful money money of Pennsylvania to me in hand paid by *Peter Eicher* of the State of Penn. at and before the ensealing and delivery of these presents the receipt whereof I do hereby acknowledge Have remissed released and forever quit claims and by those present do remiss release and forever quit claim all my Estate Share Part Right and Title of the following described Plantation and tract of land lying and being in Frederick County in the State of Maryland unto the said Peter Eicher adjoining lands of Michael Lynn, Thomas Payton, James Leech, James Davison, John Townsley and others containing two hundred and fifty three acres of land and allowed be the same more or less with the Rights of Members Hereditaments appurtenances whatsoever there to belonging so that neither I the said Conrad Brumbaugh nor any other person for me or in my name any manner of Right or title of into or out of my share or part of the above described Plantation or tract of land at any time here after shall or may have claim, challenge or demand and further I do hereby make ordain constitute and appoint Adam Gord and John Hughes of Frederick Co in the State of Maryland or either of them my true and lawful attorneys + +

In Witness whereof I have here unto set my hand and seal the 8th day of July in the year of our Lord one thousand seven hundred and ninety three.

Signed, sealed and delivered   CONRAD BOMBACH   [Seal]
in the presence of us
    John Sells Jr
    Ben Kurtz

Frederick County to Wit. On the tenth day of July 1793 came Adam Gord and John Hughes the within named attorneys before us the Subscribers two of the Justices for said County and acknowledge the within Instrument of Writing to be Act and deed of the aforesaid CONRAD BOMBACH according to the true Intent and Meaning thereof and the Act of Assembly in that case made and provided, Acknowledged before
    Jn Gwinn
    John Ross Keys"

In deed recorded "Conrad Brumbaugh, Has land of Esther Sells, now deceased, one of the Daughters of Anthony Sell late of Huntingdon County, State of Pennsylvania."

[B2] Conrad[2] and Catharine (Zell) Bombach had one son·

Abraham[3], *b* April 23, 1770, in Paxtang Twp, Lancaster Co., Pa. (now Dauphin), *m Catharine Reehm,* who *d* March 22, 1855 They had 3 ch Aaron[4], Catharine[4], and Sarah[4]

Aaron[4] *m Mira Lloyd,* dau of *John Lloyd* of Phila The eldest of their 5 ch was *Charles Carroll[5] Bombaugh,* M D, *b* in Harrisburg, Pa., Feb. 10, 1828; *d* in Baltimore, Md, May 24, 1906, grad (M D) from Harvard Univ 1850, and from Jeff Med Coll 1853, served as regimental surgeon U S A, 1861-'65; 1864-'65 was on editorial staff of *Baltimore American;* 1865 established and for thirty-three years successfully conducted the *Baltimore Underwriter*—he was an authority upon life insurance

A tombstone in St Peter's Ch Cem at Middletown, Pa., says Catharine Bombaugh *d* Dec. 18, 1833, in her 71st yr (Notes & Queries, Egle, 3d Ser., Vol. I, p 223) Whether or not this is the above Catharine[4] has not been determined

The following records are here given merely to make them accessible, but their proper place amongst the families is undetermined

---

*Further details are contained in Biog Encyc of Dauphin Co, 1896, p. 199

CHRISTIAN BOMBACH took the oath (or affirmation) of allegiance to Pa in Lebanon Twp, Lancaster Co, Pa, Oct 14, 1777. (Pa Arch, 2d Ser, Vol. XIII, p. 410)

JOHN BOMBAUGH—Ranger of the Frontier 1778-1783, Robinson Rangers, Cumberland Co, Pa (Pa Arch, 3d Ser, Vol XXIII, p 198)

JNO H. BOMBOGH—Rangers of the Frontier, following list for Westmoreland Co., Pa, mixed residence New Series, 1778-1783. (Pa Arch, 3d Ser, Vol XXIII, p. 252)

WIDDOW BOMBAUGH*—State Tax, Northumberland Co, Pa., 1778-1780, Penns Twp, valuation 311, 13, 0 (Pa Arch, 3d Ser, Vol XIX, p 410)

BUMBAUGH—There are some families using this spelling. In a few localities the later generations have changed to "Brumbaugh," and a considerable amount of information has been collected, but the replies to repeated inquiries have been so delayed that it has been decided to omit such publication

*It is not thought that this has any reference to [D2] Widow Brombach found in Va about 1760.

SECTION C.

JOHANN JACOB[1] BRUMBACH AND HIS DESCENDANTS.

[C1] JOHANN JACOB[1] BRUMBACH,* b about 1728, is said to have been an orphan and to have had £50 upon his arrival at Philadelphia, Pa , on the ship *Nancy*, August 31, 1750—see his signature on the Immigrant List He settled in the Conecocheague District, about 1 mile south of Mason's and Dixon's Line, and 4 miles north of Hagertown, then Frederick Co , Md   In 1760 he m *Mary Elizabeth Angle*, b 1740 (for Mary Elizabeth see deed of 14th March, 1780, p. 148), dau *Henry Angle* of Washington Co , Md   The latter's family in *Heads of Families, Md* , 1790, is given as three free white males over 16 years, including heads of families, two free white males under 16 years, and five free white females, including heads of families.   He built a substantial house on his tract before his marriage—the original house is standing, and with various additions and changes is shown in the recent photograph taken especially for this work reproduced elsewhere   It is probably the oldest original house in Washington Co , Md , and is occupied by the family of [C111] *Philip Napoleon[4] Brumbaugh*—the illustration shows his wife seated at the main entrance to the original building   This house is built of heavy hewn logs, 36 x 16—two rooms below and two above, with large open fire places (since closed), and very heavy oak doors and shutters   The porch and two-story addition were built during the ownership of the present occupants

IMMIGRANT LIST—AUGUST 31, 1750

"At the Court House at Philadelphia
Friday, *August* 31, 1750.

Present—Thomas Lawrence, Esquire, Mayor.

The Foreigners whose names are underwritten imported in the ship *Nancy*, Thomas Coatam Master, from Rotterdam & last from Cowes, did this day take the usual oaths

By List, 88   Persons, 270

Johannes Vollmer	Henderich Willem Stiegel
Balthas Federhoff	Christian Fautz
Johan Beinhardt Riede	Johan Jacob Weiss
Daniel Bohset	Michael Ferster

141

Bernhart Rockenstihl

Daniel Haubersack

Johan Conrad Raish

Martin Muller

Lorenz Schenck

Joseph Stahle

Johannes ? Tobias Rudolph

Hans Gorg Hetle

Martin Jommel ?

Friederich Gans

Johannes Gans

Thomas $\times$ Gan (Gans ?)

Georg Heuling

Johannes Zweigle

Friedrich   (?)

Johan Georg Bauer

Johann Bernhard Wunsch

Johann Georg Sieger

Johann Georg Musse

Michael Rieder

Andreas Brauer

Hans Georg Kuhn

Michael Hensel ?

Johann Jacob Canz

Johannes Glasser

Jonas Raub

Friederich Weiss

Wilhelm Gettling

Hans Georg Beiterman

Johann Jacob Beiterman

Georg Friedrich Beitterman

Johan Friedrich Unrath

Johan Friedrich Unrath

Heinrich Lehringer

Heinrich Lehringer

Gorg Heinrich Lutz

Gorg Heinrich Lutz

Georg Wilhelm Marx

Jeremias Horngacher

Johannes Heide

Hans Georg Benner

Andreas Rahnfelder ?

Bernhart $\times$ Gilbert

Johan Jacob Gobel

John Niclaus Gilbert

Christoff Wetzel

Johann Georg Gilbert

Frantz Kuhlwein

Johann Jacob Baum

Jacob Wurth

Hans Georg Gilbert

Andreas Singel ?

Hans Adam Herbolt

Johann Philipp Hautz

Hans Jacob Gilbert

Johann Herbolt ?

Johan Jacob Barth

Christian $\times$ Blosser

Johannes Low

Christian Giebeler

Jost Henrich Wehler

Johann Peter Gutehus

Tilman Crentz

Johann Jacob Brumbach [C1]

Johann Gitting

J. Daniel $\times$ Shneyder

Johann   ?

Johannes Rehbach

Johannes Jung

Johan Peter $\times$ Kleim

David Nuss

Johan Henrich Comrath

Johann Henrich Klein

Philip Grabeman

J. Henry $\times$ Seydenstiker

Immanuel Bager

X in above names means His X mark.

Johann Georg Marx   Johan Henrich Jung, Jr.
                                     Johann Georg Braunsberg "

Jacob [1] [a] seems at once to have dropped the "Johann" after landing, as nowhere has any later signature other than "Jacob" been found, and this was a common practice—the Census of 1790 enumerates him as "Jacob" only. Originally a Lutheran, he united with the G B B Ch, of which his wife was a member. In the Braddock campaign of the F and I. War he served as a packman, his religious scruples preventing service in actual conflict. His hearing was defective, and this tendency, together with his large stature and strong general constitution, seem to have been hereditary in some later generations. He had an unusual faculty for acquiring land, and shortly before his death in Pa., April 10, 1799,[b] is said to have owned over 6,000 acres in Bedford and Blair counties, Pa , together with large tracts of land in Frederick Co , Md. His remains were taken to the old Maryland homestead and buried in the small family graveyard   Mary d Nov. 28, 1806, and was laid beside her husband, both graves marked by rudely dressed limestones containing "J B." and "M B "   The remains of the 7 children also rest there.

Heads of Families, First Census of the United States, 1790—Md , p 118, enumerates [E2] *Jacob² Brumbach* as having 2 sons over 16, 4 under 16, and 3 dau, besides his wife, also on p. 121 [C4] *John³ Brumbagh* as having 3 dau and his wife, and immediately beneath is found [C2] *Jacob² Brumbagh* as having 4 sons under 16 and one dau besides his wife

The children seem to have united with different religious denominations, and in the main the descendants of each remained therein, [C2] Jacob² and [C7] Henry² became Pres , [C3] Mary² and [C4] John² became G B B ; [C5] Daniel² became Ref , [C6] David² and [C8] George² became Lutheran, according to [C76] David Stuckey⁴ Brumbaugh [c]

Considerable space is given to the deeds which follow because of their bearing upon questions of locality and of genealogy   Often they have been the only means of positive identification amongst our numerous families.

JACOB BROOMBACK'S PATENT "ILL WILL" 100 ACRES

Frederick &c, Know Ye that for &c, in consideration that *Jacob Broomback* of Frederick County in our said Province of Maryland hath due unto him one hundred acres of land within our said Province by virtue of a warrant for that quantity granted him by renewment the thirteenth day of July Seventeen hundred and fifty-four as appears in our Land Office and upon such conditions and terms as are expressed in our conditions of Plan-

[a] Probably a cousin of [E1] Johannes Henrich¹ Brumbach
[b] From ledger of [C7] Henry² Brumbaugh loaned by [C119] Upton S⁴ Brumbaugh, Baltimore, Md
[c] Whose excellent memory and continued interest and assistance are gratefully acknowledged

tation of our said Province bearing date the fifth day of April Sixteen hundred and eighty-four and remaining upon record in our said Province together with such alterations as in them are made by our further conditions bearing date the fourth day of December Sixteen hundred and ninety-six together also with the alterations made by our Instructions bearing date at London the twelfth day of September Seventeen hundred and twelve and registered in our Secretarys Office of our said Province together with a paragraph of our Instructions bearing date at London the fifteenth day of December Seventeen hundred and thirty-eight and registered in our Land Office

We do therefore hereby Grant unto him the said Jacob Broombick all that tract or parcel of land called *"ILL WILL*

BEGINNING at a bounded White Oak standing in the temporary line about fourteen perches to the Eastward of Thomas Longs field and running thence South forty-eight degrees West twenty-two perches, South eighty degrees East twenty-five perches, South thirty degrees East thirty-eight perches, South fifty-eight degrees and an half degree East sixty-two perches, South twelve degrees East eighty-eight perches, North fifty-six degrees East one hundred and four perches, North twenty degrees West one hundred and twelve perches, then by a straight line to the beginning tree

Containing and now laid out for One hundred acres of land more or less according to the Certificate of Survey thereof taken and returned into our Land Office bearing date the twenty-fourth day of July, Seventeen hundred and fifty-four and there remaining together with all rights, profits, benefits and privileges thereunto belonging Royal Mines Excepted To Have and To Hold the same unto him the said Jacob Broomback his heirs and assigns forever to be holden of us and our heirs as of our Manor of Conigochiege in free and common soccage by fealty only for all manner of services Yielding and paying therefore yearly unto us and our heirs at our receipt at our City of Saint Marys at the two most usual feasts in the year Viz the Feasts of the Annunciation of the Blessed Virgin Mary and Saint Michael the Arch Angel by even and equal portions the Rent of four shillings Sterling in Silver or Gold for a fine upon every alienation of the said land or any part or parcel thereof one whole years Rent in Silver or Gold or the full value thereof in such comodities as we and our heirs or such officer or officers as shall be appointed by us and our heirs from time to time to collect and receive the same shall accept in discharge thereof at the choice of us and our heirs or such officer or officers aforesaid Provided that if the said sum for a fine for alienation shall not be paid unto us and our heirs or such officer or officers aforesaid before such alienation and the said alienation entered upon record either in the Provincial Court or County Court where the same parcel of land lyeth within one month next after such alienation then the said alienation shall be void and of no effect

Given under our Great Seal of our said Province of Maryland this twenty-fourth day of July Anno Domini Seventeen hundred and fifty-four.

Witness our trusty and well beloved Horatio Sharpe, Esquire, Lieutenant General and Chief Governor of our said Province of Maryland Chancellor and Keeper of the Great Seal thereof

Land Office of Maryland, Set

I Hereby Certify, that the aforegoing is a true Copy of the Patent of "ILL WILL" 100 acres, patented to Jacob Broomback 24th July, 1754, as recorded in Liber Y & S No 8 folio 647 &c, one of the Record Books on file in this office

In testimony whereof, I have hereunto set my hand and affixed the Seal of the Land Office of Maryland, this twelfth day of April, nineteen hundred and seven

     [Seal]   E STANLEY TOADVIN,
                                     Commissioner of the Land Office

"Broomback's Lott" 50 a, lying in Frederick Co, Md, and patented to *Jacob Broomback* of Frederick Co, 21 April, 1755.

(B. C & G S, No. 3, folio 187, Land Commissioner's Office, Annapolis)

DEED OF CONROD HOGMIRE TO JACOB BROMBACK FOR "CLALAND'S CONTRIVANCE," FREDERICK CO, MD, 26 SEPT, 1753 [*]

At the Request of *Jacob Brombaek* the following Deed was Recorded October the

---

[*]Search made and record at Frederick, Md, copied by Miss Nellie Carter Garrott, Secy Frederick Co Hist. Soc

twenty Third day Anno Domini Seventeen Hundred and fifty Three To wit This Indenture made this twenty Sixth day of September in the year of our Lord God one Thousand Seven Hundred and fifty Three Between *Conrod Hogmyre* of Frederick County and Province of Maryland Blacksmith of the one Part and *Jacob Brombach weaver* of the same County and Province aforesaid of the other Part Witnesseth That the said Conrod Hogmire for an in Consideration of the sum of Sixty four pounds Current money to him at and before the Ensealing and Delivery of This Presents well and Truly Paid by the said Jacob Bromback were with the said Conrod Hogmire doth Acknowledge him self fully satisfied and contented and of Every part and Parcel Thereof doth acquit and Discharge the said Jacob Bromback his Heirs Executors Administrators for ever by this Presents hath granted Bargained and sold Aliened and Confirmed and by this Presents doth fully Clearly and absolutely Grant Bargain and sell Alien and Confirm unto the said Jacob Bromback all that Tract or Parcell of Land called *Clalands Contriuance* Beginning at a Bounded white oak standing on the head of a Dry Spring Lying Near a Tract of land Taken up by Col Cresap Belonging to Daniel Dulany Esquire and Running Thence South twenty Nine Degrees East Twenty four Perches then south fifty five Degrees East Seventy Perches then south five Degrees East Twenty six perches then South fifty four Degrees West forty perches North Eighty four Degrees West forty perches then south sixty three Degrees west sixty Six Perches then North Twenty Degrees West one hundred and forty Perches then by a straight Line to the Beginning Tree Containing and now laid out for Ninety Acres of Land more or less scituate Lying and Being in the County afore said with all appurtenances, Houses, Buildings, fences and Improvements whatsoever and the Reversion and Reversions Remainder and Remainders and Profits whatsoever of all and singular the said Premises and every part and Parcell There of To Have And to Hold this said Tract Land and Premises with all appurtenances before by this Presents Bargained and sold or Mentioned or Intended to be hereby Granted Bargained Aliened and Confirmed and Every Part and Parcel Thereof only my Lord or Lords fees Excepted to the Jacob Bromback his heirs and Assigns to the only Proper use and behoof of the said Jacob Bromback his Heirs and assigns for Ever and the said Conrod Hogmire doth warrant and for ever Defend from him his Heirs Executors administrators to the said Jacob Bromback his Heirs Executors, Administrators and assigns he the said Conrod Hogmire his Heirs Executors Administrators doth hereby Covenant promise and agree to and with the said Jacob Bromback his Heirs Executors Administrators and assigns all and singular the Before Bargained Premises with the appurtenances and every Part thereof unto the said Jacob Bromback his Heirs and assigns for ever by this presents *In Witness* whereof the above Named Conrod Hogmire hath to this Present Indenture interchangeably set his hand and seal the day and year above Written

CONROD HOGMIRE [Seal]

Signed sealed and Delivered
    In the Presence of
        Jos Smith, Thos Prather on the Back of which Deed is thus Indorsed To wit September the 26th 1753 Received the day of the date hereof the within Named Jacob Bromback the Sum of Sixty four pounds Currant Money being The Consideration Money for those and Premises with in Mentioned
    Testes Tho Prather
September the 26th day 1753 Then Came the within Named Conrod Hogmire and acknowledged the within Deed according to Law before us

JOS SMITH
THO PRATHER

Октober the 23 1753 Then Received of Jacob Bromback the sum of three shillings and seven pence half penny sterling as an Alienation fine on the within Mentioned Ninety Acres of Land by O-der of Edward Loyd, Esquire agent of the Right Honourable the Lord Proprietary of Maryland
    [Seal]   JOHN DARNALL.

"*The Resurvey* on *Clalands Contrivance*" 505 a, lying in Frederick Co., Md., and patented to Jacob Broomback of Frederick Co., 18 April, 1763

(B C. & G S., No 18, folio 313, Land Commissioner's Office, Annapolis.)

"*Timber Bottom*" 260 a, lying in Frederick Co., Md., and patented to [C1] Jacob¹ Broomback of Frederick Co., 14th Sept., 1763.

(B C & G S, No. 23, folio 35, Land Commissioner's Office, Annapolis)

"*Chance*" 23 a, lying in Frederick Co, Md, and patented to [C1] Jacob[1] Broombaugh of Frederick Co, 11th May, 1765

(B C & G S, No 28, folio 181, Land Commissioner's Office, Annapolis)

"PATENT SAMUEL WALLIS DORFANS BARN 475A 104P CUMBERLAND CO"

Thomas Penn and Richard Penn, Esqrs True and absolute Proprietaries and Governors in Chief of the Province of Pennsylvania, and Counties of New-Castle, Kent and Sussex upon Delaware To all unto whom these presents shall come Greeting Whereas in Consequence of the Application of Abraham Robinson No 167 dated the first day of August 1766 tor 300 Acres of Land near the foot of Dunnings Mountain on the head Draughts ot Yellow Creek Cumberland County, a Survey hath been made of the Tract ot Land herein after mentioned and intended to be hereby granted AND WHEREAS in pursuance ot a Warrant dated the twenty third Day of May Instant requiring our Surveyor General to accept the said Survey into his Office and make Return thereof into our Secretary's Office, in Order for Confirmation to Samuel Wallis unto whom said Robinson conveyed by Deed of the Sixteenth day of September last on the Terms of the same Warrant mentioned he hath accordingly made Return thereof thereby Certifying, the Description, bounds, and Limits, of the Land as foresaid, surveyed to be as follows, viz Situate as aforesaid called *Dorfans Barn* Beginning at a marked white oak thence by John Chandlers Land South Sixty six degrees East Three hundred and twenty eight perches to a marked white oak, thence by Barrens South five degrees West one hundred and fifty perches to a marked white oak South fifty five degrees West One hundred and thirty seven perches to a marked Pine North Seventy five degrees West Sixty eight perches to a marked Lin, South Seventy seven degrees West thirty six perches to a marked Hickory thence by Thomas Walkers Land North forty three degrees & a half West One hundred and fifty three perches to a marked Hickory thence by Dunnings Mountain North forty nine degrees West thirty five perches to a marked Chestnut oak & North fifteen degrees East Two hundred and twenty six perches to the place of Beginning Containing Four hundred & seventy five acres and One hundred & four perches and allowance of Six P Cent for Roads, &c As by the said Application, Warrant & Survey remaining in the Surveyor Generals Office and from thence Certified into our Secretaries Office more fully appears NOW at the Instance and Request ot the said Samuel Wallis that we would be pleased to grant him a Confirmation ot the same KNOW YE, that in Consideration of the Sum of Twenty three pounds Sixteen Shillings Sterling Money of Great Britain pr lawful Money of Pennsylvania, to our use paid by the said Samuel Wallis (the Receipt whereof we hereby acknowledge, and thereof do acquit and for ever discharge the said Samuel Wallis his Heirs Assigns, by these Presents) And of the yearly Quit-Rent herein after mentioned and reserved, WE HAVE given, granted, released and confirmed, and by these Presents for Us, our Heirs and Successors, Do give, grant, release and confirm, unto the said Samuel Wallis his Heirs and Assigns, the said above described Tract of Land, as the same are now set forth, bounded and limited as aforesaid With all Mines, Minerals, Quarries, Meadows, Marshes, Savannahs, Swamps, Cripples, Woods, Underwoods, Timber, and Trees, Ways, Waters, Water Courses, Liberties, Profits Commodities, Advantages, Hereditaments and Appurtenances whatsoever thereunto belonging or in any wise appertaining and lying within the Bounds and Limits aforesaid [Three full and clear fifth Parts of all Royal Mines, free from all Deductions and Reprisals for digging and refining the same; and also one fifth Part of the Ore of all other Mines, delivered at the Pits Mouth only excepted, and hereby reserved] And also free Leave, Right and Liberty, to and for the said Samuel Wallis his Heirs and Assigns, to hawk, hunt, fish and fowl, in and upon the hereby granted Land and Premises, or upon any Part thereot TO HAVE AND TO HOLD the said above described Tract of Land and Premises hereby granted (except as before excepted) with their Appurtenances, unto the said Samuel Wallis his Heirs and Assigns, To the only Use and Behoof of the said Samuel Wallis his Heirs and Assigns, for ever, TO BE HOLDEN of us, our Heirs and Successors, Proprietaries of *Pennsylvania*, as of our Mannor of Lowther in the County of Cumberland aforesaid, in free and common Soccage by Fealty only, in lieu of all other Services YIELDING AND PAYING THEREFORE yearly unto Us, our Heirs and Successors, at the Town of Carlisle in the said County, at or upon the first Day of March in every Year, from the first Day of March last One penny Sterling for every Acre of the same, or value thereof in Coin current, according as the Exchange shall then be between our

said Province and the City of London, to such Person or Persons as shall from Time to Time be appointed to receive the same AND in Case of Non-payment thereof within ninety Days next after the same shall become due that then it shall and may be lawful for us, our Heirs and Successors, our and their Receiver or Receivers, into and upon the hereby granted Land and Premises to re-enter, and the same to hold and possess until the said Quit-Rent, and all Arrears thereof, together with the Charges accruing by Means of such Non-payment and Re-entry, be fully paid and discharged WITNESS John Penn Esquire Lieutenant-Governor of the said Province, who by Virtue of certain Powers, and Authorities to him for this Purpose, inter alia, granted by the said Proprietaries, hath hereunto set his Hand, and caused the Great Seal of the said Province to be hereunto affixed at Philadelphia this twenty seventh day of May in the Year of Our Lord, One Thousand Seven Hundred and Sixty seven The Seventh Year of the Reign of King George the Third over Great Britain &c and the Forty ninth Year of the said Proprietaries Government

[Seal]   JOHN PENN

Recorded in the Office for Recording of Deeds for the City and County of Philada In Pat Book A A Vol 8 pa 330 The 4th Day of June 1767 Witness my Hand & Seal of Office afs

THEO LUSK D. Recdr

(The old f usually appears in the above where s is printed)

Samuel Wallis and Lydia his wife by deed bearing date the 4th day of September, 1782, conveyed said tract to Abel James and Henry Drinker in fee.

Abel James and Rebecca his wife, and Henry Drinker and Elizabeth his wife for five shillings in hand paid deed said tract unto Samuel Wallis on the 31st day of December, 1787.

The latter acknowledgment was taken before George Bryan, Esq, one of the Justices of the Supreme Court of the Commonwealth of Pennsylvania, and in it appears "Rebekah" James, whereas she plainly writes "Rebecca James."

Samuel Wallis and Lydia his wife by indenture bearing date the 8th June, 1797—recorded Bedford Co., Book E, p 207, etc—granted said tract in fee to Henry Drinker, etc

"Deed

• Henry Drinker & Wife (6th Aug 1803)
                    to
    Mary Brombach and
    Jacob Brombach"
Recdg &c $1-50

DEED OF [C1] JACOB[1] BRUMBAUGH, SR , TO [C4] JOHN[2] BRUMBAUGH—14 MARCH, 1780

"At the Request of *John Brombaugh* was the following deed Recorded Mch 10, 1780 Towit

This Indenture made this 14th day of March in the Year of our Lord one thousand Seven Hundred and Eighty between *Jacob Broombaugh, Senr* of Washington County in the State of Maryland, farmer, of the one part Witnesseth that he the said Jacob Broombaugh Sr for and in consideration of

the sum of Eighty pounds of current and lawful money of the State of Maryland by him the said *John Broombaugh* well and truly in hand paid before the
Ensealing and delivery of these presents the receipt whereof is hereby acknowledged by him the said Jacob Broombaugh, Sr —part of two Different
Tracts of Land as herein after Mentioned both said Tracts or parcels of land
situate in Washington County in the State of Maryland as aforesaid both of
said Tracts of land Granted by pattent unto the above named Jacob Broombaugh Sr the first parcel of Land Conveyed by Virtue of these presents by
the above Named Jacob Brombaugh Sr. unto the above Named John Broombaugh his Heirs or Assigns forever being part of a Tract or parcel of land
Called the *Resurvey on Clealands Contrivance* beginning for the said part at
the end of One hundred perches on the Seventh line of a Tract of land Called
Nicholas Contrivance Granted Edward Nichols for Seventy five Acres also
said beginning being at the end of One Hundred perches on the Twenty Seventh
line of the Original Tract Called the *Resurvey* on *Clelands Contrivance* and
running + + + to a Hickory Saplin being a corner where the division line
Starts between Said John Broombaugh and Jacob Broombaugh Sr land, and
running + + + Laid out for 100 acres of Land.

2d part small part originally granted by pattent to above named Jacob
Broombaugh Sr called *resurvey* on *Brumbaughs delight ill will* now called
timber bottom beginning for said part at the End of Sixty Six perches in the
fourteenth line of the Original Tract called *timber bottom* containing 35½
a both 140½ a

                                         Jacob Brumbaugh [Seal]"

Witness

    John Cellar
    Henry Schnelchy
    [C1] *Jacob*[1] receipts to [C4] *John*[2] for £80.
    [C1] *Jacob*[1] and *Mary Elizabeth*, wife, release dower right.   (This
seems only record of full name "Mary Elizabeth ")
    (Book B, p 313, Bedford, Pa , copied by Mr Elias Gibson.)

PATENT FROM THE COMMONWEALTH OF PENNSYLVANIA TO
    [C1] "JACOB BROOMBAUGH" FOR "RICH BARRENS"
         (225 ACRES) UPON WARRANT GRANTED
                  MARCH 14, 1785

    "To all to whom these Presents shall come, Greeting· Know ye, That in
consideration of the monies paid by *Jacob Broombaugh* of Washington County,

Maryland, into the Receiver-General's office of this Commonwealth, at the granting of the Warrant herein after mentioned, and of the sum of Eighty-five dollars and five cents lawful money now paid by him into the said office, there is granted by the said Commonwealth unto the said Jacob Broombaugh, a certain tract of Land, called "*Rich Barrens*" situate in Woodberry Town-ship, Bedford County, Beginning at a corner thence by barrens south thirty two degrees + + + thence by land of *William Dickson* + + + by land of *George Butterbaugh* + + + Containing Two Hundred twenty five acres and allowance of six per cent for roads (&c which said tract was surveyed in pursuance of a Warrant dated the 14th of March 1785 granted to the said Jacob Broombaugh with the appurtenances + + + Free and Clear of all Restrictions and Reservations, as to Mines, Royalties, Quit-rents or other-wise, excepting and reserving only the fifth part of all Gold and Silver Ore, for the use of this Commonwealth, to be delivered at the Pit's mouth, clear of all charges "

Granted by Thomas McKean, Governor, May 30, 1805 Recorded in Pat. Book P, Vol. 57, p. 107, Dept of Inter Affairs, Harrisburg

DEED OF [C1] JACOB BROMBACH, SENR TO ANN AND MARTIN HOUSER—26 AUGUST, 1785 *

"To all People to whom these Presents shall Come I [C1] *Jacob*[1] *Brom-bach Senr* of the County of Washington in the state of Maryland Yeoman send greeting whereas I the said Jacob[1] Brombach Senr obtained a warrant from the Honorable the Proprietaries of Pennsylvania bearing the Date the twenty Sixth Day of January in the year of our Lord one thousand Seven hundred and seventy five for taking up 150 Acres of Land in Morrisons Cove on Cove Run joining James Biddles 500 acre Tract on the South or North West side in Bedford Co and also I the said Jacob[1] Brombach Senr obtained one other Warrant from the said Proprietaries bearing Date the said 26 Day of January for taking up 50 acres of land in Morrisons Cove joining James Biddles 500 acre Tract in the County of Bedford as in and by the said Re-cited warrants will more fully and at large appear" + + + £100 lawful money of Pa acknowledged from Ann Houser and Martin Houser—26 Aug 1785 + + +

Jacob Brombach Senr [Seal]

Wm Beatty
David Espy
_____
*Recorded in Book B, p. 181, Bedford Co, Pa.

At request of [C1] *Jacob¹ Broombaugh* received Oct. 26, 1787, 26 Oct., 1787, Between Paul Roades of Bedford Co , Pa , farmer, and [C1] *Jacob¹ Brombaugh* of Washington Co , Md , ₤500. *Resurvey* on *Roots Hill* beginning at *Pauls purchase* on *Resurvey on Roots Hill* 84¼ a, 1st tract—2d tract *Paulas Travels* 27 a

(Book E, p 583, Huntingdon, Pa)

May 2, 1788, [C1] *Jacob¹ Brumbaugh* deeds to David Forey of Lancaster Co , Pa , for £800 *Part of Resurvey on Roots Hill* part called *Pauls Purchase* 84¼ a 1st part—*Pauls Travels* 27 a 2d part.

(Book E, p 849, Huntingdon, Pa)

Jacob Broombaugh [C1] and *John Broombaugh* [C4], both of Washington Co , Md , 26 Oct , 1787, give bond £1,000 to Paul Roades of Morris Cove in Bedford Co., Pa , 300 a tract in Morrises Cove—"which tract he the said Jacob Broombaugh formerly took out a Warrant for and has put the above named Paul Roads in possession of said land or part thereof."

Jacob Brombach			[Seal]

Johannes Brumbach		[Seal]

Witness

Jacob Rohrer

Saml Finley

(Book F, p 61, Huntingdon, Pa)

DEED FROM DANIEL CARPENTER, AND MARY, FOR "SPRINGFIELD FARM," 362 ACRES, 17 NOV. 1788, TO JACOB¹ BRUMBACH [C1]

This Indenture made the 17 day of November 1788 between Daniel Carpenter of York Town in the County of York and State of Pennsylvania, Innkeeper and Mary his wife of one part and [C1] *Jacob¹ Brumbach* of Washington County in the State of Maryland of the other part, Whereas his Excellency Benjamin Franklin, President of the Supreme Executive Council of the Commonwealth of Penna by Patent under the hand of said Benjamin Franklin and the Great seal or Commonwealth of Pennsylvania bearing date the fifteenth day of May in the year of our Lord one thousand seven hundred and Eighty six for the consideration and under the Reservations therein mentioned granted unto Daniel Carpenter his heirs and assigns forever All that tract of land called "*Springfield farm* situate on Piney Creek about seven or eight miles above the mouth in Frankstown Township Bedford Co beginning at a corner Spanish oak of Michael Krider's land, thence by the same north sixty eight degrees west two hundred and sixty eight perches to a dogwood tree thence by the Canoe Mountain south twenty two degrees west fifty perches to a white oak north seventy nine degrees west thirty perches to a large Black oak South twenty degrees West one hundred and seventy four perches to a dogwood, South seventy degrees East forty seven perches to a white oak, South twenty degrees west sixty one perches to a large white oak thence by *Pine Bariens* south twenty degrees East two hundred and twelve perches to a small hickory and north thirty degrees East two hundred and thirty four perches to the place of beginning Containing three hundred and sixty two acres and allowance of six per cent for roads &c as by the said patent Recorded in the Rolls office at Philadelphia in Patent Book No 6 page 285 reference being thereunto had may more fully appear (which said tract was surveyed in pursuance of a warrant dated the 27 day of April 1775 to John Carpenter who by deed dated May 8, 1786 conveyed the same to said Daniel Carpenter in fee) Now this Indenture witnesseth that the said Daniel Carpenter and Mary his wife for and in consideration

of the sum of three hundred and forty pounds lawful money of Pennsylvania + + + paid by the said Jacob Brumbach, &c + + +
Witnesses.

Peter Keys   Daniel Carpenter [Seal]
Frederick Budline (?)   Mary Carpenter [Seal]
    Daniel Carpenter receipts to [C1] Jacob¹ Brumbach for £340
    (Recorded 10 June, 1790, Vol A1, p 288, Huntingdon, Pa—copied by Mr Elmer E. Enyeart)

DEED FROM HEIRS OF [C1] JACOB¹ BRUMBAUGH FOR "SPRINGFIELD FARM"
TO [C2] JACOB² BRUMBAUGH OF WASHINGTON CO, MD, 10 MCH 1807

    This Indenture made the 10 day of March 1807 between [C5] Daniel² Brombaugh, [C6] David Brombaugh and [C3] George² Brombaugh all of Washington Co, Md, [C3] Mary² Ulrey and Samuel Ulrey her husband and [C4] John² Brombaugh of Bedford Co Pa of one part and [C2] Jacob² Brombaugh of Washington Co State of Md of the other part, Witnesseth that for and in consideration of the sum of one thousand six hundred and Twenty nine dollars current money of the state of Md + + + + a certain plantation or tract of land called "Springfield farm" situated on the waters of Pine Creek about seven or eight miles above the mouth in Woodbury Twp Huntingdon Co, Pa, containing 362 acres and allowance of six per cent for roads &c said tract belonging to the estate of Jacob Brombaugh by the said Jacob Brumbach, &c + + +
Witness
J Maxwell
Jacob Zimmerman
                her   [C6]   David Brombaugh   [Seal]
    [C3] Mary ✕ Ullery   [Seal]   her
                mark   Eve ✕ Brombaugh   [Seal]
           Samuel Ulrey   [Seal]   mark
           (In German)   [C8]   George Brombaugh   [Seal]
    [C5] Daniel Brombaugh   [Seal]   [C4]   John Brombaugh   [Seal]
                                                        her
                                                 Elizabeth ✕ Brombaugh [Seal]
                                                        mark

Daniel², David², George² and John² Brombaugh and Samuel Ulrey (in German) receipt to [C2] Jacob² Brombaugh for $1629
    Franklin Co Pa 16 Mch 1807 James Maxwell "one of the Associate Judges for Franklin Co" certifies to the personal appearance and signatures of [C5] Daniel² Brombaugh and Elizabeth his wife, [C6] David² Brombaugh and Eve his wife, [C8] George Brombaugh, [C4] John² Brombaugh and Samuel Ulrey
    Bedford Co Pa 1 June 1807 John Moore, "one of the Associate Judges of the Court of Common Pleas for the said county" certifies to the personal appearance and signatures of [C3] Mary² Ulrey and Elizabeth Brombaugh the wife of [C4] John² Brombaugh
    (Recorded 13 Apr, 1808, Vol LI, p 499, Huntingdon, Pa)

    "Smoak Pipe" + a, lying in Washington Co, Md, and patented to [C1] Jacob¹ Broombaugh of Washington Co, 15 Nov, 1791.

    (I. C, No E, folio 816, Land Commissioner's Office, Annapolis)

    In Bedford Co, Pa, there is another deed recorded 1805 "Between Henry² Brumbaugh [C7] and Margaret his wife of Washington Co, Md, John² Brumbaugh [C4] and Samuel Ulery and Mary² [C3] his wife + + +

    Witnesseth that whereas Jacob¹ Brumbaugh [C1] (deed) late of Washington Co., Md, father of Henry, John and Mary," etc.

DEED HENRY DRINKER & WIFE TO MARY BROMBACH AND [C2] JACOB¹
BROMBACH

    THIS INDENTURE made the Sixth day of the Eighth Month called August in the Year of our LORD One Thousand Eight Hundred and three Between Henry Drinker of

the City of Philadelphia in the State of Pennsylvania merchant and Elizabeth his Wife of the one part and *Mary Brombach* Administratrix and *Jacob Brombach* Administrator of all and singular the Goods and Chattels Rights and Credits which were of *Jacob Brambach* the elder late of Washington County in the State of Maryland deceased of the other part WHEREAS the said Henry Drinker being seized in fee of and in the tract of land herein after described and hereby intended to be granted with the Appurtenances did in the month called August in the year 1797 contract to bargain sell and convey the same unto the said Jacob Brombach the elder in his lifetime for the price or Sum of Thirteen hundred and twenty six pounds fifteen shillings lawful Money of Pennsylvania of which said purchase Monies the said Jacob Brombach the elder did in his lifetime pay unto the said Henry Drinker the sum of Three hundred and thirty eight pounds nine shillings and one penny on account and afterwards to wit on the tenth day of April in the year 1799 he the said Jacob Brombach the elder died intestate And Whereas Administration of all and singular the Goods and Chattels Rights and Credits which were of the said Jacob Brombach the elder deceased hath since been duly granted and committed to his Widow the said Mary Brombach and his eldest Son the said Jacob Brombach parties hereto And Whereas the said Mary Brombach Administratrix and Jacob Brombach Administrator aforesaid have or one of them hath since well and truly paid unto the said Henry Drinker the Sum of Nine hundred and eighty eight pounds five shillings and eleven pence balance in full of the purchase Monies aforesaid Now this Indenture Witnesseth that the said Henry Drinker and Elizabeth his Wife for and in Consideration as well of the said Sum of Three hundred and thirty eight pounds nine shillings and one penny so paid by the said Jacob Brombach the elder as aforesaid as of the said further sum of Nine hundred and eighty eight pounds five shillings and eleven pence (balance in full of the said Sum or purchase Monies of Thirteen hundred and twenty-six pounds fifteen shillings) so as aforesaid paid by the said Mary Brombach Administratrix and Jacob Brombach Administrator as aforesaid the receipt whereof is hereby acknowledged and for and in full Execution and performance of the above recited Contract of Bargain and Sale so as aforesaid made by and between the said Henry Drinker and the said Jacob Brombach the elder have and by these presents do grant bargain and sell alien enfeoff release and confirm unto the said Mary Brombach Administratrix and Jacob Brombach Administrator aforesaid and to their Heirs and Assigns All that the aforesaid Tract of Land agreed to be sold by the said Henry Drinker to the said John Brombach the elder as aforesaid Situate near the foot of Dunning's Mountain on the head draughts of Yellow Creek formerly in the County of Cumberland but now in the County of Bedford in the State of Pennsylvania called *"Dorfans Barn'* * * * Containing Four hundred and seventy five Acres and one hundred and four perches and allowances of Six pCent for Roads &c [Being the same Tract of land which Thomas Penn and Richard Penn Esquires proprietaries of pennsylvania by Letters patent bearing date the twenty seventh day of May 1767 inrolled in patent Book AA vol 8 page 330 granted and confirmed unto Samuel Wallis in fee Who with Lydia his Wife by deed thereon endorsed bearing date the fourth day of September 1762 granted the same unto Abel James and the said Henry Drinker in fee as tenants in common And the said Abel James and Rebecca his Wife and Henry Drinker and Elizabeth his Wife afterwards by their deed bearing date the thirty first day of December 1787 regranted the same unto the said Samuel Wallis in fee And the said Samuel Wallis and Lydia his wife afterwards by Indenture bearing date the Eighth day of June 1797 recorded in the Office for recording of deeds in Bedford County in Book E page 207 &c granted the same with other Lands unto the said Henry Drinker in fee and which said Tract hereby granted was afterwards by the Commissioners of Bedford County sold and conveyed to Martin Pfeiffer of the Town of Bedford Who by his deed bearing date the twentieth day of November 1799 recorded in the Office for recording of deeds in Bedford County aforesaid in Book F page 381 granted and released the same unto the said Henry Drinker in fee] Together also * * * Hereditaments & premises hereby granted with the Appurtenances unto the said Mary Brombach Administratrix and Jacob Brumbach Administrator as aforesaid their Heirs and Assigns * * * Use Benefit and Behoof of all the every the Children of the said Jacob Brombach the elder deceased and their several and respective Heirs and Assigns for Ever to be equally divided between them share and share alike as tenants in common according to the laws of the Commonwealth of Pennsylvania regulating the descent of Intestates Real Estates in force at the time of the death of the said Jacob Brombach the elder deceased Subject nevertheless to the right of dower of the said Mary the Widow of the said Jacob Brombach the elder deceased of and in the same for and during the term of her natural life and to and for no other Use Trust Intent or purpose whatsoever * * *

I do hereby acknowledge to have received from the above named Jacob Brombach the

elder in his lifetime the Sum of Three hundred and thirty eight pounds nine shillings and one penny and from his Administrators above named or one of them the further Sum of Nine hundred and eighty eight pounds five shillings and eleven pence in full of the Consideration Monies above mentioned

Witnesses to the signing   Henry Drinker
    Paul S Brown

                                             Henry Drinker   [Seal]
                                             Elizath Drinker   [Seal]
Sealed and Delivered
In the Presence of Us
    William Downing
    Paul S Brown
    The tenth day of August Anno Domini 1803 Before me the Subscriber one of the Judges of the Court Common Pleas for the City & County of Philadelphia personally came and appeared the within named Henry Drinker and Elizabeth his Wife and acknowledged the within written Indenture to be their Act and deed and desired the same may be recorded as Such The said Elizabeth thereunto voluntarily consenting she being of full age and separately and apart from her said Husband by me therein privately examined and the Contents thereof first made known unto her   Witness my Hand and Seal the day & year abovesaid
                                                     Geo. Inskeep [Seal]
Bedford County Ss
    Recorded in the office for recording of Deeds in and for said County in Book F page 348 the 21st day of October Anno Domini 1803 Witness my hand & seal of office the same Day and year
[Seal]   JACOB BONNETT Recr
    Recording &c $1-50

Mary Brumbaugh, widow and relict of Jacob[1] Brumbaugh [C1] decd, 18 June, 1803, releases her dower right in all property and is to be paid an annual payment of £35 by Jacob[2] Brumbaugh [C2], Samuel Ulry, John[2] Brumbaugh [C4], Daniel[2] Brumbaugh [C5], Henry[2] Brumbaugh [C7], David[2] Brumbaugh [C6], and George[2] Brumbaugh [C8]

                                Mary X Brumbaugh   [Seal]

Before 2 Justices of Peace
        A Ott
        Robert Douglass
    (Book P, p 122, Hagerstown, Md)

COMMISSION ON DIVISION OF ESTATE OF JACOB[1] BRUMBAUGH [C1] MARCH 23, 1804—DEATH 10 APRIL, 1799

"3d Mon in Feb 1804 Jacob[2] Brumbaugh [C2] presents petition stating that Jacob[1] Brumbaugh [C1], father, late of Washington Co, Md, died intestate 10 Apr 1799, left 7 children 6 above age of 21 and the other George[2] [C8] *under age* and widow Mary—6 are Jacob[2] [C2], Mary[2] [C3], the wife of Samuel Ulry; John[2] Brumbach [C4]; Daniel[2] Brumbach [C5], Henry[2] Brumbach [C7], and David[2] [C6]

The said Jacob[1] Brumbaugh [C1] left a Considerable Real Estate in the said County, consisting of a tract or part of tract of land called "*The Resurvey on Clelands Contrivance*" containing about 370 a, and also a part of a Tract

of land called *"Timber Bottom"* containing about 12 a and also a part of Tract of land called *"The Chance"* containing about Twelve acres + +

Petition for Commission to 5 discreet, sensible men to adjudge and determine whether the Estate of the said [C1] Jacob[1] Brumbaugh would admit of being divided without injury and loss to all the parties entitled, and to ascertain the value of such Estate in current money according to law.

Commission appointed by Wm Clagett, Esq Chief Justice of Co. Court 2 Mch 1804—issued 23 Mch 1804

Walter Boyd	4 days at 15/	£	3	0	0
John Schnebly	2 "		1	10	0
Jacob Zeller	2 "		1	10	0
Lodowick Young	2 "		1	10	0
Geo. Cellars	2 "		1	10	0
		£	9	0	0

Surveyors a/c 30/ per Day 4 days at 30 £6-0-0 Jacob[2] Brumbaugh [C2] claims to be allowed for giving notice for Commission to Saml Ulrey and Mary his wife and John[2] Brumbaugh [C4] representatives of Jacob[1] [C1] Deceased who live in Bedford Co Pa at distance 70 miles from the inheritance 4 days at 15/ per day £3-0-0 Saml Hughes atty-at-law for filing petition, advice, etc $30. £11-5-0 £29-5-0

(Washington Co, Md., records at Hagerstown, p 819)

ORDER FOR SALE OF REAL ESTATE OF JACOB[1] BRUMBAUGH [C1], AUGUST, 1806*

On application of Jacob Brumbaugh [C2] by his attorney Wm Reynolds Esq for the sale of the Real Estate of Jacob Brumbaugh [C1] late of the County of Washington in the State of Maryland, deceased, Rule that all the heirs of Jacob[1] Brumbaugh [C1] deceased shew cause at the next Orphans Court to be held at Bedford on the first Monday of August next why the Estate of said deceased should not be sold

Jacob[2] Brumbaugh [C2] who being duly affirmed saith that he served the within Rule of Court on John[2] Brumbaugh [C4], Mary[2] [C3], intermarried with Samuel Ulry, Daniel[2] [C5], Henry[2] [C7], David[2] [C6], and George[2] Brumbaugh [C8]. Affirmed in open court August 4th 1806

The Bedford Co. records also contain a deed in 1807 signed by [C2]

*(Copied from Co. Records at Bedford, Pa, by Mr. Elias Gibson)

Jacob² Brumbaugh and Catharine, [C5] Daniel² and Elizabeth, [C6] David² and Eve, and [C8] George² of Washington Co , Md , and [C4] John² Brumbaugh of Bedford Co , Pa , to Samuel Ulry (who *m* [C3] Mary² Brumbaugh) It will be noticed that [C7] Henry² and the wives of [C4] John² and [C8] George², all heirs of [C1] Jacob¹, have not signed this deed, although all were then living

   Children (7) .
[C2] + Jacob², *b* 1765, *d* 1816.
[C3] + Mary², *b* 1767.
[C4] + John², *b* 1768; *d* May 20, 1829
[C5] + Daniel S ², *b* March, 1772
[C6] + David², *b* March 17, 1776, *d* April 23, 1842.
[C7] + Henry², *b* March, 1777.
[C8] + George², *b* Sept. 9, 1783, *d* May 29, 1840

   [C2] JACOB² BRUMBAUGH (Johann Jacob¹) *b* 1765, *d* 1816, *m* *Catharine Rentch*, lived in a small stone house, and was buried on his homestead, 1 mile N. of his father's farm. He was member Pres Ch , and Admr. of [C1] Jacob's estate, and also became very extensively interested in real estate, as will be seen from the following partial list of transactions.
   Warrant to *Jacob²* [C2] and *Daniel² Brumbaugh* [C5] of the state of Maryland dated April 25, 1785 ' Patent to same Feby 5, 1805 for 407 acres of land in Huntingdon County   Patent Book, P. Vol. 55, page 269
   (Harrisburg, Pa , State records.)
   "*Save All*" 3¾ a, lying in Washington Co , Md , and patented to [C2] Jacob² Brumbaugh, Jr., of Washington Co., 20 Nov., 1802.[b]
   Thos Bolt of Washington Co., Md , 24 Nov, 1804, deeds to Jacob² Brumbaugh [C2] of same for £50. "*Long Meadow enlarged*" 4½ a.[c]
   Henry Schnebly of Washington Co , Md , 8 May, 1805, deeds to [C2] Jacob² Brumbaugh for $140. "*Garden of Eden,*" 5½ a [d]
   [C4] John² Brumbaugh and Saml Ulry and Mary² Ulry, wife late [C3] Mary² Brumbaugh of Bedford Co , Pa., and [C7] Henry² Brumbaugh of Washington Co , Md , on 30 April, 1805, deed to [C2] Jacob² who agrees to take the various lands of [C1] Jacob¹ deceased at the Commission's appraisal of £4,100, and to pay over proportionate amounts. [C4] John² Brumbaugh,

*Warrant to [C1] Jacob¹—patent—[C2] Jacob²—see [C8], p. 172
[b]I. C No S, Folio 9, Land Commissioner's Office, Annapolis
[c]Book R, p 113, Hagerstown, Md
[d]Book P, p 418, Hagerstown, Md

Saml. Ulry and [C3] Mary² received £500, paid by [C7] Henry²—they assign to [C7] Henry²

[C6] David² Brumbaugh and [C8] George² Brumbaugh of Washington Co, Md, receipt for £1200 by [C7] Henry² Brumbaugh ª

Lodwick Camerer of Westmoreland Co, Pa, deeds to David² Brumbaugh [C6] of Washington Co, Md, 17 Nov., 1805, for £500, 122½ a, "*Beech Spring*" and part of Resurvey "*Plunks Doubt*" part of "*Garden of Eden* "ᵇ

Jacob² Brumbaugh [C2] and wife Catharine of Washington Co, Md, deed to Thos. Sprigg, 15 March, 1806, for $800, 3 parts of "*Resurvey on Clelland's Contrivance*" patented to Jacob¹ Brumbaugh [C1] the elder deceased, beginning at "*Sprigg's Paradise*," 13½ a, also "*Tegerden's Delight*," 9¼ a.ᶜ

Jacob² Brumbaugh [C2] and Catharine his wife deed to Henry² Brumbaugh [C7] all of Washington Co., Md, 23 Oct, 1806, for $1,000 Resurvey on "*Clelland's Contrivance*" beginning at "*Garden of Eden*" also Resurvey on "*Long Meadow Enlarged* "ᵈ

Nov. 13, 1814, *Daniel Schnebly* was appointed Administrator of [C2] Jacob² Brumbaugh and in 1817 made distribution of his personal estate amongst his widow and children as given below.ᵉ

Children (5) of [C2] Jacob² Brumbaugh:

[C 9] + Joseph³, b Nov 16, 1783, m *Elizabeth Angle*
[C10] + John³, m *Elizabeth Cokenour*
[C11] + Jacob³
[C12] + Margaret³, m *David Angle*
[C13] + David³, m *Susanna Emrich*

[C3] MARY² BRUMBAUGH (Johann Jacob¹) b 1767 in Md ; m Elder *Samuel Ulery* ("*Ulerick*"), who was apparently the first minister of the German Baptist Brethren Church in Woodbury Twp., Bedford Co, Pa, and probably the first in that county He settled in Woodbury Twp (now Middle Woodbury) where the Brethren Church stands at New Enterprise, Pa, soon after 1780, coming with [C4] *John² Brumbaugh*. For many years he was a noted speaker and the Elder in charge of the Woodbury Church Samuel died at New Enterprise in 1822, and both himself and wife Mary² were there buried

ªBook P, p 481-486, Hagerstown, Md
ᵇBook S, p. 160, Hagerstown, Md
ᶜBook S, p 165, Hagerstown, Md.
ᵈBook S, p 433, Hagerstown, Md.
ᵉFrom data furnished by Jacob Brown [C56], Cumberland, Md—recorded at Hagerstown, Md, and other sources

[C18-vi] Barbara[5] Snoeberger writes that Mary or "Maria went for their cows one evening and became lost in the woods The wolves came near her and she had to climb a tree. The family blew horns which she could hear, but, as she could not make them hear her calls and did not dare to get down from the tree, she was compelled to stay there all night. The wolves left in the morning, and she found she was in sight of her home where she had left a nursing baby "

The name Ulery is variously spelled Eve Brumbaugh Snoeberger said: "Samuel Ulerich was the first minister of the Brethren in this place "

The Woodbury Twp., Bedford Co, Pa.,[a] assessments for 1789 show

	Acres	Horses.	Cows.	State Tax		Co Tax	
				s	d	s	d
Samuel Ulerick	200	2	2	6	6	3	3
David Ulerick	148	3	4	14	3	7	2
Daniel Ulerick	150	2	3	15	9	7	11
Stephen Ulerick	148	3	5	11	10	5	11

John Ulerick single freeman assessed £1 2s 6d state tax and 11s 2d Co tax—for some reason the highest "single freeman" assessment in the county— the other such assessments being about 10s and 5s for State and Co. taxes.

"Samuel Ullery was grantee of Commonwealth of Penna to a large tract of land in the south end of Morrison's Cove, New Enterprise, now forming part of the said grant, and his patent of 1786 was signed by Benj Franklin "[b]

A number of deeds are also noted under [C1], [C2], [C7] and [C8] in which Samuel Ulery and wife appear

Heads of Families First Census of the United States. 1790—Penna.— Bedford Co—p 21 enumerates "Samuel Ulery" as having one free white male under 16 years, and five free white females, including heads of families (his wife). It also enumerates "David Ulery" as having five sons under 16 years, his wife and a daughter (The Md Census of 1790, p. 66, enumerates "Henry Uhlry" and "Michael Uhlry" of Frederick Co)

John Ulrick[c] was the owner of the Neff mill at Roaring Spring, Blair Co., Pa , and sold it to George B Spang in 1822 Christena, w of John Ulrick, d July 1, 1817, as shown by the tombstone inscription. John seems to have been a brother of Samuel Ulrick who m [C3] Mary[2] Brumbaugh.

"Daniel Olery" Dec. 1, 1795, deeds 309 a, called "Hopkinses Traverses,"

---

[a]See page 53.
[b]P. S. Brown, Esq , Kansas City, Mo.
[c]Reported by [C76] David Stuckey[4] Brumbaugh, Roaring Springs, Pa , who says the name was later changed to Ulery

to "John Broombaugh." (See p. 163.) Both signatures to this deed were probably misread, being in German

MONTGOMERY, VIRGINIA.

January 17, 1798, "Thomas Proctor of the City of Philadelphia in the State of Pennsylvania, Esquire," deeded to "Mary Broomburgh of Washington County, Maryland," one certain Lot or piece of ground in the Town of Montgomery in the State of Virginia Marked in a General Plan of the said Town No. 1334 situate on the South side of Washington Street in the said Town" This deed was acknowledged before Thomas Smith, Esq, one of the Associate Judges of the Supreme Court of Pennsylvania, February 3, 1798, and witnessed by Sarah A Chailton and Daniel Grant.

The Library of Congress, and the Virginia State Library at Richmond, Va, are unable to afford any information as to the location or history of the "Montgomery, Virginia." The town was platted of considerable size to contain at least 1334 lots. The deed was evidently intended for [C3] Mary[2] Brumbaugh, born in 1767, and lived in Washington Co, Md., until her marriage to Samuel Ullery, a minister of the German Baptist Church, and one of the first ministers of that denomination in Bedford Co, Pa. German names were very often mis-spelled in legal documents through misinterpretation of speech or writing

DEED FOR "DORPHAN'S BARN" TRACT, 1807.*

[C3] Mary Ulry, late Mary[2] Brumbaugh and Samuel her husband, [C4] John[2] Brumbaugh, [C8] George[2], [C6] David[2] of Bedford Co, Pa, and [C2] Jacob[2] and [C5] Daniel[3] of Washington Co, Md, acknowledge receipt of $4,990 50 from [C8] George[2] and [C6] David[2] Brumbaugh and convey their interest in *"Dorphan's Barn"* on the headwaters of Yellow Creek, Woodbury Twp., being part of [C1] *Jacob[1] Brumbaugh's* tracts, and containing 550½ acres.

Executed March 16, 1807, in Franklin Co, Pa, by Samuel Ulry, John Brumbaugh, Daniel and Elizabeth Brumbaugh. Jacob and Cathrine Brumbaugh, and on May 28, 1807, in Bedford Co, Pa, by Mary Ulry and Elizabeth, wife of John Brumbaugh

[C2] Jacob[2] Brumbaugh and Cathiena, [C5] Daniel[2] Brumbaugh and Elizabeth, [C6] David[2] Brumbaugh and Eve, and [C8] George[2] Brumbaugh,

---
*Recorded in Book G, p. 461, Bedford Co, Pa

all of Washington Co , Md , and [C4] John[2] Brumbaugh of Bedford Co , Pa.,
in 1807 for $1,333 49, "money of Pennsylvania," convey to *Samuel Ulry* of
Bedford Co , Pa., a tract of the late [C1] *Jacob[1] Brumbaugh*, deceased, late
of Md., situate on the waters of Three Springs in Woodbury Twp , Bedford
Co , Pa , half of tract land by Jacob Brumbaugh and Samuel Ulry and tract on
Waters of Yellow Creek and west side of Tussey's Mountain—231¾ acres.[a]

[C7] Henry[2] Brumbaugh of Washington Co , Md., "farmer," quit claims
to [C4] John[2] Brumbaugh and Samuel Ulry of Bedford Co , Pa., his interest
in 225 acres known as *"Rich Barrens,"* west of *"Hickory Bottom."* Sealed in
presence of George Brumbaugh.[b]

> *Children* (4), *surname Ulery* (*"Ulerick"*) :
> i Mary[3] , *m David Studebaker, s Jacob Studebaker;*[c] the former was a
>   minister of G B B Ch , and lived in Ohio.
>   *Children* (7), *surname Studebaker:*
>   (1) Jacob[4]; (2) John W[4]; (3) Catharine[4], (4) Elizabeth[4]; (5)
>   Sarah[4], (6) Abraham[4]; (7) David[4]
> ii Elizabeth[3]; *m Jacob Brown*, farmer, member G B B Ch.; they moved
>   to a farm near Libertyville, Jefferson Co , Iowa, where both died.
>   "Grandfather and all his family, except ours, moved to Jeffer-
>   son Co , Iowa, about 1846, and his descendants from there scattered
>   throughout the far West. I could not trace them "—P. S. Brown,[d]
>   Kansas City, Mo
>   *Children* (9), *surname Brown:*
>   (1) Hannah[4], *b* Jan 10, 1807, at New Enterprise, Bedford Co ,
>   Pa ; 1824 *m* Elder *Leonard Furry*, *b* July 15, 1806, at Eliz-
>   abethtown, Lancaster Co , Pa.—his grandfather ("Fohrer")
>   is said to have emigrated from Switzerland—originally a
>   Lutheran, he united with his wife's church, G. B. B   He was
>   elected Elder of Clover Creek Congregation and in his zealous

---

[a]Book G, p 159, Bedford Co , Pa
[b]Same reference, p 163.
[c]According to [C18] Eve[1] (Brumbaugh) Snoeberger   Eld. Jacob Gump, Churubusco,
Ind., and Emma A (Miller) Replogle, Huntingdon, Pa, also furnished considerable infor-
mation concerning these families
   The children (9) of Jacob Studebaker [w, a dau of Jacob Snider (Snyder), buried in
Studebaker cem in Miami Co , O] were John, who *m* [C3-iv] Hannah Ulery, David, who *m*
[C3-i] Mary Ulery , Jacob, who *m* Catharine Puterbaugh, Abraham, *b* May 1, 1790 *d* June
6, 1854, *m* Elizabeth Steele, Samuel, Margaret, *m* Jeremiah (or Daniel) Gump, Hannah, *m*
David Puterbaugh, Mary, *m* George Harshberger, Sarah, *m* David Rench, and Barbara, *m*
—— Ritchey
   [d]Persons interested in these lines should communicate with him and assist in completing
the data he has gathered

ministerial duties traveled extensively as far as Kans—attended all annual meetings, served once on its Standing Committee, contributed extensively to the *Gospel Visitor* He *d* Dec. 8, 1877, and Hannah *d* April 11, 1883, both bur at New Enterprise, Bedford Co, Pa

Children (8), *surname Furry*

(a) Susan[5], *b* Jan 3, 1826, *d* Oct 30, 1837

(b) Jacob Brown[5], *b* Nov 20, 1827, *d* Dec 15, 1905, deacon G. B. B; *m Elizabeth Burger*

(c) John Brown[5], *b* May 24, 1829; *d* Dec 18, 1863, *m Elizabeth Snowberger*, lived at New Paris, Bedford Co, Pa

(d) Magdaline[5], *b* Aug. 25, 1831, *m* [C97] *Jacob Snyder*[4] *Brumbaugh* as his 1st w, she *d* April 5, 1850

(e) Elizabeth[5], *b* Jan 14, 1834, *m* (1) *Levi Holsinger*, and *m* (2) *Elias Davis* Elizabeth[5] *d* July 27, 1860, they lived at New Paris, Bedford Co, Pa

(f) Samuel Brown[5], *b* Feb 17, 1836, Jan. 1, 1861, *m Mary Ann Shelley*, *b* Jan 25, 1842; dau *John* and *Frances* (*Byers*) *Shelley*, he is Elder in Brethren Ch, and res at Martinsburg, Pa. He furnished the data for the Furry family, (9 ch), of whom Rev. John Edward, *b* Feb. 21, 1862, is minister of Brethren Ch. (G B B)

(g) Catharine[5], *b* 1838; *m Samuel M. Burger;* s *Samuel* and *Elizabeth* (*Moon*) *Burger*, and sister of *Elizabeth Burger*, who *m Jacob Furry*. There were 9 ch, of whom Hannah Amanda[6] Burger, *b* Sept 3, 1861; *m* [C366] *Cyrus Edward*[5] *Brumbaugh*

(h) Sarah Ann[5], *b* June 27, 1843, *d* Oct. 12, 1848

(2) Samuel Ulery[4] Brown, *m Fannie Hoover.*

(3) Jacob Ulery[4] Brown, *m Annie Hoover*

(4) John Ulery[4] Brown, *m Delilah Miller.*

(5) Elizabeth[4] Brown, *m John Burger.*

(6) Sarah[4] Brown, *m George Replogle.*

(7) Mary[4] Brown, *d y.*

(8) Henry[4] Brown; *m* —— *Shelly*

(9) George[4] Brown, *m Catharine Fishel*

iii Catharine[3] Ulery, *m John Snider*,* *b* 1770. "John Snider" was as-

*Record from Bible furnished by [C3-iii-2-(a)] Mary[5] Snider Ober, Roaring Spring, Pa

sessed in Woodbury Twp , Bedford Co , Pa , in 1789 for 950 a, 3 h, 8 c, and a State tax of £1 19s 10d, also a Co tax of 19s 11d   He was a farmer, member G B B Ch , d 1855, and was buried in Snake Spring Twp , Bedford Co , Pa.

   Children (4), *surname Snider*

(1) John⁴ , lived Snake Spring Twp , Bedford Co , Pa   Ch Samuel⁵, Isaac⁵, Caroline⁵, Maria⁵, Malachia⁵, Charles⁵, Mary⁵

(2) Jacob Ulery⁴ Snider, *b* Jan 3, 1812, in Snake Spring Twp , Bedford Co , Pa . a farmer, member G B B Ch . *m* (1) *Catharine* (*Elizabeth* ?) *Baker*, dau *John Baker; d* 1843, *m* (2) *Lovina Gruber*, *b* Oct 30, 1818, in Blair Co , Pa , dau *Nicholas* and —— (*Daniels*) *Gruber.* Lovina *d* Sept. 6, 1900 (81-10-6), and was buried at New Enterprise, Bedford Co , Pa   Jacob⁴ *d* July 22, 1896 (84-6-19), in South Woodbury Twp , Bedford Co , Pa.

       Children by 1st m (2), *surname Snider* *

       (a) Mary⁵, *b* Jan 18, 1842, *m William Smith Ober, b* 1843, s *Joseph* and *Anna* (*Smith*) *Ober*, address Roaring Spring, Pa. (Ch 3)

       (b) Catharine⁵, *b* Sept. 28, 1843, *m Samuel Teeter*
            Children by 2d m (7), *surname Snider*

       (c) John Gruber⁵, *b* Sept. 29, 1844, *m* [C78]+ *Evaline Dorothy⁴ Brumbaugh*, b Dec 6, 1846, (7 ch)

       (d) Susanna⁵, *b* Feb 10, 1847, *d* Nov 1, 1867

       (e) Elizabeth⁵, *b* Aug 6, 1849

       (f) Rebecca⁵, *b* April 20, 1852, *d* Aug 19, 1892, *m* —— *Furry*

       (g) Jacob Gruber⁵, *b* July 28, 1854

       (h) Lovina⁵, *b* March 5, 1857

       (i) David Gruber⁵, *b* April 29, 1860

   (3) Elvina⁴ Snider; *m Samuel Furry*

   (4) David⁴ Snyder

   (5) Margaret Snyder; *m Jacob Kaufman*

   (6) Maria Snyder; *m Henry Walter.*

   (7) Samuel Snyder

  iv Hannah³ Ulery; *m John Studebaker*, bro. of *David*, who *m Mary Ulery*

---

* "All the information I could get was very limited   John Snider, whose wife was Ulery and was the only member of the Ulery family I learned to know, was son of Jacob Snider. My father was a son of Joseph Snider and no intermarriages in our family with the Ulery family " "I have passed the 88th year of my life "—Simon Snyder, April 25, 1910

[C3-1]; farmer, member G B. B Ch, lived on the Jackson Stuckey farm in Morrison's Cove—John was *b* in Snake Spring Valley, Bedford Co, Pa —and they moved to Southern O in 1816   Hannah *d* Oct., 1862, and was bur at Eaton, Delaware Co, Ind

Children (14 at least), surname Studebaker·

(1) Samuel⁴, *b* about 1808
(2) Jacob, *b* about 1811, *d* 1880, *m. Catharine Dietrich*
(3) John⁴, *b* 1812; *m Nancy Rudy* ª
(4) David⁴, *d* July, 1863, *m Martha Leavel*
(5) George W, *b* March 2, 1818, *d* July 22, 1905, at Fredonia, Wilson Co, Kans
(6) Daniel, *b* 1819, *m Elizabeth Jacobs*
(7) Stephen, *m Susan Dietrich*
(8) Isaac, *d* age 9
(9) Mary, *m Eli Gump.*
(10) Elizabeth, *m J. O. Nodle.*
(11) Margaret, *m Henry Bosler*
(12) Catharine, *m Conrad Warner.*
(13) Hannah, *m John Hamel*
(14) Lydia, *m James Wirt.*

[C4] JOHN² BRUMBAUGH (Johann Jacob¹) *b* 1768; lived near New Enterprise, Bedford Co, Pa., settling in Morrison's Cove on the headwaters of Yellow Creek soon after 1789, farmer, and minister in G B B. Ch.; *m Mary Elizabeth Miller.*ᵇ John² *d* May 20, 1829, Elizabeth *d* May 5, 1834, both aged 62 years.

John² Brumbaugh [C4] of Washington Co., Md, deeds to David Dunweddie, both of same place, on April 1, 1789, for £288, *Resurvey on Clelands Contrivance* and part of *Mary's Garden,* 53½ a, (John Brumbaugh and Jacob Brumbaugh lands adjoin), and part of *Timber Bottom,* 18 a, 67 P.

"Johannes² Brumbach"   [Seal]

Elizabeth his wife releases dower right, before H. Shryok and Alex. Clagett, Justices of Peace of Washington Co

(Book F, p 356, Hagerstown, Md)

ª Mrs Fannie⁵ (Studebaker) Quinter, *b* 1837, wid Eld James Quinter), Huntingdon, Pa, dau, has materially assisted with facts, as has also Eld Jacob Gump, Churubusco, Ind
ᵇ Sister to Martin Miller of Morrison's Cove, according to [C69] David Stuckey⁴ Brumbaugh
Note.—After above is in type it is found generation numbers have been omitted in (2), (5), etc

"*Mary's Garden* 5 a, lying in Washington Co , Md , and patented to John Broombaugh [C4] of —— Co , 15 Nov , 1790

(I C , No E, folio 570, Land Commissioner's Office, Annapolis.)

Conrod Bromboch and John Martin of Woodbury Twp , Bedford Co , Pa., in 1791 convey a tract of land to John Bromboch [C4] yeoman of Washington Co , Md.

(Book C, p 537, Bedford Co , Pa)

Conrod Bromboch in 1791, Book C, p. 537, deeds a tract, and Conrod Bromboch and John Martin in 1791, Book C, p 539, deed another tract to Henry Engle.

Henry Schnebly and Elizabeth his wife of Washington Co , Md , on 28 Jan., 1791, for £28 deeds to John Brumbaugh [C4] of Franklin Co , Pa , 8 a, situate in Franklin Co , Pa , and 13 a in Washington Co , Md —a *Resurvey* on *Plunks Doubt*, 106 a, showing a lack of 13 a   (Book G, p 308, Hagerstown, Md.)

John[2] Brumbaugh [C4] and Mary Elisabeth, wife, of Franklin Co , Pa , 13 April, 1801, deed to Jacob Speigler of same for $2,665 65 *Resurvey* on *Plunks Doubt* granted by patent Lord Baltimore to Henry Schnobly then in Frederick Co , Md , and now in Franklin Co., Pa , and partly in Washington Co., Md , 18¼ a, exclusive of allowances.

Witnesses	Johannes Brumbach	[Seal]
Wm Lee	Mary Elizabeth ✕ Brumbach	[Seal]
A Olt.		

(At one point in this deed there is an erroneous reference to "the said *Jacob* Brumbach.)

(Book O, p 71, Hagerstown, Md)

"Daniel Olery" of Woodberry Township, Bedford Co , Pa , yeoman, on 1 December, 1795, deeds to "John Broombaugh," yeoman, of the same township, a tract of 309 acres called "*Hopkinses Traverses*," in Frankstown Township, Morrison's Cove—part of tract belonging to Daniel Olery, deceased—corner of Abraham Teter and John Olery, executors of John Teter

(*Book D, p 613, Bedford Co , Pa , records*)

John Broombaugh and Mary, his wife, of Woodberry Twp , Bedford Co , Pa., yeoman, on 16 April, 1796, deed to Jacob Shineberger, yeoman, of the same township and county, a tract in Morrison's Cove called "*Hopkinses Traverses*," containing 309 acres   "The late Proprietors of the province of pennsylvania by their Patent dated 12 April, 1770, Recorded in Rolls office Patent Book AA, Vol II, page 272, dated 14 April, 1770, confirmed to Samuel Wallace of Philadelphia—Gentn a tract in Morrison's Cove" etc.   Samuel Wallace and Lydia his wife convey ——.   Thomas Mifflin, Governor, by Patent

of 4 June, 1793, enrolled in Patent Book 19, p 339, on 5 June, 1793, confirms
to "Daniel Olery" a tract called "*Greenfield*," adjoining this tract "*Hopkinses
Traverse*"—part of estate Daniel Olery, dec —being son to Daniel Olery, dec
   (*Recorded in Book D, p. 529, Bedford Co records*)

Doctor Henry Schnebly of Washington Co , Md , on 18 April, 1801, for
£8 deeds to John Brumbach [C4] of Washington Co., Md , *Garden of Eden,*
patented to Henry Schnebly.
   (Book O, p 11, Hagerstown, Md)

John Brumbach [C4] of Franklin Co , Pa , on 20 April, 1801, deeds to
Robt. McKee of Washington Co , Md , *Resurvey on Claylands Contrivance* and
Marys Garden "contiguous" 53⅞ a and *Timber Bottam*—by deed 14 Sept ,
1780, David Dunwiddie 4 a 7 P —— for £221 17s 3d.
   (Book N, p. 447, Hagerstown, Md)

[C7] Henry[2] Brumbaugh of Washington Co , Md , in the presence of
[C8] George[2] Brumbaugh, in 1807 deeds certain lands to [C4] John[2] Brumbaugh and Samuel Ulry ' (See [C3].)

[C4] John[2] Brumbaugh of Township of Woodberry, Bedford Co , Pa , for
$83 50 releases his interest in *one fourth of one seventh part of the tract ad-
joining Canoe Mountain* on the N W etc —heir of the late [C1] Jacob[1]
Brumbaugh, Senr , of Washington Co , Md

Executed in Bedford Co , Pa , 25 August, 1825, before James Shirley, J P

HEIRS OF [C4] JOHN[2] BRUMBAUGH CONVEY THEIR INTEREST
IN 103 ACRES TO CHRISTIAN KOCHENDAFER—
APRIL 2, 1832.[c]

[C14] Daniel[3] Brumbaugh and Elizabeth, [C16] David[3] and Mary, [C17]
Jacob[3] and Susannah, David Snowberger and [C18] Eve[3]. his wife, of Woodberry Twp , Bedford Co , Pa , acknowledge receipt of $978 50, paid by Chris-
tian Kochendafer, and convey their interest in 103 acres adjoining David
Snowberger on S and E, Daniel Brumbaugh on W , David Brumbaugh on N —
being part of a larger tract struck off by [C4] John[2] Brumbaugh in his lifetime for Christian Kochendafer and Eve, his wife.
   Children (5).
[C14] + Daniel[3], b 1791 ?; d Aug 11, 1885.

ᵃRecorded in Book G, p. 463, Bedford Co , Pa —search made by Mr. Elias Gibson,
Bedford, Pa
  ᵇRecorded in Book VI, p 140, Huntingdon Co , Pa
  ᶜRecorded Book R, p 129, Bedford Co., Pa. Page 130 gives another deed from the same
parties, and the names "Rinchart Replogel" and "Rinehart Rippleogel" also appear therein

[C15] + Mary³, b Oct , ——, d July 27, 1882.

[C16] + David³, b Sept 5, 1797, d Nov. 15, 1874.

[C17] + Jacob S—³, b March 14, 1800, d Nov. 25, 1865

[C18] + Eve³, b July 12,* 1806; d Sept. 15, 1893.

[C5] DANIEL S ² BRUMBAUGH (Johann Jacob¹ b 1772 in Frederick Co , Md (now Washington Co), farmer; m Elizabeth Long, b Jan , 1779 Daniel² d Aug 24, 1824, and rests in the cemetery of the Salem Ref. Ch. in Washington Co , Md , together with the remains of Elizabeth, who d Feb. 6, 1861.

"Albania" and "Rich Barrens" patented from the Commonwealth of Penna. Nov. 17, 1788, and May 30, 1805, to [C1] Jacob¹ Broombaugh deceased and father of [C5] Daniel² Brumbaugh, deceased, and 15½ acres of above land was allotted by Writ of Partition Nov Term Nov. 4 to said [C5] Daniel² Brumbaugh, deceased, and at Aug. Term, 1830, [C8] George² Brumbaugh was assignee of [C21] Daniel³ Brumbaugh, eldest son of said [C5] Daniel² Brumbaugh, and together with the children and legal representatives of said [C5] Daniel² Brumbaugh, deceased (who died intestate)—partition and [C8] George² Brumbaugh of Washington Co , Md , assignee of eldest son of said deceased, etc [b]

John Brumbaugh deeded lands (335¾ acres) to above named [C5] Daniel² Brumbaugh.

[C8] George² Brumbaugh and Louisa, w, by deed of March 29, 1836, convey the above tracts to Samuel Haffley—Davis Gibboney and w Mary.[c]

TOMBSTONE INSCRIPTIONS, CONOCOCHEAGUE DISTRICT, MD.

"Salem German Reformed Church in Conococheague Dist. is located 4 mi. S.E of Cearfoss P O. It is a stone building of moderate dimensions and in the church yard are buried the following persons :[d]

[C5] Daniel S Brumbaugh, d Aug 24, 1824, aged 52 yrs , and his w Elisabeth, d Dec 12, 1860, aged 81 yrs 11 mos

[C19] Susannah³ Brumbaugh, b May 28, 1799, d Feb 6, 1861.

Children (9)

[C19]   Susanna³, b May 28, 1799, d Feb. 6, 1861.

[C20] + Elizabeth³

According to Barbara [C18-vi] Snoeberger.
[b]Deed Book 94, p 332, Bedford, Pa
[c]Deed Book N, pp. 289-90, Bedford Co , Pa.
[d]History of Western Md—Scharf, Vol II, p. 1289.

[C21] + Daniel³, *b* Aug 6, 1803

[C22] + Louisa³, *b* Sept 3, 1808, *d* Nov. 6, 1886

[C23]   Maria³, *m John Bosteller;* both *d*, (descendants—no replies)

[C24] + Samuel David³, *b* June 11, 1813

[C25]   Thomas Jefferson³, *m Mary Reader* of Washington Co , Md.; accidentally drowned in Mo river, (3 ch).

[C26]   Isabella³, *d* y, *m William Bentz* of Funkstown, Md ; (1s—Clay⁴)

[C27]   Rosanna Caroline³

[C6] DAVID² BRUMBAUGH (Johann Jacob¹) *b* March 17, 1776; 1805 *m Eve Kissecker,*ᵃ *b* March 6, 1789, at or near Hagerstown, Md.; dau *Simon Kissecker, b* May 20, 1747, and *d* May 25, 1818.

He farmed in Washington Co., Md , where he owned some slaves—never sold one, and later liberated them One of the latter was Samuel Cole of Hagerstown, Md In 1827 the entire family moved from Md into Franklin Co , Pa., upon a farm in Antrim Twp He built a house at Middleburg, now called State Line, Pa —this house was later used as a public house, or hotel, which Eve largely conducted while David² directed the farming of his 300-acre tract S.W. of McConnelsburg About 100 acres of this were cleared and the balance consisted of heavily wooded land and contained several fine springs He was very fond of spending his summers on this mountain land, and it was a great treat for the grand-children to join him there Simeon³ farmed the old homestead farm in Washington Co , Md., during a portion of this time

David² Brumbaugh founded the town of Middleburg, now called State Line, Pa.

CONSTABLE'S BONDS.

[C6] David² Brumbaugh and Thomas Shuman of Washington Co , 19 July, 1803, bond to State of Md $250

(Book P, p 182, Hagerstown. Md)

[C6] David² Brumbaugh and [C8] George² Brumbaugh of Washington Co., Md., 4 Oct , 1804, bond to State of Md $250.

(Book P, p. 889, *ibid*)

[C9] Joseph³ Brumbaugh and [C8] George² Brumbaugh of Washington Co., Md (date omitted in transcribing), bond to Md $800.

[C9] Joseph³ Brumbaugh and [C8] George² Brumbaugh of Washington Co., Md , 20 July, 1809, bond to State of Md. $250.

(Book T, p 536, *ibid.*)

(Book W, p 173, *ibid.*)

ᵃName also spelled *Kiesecker* and *Kisecker.*

SUPERVISOR'S BOND

[C6] David² Brumbaugh and Tho Keller of Washington Co., Md., Nov 9, 1818, bond to State of Md. ——.

(Book DD, p 165, *ibid*)

The parents were members Luth. Ch , and all the children were baptized into that faith, but later united with different denominations. David² *d* April 23, 1842, and Eve *d* July 22, 1845—the remains of both rest in Rose Hill Cem , Hagerstown, Md

[C6] David² served as a private in the battle of Bladensburg, War of 1812.*

In Record Book AC, p 235, Bedford Co , Pa , we find that the heirs of [C6] David² Brumbaugh acknowledge the receipt of $4,935 10 and convey to [C28] Simon³ Brumbaugh[b] a tract of land under date of Oct 11, 1851 The signatures of the heirs are given in the order and manner of signature (excepting the identification numbers and the addition of the full middle names) ·

[C30]   Elias David³ Brumbaugh

[C31]   Nathan Henry³ Brumbaugh.

[C32]   Elizabeth L ³, intermarried with Wm Logan.

[C33]   Jacob Benjamin³ Brumbaugh

[C35]   Catharine Jane³ Brumbaugh, intermarried with Joseph Newman.

[C36]   Ann Maria³ Brumbaugh

[C37]   Judiana Dorothv³ Brumbaugh, intermarried with Henry Cook

[C13]   David Brumbaugh, guardian to [C39] George Washington³ Brumbaugh.

Received from [C28] Simon³ Brumbaugh, one of the heirs of the deceased —lands in Franklin Co , Pa.

Children[c] (12)

[C28] + Simeon K—³, *b* Sept 27, 1806, *d* July 14, 1892.

[C29]   George³, *b* Nov 12, 1808, *d* y.

[C30] + Elias David³, *b* April 22, 1811, *d* Sept 14, 1893

[C31] + Nathan Henry³, *b* May 24, 1813

[C32] + Elizabeth L ³, *b* Nov. 15, 1815

[C33] + Jacob Benjamin³, *b* June 23, 1818, *d* Feb. 4, 1903.

[C34]   Ann Maria³, *b* May 20, 1820, *d* y.

---

*According to [C69] David Stuckey⁴ Brumbaugh The official records have been searched, but the rolls do not seem to contain his name.—Adj. Gen

[b]Simeon³ often wrote his name "Simon," as in this deed, and oftener simply "S Brumbaugh "

[c]From [C6] David² Brumbaugh's Bible—record furnished by Mrs. Rebecca (Clopper) Brumbaugh, who preserves the volume.

[C35] + Catherine Jane³, b June 11, 1822
[C36]   Ann Maria³, b Dec 6, 1824   (See [C168])
[C37] + Indianna Dorothy³, b March 17, 1827
[C38]   Elenora Louisa³, b July 22, 1829, d y.
[C39] + George Washington Andrew Jackson³, b July 8, 1833, d July 5, 1907

[C7] HENRY² BRUMBAUGH (Johann Jacob¹) according to his own record[a] "born in the beginning of March, 1777", March 28, 1798, m *Margaret Rentch*,[b] b Nov. 25, 1781. They lived upon a farm in Washington Co, Md, near Hagerstown, about 1847 these parents went to visit their son *Otho²* [C42] at his home near West Manchester, now in Preble Co, O, using a "one horse shay" Henry² carried a quantity of large red clover, the first of this famous clover to be introduced into that region He was a large, powerful man of dark complexion, a man of considerable influence in his neighborhood, and was the owner of some slaves, as will be seen from his reproduced record.[*]

Henry² d 1856, and was buried on the old paternal homestead beside his father [C1] Johann Jacob¹ Brumbach.

DEED OF [C5] HENRY² BRUMBAUGH AND MARGARET TO [C4] JOHN² BRUMBAUGH AND SAMUEL ULRY AND [C3] MARY²—APRIL 26, 1805

"This indenture made this twenty sixth day of April in the year of our Lord one thousand eight hundred and five Between Henry Brumbaugh and Margaret his wife of Washington county and State of Maryland of the one part and John Brumbaugh and Saml Ulrey and Mary his wife, late Mary Brumbaugh of Bedford County in the Commonwealth of Pennsylvania of the other part Witnesseth that whereas [C1] Jacob Brumbaugh, late of Washington County and State of Maryland (decd) father of the above named Henry, John, and Mary died intestate, seized in his demesne as of fee of certain tracts or parcel of tracts of Lands in Bedford and Huntingdon counties in the State of Pennsylvania and whereas the said Henry Brumbaugh one of the heirs and legal representatives of the said deceased hath or claimed to have a share or title to one Seventh part of all the lands lying and being in Bedford and Hunt-

---

*Account book containing the autographic record reproduced in Plate 51—preserved and handed to the author by [C119] Upton S—' Brumbaugh

[b]Heads of Families—First Census of the United States, Md, 1790, p 118, for Washington County, immediately beneath "Jacob Brumbach" contains the entry Andrew Rentch, with a family consisting of 2 s over 16, 1 s under 16, 5 free white females, including wife and 15 slaves John, Jacob and Peter Rentch are also enumerated in the same county

ingdon Counties aforesaid whereof the said Jacob Brumbaugh died Seized, is willing to transfer all his Right therein to the above named John Brumbaugh and Saml Ulrey   Now this Indenture witnesseth the said Henry Brumbaugh and Margaret his wife, for and in consideration of the some of One Hundred Pounds current Money of the State of Maryland to him in hand Paid by the John Brumbaugh and Saml Ulrey before the sealing and Delivery of these presents + + + + and assigns all his the said Henry Brumbaugh his right title interest claim property and demand of in and to all and Singular, the Lands and Premises in Bedford and Huntingdon Counties in the State of Pennsylvania whereof the said Jacob Brumbaugh deceased died seized (except two hundred and twenty five acres, lying and being in Bedford County) + + + +.   In Witness whereof the said Henry Brumbaugh and Margaret his wife have hereto set their hands and affixed their Seals the day and year first herein before mentioned.

Henry Brumbaugh   [Seal]

Margaret Brumbaugh   [Seal]

Signed Sealed and Deld
in the presence of
George C. Smoot
Jacob Schmebely
    State of Maryland, Washington Co , 26th April, 1805—executed before Jacob Schmebely and Robert Douglas "the subscribers, two Justices of the peace in and for the Co aforesaid "
    To all people, to whom these presents shall come, Know ye that [C7] Henry[2] Brumbaugh of Washington Co., Md , "farmer, for divers good causes and considerations him thereunto moving" + + + and forever quit claim unto [C4] John[2] Brumbaugh and Samuel Ulry of Bedford Co , Pa , + + + a certain Tract of Land lying and being in Bedford Co , Pa , containing 225 acres and allowances and known by the name of *"Rich Bernse"* (Rich Barrens) west of the *Hickory Bottom,* + + +   In Witness whereof the said [C4] Henry[2] Brumbaugh, hath hereunto set his hand and affixed his seal, this twenty fourth day of February in the year of our Lord one thousand eight hundred and seven

[C7] Henry[2] Brumbaugh   [Seal]

Sealed and delivered
in the presence of [C8] George[2] Brumbaugh
    (Recorded Bedford Co , Pa , Book G, p. 195—copied by Mr Elias Gibson)

BILL OF SALE—HENRY BRUMBAUGH TO GEORGE BREADY, 20 DECEMBER, 1811.*

"At the request of George Bready the following Bill of Sale is recorded 20th December, 1811, to wit Know all men by these presents that I, Henry Baumbaugh of Frederick County and State of Maryland, for and in consideration of the sum of thirty dollars current money to me in hand paid by George Bready of the County and State aforesaid at and before the sealing and delivery hereof the receipt whereof I do hereby acknowledge, have granted bargained and sold and by these presents do grant bargain and sell unto the said George Bready his Heirs Executors and administrators and assigns two small shoats, one large iron kettle, two iron pots, one pan, one dutch oven, one chest, one table, one doz. of cups and saucers half doz of plates, one wolling wheel, one spinning wheel and reel, To Have and To Hold the same described property above bargained and sold to the said George Bready his executors, administrators and assigns for ever to his and their only proper use and benefit and I the said Henry Baumbaugh for myself, my executors and administrators shall and will warrant and forever defend by these presents to the said George Bready his Executors, Administrators and assigns, to the said described property, against me, my executors and administrators and against all and every other person or persons whomsoever, claiming the same or any part thereof In testimony whereof I have here unto set my hand and affixed my seal this 20th day of December in the year of our Lord one thousand eight hundred and eleven

Henry Baumbach   [Seal]

Signed, sealed and delivered
in the presence of
    Frederick Nusz
    Henry Kuhn

Frederick County to wit on the 20th Day of December 1811 Henry Baumbach appeared before the subscriber one of the Justices of the peace of the County aforesaid and acknowledged this Instrument of writing to be his act and deed and the property hereby intended to be conveyed to be the right and estate of the said George Bready, his Heirs and Assigns forever according to the true intent and meaning thereof and the act of Assembly on that case made

Henry Kuhn.

TAKEN FROM COVER OF "HENRY BRUMBAUGH HIS ACCOUNT BOOK, MARCH 24, 1813—PRISE $5."

"1827 This is to certify that Mr Henry Brumbaugh has subscribed for a copy

*Copied from Frederick Co., Md, records by Miss Nellie Carter Garrott, Secy Frederick Co Hist Soc

of Henry's Exposition for which I will take any kind of Produce that
will answer for my family

Dec 28 Delivered the 5 vol of Henry	0.00

Yours Blud

—1828   Mr Blud Dr

"Jan 16 to 170 lbs of Beaf at 4 cents	$ 6 80
"June 4 Delivered the 6 vol of Henry .	0 00
Novem 19 to 1 fat hoge wade 210 lbs at 5 cents	
per lb and the rising prise	10 50
By 1 wallem of Henry .	$17.30

Duos of father on the 11 of Aprile 1799
Duos of Mother on the 28 of November 1806
Duos of Mother Law Rench the 4 Day of —— 1812
Frost on the 12 of July 1814
1815   January 2 Ciled 1 hog wait 483 lbs"

Children (8):

[C40] + Elizabeth[3], *b* Dee. 29, 1799, *d* 1832.
[C41] + Casandra[3], *b* Oct 23, 1804; *d*
[C42] + Otho[3], *b* July 28, 1807; *d* 1881.
[C43] + Andrew[3], *b* Oct. 5, 1809
[C44]   Upton[3], *b* Sept 16, 1812, *d* Sept 24, 1838
[C45]   Elvina[3], *b* Sept. 11, 1815, unm; *d* Bedford, Pa
[C46] + George[3], *b* June 30, 1818.
[C47] + Calvin[3].

[C8] GEORGE[2] BRUMBAUGH (Johann Jacob[1]) *b* Sept. 9, 1783, in
Frederick Co., Md, *m Louisa Gelwicks*, *b* Aug 11, 1778, lived in Hagerstown,
Md., on East Franklin St, next to the present market house: by occupation a
brewer mostly of beer, which he wholesaled, became quite wealthy; himself and
wife were members of St. John's Lutheran Ch., Hagerstown. He *d* May 22,
1837, aged 53 yrs. 8 mos 13 ds., his wife *d* March 29, 1840, aged 61 yrs.
7 mos. 18 ds, both buried in Rose Hill Cem, Hagerstown, Md. (No issue.)

[C3] Mary[2] Ulry of Bedford Co, Pa, Dee 8, 1825, for $150, deeds to
[C8] *George[2] Brumbaugh* of Washington Co, Md, 407 a in Morrison's Cove,
Woodbury Twp, Huntingdon Co, Pa, taken up by [C1] Jacob[1] Brumbaugh,
Sr, late of Washington Co, Md, surveyed Aug 26, 1785, on warrant in name
of [C2] Jacob[2] and [C5] Daniel[2] Brumbaugh, dated April 25, 1785, and tract

adjoining 30 a [C1] Jacob¹ Brumbaugh, Sr., bought of Henry Clapper June 2, 1787. (See [C1], p 155.)

(Huntingdon Co , Pa , Deed Book U 1, p 41.)

RELEASE OF [C6] DAVID³ BRUMBAUGH, JUNR , TO [C8] GEORGE² BRUMBAUGH—3 NOVEMBER, 1827.ᵃ

[C6] David³ Brumbaugh Junr of Washington Co., Md , for $500 00 paid by [C8] *George² Brumbaugh* of the same place—David³ being one of the co-heirs of [C2] Jacob² Brumbaugh Junr, deceased—releases his interest in the parcel of land situate on *pine creek* in Morrison's Cove, Woodberry Twp., Huntingdon Co , Pa., containing 379 acres taken up by [C1] Jacob¹ Brumbaugh Senr, late of Washington Co , Md , dec'd,—surveyed 26 Aug 1785 on Warrant in names of "Jacob and [C5] Daniel² Brumbugh" dated 25 April 1785 and the tract adjoining containing 30 acres which said [C1] Jacob¹ Brumbug Senr deed bought of Henry Clapper 2 June 1787"

(Signed one name only)   David Brumbaugh   [Seal]

Executed in Franklin Co , Pa , before Wm Wood, J P., 3 Nov , 1827

DEED OF [C8] GEORGE² BRUMBAUGH TO SAMUEL ROYER— NOVEMBER 6, 1827 ᵇ

[C8] George² Brumbaugh recites that [C1] Jacob¹ Brumbaugh late of Washington Co., Md , died intestate leaving children [C2] Jacob², [C3] Mary² married Samuel Ulry, [C4] John², [C5] Daniel², [C7] Henry² and [C8] George². [C1] Jacob¹ had the tract at Pine Creek, Huntingdon Co , Pa , surveyed 26 Aug , 1785, on warrant in name of Jacob and [C5] Daniel² Brumbaugh, dated 25 April, 1785, containing 379 acres, and the adjoining tract bought of Henry Clapper 2 June, 1787, containing 30 acres—[C8] George² secured by purchase the share of his brother [C6] David², sister [C3] Mary², and nephew [C9] Joseph³—and for a consideration of $1631 00 sells to *Samuel Royer*.

Deed executed by [C8] George², alone, in Franklin Co , Pa , 6 Nov , 1827

[C3] Mary² Ulry of Bedford Co , Pa.. for $150, quit claims to [C8] George² Brumbaugh of Washington Co., Md ᶜ

[C9] Joseph³ Brumbaugh of Washington Co., Md., quit claims to [C8] George² Brumbaugh of same.ᵈ

ᵃRecorded in Book VI, p 138, Huntingdon Co , Pa.
ᵇRecorded in Book VI, p. 138, Huntingdon Co., Pa.
ᶜRecorded in Book U1, p. 40, Huntingdon Co , Pa.
ᵈRecorded in Book U1, p. 41, Huntingdon Co , Pa

David Angle and Margaret, "late Margaret³ Brumbach" [C12] quit claim to [C8] George² Brumbaugh on 24 March, 1828.[a]

[C9] JOSEPH BRUMBAUGH ([C2] Jacob², Johann Jacob¹) b Nov 16, 1783, in Washington Co, Md ; about 1812 m *Elizabeth Angle*, b at Welsh Run Aug. 5, 1793   Joseph³ was a farmer, and his farm extended on both sides of State Line, mainly lying in Washington Co, Md, and near Middleburg Himself and w were members of Ger. Ref. Ch.; they moved to a farm near Wheeler, Porter Co, Ind, where he d 1859; Elizabeth d 1868, near Whiteside, Ill., and was buried near the same place [b] "The Angle family were also numerous and respectable '"[a]

"*Joseph Brumbaugh* + + +   The farm being divided by the 'old Province line,' in the same manner as my own old home farm, about 100 miles west—a strange coincidence.   The farm has passed out of the hands of the family long since, the same as the Brown farm   It is a singular fact that not one of the ten children has lived in Washington county for over twenty years; indeed, the Brumbaugh race has become quite meagre in its native county Gone West   Many of them, however, of the race live in Southern Pennsylvania.   Father Joseph Brumbaugh was a plain, unassuming man, deservedly respected by those who knew him.   He was a careful, watchful parent, and a faithful husband.   He bore arms for his country in the War of 1812; was one of the defenders of Baltimore.   His wife bore an excellent character, was highly respected and proud of the Angle and Brumbaugh names   I honor her for it."[d]

[C9] JOSEPH³ BUYS A NEGRO GIRL NAMED MATILDA AUG 27, 1817.[e]

"For the consideration of five hundred dollars in hand paid, I have this day sold to Joseph Brumbaugh of Washington Co, Md., a Negro girl named Matilda, a slave for life about sixteen years of age whom I warrant to be sound and defend from all persons claiming   In Witness hereof I have hereunto subscribed my name this 27th day of August in year of our Lord one thousand eight hundred and Seventeen

Saml Crumbaugh"

Witness. G. Bower

---

[a]Recorded in Book VI, p 139, Huntingdon Co, Pa
[b], [c] and [d] "*Brown's Miscellaneous Writings*"—Jacob Brown, Cumberland, Md, 1896, p. 324 —see also [C56]—to which the interested reader is referred
[e]Recorded at Hagerstown, Washington Co, Md, Book CC, p. 180   On the same page is recorded the sale of a negro girl, Anna, 12 years old, for $300 to another person

JOSEPH³ BRUMBAUGH [C9] TO GEORGE BRUMBAUGH, AUG. 26, 1825.

Joseph Brumbaugh of Washington Co, Md, acknowledged receipt of $70 paid by [C8] George² Brumbaugh of Washington Co, Md, and on Aug 26, 1825, conveys *Pine Creek* in Morrison's Cove, Franklin Twp, Bedford Co., Pa, now Huntingdon Co, Pa, consisting of 407 a, surveyed Aug 26, 1785, warrant in name of [C2] Jacob² and [C5] Daniel² Brumbaugh, dated April 25, 1785, also tract adjoining above 30 a, which said [C1] Jacob¹ Brumbaugh bought from Henry Clapper 2 June, 1787

(Acknowledged in Franklin Co, Pa, before Lewis Denig, J P., and recorded at Huntingdon, Pa, in U 1, p 41)

Children (10)

[C49]   Catharine Susannah⁴, *b* April 8, 1813; *d* Nov 18, 1882, *m John Rench* of Cumberland, Md. (No ch)

[C50]   Eliza Jane⁴, *b* June 19, 1814, *d* 1855; *m Frederick Angle* of Welsh Run, Md.

[C51] + Alexander⁴, *b* Oct 27, 1815.

[C52] + Julia Ann⁴, *b* Oct 26, 1819; *d* 1885 at Attica, O.

[C53] + Emily⁴, *b* May 28, 1822, *d* 1891.

[C54] + Mary⁴, *b* Jan 8, 1824, *d* Aug 24, 1894

[C55]   Oliver Perry⁴, *b* July 17, 1825, *d* 1847

[C56] + Eleanor⁴, *b* Dec 8, 1827, *d* July 27, 1889

[C57]   Joseph⁴, *b* Aug 31, 1829, *d*   .

[C58]   Louisa Davis⁴, *b* July 2, 1832, *d* 1885; *m Samuel Venrich*

[C10] JOHN³ BRUMBAUGH ([C2] Jacob², Johann Jacob¹); *m Elizabeth Cokenour* (Census of 1790 spells this name Kochenouer and Kochenauer). Lived in Middle Woodbury Twp, Bedford Co, Pa.

Children (3)

[C93]   Jacob⁴, *m Mary McGee*, moved to Moulton, Appanoose Co, Iowa

[C94] + Joseph⁴, *m Catherine Gossard*.

[C95]   David⁴, *m Maggie Lydie*, lived in Blair Co, Pa, and bur. near Martinsburg, Pa

[C11] JACOB³ BRUMBAUGH ([C2] Jacob², Johann Jacob¹)

Of Jacob³ the only information thus far obtainable is contained in a letter written many years ago by the late [C389] *Andrew M. Brumbaugh*, M D, of Dahlgren, Ill, a grandson, and even he was somewhat uncertain—he also said there were many uncles and aunts but that he could recall only the

names of those given below, never having given any attention to family matters.[a]

   Children ("many more")·

[C123] + Philip D.[4]
[C124]   John.[4]
[C125]   Joseph[4].

[C12] MARGARET[3] BRUMBAUGH ([C2] Jacob[2], Johann Jacob[1]);
m David Angle

   March 24, 1828, David Angle and Margaret, "late Margaret Brumbach, one of the heirs of [C2] Jacob Brumbach," for $70 00 convey an undivided one fourth part of the tract in Huntingdon Co , Pa , near the Waters of Piney Creek, adjoining the lands of Daniel Royer and others—the land taken up by [C1] Jacob[1] Brumbach, Senr , by warrant in names of [C2] Jacob[2] and [C5] Daniel[2] Brumbach, dated April 25, 1785, 379 a and adjoining 30 a.

   Executed in Washington Co , Md , before John Marshal, J P., and recorded in Book VI, p 139, Huntingdon Co., Pa

[C13] DAVID[3] BRUMBAUGH ([C2] Jacob[2], Johann Jacob[1]) *b* about May 25, 1802, *m Susanna Emrich*, dau *Ludwig* and *Susanna (Eminger) Emrich*. Ludwig was s of *Valentine*, and latter was s of *Conrad Nicholas Emrich*, *b* in Hesse Darmstadt in 1700, said to have landed in Phila in 1736

   "David Brumbaugh, brother of father Joseph, was a prominent and respectable man in Washington Co , especially in agricultural matters and insurance business   He had two sons and as many daughters   Jerome became a member of the Washington Co bar, but promptly located in Kansas, where he did well.   Was at one time Attorney General of the State.   He died some years ago, leaving a widow, who soon followed him.   The Brumbaugh family are too numerous and scattered to permit more than a general reference to them + + +."[b]

   David[3] was one of the incorporators and First Pres of Washington Co , Md., Agricultural and Mechanical Assn , which was chartered in 1854, and the first fair was held on the edge of Hagerstown along the Williamsport pike He owned and operated the Lehman Mill in Leitersburg Dist for 6 yrs —it is the third largest mill in Washington Co , Md , outside of Hagerstown. The

----

[a]The author thinks this classification a probable error—possibly in family, probably in generation at least—as [C389] Andrew M—[4] Brumbaugh, *b* 1831 would place him in the fourth generation rather than the fifth—the correspondence could not be pursued owing to the death of the writer and the fact that none of the surviving family will reply to letters
   [b]Cumberland, Md , Sept 24, 1886—"Brown's Miscellaneous Writings—Jacob Brown," p 325.   See also [C56]

present brick and stone mill was erected in the spring of 1869, when the old
stone mill was torn down—the latter was one of the first to be erected in the old
Frederick Co, having been built in 1760 by Mr Sprigg, who owned nearly
1,000 a of land ("Spriggs Paradise"), and he was an extensive slave owner
An old negro, Chatham, who d at age 104, carried the clay used in building the
old mill.[a] David[3] d Dec 6, 1878, aged 76 yrs. 6 mos. 11 ds

"DEATH OF DAVID BRUMBAUGH.[b]

"This worthy and much esteemed citizen and native of our county, one of
a numerous and influential family, an honest man and a true Christian, if we
may judge of his life by his actions, died at his home near the Pennsylvania
State Line on Friday night last, December 6, aged 76 years, 6 months and 11
days   His death was caused by old age, the wearing out of nature   We believe until he lost his wife, a few years since, he scarcely knew what it was to
be sick a day.   That loss, followed soon after by the death of a son, of whom
he had just cause to be proud, and in whose career was stored pretty much
all of his earthly treasures during his latter years, broke his almost indomitable spirit, and he gradually sank under the repeated blows of affliction.

In the early days of his life, out of a numerous family of solid and influential men, all of who were active politicians, Mr. David Brumbaugh was the
only one who was a Whig, the others of the name in this locality being all
decided Democrats   He was also as decided a Presbyterian, and through
sunshine and storm alike he as regularly wended his way to Hagerstown
to church, as on Tuesday he did, in later years, to the office of the Mutual
Insurance Company, of which he was Surveyor and Actuary   Up to the day
of his death he was devoted to his church, but when the 'Know Nothing' party
supplanted the old Whig party he connected himself with the Democratic party
of the nation and died in that political association.   A man of deep convictions and marvelous regularity of habits, he was always conspicuous in public
enterprises and thoroughly earnest in his work.   He was born upon a farm
and reared with agricultural predilections, and was, if not absolutely the
father of the Agricultural Association of our county, more entitled to that
honor than perhaps any one man connected with it, as he was from its birth.
For many years, and until age began to paralyze his energies, he was its
President, and continued to be its Vice-President until near his death.   In this
connection he was Correspondent of the Agricultural Bureau at Washington

<hr>

[a]Extracted from History of Washington Co, Md—Williams, Vol II, p 1275, etc
[b]Newspaper clipping preserved by Elizabeth (Waterson) Brumbaugh [C169], mother of
[C426] Alberta Jessie[5] (Brumbaugh) Day, and furnished by the latter

for many years, and was the only agricultural statistician our county has
ever had   In this field his death will be a loss to the whole county

"For many years before his death, as we have said, he was Surveyor of the
old Mutual Company of our county, and as such visited and familiarized himself with the people of every section of the county; there is probably not a
man in our county who did not know David Brumbaugh   In early life he was
a man of property, and one of the most intelligent and prosperous of our
farmers. Had he confined himself exclusively to practical farming, he no doubt
would have died among the rich men of our county   As it was, he was poor
With a very active mind and more than ordinary education, and of a generous
nature towards his fellow men, in early life he divided his talent and attention
between his legitimate business and that of surveying and assisting his neighbors in conveyancing, and finally to farming attempted to add the milling
business; which multiplicity of occupations was too much for him, and he lost
his property, but never the love and respect of his fellow beings   Then it was
he became connected with the Insurance Company, and at his funeral, which
took place last Sunday at State Line, as a mark of well-merited respect, Messrs.
M. S Barber, H K Tice, Alex Neill and Buchanan Schley, officers of the
company, were in attendance. Among the pall bearers were two of his brethren
in the church, Messrs. P B Small and Joseph B Loose, whilst the funeral
services were solemnized by the Rev. J C Thompson, of the Presbyterian
Church of our place, of which the deceased was a member. The whole surrounding people turned out to pay the last sad rites to the memory of their
friend "

[C164]   Rebecca⁴; m John Snyder, carpenter, moved to Ohio; (8 ch).
[C165] +   Eveline⁴, m Joseph or Peter Binkly
[C166]   David I ⁴; m Maggie Stine
[C167]   Laura⁴; m R— Risinger.
[C168] +   Hiram Emmich⁴; m [C36] Ann Maria³ Brumbaugh
[C169] +   Jerome David⁴, b 1833, m Elizabeth Waterson

[C14] DANIEL³ BRUMBAUGH ([C4] John², Johann Jacob¹) b
1791 (?), m Elizabeth Teeters, dau John Teeters, and sister of Susannah
Teeters, who m [C17] JACOB S—³ BRUMBAUGH, b March 14, 1800,
moved from Bedford Co, Pa, to Richland Co, O, in 1833, and to Noble Co.,
Ind, about 1850, living near Kendallville, Ind ; he d Aug 11, 1885.

         Children (4):
[C60] John⁴, last ad Custer Co, Neb.
[C61] Martin⁴; last ad. Minn

[C62] David⁴; last ad Lincoln, Ill

[C63] Susan⁴, last ad. Kendallville, Ind , *m —— Bloomfield.*

[C15] MARY³ BRUMBAUGH ([C4] John², Johann Jacob¹) *m Christian Kochenderfer.* She was known far and wide as a "great doctor woman" (midwife), and *d* at New Enterprise, Bedford Co , Pa , July 27, 1882

April 2, 1832, [C14] Daniel³ and his w. Elizabeth³, [C16] David³ and Mary, [C17] Jacob³ and Susannah, David Snowberger and [C18] Eve³, the other heirs of [C4] John Brumbaugh conveyed their interest in 103 acres in Bedford Co , Pa , to Christian Kochenderfer.ᵃ

[C14] Daniel³ Brumbaugh deeds to Christian Kochenderfer, ——, 1834.ᵇ

[C16] David³ Brumbaugh deeds to same, ——, 1834 ᶜ

Children (12), *surname Kochenderfer*

  i   John⁴, *b* Dec 18, 1814, *d* Jan 2, 1867, *m Catharine Zook.*

  ii   Susanna⁴, *b* May 25, 1816, *d*, *m Benjamin Yoder*

 iii   Catharine⁴, *b* July 4, 1817, *d*. *m Oliver Reasy*

 iv   Elizabeth⁴, *b* March 29, 1821, *d* Feb 24, 1864.

  v   Mary⁴, *b* March 4, 1824, *m Henry Weaver*, Loysburg, Pa

 vi   Samuel⁴, *b* Dec 12, 1825; *d*

 vii   Eve⁴, *b* July 12, 1828, *d* Jan 11, 1906, unm.

viii   Adam⁴, *b* July 12, 1828, *d* y.

 ix   Barbara⁴, *b* July 20, 1830, *m George Albright*, res. Polo, Ill (8 ch)

  x   Christian⁴, *b* May 25, 1832

 xi   Martin⁴, *b* Jan 13, 1834, *d* July 23, 1847

 xii   David B ⁴, *b* May 22, 1836; *m Mary Ann Moore*; res. Cedar Rapids, Nebr. (7 ch)

[C16] DAVID³ BRUMBAUGH ([C4] John², Johann Jacob¹) *b* Sept 5, 1797, in Bedford Co , Pa., March 31, 1822, *m Mary Snyder, b* April 26, 1802, in Snake Spring Valley, Bedford Co , Pa , dau *Jacob* and *Catharine (Ulery) Snyder*, a successful farmer, baptized in G B B Ch. Sept 26, 1823, and elected to ministry in the same denomination Jan 12, 1827, both were faithful church workers. Mary *d* Sept. 26, 1860, and David³ *d* Nov 15, 1874, at New Enterprise, Pa The old family Bible was destroyed by fire.

Mrs Mary Susan⁵ (Eshleman) Gates [C101-i] relates the following incident concerning her grandfather [C16] David⁷ Brumbaugh:

"When his boys were young he was one day blasting rocks for a limekiln

ᵃRefer to [C4]—Record Book R, p 129, Bedford Co , Pa
ᵇRecord Book R, p 129, Bedford Co , Pa
ᶜSame, pp. 129-130, same

and thought it would be a good thing to demonstrate the power of powder. He placed some on a shovel and called the boys around him, saying· 'Now bura gook was fulfer doot'—('Now boys come and see what powder does')—whereupon the powder 'went off' and also his beard, which was long after the manner of the men of those long past years "

David³ lived on a large tract over a square mile in extent about one mile west of New Enterprise, Bedford Co , Pa   The "mansion part" now has but about 300 acres   The old house, greatly altered and modernized, is herewith shown, and is about 100 years old. "One part of it was used as a meeting place of the Brethren before they had a church in that community, and as they now have the second church on the same foundation for over 80 years you can see how long since they worshiped in the old David Brumbaugh house." *

See [C3-iii], this name is also written "Snider "

WILL OF [C16] DAVID³ BRUMBAUGH.[b]

The last will of [C16] David³ "of South Woodbury" was dated Feb. 26, 1862. and executed before James B Noble and John I. Noble, witnesses   It provided that he should be buried in the cemetery "near Daniel Snoeberger's belonging to our Meeting House by the side of my wife." He gave bequests to his "grand-daughter Susan⁵ Eshleman [C101-1], daughter of my daughter [C101] Susan⁴ now deceased " The will further mentions his daughter [C98] Elizabeth⁴ Pechtel ('Bechtel') deceased, his sons [C97] Jacob (Snyder⁴), [C99] Martin (Snyder⁴), [C100] John (Snyder⁴), [C102] David (Snyder⁴), and [C105] Simon (Snyder⁴), the youngest—Jacob resides on the Mansion farm"—and daughters [C96] Catharine⁴ Hoover, [C103] Mary⁴ Replogle and his grandchildren [C98-1] Simon⁵, [C98-11] Jackson⁵ and [C98-1v] Nancy Pechtel ("Bechtel")   He holds interest in mountain land in partnership with his s [C97] Jacob⁴ and Samuel Kochendarfer.   To [C96] Catharine⁴ he bequeathed "my large German Bible" and to "my son Simon large English Bible." [C100] John Snyder⁴ and [C102] David Snyder⁴, sons, were executors.   David³ d Dec 15, 1874, 10 A M.

Children (10)

[C 96] + Catharine⁴, b Dec 7, 1823: d Dec 7, 1865
[C 97] + Jacob Snyder⁴, b Dec. 11, 1825; d Feb 22, 1894
[C 98] + Elizabeth⁴, b Jan. 19, 1828; d July 4, 1861
[C 99]   Martin Snyder⁴, b Feb. 19, 1830, d 1878, m Esther Replogle; (no issue).

---

*Letter from Mary (Eshleman) Gates, Bedford, Pa , who furnishes considerable information.
[b]Recorded in Will Book 5, p 187, Bedford Co , Pa

[C100] + John Snyder[4], *b* Jan. 16, 1832, *d* Feb 20, 1903
[C101] + Susan[4], *b* Dec 13, 1835, *d* May 16, 1858
[C102] + David Snyder[4], *b* March 20, 1838
[C103] + Mary[4], *b* May 31, 1840, *d* May 31, 1904.
[C104]   Delilah[4], *b* Dec 27, 1842, *d* Oct. 22, 1846
[C105] + Simon Snyder[4], *b* Sept 12, 1845, *d* Jan. 14, 1910

[C17] JACOB S—[3] BRUMBAUGH ([C4] John[2], Johann Jacob[1]) *b* March 14, 1800, in Bedford Co., Pa., together with his bro [C14] Daniel[3] he moved from Bedford Co to Richland Co, O, and later to Noble Co, Ind, where both *d*—Jacob[3] *d* Nov 28, 1865 Jacob[3] *m Susannah Teeters*, sister of *Elizabeth Teeters*, who was the w of [C14] DANIEL[3] BRUMBAUGH (two sisters married two brothers), and both daughters of *John Teeters*.

[C133]   Elias[4], *b* Jan 2, 1822, in Pa.; *d* Jan 1, 1850, in Noble Co, Ind.
[C134] + Samuel[4], *b* Dec. 27, 1824
[C135] + Jacob[4], *b* Aug. 1, 1834
[C136]   Mary[4]; *m* —— *Flory*
[C137]   Daughter[4].
[C138]   Daughter[4].

[C18] EVE[3] BRUMBAUGH ([C4] John[2], Johann Jacob[1]) *b* July 12, 1806; 1823 *m David Snoeberger*[a], s *Theodore* (*b* in Switzerland) and *Elizabeth (Miller*[b]*) Snoeberger*; lived together upon the old [C4] JOHN[2] BRUMBAUGH homestead in South Woodbury Twp, Bedford Co, Pa, for 54 yrs., and Eve[3] survived her husband 16 yrs —David *d* March 24, 1877, aged 79 yrs 24 ds, and Eve[3] *d* Sept. 15, 1893, aged 87 yrs 1 mo 25 ds
    Both united with the G B B Ch. early in their married life and remained quite active therein until their death. Their home in the early days was often used for church services, and visiting brethren and sisters were ever welcome— no person was ever sent away empty handed, and the orphan was ever an especial object of solicitude upon their part Eve read extensively, only in the German language, and retained her excellent memory and active interest in all of life's activities until the end of her long life
    [E344] Andrew[5] Brumbaugh visited Eve[3] at her home in 1891 and then made extensive notes based upon her exceptional memory and extensive knowledge of family matters These notes have proven of great assistance in un-

---

[a]Barbara[3] Snoeberger (VI) says· "Father's family and his brother John always spelled the name 'Snoeberger' I think all the rest of the family 'Snowberger' The original name was 'Schnaebarger' 'Snowberger' is the usual spelling used "
[b]Sister of Martin Miller.

raveling many a genealogical problem   He described her as then being "85 years old, robust and tall, very much resembling the old ancestors of our line of Brumbaughs." She said "I always understood from my father that my grandfather, [C1] *Jacob*[1], was a cousin to [E1] *Johannes*[1] *Henrich*, and his son *Johannes*[2] [E4] was called the stocking weaver." This makes [C1] JOHANN JACOB[1] BRUMBACH and [E1] JOHANNES HENRICH[1] BRUMBACH cousins, and is the only definite information yet discovered bearing upon this point, but especial attention is directed to the occurrence of Johann Jacob Brombach in the foreign records elsewhere reproduced.

Children (10), *surname Snoeberger*

i   Elizabeth[4], *b* April 21, 1825, *d* Feb, 1898; *m Samuel Stayer, d* March 21, 1880, s *David* and —— *(Snyder) Stayer*, lived at Roaring Spring, Blair Co, Pa.

Children (5), *surname Stayer*

(1) David[5]; lives at Denton, Md, *m* (1) *Hannah Stuckey*, who *d* soon after marriage; *m* (2) —— *Ober*   (Several ch.)

(2) Andrew Snowberger[5], M D, *b* May 21, 1848. *m* [C79] + ROSE KISSECKER[4] BRUMBAUGH, *b* May 22, 1848. (See the latter for fuller information)

(3) Susanna S[5], *b* Aug. 2, 1851, Dec 24, 1871, *m Daniel S—*[5] *Replogle, b* Feb 19, 1847   (See [E3009-iii-(2)].)

(4) Joseph[5], graduated at Millersville (Pa.) State Normal Sch ; teacher; Dist Atty Bedford Co, Pa, *m Susan Shelly;* both *d*

Children:

(a) Rev. Abraham Lincoln[6], 129 W 10th St, Newton, Ks.

(b) Mary[6], (c) Eva[6], (d) Charles[6]; (e) Susan[6].

(5) Mary[5], lives in Philadelphia, Pa

ii   Susanna B[4] Snowberger, *b* May, 1828; *d* 1907, *m James H Graham;* lived and *d* at Butler, Pa.   (Numerous descendants)

iii   Andrew B[4], *b* 1830, *d* 1875, *m Mary Holsinger*, both *d*

(1) Jacob Snowberger[5], J P New Enterprise, Pa.

iv   Nancy[4], *b* 1832, *m Jacob Horner;* res Los Angeles, Cal.

Children (12—6 adults), *surname Horner*

(1) Mary Elizabeth[5], ad Altoona, Pa.

(2) Amanda[5]; Apr. 10, 1888 *m Edward McPherson Pennell, b* Bedford, Pa, Apr 23, 1860, *s Eben* and *Barbara Mary Anna (Over) Pennell*   Mr. Pennell attended Bedford Academy and Millersville State Normal Sch., admitted to Bed-

Co. (Pa) Bar Mch 10, 1885, Dist Atty 1888-1894, deacon and elder St. John's Ref Ch and trustee Theolog Sem of Ref. Ch , Lancaster, Pa.; ad Bedford, Pa   All old "B. N. C." students will well remember "Amanda Horner," when that institution was in the "Burchnell Building" Later graduated from Millersville State normal   Both herself and husband have shown much interest in this publication

Children (3)

(a) Eben Horner, *b* Oct 15, 1889.

(b) Cornelia, *b* Aug 28, 1894

(c) Miriam, *b* Mch 18, 1896, *d* Dec. 11, 1903

(3) Florence[5]; grad of Millersville State Normal; *m Leon Lush;* ad Okaton, Lyman Co , S Dak

(4) Annie[5]; teacher, grad. Millersville State Normal, ad. Los Angeles, Cal

(5) Ida[5], teacher, grad. Millersville State Normal, ad Los Angeles, Cal.

(6) David L [5], *m Margaret Simmonds,* clerk, ad Altoona, Pa

v   Joseph[5], *b* 1834, *d* 1899, lived at Loysburg, Bedford Co., Pa., (8 ch)

vi   Barbara[5], *b* 1836, assisted maternally with facts concerning her family, etc., unm, member G B B. Ch ; residence, 810 Oakland Ave, Madison, Wis

vii   Mary A [5], *b* 1844; *m* Prof *Samuel M Smeigh,* Denver, Colo.

[C20] ELIZABETH[3] BRUMBAUGH ([C5] Daniel[2], Johann Jacob[1])
m Thomas Spickler, b June 18, 1800, *d* Sept 23, 1834

Children (2), *surname Spickler:*

i   Thomas[4], lived in Washington Co , Md., *m Susan Middlecauff,* also of the same county, both *d.*

ii   Mary Louisa[4], *m David Long Martin;* lived at Middleburg, Franklin Co., Pa

Children (3 s and 2 dau), surname Martin.

(1) William[5], *m* (1) MARGARET PERMELIA[4] BRUMBAUGH [C118], *b* June 17, 1847, and *d* 1878 (dau [C43] Andrew[3]), *m* (2) SUSAN MARIA[4] BRUMBAUGH [C149], *b* Dec 5, 1848.

(2) Alice[5]; *m* [C111] PHILIP NAPOLEON BRUMBAUGH, *b* Sept 18, 1847; (11 ch)

iii   Elizabeth[4]; unm; *d*

[C21] DANIEL³ BRUMBAUGH ([C5] Daniel², Johann Jacob¹) *b* in Washington Co., Md, Aug 6, 1803, 1823 *m Annie Gray, b* in Md Aug 5, 1805; dau *Peter* and *Susan (Bowman) Gray.* In 1827 moved to Bedford Co, Pa., and in Dec, 1863, moved to Darke Co, O, where Daniel³ *d* Jan 29, 1882, at Greenville, Darke Co, O —Annie *d* about 1874 at Delisle, in the same county, and their remains rest in Zion Cemetery, near Greenville, O.

    Children (10) ·

[C65]   Mary Elizabeth⁴, *b* Sept 16, 1825, unm, Pikeville, Darke Co., O.

[C66] + Havana Catharine⁴, *b* Sept 28, 1827, *d* about 1904

[C67] + Rosanna Caroline⁴, *b* Sept 27, 1829; *d* Dec 19, 1902, unm·

[C68] + Samuel David⁴, *b* Jan 7, 1832, *d* March 18, 1868

[C69] + John Peter⁴, *b* May 29, 1835, *d* Nov. 26, 1899, unm

[C70]   Daniel Simon⁴, *b* July 25, 1837, unm

[C71] + Joseph Nathan⁴, *b* Oct 16, 1839

[C72] + Nancy Jane⁴, *b* Oct 30, 1841, *d* May, 1906

[C73]   Eliza Louisa⁴, *b* Nov 18, 1844

[C74]   Susanna Bell⁴, *b* April 29, 1846

[C22] LOUISA³ BRUMBAUGH ([C5] Daniel², Johann Jacob¹) *b* Sept. 3, 1808, about 1839 *m Samuel Bloom, b* Sept 27, 1808, at Bloomfield, Pa. He moved to Hagerstown, Md, in 1838, and at the latter place was a cabinet maker until his *d,* Aug 20, 1872 He was a hard-working, industrious and public-spirited man, member Ref Ch : Repn Louisa *d* Nov 6, 1886; both are buried in the cemetery of Zion Reformed Church of Hagerstown, Md. Both the cemetery and the church were substantially remodeled in 1896 by the son [iii] *Samuel Martin⁴ Bloom* at his own expense, and, as he stated in a communication to the church officers, "out of his interest in and regard for the ancient and historic church, and as an act of filial respect and affection in memory of his parents who lie in its graveyard " ' This example should be followed by many others throughout our broad land, rather than permit the existence of so many neglected last resting places of the worthy ancestors.

    Children (3), *surname Bloom·*

  i   George Daniel⁴, *b* 1838, *d* 1899

  ii   Evaline Louisa⁴, *b* July 27, 1840, *m Elias G. Kauffman* Evaline *d* Jan. 12, 1892

 iii   Samuel Martin⁴, *b* 1846, unm , Repn ; member Ref Ch., resides at Hagerstown, Md, where he was educated in the public schools;

'Part of this data is taken from "Historical & Biographical Record of Washington Co., Md.—Williams, Vol. II, p 678

learned the trade of cabinet maker under his father, and worked in the latter's shops until he was of age; he then chose the grocery business, and on April 14, 1865, with $800 00 cash, principally borrowed money, opened a small retail store on the S W. corner of Potomac and W. Franklin streets, having a one-horse wagonload of groceries This business steadily increased, and in 1878 he sold out and established his present large wholesale grocery business upon the site of his father's cabinet-maker's shop. In 1888 he added the wholesale notion business, and the firm of S. M Bloom & Co , wholesale grocery and dry goods jobbing house, conducts probably the largest wholesale grocery and notion business in the rich Cumberland Valley.

In 1884, as a Repn , he was elected Mayor of Hagerstown, and "served with marked general satisfaction", 1887 was elected Co Commissioner, and "served with skill and acceptability", 1890 elected president of the First Natl Bank of Hagerstown; is also president of Board of Managers Wash Co Orphan Asylum.

In 1901 he gave grounds opposite his fine residence as a site for a park to contain a Spanish cannon captured at Santiago, Cuba, the cannon is beautifully mounted and was dedicated July 4, 1901, the grounds are called "Bloom Park", ad. Hagerstown, Md

[C24] SAMUEL DAVID[3] BRUMBAUGH ([C5] Daniel[2], Johann Jacob[1]) b June 11, 1813, m Eliza Kissecker, b Sept , 1814, dau Nicholas and Rosanna (Kritzer) Kissecker—Nicholas was s of Nicholas (b Dec 16, 1744, d Aug. 6, 1803) and Anna Margaret (Livinggood) Kissecker (b May 29, 1755—see below*). Samuel David[3] was educated in the public schools, and farmed the old Md. homestead, where he d March, 1876, Eliza d Nov , 1891, and was buried in Greencastle Cemetery, Franklin Co , Pa

"EXTRACT OF A LETTER FROM AN OFFICER IN THE PROVINCE SERVICE, DATED AT TULPEHOCKEN THE 8TH INSTANT *

"Mr Kern and I have just got to Shearman's, and are informed, that a Woman was killed and scalped last Night by the Enemy, about three Miles from hence, we are now setting off in Pursuit of them The List of killed with one Prisoner, is as follows, viz At Swetara, two young Men, Brothers, named

---

* "Extract of a Letter" and many facts concerning descendants in this line have been furnished by Dr D W Nead, Buffalo, N Y , who has extensive Livinggood and related genealogies about ready for publication , and also numerous facts have been furnished by [C76] David Stuckey[4] Brumbaugh, Roaring Spring, Pa

Schaterly, Michael Souder, and William Hart, killed, a Widow Woman carried off. In Tulpehocken, one Levergood, and his Wife, killed. At Northkill, the Wife of Nicholas Geiger, and two Children, and the Wife of Michael Titleser, all killed and scalped. The Indians are divided into small Parties through the Woods."

From No 1529 of The Pennsylvania Gazette, dated April 13, 1758, printed by B Franklin, Post-Master, and D Hall, at the New Printing Office, near the Market

"One Levergood and his wife were Jacob Lowengut *(Lay-fen-goot)* and his wife. Their son Jacob's daughter, *Anna Margaret Livingood (b* May 29, 1755; *d* Nov 20, 1824), *m Nicholas Kissecker (b* Dec 16, 1714, *d* Aug 6, 1803), and their daughter Anna Catherine Kissecker (*b* Oct 31, 1780, *d* Oct. 31, 1854), *m* Dec 24, 1805, Daniel Wunderlich (*b* Jan 21, 1779, *d* March 3, 1844)."

Children (9)·

[C107] + Margaret Evahne[4], *b* Jan 3, 1838, *d* May 30, 1871.

[C108] + John Nicholas[4], *b* May 22, 1840, *d* Dec 9, 1909.

[C109] + Susan Isabella[4]

[C110]   Martha[4], *d* y

[C111] + Philip Napoleon[4], *b* Sept 18, 1847.

[C112]   Rosa[4], *d* y

[C113]   Theodore[4], *d* 1848

[C114]   Andrew[4], *d* at age 7.

[C115]   Adam[4], *d* 1862.

· [C28] SIMEON K—[3] BRUMBAUGH ([C6] David[2], Johann Jacob[1]) *b* Sept 27, 1806, north of Hagerstown, Md , Jan. 24, 1842, at Woodbury, Bedford Co , Pa., *m Christiana Stuckey, b* Jan 2. 1825, at Woodbury, Pa., dau *David* and *Margaret (Brake) Stuckey David Stuckey* was s of *Simon* and *Rose (Snyder) Stuckey*, and Simon was a brother of *Daniel Stookey,*[*] who m *Barbara Whetstone*. Simeon[3] was also called "Simon" and "Simmie" He usually wrote his name merely "S " (See picture reproduced) He was a farmer, Dem ; member Luth. Ch.; and acquired considerable property Simeon[3] *d* at Roaring Spring, Blair Co , Pa., July 14, 1892, and Christiana *d* at the same place Feb 11, 1906

Children (7):

[C76] + David Stuckey[4], *b* April 2, 1843

---

[*]See [C77] Maria Louise[*] (Brumbaugh) Stookey and Dr Lyman Polk Stookey "The name 'Stuckey' is believed to have been changed through a clerical error in a deed, and the name was retained rather than resort to a court to have the name on the deed corrected "—Lyman Brumbaugh Stookey.

[C77] + Marie Louise⁴, *b* Oct 26, 1844
[C78] + Evaline Dorothy⁴, *b* Dec 6, 1846
[C79] + Rose Kissecker⁴, *b* May 24, 1849
[C80] + Simon Smucker⁴, M D , *b* July 17, 1852
[C81] + Margaret Christena⁴, *b* Sept , 1856, *d* Dec., 1883.
[C82] + Grace Eleanore⁴, *b* Nov. 20, 1861

[C30] ELIAS DAVID³ BRUMBAUGH ([C6] David², Johann Jacob¹)
b April 22, 1811, in Md ; Sept 27, 1836, *m* (1) *Marinda Etta Benner, who d*
Aug 26, 1878, dau *Henry* and *Elizabeth (Showman) Benner.* He *m* (2) *Mrs.*
Elizabeth Deshong, a widow, residing near McConnelsburg, Pa   Elias David³
d Sept 14, 1893.
          Children by 1st m (4, 2 infants, names not secured):
[C116]   Laura Elizabeth⁴, *d* age 8
[C117] + Emeline⁴, *b* Aug. 28, 1843, *m* *Webster Hartle*

[C31] NATHAN HENRY³ BRUMBAUGH ([C6] David², Johann Ja-
cob¹) *b* May 24, 1813, in Washington Co , Md., *m* *Lavinia Myers, b* Jan. 5,
1819, in the same county; dau *Jacob* and *Susan (Zent) Myers.* Lavinia
(called "Eveline") *d* May 28, 1902, and both are buried in the Cedar Hill
Cemetery at Greencastle, Franklin Co , Pa. Nathan³ and Lavinia were mem-
bers Ref Ch. of State Line (Greencastle), and during his earlier and middle
life he had been a successful farmer, but during the last twelve or fourteen
years he enjoyed the well-earned rest which came in his retired life.
          Children (9)
[C146] + David⁴, *b* Nov. 29, 1841
[C147]   Jacob Theodore⁴, *b* March 28, 1844, *d* y.
[C148] + Eveline Maria⁴, *b* May 8, 1846
[C149] + Susan Maria⁴, *b* Dec 5, 1848
[C150]   Elias II—⁴, *b* Feb 27, 1851, *d*
[C151] + William⁴, *b* June 13, 1853
[C152] + Emma⁴, *b* Dec. 12, 1854.
[C153]   Charles⁴, *b* Dec. 31, 1858, accidentally shot in Philadelphia.
[C154]   John⁴, *b* Sept. 5, 1861, moved to Washington.

[C32] ELIZABETH L ³ BRUMBAUGH ([C6] David², Johann Jacob¹)
b Nov 15, 1815; *m* *William Logan*, he lived in and near State Line, Pa , following the trade of a carpenter, he next bought a farm across the "line" in
Md., and three children were there born, after some years the family moved
upon a well-timbered farm in Richland Co , O.

Children (6), surname Logan

i Eve[4], *m C C Coleman, d* —, son (1) William
ii Annie Eliza[4]
iii John[4], *m*, res Plymouth, O , (1 dau).
iv Jacob[4], lives at Mansfield, O.
v David R—[4], *m* [C174] IDA LOUISA[4] BRUMBAUGH: residence, State Line, Pa
vi George[4], lives at Mansfield, O ; (2 dau).

[C33] JACOB BENJAMIN[3] BRUMBAUGH ([C6] David[2], Johann Jacob[1]) *b* June 23, 1818, in Washington Co , Md , when he was nine years old his parents moved to Antrim Twp , Franklin Co , Pa., where they *d* in 1842 and 1845. Jan 1, 1856, he *m Rebecca Clopper*, *b* on a farm near Wingerton, Franklin Co , Pa , March 15, 1834, dau *Samuel* and *Maria (Gordon) Clopper* In 1857 they moved to Middleburg, Franklin Co. (now State Line), and there kept a hotel and also conducted a farm of 170 acres in the immediate vicinity; Rebecca practically managed the hotel, in 1870 they moved to Lemaster, same county, and there spent the remainder of Jacob's life

The *Public Opinion*[*] in announcing his death on Feb 4, 1903, after a protracted illness with a complication of diseases, in his eighty-fifth year, said in part

"Mr Brumbaugh was, therefore, reared to manhood in this county, during a long, honorable and useful life, taking an interest in its history and progress, and in everything relating to the welfare of his fellow citizens A successful farmer and business man and prudent in the management of his affairs, he had the confidence of the community in which he resided, and was a safe counsellor whose advice was sought by neighbors.

"Charitable and kind-hearted, Mr Brumbaugh's generosities were many and unostentatious. His supreme happiness was in being in company with congenial friends, and his knowledge of current affairs made him interesting and the life of the party After his retirement from the farm and on his removal to Lemaster ten or more years ago, where he spent the evening of his life, there as at his old home he quickly gathered about him troops of those with whom he would spend a pleasant hour As one after another of some of these were called hence, he felt their loss as one personal, and their memory was ever dear to his heart. Himself ever honorable and truthful, he spoke ill of no one

"In politics a Democrat, Mr Brumbaugh had the courage of his convictions, but he had respect for those who differed with him He was well known

---

*Chambersburg (Pa) *Public Opinion* of Feb 6, 1903.

for his uprightness and integrity, and served with credit as a member of the Board of County Commissioners, to which body he was elected in 1869 For years he was one of the master spirits of his party, and later was a candidate for County Treasurer, being defeated by his Republican opponent, the late J. N. Flinder, by a small majority "

Jacob Benjamin[3] was buried in the Greencastle Cemetery, Franklin Co., Pa ; Rebecca, his widow, lives near Greencastle, Pa , and has assisted by repeatedly furnishing extensive facts for this publication, and by the purchase of copies of the latter

JOHN BROWN INCIDENT.[*]

"The venerable J B Brumbaugh, of Peters Township, one of the well-known and highly esteemed residents of Franklin County, conversed very entertainingly about famous John Brown, whilst in the *Opinion* office recently, and thus furnished data for a first-class article of unpublished history.

"Mr Brumbaugh followed his father in keeping a hotel or wayside inn at Middleburg, in Antrim Township, this county, in the latter part of the fifties Because of this fact he was not aware until too late that he had entertained one of the famous characters in our national war history

"Late one night in October, 1859, he was called and was met at the door by a gray-bearded, pleasant spoken old gentleman who desired entertainment A young man was with him Their horse was put up and after breakfast the next morning they departed In this case, as well as at subsequent times, the stranger paid his bills in gold Mr Brumbaugh said that the stranger, whom they called 'Pap,' and who afterward proved to be the famous John Brown, made his hostelry his stopping place from that time on, was a fluent talker, and as orderly and pleasant a guest as ever stopped at his place On one occasion 'Pap' had assisted at an apple butter boiling During all his lodging Brown had slept in a certain bed. + + + +

"At different times one of his sons accompanied John Brown, Mr Brumbaugh continued He well remembers the incidents of Sunday and Monday evening before the State election After breakfast Monday morning Brown and his son, before departing, remarked that if any person called for them during the day to inform the party that he would be back in the evening No person called during the day, but in the evening visitors turned up Two genteel looking men drove up to the house, had their horses put up, got supper, asked for a room with two beds and very soon after retired When John Brown returned he greeted the strangers, one of whom was another of his sons The whole night the men engaged in animated conversation Mr and Mrs Brumbaugh were interrupted in their slumbers by the mumbling, and mine host B feels sure that that night the plans were laid for the raid at Harpers Ferry the following Sunday

"The two strangers left Tuesday morning at 4 o'clock for Chambersburg, whilst John Brown and son, after breakfast, made their way toward Harper's Ferry. In the evening the son returned, left his horse at Middleburg, and left for Chambersburg on foot Wednesday he returned with two men and a horse and wagon, and after supper proceeded towards Harper's Ferry. This was the last that Mr Brumbaugh saw of the Browns at Middleburg

"The events at Harper's Ferry the following Sunday, when Brown and his party were routed and captured, but not until great efforts is history and well known John Brown, after a fair trial, was hanged at Charlestown, W Va, December 2 Mr Brumbaugh felt a hesitancy about witnessing the execution of Brown, but in April of the following year witnessed the execution of Stephen and Hazlett, who participated with Brown in the fight Mr. Brumbaugh says they were fine looking men and died game."

Children (7):
[C172] + Mary Catherine[4], b Nov 10, 1856.
[C173] + Snively Strickler[4], b Dec 28, 1858

*From *Public Opinion*, Chambersburg, Pa, of July 2, 1897

[C174] + Ida Louisa⁴, b July 10, 1860   (See [C32-v])
[C175] + Elias Guilford¹, b Nov 27, 1862.
[C176] + Anna Eva⁴, b Jan. 16, 1864
[C177] + Eliza Jane⁴, b Dec 25, 1867.
[C178]   George Washington⁴, b Nov 12, 1870; d Sept. 4, 1884

[C35] CATHERINE JANE³ BRUMBAUGH ([C6] David², Johann Jacob¹) b June 11, 1822. m Joseph Newman, who d and was bur in Luth Cem. at Hagerstown, Md.   After his d his w continued farming, until the ch left home, when she bought the old State Line hotel, home of her parents, and lived there until her d, Dec 30, 1904 (80 yrs 19 ds)   She was a member of Luth Ch. of Greencastle, Franklin Co , Pa , and was bur. beside her husband
    Children (5), surname Newman.
  i Jacob⁴, d at age 21
  ii Anna Amelia⁴, m Isaac Myers; the former was a member of Ger Ref. Ch. and the latter of Riv Br Ch   Anna d Dec. 30, 1908, from pneumonia, and Isaac d Dec 30, 1909, from disease of the heart; both were buried in the Greencastle (Pa) Cemetery; (11 ch).
  iii Elizabeth⁴, b April 13, 1857, m George Koontz; address State Line, Pa , where he owns a fine farm bought of [C35] CATHERINE JANE³ BRUMBAUGH, (17 ch)
  iv Maria⁴, m William J Pensinger   Maria⁴ was a member of Luth Ch. and d Aug 1, 1909, from pneumonia and disease of the heart, survived by one son and her husband, whose address is Greencastle, Pa , R R 4
      Issue (1 s)
      (1) Lester Leroy⁵ Pensinger, m Mary Snider; (no ch)
  v Ella Louise⁴, m Jacob Saurbaugh, farmer; address Zullinger, Franklin Co., Pa
      Children (3), surname Saurbaugh.
      (1) Ottie⁵, m George Gilbert of Waynesboro, Pa
      (2) Sarah Newman⁵; m John Miller of Waynesboro, Pa.; (2 ch).

[C37] INDIANA DOROTHY³ BRUMBAUGH ([C6] David² Johann Jacob¹) b March 17, 1827—also written "Judianna"; m (1) Henry D Cook and lived at Mansfield, O : m (2) —— Kyle, m (3) —— Clark.
    Children (3):
  i Mary⁴; m —— Dickinson, Mansfield, O.
  ii Ellen⁴, m —— Dickinson, Mansfield, O., brothers
  iii Jacob⁴.

[C39] GEORGE WASHINGTON³ BRUMBAUGH ([C6] David², Johann Jacob¹) *b* July 8, 1834—his name is recorded in the family Bible "George Washington Andrew Jackson," but he dropped the latter half of the name, *m Eliza Hartman*, lived at Greencastle, Franklin Co, Pa, where he *d* July 5, 1907. He left an estate estimated at $50,000, which was devised to church and charity, his only child having recently *d*, but the bequests lapsed because death occurred less than 30 days from signature of the will—the Orphans' Court of Franklin Co, Pa, has appointed an auditor and the estate will be divided amongst the next of kin.

One daughter.

[C167] Susan⁴, *d* May 30, 1907.

[C40] ELIZABETH³ BRUMBAUGH ([C7] Henry², Johann Jacob¹) *b* Dec. 29, 1799, *m Peter Miller*, *b* Oct., 1791, farmer, lived at Sharpsburg and Fairplay ("Timmelton"), Washington Co, Md. (then Frederick Co) Elizabeth³ was member G B B Ch.; Peter was member Ger Ref. Ch., but united with G. B. B Ch ; he owned 2 slaves as house servants and liberated them. Elizabeth *d* 1832, and Henry *d* Feb. 14, 1856, after many years of suffering from rheumatism, they are buried on the old Brumbaugh homestead, north of Hagerstown, Md.

MARRIAGE PORTION OF [C40] ELIZABETH³ (BRUMBAUGH) MILLER.ᵃ

The following interesting record shows the goods and chattels from her home, with which Elizabeth³ commenced housekeeping

ᵇ ELIZABETH MILLER, DR.ᵇ

1820		
May to	1 Negro girl Nancy and 1 boy William	$350 00
"	1 bay horse	80 00
"	3 Milk Cows	45 00
"	1 bed Sted and Cord	12 75
"	6 Silver tee Spoons	5 00
"	6 knives and forks	2.25
"	15 yards of bed ticken	7 50
"	1 Sid saddel	20.00

ᵃ and ᵇCopied from [C7] Henry² Brumbaugh's ledger—evidently a memorandum account —no further entry Furnished by [C119] Upton S—ᵉ Brumbaugh, Baltimore, Md

1820

May to	45	lbs of fathers at 60 cents	$27 00
"		Do 30 lb at 50	15.00
"	12	yards of bed ticken	6 00
"	9	table Cloths	22.50
"	7	Sheats	14 00
"	8	blankeds	28 00
"	3	quilts	18 00
"	9	yards of linnen for Piller Cases	3 33
"	1	tee kittel	5.00
"	6	towels	1 50
"	4	Sheap and 3 lams	8.00
"	1	Mahony Burow	25 00
"	1	Dining tabel	8 00
"	1	brackfest tabel	5 00
"	6	winser Chares	6.00
"	6	Chares and Spinning weal	16 50
"	1	bedstead and Coid	5.00
"		tin ware bought at Shavers	5.49
"	13	Crocks	1.00
"		Sundres bought at Hagers as will apeaie By bil	34 29
			$665 11

May to	12	Spones	$2.25
"	1	gridiorn and 1 gridiorn 1 Cillett	1.75
"	7	yards of Muslen	1.75
"	8	yards of Muslen	2 00
"	1	Washbasked and 1 Soing basked	1.50
"	2	tubs 1 Churn 2 buckeds 1 butter tub	8 87½
"	1	Stone of Cuitens and 3 yards	13 00
"	1	doghtray and 1 frying pan	4 00
Nov 14 to	1	fat Steare	13 00
"	2	Woollen Counterpins	10 00
"	2	Ieren Pots and one duch oven and 1 Collender	6 50
"	1	Ieien Cittel	5 00
"	8	geas	2.00
"	2	flat Ierns	1.10

1822	June 11	to Cash	$ 1.50
		" 1 Coffin for your Chile mad by Mr Curry	2 50
1823		" 1 fameley Bibele	3 50
		" 3 munths work of Anteny	15 00
1824	Deem	" 1 Sam and himn Book	1 00
		" 1 Cow and Calf	10 00

Children (6), *surname Miller.*

i   Calvin⁴, *d* y.

ii   Upton⁴, *b* March 26, 1822, *d* April 18, 1902, *m* (1) *Louise Davis*, *m* (2) *Kate Newcomer*

iii   Daniel⁴ Miller, *b* March 22, 1824, *d* Sept. 16, 1905, in Ogle Co, Ill In 1849 he *m Mary Lambert*, *b* 1833 at Eakles Mills, Washington Co., Md ; dau of *Elizabeth (Poffenbarger) Lambert.*

    Children (5).

    (1) Albertis⁵, *b* 1851, *m Susan Reichard.*

    (2) Clara⁵, *b* 1854, *m John Miller*

    (3) Susan⁵, *b* 1857, *m Fred Mathias.*

    (4) Jacob⁵, *b* 1859, *m Amelia Miller.*

    (5) George Arthur⁵, *b* Jan. 31, 1864, at Mt Morris, Ill , May 19, 1891, *m Mina E. Vandervort*, educated in public sch , Mt Morris College, 1881-'82, Carthage (Ill) College, 1887-'90 (Academic grad. 1886) ; Eureka (Ill.) College, 1890 (A B)—theological graduate same, 1890, A M. from same, 1893, attended same 1900-'01 ; Chicago Univ., 1904. Was farmer until 1885, teacher until 1888, minister 1887 to present in Christian Church, Pastor Chr Ch , Monroe, Wis , 1890-91, Normal, Ill., 1891-94 ; Covington, Ky , 1894-1906, Ninth St Chr. Ch , Washington, D C , 1907, Editor Intermediate S S Commentary Standard Pub Co 1901- —, Mrs Miller *d* at Washington, D C , Sept 27, 1910 ; residence, 338 10th St. N. E , Washington, D C

iv   Andrew⁴ Miller, *b* March 24, 1826, at Caseytown, Washington Co , Md.; *m* July 15, 1850, *Easter Ann Smith*, *b* 1830, dau *John* and *Sarah Smith*; Easter *d* March 11, 1899, and was buried at Mann Church, Washington Co , Md. Andrew is undertaker and lived at Boonesboro, Md.

    Children (5).

    (1) Alice⁵, *b* Aug 15, 1851, *d* April 13, 1861 ; unm.

(2) Hamilton Pierce[5], *b* March 1, 1853, *d* June 1, 1895

(3) Sarah E [5], *b* July 11, 1855, *d* Jan. 28, 1877

(4) Sue S.[5], *b* Sept 17, 1862, March 24, 1904, *m John H. Nazarene,* Boonesboro, Md.

(5) Thomas H.[5], *b* Aug 7, 1863, res Fairplay, Md

v   Jonathan[4] Miller, *b* April 18, 1826, *d* Nov, 1903, *m Lucinda Curfet,* lived Martinsburg, W. Va —only son to enter either army, and he entered the Southern one.

vi Elizabeth[4] Miller, *b* and *d* 1832

[C41] CASANDRA[4] BRUMBAUGH ([C7] Henry[2], Johann Henrich[1]) *b* Oct 23, 1804, *m* (1) *John Spickler.* After his *d* she *m* (2) *Absalom* (or *David?*) *Johnson,* and they moved to a point near Rockford, Ill   Henry[2] never forgave her for this *m.*   Further details unobtainable   There were 5 ch as issue 1st *m,* of whom but the name of i *Calvin B Spickler* has been obtained

MARRIAGE PORTION OF CASANDRA[3] (BRUMBAUGH) SPICKLER '

The following memorandum account has been copied from [C7] Henry[2] Brumbaugh's ledger and also shows the goods and chattels with which she commenced housekeeping

CASANDRA SPICKLER '

1822

March 25 To	1 Side Saddel and Bridel	$18.50
"	13 yds Bedtickin	5.20
"	7 yds to Linnen	1.75
"	4 yds Camerrick muslen	1.50
"	6 Silver teespones	4 50
"	2 wollen Counterpins	10 00
"	4 Pare of Blankets	36 00
"	3 quealts	18 00
"	4½ yards of to linnen	1.12½
"	1 Negro girl adled and a boy James	350 00
"	1 Bay Mare	70.00
"	1 old Chafe Bag	1 00
"	75 lb of fethers	37.50
"	12 Chares	12 50
"	1 Spinning weal	3.00

*Furnished by [C119] Upton S—' Brumbaugh, Baltimore, Md

1822

March 25 To	1 Burow	$10.00
"	1 Bedsted	3 25
"	1 Dining tabel	5 00
"	1 Cichen do	1 00
"	1 ——	1 50
"	1 fring pane .	1.62½
"	Sundres bought at Shumens	11 47¾
"	Furneture Bought at Curres	31 00
"	Sundres bought at Websters	13 68½
"	Sundres bought at Hagers	24.40
"	teepot and 1 Shuger Bole	1 27½
"	1 lookinglase	4 50
"	9 tabel cloths	22 50
"	6 Sheats	12 00
"	83 lbs of Baken at 8 c	6 64
"	2 Bed cords	1.00
"	6 towels .	1 50
"	3 Cows	40 00
"	4 Sheap and 5 Lams	9 00
"	12 yards of bedticken	5 00
"	2 baskeds	1.25
"	1 Iron Cittle	5.50
"	1 Butter Churn	2 00
March 25 To	8 yards ——	$2 00
1823		
Nov. 4 "	1 Staned of Curtens	9.50
1828		
Sept. 3 "	cash	20 00
1830		
Oct. 8 "	10 bushels of Sead Wheat $2 per bu	20 00

$787 54

[C42] OTHO[3] BRUMBAUGH ([C7] Henry[2], Johann Jacob[1]) *b* July 28, 1807, *m Catharine Bookwalter*, dau *Gerhard ("Garrett") Bookwalter* of Hagerstown, Md, a miller Gerhard's father came from Switzerland in a vessel which was lost, including his entire family, excepting a brother and himself Otho[3] was a Captain in the "Hagerstown Regulars," ˚ and lived on the homestead farm in Washington Co, Md, until in 1829 the family moved to Mont-

gomery Co , O., they went by carriage to the Ohio River, went down the latter
on a flat-boat to Cincinnati, then up to Liberty, O.,,to Bookwalter's, soon
after the family located on a farm in Preble Co , where West Manchester stands
and where both the parents *d*—Otho in 1881   Catharine was a member G. B
B. Ch , but Otho[3] is said never to have made any profession of religious faith
          Children (10)
[C83] + Margaret[4], *b* 1828.
[C84] + Gerhard[4], *b* 1829
[C85] + Theophilus[4], *b* 1831
[C86] + Maria[4], *b* 1833.
[C87] + Henry[4], *b* 1835
[C88] + Calvin[4], *b* 1837.
[C89] + George[4], *b* Nov 7, 1840.
[C90]   Elvina[4], unm, *d* in Kans
[C91] + Upton E—[4]
[C92] + Levi[4], *b* June 17, 1850, *d* Sept 20, 1880.

  [C43] ANDREW[3] BRUMBAUGH ([C7] Henry[2], Johann Jacob[1]) *b*
Oct. 5, 1809, 1846 *m Susan Lynch, b* 1826; dau —— and *Permelia Lynch*
  It is related of Andrew[3] that he quarreled with his father and went to
N. C., where for a time he lived as overseer on a large plantation. A reconcilia-
tion took place, and he returned, buying part of the ancestral homestead in
1848 (near Middleburg, about four miles north of Hagerstown, Md.)   He *d*
in 1856, and his remains rest beside those of Henry[2] [C7] and Jacob[1] [C1]
Susan later *m* ——, a minister; details not obtained.
          Children (5)
[C118] + Margaret[4] Permelia, *b* June 17, 1847; *d* 1878
[C119] + Upton S—[4], *b* April 1, 1849
[C120]   Alice[4], *b* 1851, *d* 1866.
[C121]   Sallie[4], *b* 1854, *d* 1885; *m Norman Shindell*, (1 ch).
[C122]   Henry Clinton[4], *b* 1856, *d* Easter, 1863.

  [C46] GEORGE[3] BRUMBAUGH ([C7] Henry[2], Johann Jacob[1]) *b*
June 30, 1848, in Washington Co , Md ; *m Mary Ann Sharp* of Sharpsburg,
Va., moved to Preble Co , O , in 1852, and to Montgomery Co in 1856, where
he was a farmer, *d* 1858; Mary *d* 1888; both buried South of Dayton, O
          Children (7).
[C156]   Annie E [4], *b* 1842; *d* 1885, *m Daniel Meade*, (6 ch)

—————
*According to [C91] Upton E—[4] Brumbaugh.

[C157] + William Greenberry⁴, *b* March 14, 1844.

[C158]   Margaret Virginia⁴, *b* 1846, *m James B Young;* res Dayton,
             O , (no issue)

[C159] + John Henry⁴, *b* 1848

[C160]   Emma P.⁴, *b* 1850, *m David M. Young;* farmer near Dayton, O

[C161] + Charles S ⁴, *b* 1852.

[C162] + Andrew Wesley⁴, *b* 1855

   [C47] CALVIN³ BRUMBAUGH ([C7] Henry², Johann Jacob¹) *b* near
Hagerstown, Md ; moved early in life to Millersburg, Holmes Co , O , *m Agnes
Emeline Pinkerton*, dau *John* and *Nancy Pinkerton* of Mt. Vernon, Knox Co ,
O.; *d* in California in 1858   Agnes *m* (2) *Jacob Myers* of Agency City, Iowa,
and *d* at Moline, Ill., Feb 15, 1909
              Children (3), *b* at *Millersburg, O..*

[C180] + John Henry⁴, *b* 1851

[C181] + Eli Harrison⁴, *b* 1853, *d* Jan 19, 1902.

[C182]   Upton Ross⁴, *b* 1855, *d* 1900; unm.

   [C51] ALEXANDER⁴ BRUMBAUGH ([C9] Joseph³, [C2] Jacob²,
Johann Jacob¹) *b* Oct 27, 1815, 1851 *m Elizabeth Hawthorn*   He was an
atty.-at-law and lived at Marysville, Marshall Co , Kansas.
              One daughter.

[C186] + Emma Jane⁵, *b* March 17, 1864.

   [C52] JULIA ANN⁴ BRUMBAUGH ([C9] Joseph³, same ancestry as
[C51]) *b* Oct 26, 1819, *m Abram Rush*, a minister , lived near "Zearfas, Md.";
moved to Ohio, and Julia Ann⁴ is reported to have *d* at Attica, Seneca Co ,
that State   They had children

   [C53] EMILY⁴ BRUMBAUGH ([C9] Joseph³, same ancestry as
[C51]) *b* May 28, 1822, near Hagerstown, Washington Co , Md , *m Abraham
Stouffer, b* 1822 in Lancaster Co , Pa.; *s Abraham Stouffer*   Abraham, Jr ,
was a mechanic, Dem ; member M E Ch , and *d* 1887 near Salt Creek, Mich.;
Emily⁴ *d* 1891 and was buried in Robbins Cemetery at Salt Creek.
      Children (2), *surname Stouffer·*
   i Laura Virginia⁵, *b* 1843 on a farm in Porter Co , Ind , 1866 *m* (1)
       Amos Kendall Robbins, b 1840, *d* 1879.   June 9, 1881, Laura⁵ *m*
       (2) *John August Gustafson*, who *d* May 24, 1887.   She *m* (3) Nov
       27, 1890, *Alonzo Elvin Deval, b* Nov 6, 1850; address is Valparaiso,
       Ind., R. R. 4, Box 54

One daughter by 1st m

(1) Olive May[6] Robbins, *b* Nov. 2, 1871, *m Charles Howard Johnston;* La Porte, Ind, R R. 7, Box 19

One son by 2d m.

(2) Edward Vancouver[6] Gustafson, *b* Nov. 29, 1882, *m Lydia Mae Galloway,* Chesterton, Ind, R R. 1.

(3) Blanche Irene[6] Gustafson, *b* March 26, 1885; *m John Nicholas Laheyn,* Valparaiso, Ind.

ii Mary Ellen[5], *b* Dec 28, 1851, near Valparaiso, Porter Co, Ind ; Aug 13, 1871, *m Andrew C Harris,* address Wolverine, Mich, Box 52.

Children (3), surname Harris.

(1) Cora P[6], *b* 1874; *m Barnes Napier;* address 3442 54th St., Elseten Sta, Chicago, Ill

(2) Mable G[6], *b* 1877, *m* —— *Marine;* address 1373 Angus St, Fresno, Cal

(3) Laura F[6], *b* July, 1879, *m* —— *Chase;* address Wolverine, Mich.

[C54] MARY[4] BRUMBAUGH ([C9] Joseph[3], same ancestry as [C51]) *b* in Washington Co, Md, Jan. 8, 1824, May 3, 1884 *m Edward Lacy Betts, b* Dec 13, 1821, in Bucks Co, Pa.; *s Zachariah* and *Maria (Mitchell) Betts* Edward was a farmer; Repn.; member Luth Ch ; enlisted in Co. E, 1st Mich. Sharp Shooters, and was discharged June 23, 1865 The family resided in Bloomfield Twp, near La Grange, Ind, where he *d* March 1, 1894, and Mary[4] *d* Aug 24, 1894, both were buried in Greenwood Cemetery

Children (6), surname Betts.

i Annie A.[5], *b* Aug 16, 1850

ii Laura[5], *b* Sept 16, 1854, Oct. 8, 1876, *m Hiram Crowl, b* June 15, 1851, in Putnam Co, O , *s Samuel* and *Lucinda Crowl;* farmer, Repn , memb Christian Ch

Children (2), surname Crowl.

(1) Ray E.[6], *b* May 19, 1883

(2) Olive M[6], *b* Dec 25, 1886.

iii Fremont[5], *b* Aug 18, 1857, *d* Feb 12, 1861.

iv Carrie[5], *b* Sept 10, 1860, *d*

v Etta[5], *b* July 23, 1863.

vi George W.[5], *b* March 23, 1866; Aug 18, 1895, at Centerville, Mich, *m Bertha A Gonser,* who *d* from consumption March 26, 1909, address La Grange, Ind.

Children (3).

(1) Ethel M , *b* May 20, 1896, *d* May 1, 1890

(2) Lester L., *b* Oct 3, 1903

(3) Forest G , *b* March 24, 1907; *d* March 20, 1908.

[C56] ELEANOR⁴ BRUMBAUGH ([C9] Joseph³, same ancestry as [C51] *b* Dec 8, 1827: *d* July 27, 1889 .

"I shall now speak of the most important step, and part of my life. Was married to ELEANOR BRUMBAUGH on the 20th of May, 1851, in Grants-ville, Md., by the Rev Henry Knepper, in the German Reformed church We lived together in that place three years, before moving to Cumberland Our first two children were born there + + +."[a]

"Eleanor[b], wife of Jacob Brown, *d* at their residence in Cumberland, Md , on the 27th day of July, 1889, after an illness of over two weeks, age 61 Her children were all present at her death and funeral, which took place at 5 P. M on the 28th in Rose Hill Cemetery. She leaves surviving her husband, Jacob Brown, and five children, all of age, three daughters and two sons—two daughters and one son unmarried She was married to her surviving husband May 20, 1851, and has lived in Allegheny County ever since, nearly all the time in Cumberland She was born and reared in Washington Co , Md . the sixth daughter of the late Joseph and Elizabeth Angle Brumbaugh, two ancient families of great respectability Her immediate family left that country many years ago The survivors are one brother, Alexander, in Kansas; two sisters, Mary and Emily, in Indiana, all her seniors She was a full cousin of Catherine Angle McComas, mother of Congressman McComas, and she a daughter of the late Henry Angle, one of Washington County's most respected citizens The deceased, in life, was retiring and modest, amiable, quiet and kind in her disposition, yet energetic, wise and intelligent in her chosen sphere in life—thoroughly domestic and practical by nature and cultivation. Her house a model of industry and prudence, where her friends were sure of a hearty welcome and real hospitality She was intensely devoted to her family, and took but little share in the world's pleasures—hers were at home "

Jacob Brown was *b* April 7, 1824, on the "old Brown farm" of 103 acres midway between the Little Meadows in Md. and Salisbury in Pa.—part in Pa. and mostly in Md., s *Samuel Brown*, *b* Nov. 15, 1770. who was s of *Willie Brown*, *b* at the head of Elk River, Delaware Co , Pa —and of *Martha* ——. His mother was *Amy (Penrod) Brown*, *b* March 7, 1783; dau

---

[a]"Brown's Miscellaneous Writings"—Jacob Brown, Cumberland, Md , 1896, p 323
[b]Same reference, p 228

John Penrod, who lived, as well as latter's parents, on a farm three miles S. of Somerset, Pa   Jacob Brown has written *"Brown's Miscellaneous Writings"*—Cumberland, Md , 1896, and the full details concerning his family are given in pp. 309-323 This very interesting volume deals with many subjects (historical, biographical, etc)—unfortunately, the edition is exhausted and it is out of print.

Judge Brown was educated in the "old time schools" and attended Washington College in 1845 and '46, was admitted to the bar of Cumberland, Md , in 1849, and is the oldest member of that bar—he has retired from the active practice of law He is especially well acquainted with genealogical matters in Md and for his active assistance the writer is glad to here express appreciation.

> *Children* (7), *surname Brown.*

- i Emma Elizabeth[5], *b* Aug 9, 1853; *m Daniel Chisholm*
- ii Katharine Jane[5], *b* March 8, 1855, unm.; Cumberland, Md.
- iii Georgia[5], *b* Jan 15, 1857; *m George W McLaughlin*, *d* Oct 9, 1884, at Keyser, W Va   "On account of her many rare womanly traits, she earned many close and dear friends."
     > *One son·*
     (1) George Brown McLaughlin, *b* Oct 15, 1884
- iv Joseph[5], *b* May 25, 1859; *m Thearesa Seaders*, residence, Cumberland, Md
     > *Children* (2):
     (1) Eleanor T.[6]
     (2) Elizabeth B [6]
- v Frances Louisa[5], *b* March 31, 1863; *m Arthur O De Moss*, res. 219 B St., Roland Park, Baltimore, Md.
- vi David Newton[5], *b* Oct 14, 1865; unm ; res. Cumberland, Md.
- vii Ida Eleanor[5], *b* March 21, 1869; *d* May 20, 1879

[C66] HAVANA CATHARINE[4] BRUMBAUGH ([C21] Daniel[3], [C5] Daniel[2], Johann Jacob[1]) *b* Sept 28, 1827, *m Michael Croft*, and lived in Blair Co., Pa , where both *d* about 1904

> *Children* (3), *surname Croft*

- i Joseph Napoleon[5], *m Jennie Hite*, res Roaring Spring, Pa.; (1 ch)
- ii Daniel Michael[5]; *m Ellen Stiffler*, res. Hollidaysburg, Pa., asst. supervisor P R. R., (2 ch).

[C67] ROSANNA CAROLINE[4] BRUMBAUGH ([C21] Daniel[3], same ancestry as [C66]) *b* Sept 27, 1829, unm., by her own toil and careful atten-

tion to business she obtained free of debt a beautiful farm of 70 acres two miles E of Greenville, Dark Co , O , where she *d* Dec 19, 1902

[C68] SAMUEL DAVID⁴ BRUMBAUGH ([C21] Daniel³, same ancestry as [C66] *b* Jan 7, 1832, near Hagerstown, Washington Co , Md.; Dec. 8, 1853: *m Elizabeth Darner*, *b* June 24, 1831, at Beaverstown, Montgomery Co., O.; dau *Jacob Darner*   Samuel David⁴ was a farmer and lived near Greenville, Darke Co , O , Dem , member Ger. Ref. Ch.   He was commissioned July 4, 1863, First Lieut Co. E , 3d Regt., Ohio Inf   He *d* March 18, 1868, and was buried in the Greenville Cemetery, Darke Co., O.   Elizabeth *d* May 25, 1912.

     Children (5):

[C200] + John Franklin⁵, *b* Nov. 12, 1854; *d* Sept. 10, 1898.
[C201] + Daniel Harmon⁵, *b* Oct 11, 1856.
[C202] + Virginia Bell⁵, *b* Dec 21, 1859.
[C203] + Clement Laird⁵, *b* Feb. 28, 1863.
[C204] + William David⁵, *b* Aug 1, 1866

[C69] JOHN PETER⁴ BRUMBAUGH ([C21] Daniel³, same ancestry as [C66]) *b* May 29, 1835, unm , farmer, *d* Nov 26, 1899   [C67] Rosanna⁴, [C69] John Peter⁴, [C70] Simon Daniel⁴ and their parents all lived upon the same farm until the latter died—the survivors continue to live together, address Greenville, Darke Co., O.

[C71] JOSEPH NATHAN⁴ BRUMBAUGH ([C21] Daniel³, same ancestry as [C66]) *b* Oct 16, 1839, *m Minnie Lease*, he owns and operates a farm five miles E of Greenville, O

     Children (7):

[C238] Annie⁵
[C239] Daniel⁵.
[C240] Joseph⁵
[C241] Grover Cleveland⁵.
[C242] Lewis⁵.
[C243] Samuel David⁵.
[C244] Minnie⁵.

[C72] NANCY JANE⁴ BRUMBAUGH ([C21] Daniel³, same ancestry as [C66]) *b* Oct. 30, 1841, *m Mathias Imler;* farmer; address Greenville, Darke Co , O   Nancy Jane⁴ d May, 1906.

Children (6), *surname Imler:*

i Cora Bell[5]
ii Maggie E[5]
iii Anna May[5].
iv Alice Nellie[5]
v John B [5]
vi Harry B [5]

[C73] ELIZA LOUISA[4] BRUMBAUGH ([C21] Daniel [3], same ancestry as [C66]) *b* Nov 18, 1844, *m John McNutt*, address Greenville, O.

Children (5), *surname McNutt*

i Joseph[5].
ii Harvey[5].
iii John[5].
iv Havana[5].

[C74] SUSANNA BELL[4] BRUMBAUGH ([C21] Daniel[3], same ancestry as [C66]) *b* April 29, 1846, *m Phillip Hartzell* of Darke Co , O.

Children (4), *surname Hartzell*
(2 *d* y in Washington Co , Md.)
iii Orpha Gray[5], *d*; iv Annie Bell[5], *d*.

[C76] DAVID STUCKEY[4] BRUMBAUGH ([C28] Simeon K—[3], [C6] David[2], Johann Jacob[1]) *b* April 2, 1843, on the Brumbaugh homestead in Bloomfield Twp., Bedford Co., Pa., and spent his youth on the farm, attending public school in the winters, attended Allegheny Seminary, Rainsburg, Pa., in the Spring of 1860 and 1861; taught public schools in Pennsylvania and Illinois for twelve consecutive terms, commencing at Henrietta, Pa., in the Winter of 1860-61, studied law under Marshall W. Weir, Esq , of Belleville, Ill., and was admitted to the practice of law in the Supreme Court of Illinois June 9. 1869, admitted in Pennsylvania in 1871; has resided at Roaring Spring. Blair Co , Pa , since 1871, excepting two years' residence in Altoona, Pa. He was elected to the office of J P , and has served in that office almost continuously since 1880; united with the Luth Ch in his sixteenth year, and has long held the office of deacon and elder, has also frequently been a delegate to the General Synod (Luth), was director of the Lutheran Theological Seminary at Gettysburg, Pa , for fifteen years A Repn in politics, his first vote was cast for Abraham Lincoln in 1864, has frequently been a delegate to the State and County Republican conventions, and believes that good citizen-

ship includes the duty of helping to select and elect good local public officers, always an advocate for temperance, he is a total abstainer. He also heartily favors thorough and practical education, and has given much care to the education of his children

April 23, 1870, David Stuckey⁴ m (1) *Emma R Madara*, b in Bloomfield Twp , Bedford Co., Pa., dau *James* and *Jane Madara*   Emma d June 10, 1871   May 24, 1877, he m (2) *Fannie Louisa Cowen*, b ⸺, in Taylor Twp , Blair Co , Pa ; dau *John* and *Barbara (Hoover) Cowen*   Fannie d Nov 21, 1908, at Roaring Spring, Pa , after an illness from nephritis extending over about three months. She was an active and faithful member and worker in St Luke's Lutheran Church in her home town, and her death was a decided loss, not only to the family, but also to the community where she was so favorably known.

> *Daughter by 1st m*

[C206] + Emma Jane⁵, b June 1, 1871; m *Charles T. Holsinger*, d March 21, 1900.

> *One son, surname Holsinger:*
> Roy⁶.
> *Children (6) by 2nd m.*

[C207] + Arthur St. Clair⁵, M D , b Aug 23, 1879.
[C208] + Maude Edna⁵, b June 27, 1882.
[C209] + Sarah Barbara⁵, b Aug 27, 1883.
[C210] + Roland Edward⁵, b Nov 9, 1885
[C211]   Ruth Margaretta⁵, b Oct. 11, 1892.
[C212]   Luther Truman⁵, b July 1, 1894

[C77] MARIE LOUISE⁴ BRUMBAUGH ([C28] Simeon K—³, same ancestry as [C76]) b Oct 26, 1844, in Roaring Spring, Blair Co., Pa ; educated in public schools and in Millersville State Normal School (1862-'64); teacher in public schools of Pa (1864-'67), Sept, 1867, m *Lyman Polk Stookey*, M D , b 1845 in Belleville, Ill , where he lived, practised medicine and d in 1901   Dr Stookey was s *Moses* and *Elizabeth (Anderson) Stookey;* (of *Daniel** and *Barbara (Whetstone) Stookey*, of *Daniel (?) Stookey)*. He was educated in public and private schools of Ill , Shurtleff College (1863-'66); graduated Mo. Med College 1872 (M D.)—now Med Dept Univ of Mo , student assistant in Anatomy 1871-'72, president Southern Ill Med Assn ;

---

*Daniel Stookey was brother of Simon Stuckey, who m Rose Snyder—ancestors of Christine Stuckey, who m SIMEON K—³ BRUMBAUGH [C28]   "The name 'Stuckey' is believed to have been changed through a clerical error in a deed, and the name was retained, rather than resort to a court correction of the error "—Lyman Brumbaugh Stookey

president St. Clair Co Med Soc.; author of some papers on internal medicine, member Belleville (Ill) Baptist Ch   Mrs Brumbaugh survives him and lives at Hermosa Beach, Los Angeles, Cal

Children (5), *surname Stookey*

i   Mary[5], *b* 1874, *d* 1878

ii Lyman Brumbaugh[5], M D , *b* at Belleville, Ill , July 30, 1878, edu-cated in public schools, graduated from Belleville·High School 1893; attended Chicago Univ , and Yale, graduating (A.B.) from latter in 1900, also received A M and Ph D (1904) from same, 1901-'02 Graduate Scholarship in Physiology at Yale, 1902-'04 Associate in Physiology and Bio-chemistry in N Y. State Path. Lab., 1904-'05 student in Med Dept. (Graduate School) of Univ. of Strasburg, Germany, Professor of Physiology Univ. of South-ern Cal. 1905—; Amer. Ed. International Yearbook of Chem Physiology and Chem. 1905—. fellow Amer. Assn. A of S. 1906. author of over thirty original contributions to physiological and medical subjects; member Amer Chem. Soc., Amer. Soc. Biolog Chemists, Amer Physiolog Soc , Soc. Experimental Med and Biology.   Dec 31, 1903, at Belleville, Ill , *m Margaret Powell* Address University Club, Los Angeles, Cal

iii Bayard[5], *b* and *d* 1882

iv Adele[5], *b* at Belleville, Ill , 1884, where educated in the public schools, graduated from Hosmer Hall, St Louis, 1901, pursued advanced study in French in N Y. 1901-'02. studied and traveled in Europe 1902-'06; attended Univ of Southern Cal , 1906-'08, taking A B degree in 1908, (A.M 1909), assistant in French in Univ. of Southern Cal , and graduate student 1908-'09, instructor in French and Italian at same institution 1909-'10, Jan. 31, '11, *m Alanson Halden Jones, M. D* , ad. 222 Bradbury Bldg , Los Angeles, Cal.

v   Byron Polk[5], *b* at Belleville, Ill , in 1887; there educated in the pub-lic schools, at Smith Acad , St Louis, —— Park Acad , Chicago; Strasburg (Germany) Gymnasium 1904-'05; student Univ. of Geneva, Switzerland, 1905-'07, assistant in Compar Anat. in Univ of Geneva 1906-'07; attended Univ. of Southern Cal 1907-'08, re-ceiving A B degree; attended Harvard Univ. 1908-'09, receiving A M. degree (*magna cum laude*), student Med. Dept. Univ. of Southern Cal. and assistant in Anatomy 1909—.   Address Her-mosa Beach, Los Angeles, Cal.

[C78] EVALINE DOROTHY[4] BRUMBAUGH—"EVA" ([C28] Simeon K—[3], same ancestry as [C76]) *b* Dec 6, 1846; March, 1868, *m* Rev *John Gruber*[5] *Snider,** *b* Sept 29, 1844, s [C3-iii-(2)] *Jacob Ulery*[4] and *Lavina (Gruber) Snyder* (see p. 161); a minister in the Progressive German Baptist Church, residence formerly in Taylor Twp, Blair Co, Pa, but now in Courtland Republic Co, Kans

> *Children* (7), *surname Snider**

> i   Lillie Viola[5], *b* Jan 17, 1869, *m Harry A. Madara*, farmer; residence near Roaring Spring, Pa

> ii Ida Florence[5], *b* Sept 24, 1870; *m Emanuel D Moek*; residence 1005 Logan Ave, Tyrone, Pa

> iii Simon Jacob[5], M D, *b* March 25, 1872, June 3, 1900, *m Ella L Fogelberg*, dau *Andrew* and *Belle (Myers) Fogelberg*, he graduated Millersville (Pa.) State Nor. Sch. 1894 (B E); graduated Medico Chirurgical Med College 1897 (M D), located in Altoona, Pa., until April, 1898, enlisted as Hosp Steward 4th Regt, Pa Vol Inf, Span -Amer War; upon mustering out of his Regt. resumed practice in Altoona, and in March, '99, moved to Courtland, Kans., where he has since engaged in regular medical and surgical practice, Repn , member Prog Breth. Ch

>> *Children* (3):

>> (1) Marjorie May[6], *b* Oct. 24, 1902, *d* Feb 7, 1904
>> (2) Simon Fred[6], *b* June 26, 1905
>> (3) Louis Holland M [6], *b* Oct 14, 1906

> iv Lavinia May[5], *b* Aug 5, 1876, trained nurse; *d* Feb. 24, 1905
> v   Grace Evelyn[5], *b* Dec 3, 1879, residence Tyrone, Pa
> vi Lyman Edgar[5], *b* Oct 12, 1881; residence Altoona, Pa , unm
> vii John Blaine[5], *b* July 17, 1884, graduated State College, Pa , 1908—employed in U S Treasury Assay Office, New York City.

[C79] ROSE KISSECKER[4] BRUMBAUGH ([C28] Simeon K—[3], same ancestry as [C76]) *b* May 22, 1848, in Bloomfield Twp, Bedford Co, Pa.; June 30, 1870, *m Andrew Snowberger*[5] *Stayer, M D.* [C18-i-(1)], *b* May 21, 1848, in South Woodbury Twp, near New Enterprise, Bedford Co , Pa., s *Samuel* and *Elizabeth (Snowberger) Stayer* [C18-i].

"His great-grandfather was born in France, and when but a lad accompanied Gen. Lafayette to this country. He served through the Revolutionary campaign, and after the war made his permanent settlement in Bedford Co ,

---

*Only John Gruber Snider and his children spell the name "Snider," the others use "Snyder"

where he passed the remainder of his days   Dr Stayer's maternal ancestors were Swiss, his great-grandfather (Snowberger) having emigrated from Switzerland to Bedford Co , Pa " *

Dr Stayer was reared upon the old Stayer homestead; attended the common schools, Bedford Co Normal School, Millersville State Normal School—teaching winters—1869 began the study of medicine under Dr. Charles Long, of South Woodbury , 1870 attended Med. Dept Mich State Univ , and graduated (M D) March 12, 1873, from Jefferson Med College; March 18 he located at Roaring Spring, Blair Co , Pa., and continued there in active and very successful general practice until Aug. 15, 1893, when he removed to Altoona, Pa , address 613 15th St , that city   He is a member of the Blair Co. Med Soc , Penna State Med Soc , Amer Med Assn., and Assn of Mil Surgeons of the U S

He served as school director for Taylor Twp , Blair Co , Pa., 9 years, for Roaring Spring, Pa , 6 years, for Altoona, Pa., 10 years; member Pa Leg Sessions 1891 and '93, Maj and Surg 5th Regt , Pa Vol., Spanish-Amer. War, May 5, 1898, to Nov 7, 1898, Maj and Surg 5th Regt , N. G. Pa., 1885 to Jan , 1904, Lieut -Col and Surg in Chief Div N G Pa. Has passed the chairs in all Masonic bodies, except the Scottish Rite, also in the I O. G T. , Repn., memb Luth. Ch , and also much interested in S S work

Children (3), *surname Stayer.*

i Edgar Simon[5], *b* Nov 7, 1874; ed com schs , Roaring Spring High Sch , Penna Col., Gettysburg, Pa , 1890-'91, Wittenberg Col , 1891-'94, grad.' June 14, '94 (A B), taught in pub sch. and studied law; memb Co. C, 5th Regt., N. G. Pa., 1890 to '93, etc , mustered into U. S. service May 11, '98; mustered out Nov. 7, '98, apptd. 1st Lieut 28th Regt , U. S Vols., July 13, '99; Quartermaster of Regt until it was mustered out at San Francisco May 1, 1901—served through various battles in the Philippines, as 1st Lieut , 23d U. S Inf., April 2, 1902, returned to Philippines—returned to U. S with Regt. June 14, 1905; served at Madison Barracks, N Y , San Francisco, Cal , April, 1906, Jamestown Exposition; Aug. 15, 1907, Prof of Military Science and Tactics at Delaware College, Newark, Del , since March 12, 1911, Capt , 23d Inf U. S A., stationed at Ft Benjamin Harrison, Ind.

ii Morrison Clay[5], M.D , *b* July 12, 1884, *m Edna Keller;* grad. Altoona High School 1899, La Fayette College (A B) 1903, Jefferson Med. Col (M D), 1906, was one of the resident physicians

*History of Blair Co , Pa —Africa, 1883, p 224

at St. Agnes Hospital, Phila., for five months after graduation;
engaged in practice of medicine at 1131 7th Ave , Altoona, Pa ,
until Oct , 1908, when he became Surgeon in U. S A , with rank of
1st Lieut   During the Span.-Amer War he served as private in
Hosp Corps U. S A , and was honorably discharged Dec 7, 1898

iii   Clara Mabel⁵, *b* March 12, 1886; graduated from Altoona High Sch.
in 1903 , pursued various studies at Lausanne, Switzerland, in 1904,
and spent 1905 in Germany; graduated from Wellesley College
1910.

[C80] SIMON SCHMUCKER⁴ BRUMBAUGH, M.D ([C28] Simeon
K—³, same ancestry as [C76]) *b* July 17, 1852, at the homestead in Bloomfield Twp , Bedford Co , Pa . attended public schools, Martinsburg Acad ,
taught several years in Pa. and Ill ; graduated Mo Med Col , St. Louis, Mo ,
1878 (M D) ; began practice at Pipersville, Bucks Co , Pa., and there remained
in a large practice for nearly 20 years; after a year of rest at Hopewell, N. J ,
he removed to 2923 N 12th St . Phila , Pa , where he has since been actively
and successfully engaged in medical practice   He is conservative in politics , a
Dem.; member Pres Ch.; an earnest S S worker, as Supt and teacher   He
erected a chapel at Pipersville, Pa , for S. S. work at his own expense, 1880 *m*
Elizabeth Morgan •
    *Children*ᵇ (5)
    (a) Emma⁵, *d* y.
    (b) May Irene⁵; grad N J State Normal Sch.—taught, *m* —— *Mor-.*
        gan; lives in Phila , Pa
    (c) Christine Grace⁵. grad East Stroudsburg State Nor. Sch ; *m C. N.*
        Sperling, res Phila , Pa.
    (d) Howard S.⁵, *b* 1884, *m Harriet Archibald;* ad. 1126 Chestnut St ,
        Phila., Pa
    (e) Roy T ⁵; student in Penna. College, Gettysburg, Pa

[C81] MARGARET CHRISTENA⁴ BRUMBAUGH ([C28] Simeon
K—³, same ancestry as [C76]) *b* Sept , 1856; *m Frederick Schneider,* Margaret⁴ *d* Dec., 1883
    Children (3), *surname Schneider.*
    i Frederick⁵, ii Flora⁵, iii Infant, *d* y

[C82] GRACE ELEANORE⁴ BRUMBAUGH ([C28] Simeon K—³,
[C6] David², Johann Jacob¹) *b* Nov. 20, 1861; *m George Yingling*

• and ᵇAll information kindly furnished by [C76] *David Stuckey⁴ Brumbaugh* after his
brother failed to reply, and received too late to assign numbers to the children

Children (3), *surname Yingling*
i Christiana⁵, ii Lena⁵; iii Simon⁵

[C83] MARGARET⁴ BRUMBAUGH ([C42] Otho³, [C7] Henry², Johann Jacob¹) *b* in Washington Co, Md, ——, 1828, *m George Washington Brown;* they moved to Cherubusco, Ind, later moved to a farm near Goshen, Noble Co, Ind, where they yet live, both members G B B Ch.

Children (8), *surname Brown*

i William⁵, *b* May 24, 1848, *m Mary Zumbrum.*
Children (5):
(1) Syntha Ann⁶, *m* —— *Darr,* Syracuse, Ind.
(2) Sabia Anthum⁶; *m* (1) —— *Gump,* (2) —— *Babcock*
(3) Lilly Viletta⁶; *m* —— *Bear*
(4) George Washington⁶.
(5) Albert⁶

ii Otho⁵, *b* April 24, 1850; *m Barbara Royer*
Children (5):
(1) Rose⁶; *m* GEORGE BRUMBAUGH, Syracuse, Kosciusko Co, Ind
(2) Franklin⁶; unm
(3) Charles⁶, *m*, residence Ft Wayne, Ind
(4) William⁶, *m*, ——, Kans
(5) Iva⁶, unm; residence Syracuse, Ind

iii George⁵, *b* April 19, 1853, *m Annie McCoy,* (3 ch).
iv Sarah Catherine⁵, *b* Nov. 1, 1856, *m* —— *Southwick,* (no issue).
v Frances Ellen⁵, *b* Dec. 28, 1858, *m Aaron Eagley;* (3 ch).
vi Lydia Alice⁵, *b* May 24, 1861, *m Samuel Block;* (7 ch).
vii Effie⁵, *b* June 12, 1863, *d* Sept 7, 1864
viii Laura⁵, *b* Aug 30, 1865; *m W. H Spitler;* (5 ch)

[C84] GERHARD⁴ BRUMBAUGH ([C42] Otho³, same ancestry as [C83]) *b* 1829; his parents started to Ohio when he was but nine weeks old; he *m Hester Brown,* and they lived in Union City, Randolph Co, Ind, where he *d.*

Children (12; 5 s and 7 dau)

i Alice⁵, *m* —— *Smith,* residence, Piqua, O
ii Daughter, *m W W Fowler,* Union City, Ind
iii Nora B⁵; *m Harvey Skidmore,* Anderson, Ind

[C85] THEOPHILUS⁴ BRUMBAUGH ([C42] Otho³, same ancestry as [C83]) *b* 1831; *m Elizabeth Gates,* they lived at Redkey, Jay Co., Ind The-

ophilus[4] served during the Rebellion in a Co of Ohio Inf Both are deceased
Children (10, 4 sons and 6 dau):

[C251] Elmer George[5], lives at Owensboro, Ky.
[C252] Libby[5], m John Deem, lives at 116 Richmond Ave., Richmond, Ind
[C253] Willis[5], unm, lives 6065 Princeton Ave, Chicago, Ill
[C254] Mallusa[5], m Dora Price; lives at New Paris, Preble Co, O
[C255] Olive[5].
[C256] Dora[5].

[C86] MARIA[4] BRUMBAUGH ([C42] Otho[3], same ancestry as [C83])
b 1833; m Laborius A Gates—deceased Maria[4] lives in Butler Co, Kans.
Children (8, 6 sons and 2 dau), surname Gates.
i Charles[5], ii Leo C.[5], Los Angeles, Cal

[C87] HENRY[4] BRUMBAUGH, M D ([C42] Otho[3], same ancestry as
[C83]) b 1835, m Elizabeth Coovert, both deceased.
Children (5, 4 s and 1 dau):
[C298] Gerhart[5]; m.
[C299] De Soto[5], d.
[C300] Ella[5]; m Irvin Stanton.
[C301] Balboa[5], m and d

[C88] CALVIN[4] BRUMBAUGH ([C42] Otho[3], same ancestry as
[C83]) b 1837, m Lorinda Esta Collins; he d in Kans., she lives in same State.
It is said Calvin[4] served during the Rebellion in Co E, 5th O. Vol Cav.
Children (8, 3 s and 5 dau)—details unobtainable

[C89] GEORGE[4] BRUMBAUGH ([C42] Otho[3], same ancestry as
[C83]) b Nov 7, 1840, at West Manchester, Preble Co., O ; July 1, 1866, m
Lovinda McKinstry, b at Eaton, Preble Co, O, dau Jacob and Mary (Odell)
McKinstry He taught in the public schools for thirteen years, then became
a farmer In 1888 he moved into Eaton, Preble Co, O, and has since lived
there, being a dealer in real estate; Dem, Protestant.
Children (3):
[C386] + Lawrence McKinstry[5], b Dec 22, 1867
[C387] + Virgil Victor[5], b Aug. 18, 1874
[C388] + Zenobia Ernestine[5], b Dec 19, 1876

[C91] UPTON E—[4] BRUMBAUGH ([C42] Otho[3], same ancestry as
[C83]) b in Preble Co, O, m (1) Sarah M. McKinstry, dau William and

Rebecca (Gray) McKinstry, m (2) *Sarah E. Hasty*, dau *Robert Hasty*
Served in 13th O Inf, 48th O Arty, and 22d Ind. Vol Inf during the War
of the Rebellion, Dem, Spiritualist; cement worker; residence, 412 W. 6th
St., Marion, Grant Co., Ind.

Children (8, 5 dau and 3 s).
[C405] Hope⁵.
[C406] Richard⁵.
[C407] Charles N⁵; m, residence, Logansport, Ind
[C408] Pearl⁵; m —— Cronkite, Indianapolis, Ind
[C409] Lee⁵; unm

[C92] LEVI⁴ BRUMBAUGH ([C42] Otho³, same ancestry as [C83])
b June 17, 1850, at West Manchester, Preble Co, O.; Sept. 3, 1874, m *Rebecca Hoover*, b Dec 5, 1852, at Miamisburg, Montgomery Co., O., where
they resided, dau *Frederick* and *Elizabeth (Bolten) Hoover*. He was an atty.;
Dem; and d Sept 20, 1880.

Children (3):
[C421]   Ada⁵, b Sept 3, 1875; m *Milton Snyder*
[C422] + Robert Nevin⁵, b Feb 16, 1878.
[C423]   Leona⁵, b Nov 23, 1880; d Nov. 27, 1885.

[C94] JOSEPH⁴ BRUMBAUGH ([C9] John³, [C2] Jacob², Johann
Jacob¹) m *Catharine Gossard*, lived in Washington Co, Md

Children (13)
[C305] John⁵, m *Emma Wolf*
[C306] George⁵, m *Mary Blosser.*
[C307] Jacob⁵; m *Sarah Bechtle*
[C308] Joseph⁵; unm
[C309] Charles⁵, unm.
[C310] Daniel⁵; d y
[C311] Mary⁵, m *Daniel Mertz*
[C312] Nannie⁷, m *Christian Shenck.*
[C313] Sarah⁵, m *George Jackson.*
[C314] Eliza⁵, m *Wm T Andrews*
            i John Albert Andrews.
[C315] Katie C.⁵, m *Wm. T. Adams.*
            i Eva Glendora Adams
[C316] Victoria⁵.
[C317] David⁵.

[C96] CATHARINE[4] BRUMBAUGH ([C16] David[3], [C4] John[2], Johann Jacob[1]) *b* Dec 7, 1823, *m* *Rudolph Hoover*, *b* Dec. 17, 1820, in Lancaster Co , Pa.; s *Martin Hoover*, *b* 1777, and *d* March 17, 1855, and *Maria (Eshleman) Hoover*, *b* 1778, and *d* Oct 6, 1868   Catharine[4] *d* Dec. 7, 1865, from "dropsy "   Rudolph *m* (2) *Annie Coble*   He was a farmer; Dem ; memb. G. B. B Ch ; and lived at Woodbury, Bedford Co , Pa.; *d* July 21, 1899.

Children (10), *surname Hoover*

i   Mary[5], *b* June 9, 1844, *m James Matthews*, she *d* July 21, 1870, from consumption

    (1) Mary Malinda[6] Matthews, *b* Jan , 1869, *d* May 16, 1870.

ii   Martin[5], *b* 1816, *d* May, 1850

iii   Elizabeth[5], *b* Dec. 25, 1848; *d* May 18, 1870, from typhoid fever; unm

iv   Malinda[5], *b* Jan. 31, 1850, Dec. 27, 1870, *m Thomas M Ake*, s *Joseph* and *Nancy (Edwards) Ake;* he *d* March 25, 1907

      Children (2), *surname Ake:*

    (1) Myrtle[6], *b* Sept 22, 1871, *m Frederick A. Geib*

    (2) Margaret[6], *b* July 17, 1877, unm.

v   Elias[5], *b* Feb. 17, 1853, *m Lottie Long*, who *d* Dec. 18, '05, (no issue)

vi   Susan[5], *b* April 16, 1855, Aug 24, 1873, *m Thomas Imler*, *b* Aug , 1852. Susan *d* Aug 19, 1890, from typhoid fever, and Thomas *d* Nov. 30, 1908, from "dropsy."

      Children (3), *surname Imler.*

    (1) Harvey[6], *b* July 31, 1874

    (2) Blanche[6], *b* Oct 13, 1876

    (3) Thomas[6], *b* July 4, 1883

vii   Anna Belle[5], *b* April 24, 1857   Dec. 14, 1882, *m W. W. Coble*, *b* June 7, 1855, and *d* Jan 3, 1900

      Children (7), *surname Coble*

    (1) Lottie B [6], *b* Feb 7, 1884, *m E F. Linderer.*

    (2) Clyde H.[6], *b* Sept 12, 1885; *m Sadie Peters.*

    (3) William H [6], *b* Sept 24, 1888.

    (4) Ralph C.[6], *b* Jan 29, 1890

    (5) Myrtle B [6], *b* March 30, 1892

    (6) Edna V.[6], *b* Sept 24, 1894.

    (7) Hugh D.[6], *b* May 26, 1896

viii   Jennie[5], *b* July 14, 1860, Dec 4, 1881, *m William Hartman*

      Children (8), *surname Hartman:* Josie, Clarence, Andrew, George, James, Lillian, Robert, Chalmers.

ix   George B⁵, *b* Sept 30, 1863, *m Mary Summers*
     Children (4) Elsie, Clara, Margaret, Rudolph
x   Catharine⁵, *b* Sept 26, 1865; Feb, 1875, *m William Cromwell*, resi-
     dence, 344 E Pitt St, Bedford, Pa
     Children (5), *surname Cromwell.*
     (1) Harry Rudolph⁶, *b* Jan 3, 1887.
     (2) Margaret Cathryn⁶, *b* April 29, 1895 ·
     (3) Helen Isabell Hoover⁶, *b* Sept. 19, 1897.
     (4) Lydia⁶ *(née* Hearne), M.D.
     (5) W Ralph⁶.

[C97] JACOB SNYDER⁴ BRUMBAUGH ([C16] David³, same ancestry as [C96]) *b* Dec. 11, 1825, in South Woodbury Twp, Bedford Co, Pa ;
farmer, member G B B Ch , resided at New Enterprise, Bedford Co, Pa,
where he *d* Feb 22, 1894, Jan 28, 1849, *m* (1) *Magdaline Furry, b* July 17,
1831; dau *Leonard* and [C3-11] *Hannah⁴ (Brown) Furry* Magdalena *d*
April 5, 1850; 1857 *m* (2) *Susannah Pote, b* Oct 21, 1831; dau *John* and
Mary (Baker) Pote, Susannah d June 17, 1868; Oct. 6, 1869, he *m* (3)
Francina Straley, b Jan. 14, 1845, and the latter is reported as living at——.

Being the oldest son, he showed special ability in farming, and before
attaining his majority he was assigned a portion of his father's farm as tenant
and foreman

In 1857 he commenced farming on a larger scale, but living on his original
rented farm, he filled several Twp. offices, bought and sold timber lands, and
accumulated a considerable fortune   Upon David's³ death he paid for the
rented farm, and soon after bought the mansion part of the old Kochendarfer
estate, residing upon the latter until his death.   Soon after his second marriage both himself and his wife united with the German Baptist Brethren
Church

His body and general constitution were especially rugged, and his life
was quite active, he died from a relapse of La Grippe.   "He was kind and
charitable to the poor, strict and stern in business dealings, and possessed of a
remarkable memory."

        Son by 1st m·
[C320] + John Furry⁵, *b* March 16, 1850.
        Children by 2d m (8)
[C321] + Caroline Pote⁵, *b* Dec. 16, 1852, *d* June 19, 1878
[C322]   Nancy Pote⁵, *b* April 25, 1854, *d* June 18, 1865.
[C323] + Alison Pote⁵, *b* Feb 14, 1856
[C324] + Jacob Pote⁵, *b* March 7, 1858

[C325] + Mary Jane Pote⁵, *b* Aug 7, 1860.
[C326]   Susan Pote⁵, *b* Dec. 10, 1862, *d* June 12, 1865
[C327] + David Pote⁵, *b* Jan 10, 1865.
[C328] + Martin Pote⁵, *b* April 12, 1867.
            Children by 3d m (3).
[C329] + Daniel Straley⁵, *b* Oct. 1, 1870
[C330] + Franklin Straley⁵, *b* March 2, 1872
[C331]   Annie Straley⁵, *b* March 17, 1874, unm

[C98] ELIZABETH⁴ BRUMBAUGH ([C16] David³, same ancestry as
[C96]) *b* Jan 19, 1828, in Huntingdon Co., Pa., Dec 26, 1852, *m Andrew
Bechtel*, *b* in the same county Dec. 20, 1829; s *Peter* and *Elizabeth (Snow-
berger) Bechtel*   Elizabeth⁴ *d* July 4, 1861   Andrew on Oct. 13, 1861, *m* (2)
Elizabeth Frederick, *b* in Knox Co., O., Sept. 2, 1829, dau *Jacob* and *Esther
(Pringle) Frederick*—Jacob *b* in Huntingdon Co, Pa, Nov 2, 1793, and Es-
ther *b* May 23, 1795   Andrew was a farmer, member G B B. Ch , and *d* Feb.
3, 1907, near Ankenytown, Knox Co., O.
        Children by 1st m (4), surname Bechtel:
    i   Simon⁵, *b* Knox Co, O, May 26, 1854; May 10, 1877, *m Mary Ellen
        Swank*, *b* March 20, 1856
            Children (5).
        (1) Dore⁶, *b* June 3, 1878
        (2) Sylvia⁶, *b* Nov. 4, 1879, *d* March 24, 1880.
        (3) Walter⁶, *b* April 7, 1881; *d* Aug 26, 1888.
        (4) Alva⁶, *b* Jan. 30, 1883, *m Zella Leedy.*
        (5) Edna⁶, *b* May 29, 1888
    ii Jackson⁵, *b* Jan. 21, 1856, May 25, 1882, *m Martha Hess*, *b* March
        6, 1858, residence, Belleville, O
            Children (4):
        (1) Iva May⁶, *b* May 13, 1883
        (2) Oscar Hess⁶, *b* Sept. 10, 1884.
        (3) Elmer Hess⁶, *b* July 30, 1896
        (4) Lola Pernie⁶, *b* Oct 10, 1898
    iii Mary Ann⁵, *b* Jan 10, 1858, *d* Feb. 7, 1858
    iv Nancy Jane⁵, *b* Dec. 23, 1859, June 13, 1882, *m Solomon Jay Work-
        man*, farmer, address Fredericktown, O
            Children (4), surname Workman:
        (1) Celesta Gertrude⁶, *b* Sept 11, 1884; *d* Oct. 20, 1889.
        (2) Ernest Andrew⁶, *b* June 14, 1886; *m Effie Secord*
        (3) Clarence Earl⁶, *b* Feb. 24, 1891.

(4) Mabel Elizabeth⁶, *b* April 5, 1901.

Children by 2d m of Andrew (4), surname Bechtel.

v Isaac⁵, *b* Aug 6, 1862, *d* June 21, 1864

vi Lewis⁵, *b* Sept. 15, 1864

vii Sarah⁵, *b* Sept 25, 1866

viii Minnie⁵, *b* July 6, 1870

[C100] JOHN SNYDER⁴ BRUMBAUGH ([C16] David³, same ancestry as [C96]) *b* June 16, 1832, at New Enterprise, Bedford Co , Pa ; March 17, 1857, *m* *Delilah Ober*, *b* Jan. 18, 1839, at New Enterprise, Pa ; dau *Jacob* and *Hannah (Stevens) Ober;* he was farmer; member G. B B Ch.; *d* Feb. 20, 1903, and was buried at New Enterprise.

Children (9):

[C366] + Cyrus Edward⁵, *b* June 12, 1858.

[C367] + David Irvin⁵, *b* Jan. 12, 1861.

[C368] + Charles Ober⁵, *b* March 25, 1863

[C369] + Harry Ober⁵, *b* Oct. 16, 1866

[C370] + Nannie May⁵, *b* March 25, 1869

[C371] + William Ober⁵, *b* March 19, 1872.

[C372] + John Shannon⁵, *b* Feb 18, 1875.

[C373] Hannah Virgie⁵, *b* April 29, 1878, *d* Oct. 2, 1894, at New Enterprise

[C374] Robert Anson⁵, *b* Aug 3, 1880, *d* Dec 17, 1900, at Pittsburg, Pa.

[C101] SUSAN⁴ BRUMBAUGH ([C16] David³, same ancestry as [C96]) *b* Dec. 13, 1835, near New Enterprise, Bedford Co , Pa.; Jan. 6, 1857, was *m* by Rev Jacob Miller to (1) *David Deahl Eshleman*, *b* Sept. 29, 1832, near Woodbury, Bedford Co , Pa , s Rev. *John Eshleman* and *Susan (Deahl) Eshleman*, he was a surveyor, school teacher, Repn., member G. B. B Ch Susan⁴ *d* May 16, 1858, and was buried in the cemetery 1½ miles N E of Woodbury. David *m* (2) *Catharine A. Lutz* at Woodbury, Pa , by this *m* there were *b* *Minnie May*, June 15, 1862, and *Anna Alsamena*, April 2, 1864—both *m* David *d* Sept 15, 1864, at Shirleysburg, Huntingdon Co , Pa , and was buried near the Germany Valley Meeting House, same county

Mrs. Mary Susan⁵ (Eshleman) Gates [C101-1] relates the following incident concerning her mother [C101] Susan⁴ (Brumbaugh) Eshleman:

"When about 15 years old she was one day left at home while her parents spent the day away from the home. Her father was considered about the richest man in the community, and doubtless had plenty so that a neighboring family thought there was more than was needed—frequently relieving them of

their substance. On this day mother saw two women slipping into the smoke house—she, too, 'skipped' in a round about way and shot the bolt of the door. When the folks came home in the evening she said: 'Come into the yard and see the nice birds I caught!" You can imagine the rest."

She also says: "On the Brumbaugh farm, which has been in possession of some of the name for well on 200 years, is a cave of interest. When my great-grandfather, John² Brumbaugh [C4], first bought the land from the Indians it was a hiding place of theirs. On the wall of one room is a carved picture in relief of an Indian woman nursing her child   There is also an interesting story of a panther that I heard when I was a small child."

Daughter by 1st m

i   Mary Susan⁵ Eshleman, *b* March 19, 1858, March 16, 1879, *m Samuel F. Gates, b* April 3, 1851, at McKees Gap, Blair Co , Pa ; s *Henry C* and *Elizabeth (Chaney) Gates*   Samuel was Sheriff of Bedford Co , Pa , 1900-'02, and Mary was Matron, he *d* May 23, 1906, at Bedford, Pa   Mary resides at Rochester, Pa.

Children (3), *surname Gates*

(1) Laura Bella⁶, *b* Feb. 23, 1880; *m Dr. George Wells Potter,* res , St. Augustine, Fla , son *David Wilfred Potter, b* Jan 15, 1906.

(2) Anna Vincent⁶, *b* Dec 13, 1881, May 10, 1911, *m Charles W Waggoner,* res, Rochester, Pa.

(3) Samuel Eshleman⁶, *b* May 3, 1884, *d* July 21, 1885

[C102] DAVID SNYDER⁴ BRUMBAUGH ([C16] David³, same ancestry as [C96]) *b* March 20, 1838, at New Enterprise, Bedford Co , Pa.; educated in the public schools and attended the Rainsburg Seminary three terms ; taught school two terms, live stock dealer, drover and shipper for many years, and for over twenty-one years has followed merchandising, firm name S. L. Buck & Co.; has also served four years as P M at New Enterprise. Pa , which has continuously remained his address

He has held Twp offices. Early in life he was nominated for the office of J. P , duly elected by a good majority, only to be informed by the Governor that there was no vacancy, as the incumbent had a year to serve   He says, "I was very glad for that, and never more allowed my name to go for J P "

Jan. 3, 1866, David⁴ *m Mary Melissa Buck, b* April 2, 1846, dau *David F.* and *Barbara (Longenecker) Buck,* both herself and husband members G. B B. Ch   Mary *d* Dec 17, 1891.   Her will* is dated Dec. 16, 1891, and

---

*Will Book 7, p 129, Bedford Co , Pa   The "Old Store House" was built by her father, is quite a prominent house, and yet stands

recites that she is late of South Woodbury Twp.—that the "Old Store House in New Enterprise is not to be sold until my youngest daughter Lottie is age 18." It further mentions her husband, David Snyder[4], and four ch : Ira[5], Samuel[5], Effie[5], and Lottie[5], and gives her cow "Pattie" to Effie and Lottie Charles L Buck, eldest brother, was appointed executor.

      Children (6) :

[C397] + Ira Miley[5], *b* Dec. 1, 1866.

[C398]   Myrtle[5], *b* June 1, 1868, *d* May 19, 1873.

[C399] + Samuel Longenecker[5], *b* Dec 8, 1869.

[C400]   Mary Effie[5], *b* March 10, 1875

[C401] + Charlotte Amanda[5], *b* Sept. 25, 1877.

[C402]   Edgar[5], *b* Feb. 23, 1880, *d* July 8, 1881.

    [C103] MARY[4] BRUMBAUGH ([C16] David[3], same ancestry as [C96]) *b* May 31, 1840, Jan, 17, 1860, *m Rinehart Long Replogle*, *b* Aug 22, 1836, s *Rinehart* and *Elizabeth (Long) Replogle*,* all *b* at or near New Enterprise, Bedford Co., Pa., he was a farmer; Repn.; and himself and w members G B B Ch   Rinehart *d* March 8, 1908, and Mary *d* May 31, 1904, aged 64 years; both interred at Woodbury, Bedford Co , Pa , where the family lived.

      Children (14), *surname Replogle.*

  i Esther[5], *b* Feb 3, 1861, Feb 3, 1884, *m John R Stayer*, *b* Aug 14, 1858; farmer, Proh., member G B B Ch , residence, Woodbury, Pa.

      (1) Elsie[6] Stayer, *b* June 28, 1891.

      (2) Della[6] Stayer, *b* July 28, 1894, *d* Nov 29, 1897.

      (3) Rena[6] Stayer, *b* Feb 22, 1899

  ii Charles[5], *b* Sept 15, 1862, *m Annie Mock*, residence, Altoona, Pa

  iii Annie[5], *b* Sept. 2, 1864, *m John A. Sell*, Woodbury, Pa

  iv Lecta[5], *b* March 5, 1866, *m Wilson Mentzer*, S Altoona, Pa.

  v Delilah[5], *b* Jan 10, 1868; *d* Oct 25, 1875.

  vi Martin[5], *b* Aug 13, 1869, *d* Oct 15, 1870.

  vii David[5], *b* April 24, 1871, *m Olive Bloom*, Woodbury, Pa

  viii Joseph[5], *b* Nov. 22, 1872; *m Gertrude Gardner*, Altoona, Pa

  ix Cyrus Brumbaugh[5], *b* July 19, 1874, *m M—— Stayer;* grad N E. Class '97, Juniata College, member firm "Replogle Bros ," grocers, Altoona, Pa.

  x Mary[5], *b* Dec 10, 1876, *m George H. Miller*, Woodbury, Pa.

*See [E3009] for further facts concerning *Rinehart Replogle,* and details concerning another s *Daniel Replogle,* who *m* NANCY[2] BRUMBAUGH [E3009] of [E5] George[3]

xi Elizabeth⁵, *b* May 26, 1879, residence, Altoona, Pa

xii Rinehart⁵, *b* July 8, 1881, *m Eliza Hershberger Working*, Altoona, Pa.

xiii Infant son, *b* July 18, 1883, *d* y.

xiv Lena⁵, *b* June 21, 1888, *d* Jan. 31, 1896

[C105] SIMON SNYDER⁴ BRUMBAUGH ([C16] David³, same ancestry as [C96]) *b* on the farm near New Enterprise, Bedford Co., Pa, Sept 12, 1845; Dec. 21, 1875, *m Elizabeth Imler, b* 1849 at Imlertown, the same county; dau *Thomas* and *Susan (Yont) Imler.* He owned and lived upon the *David³ Brumbaugh* [C16] homestead, on which he conducted a small store and P. O, the latter called "Brumbaugh" until it was recently discontinued when the R. F. D route from New Enterprise was established. Elizabeth lives in Bedford, Pa. (1911).

The following extract is taken from the *Martinsburg (Pa) Herald* of Jan. 21, 1910:

"Simon Snyder Brumbaugh, a prominent and highly esteemed citizen of Bedford county, died at his home near New Enterprise Friday, Jan 14, at 6:45 P M., 1910, after an illness extending from the middle of May, 1909 The best of medical assistance was given him and all that careful nursing administered by loving hands could do was done in the hope of his gaining health and strength.

"In October he underwent an operation at Jefferson Hospital, Philadelphia, which seemed to benefit him for a time. Through all his sickness he was a patient sufferer, bearing it all with Christian fortitude Early Thursday morning he took a turn for the worse and passed peacefully away, the wife and children all being present. * * *

"In his earlier life he was a huckster. He was elected steward of the Bedford County Almshouse and served six years About twenty-five years ago he purchased the Aaron Reed distillery and was engaged in that business at the time of his death In business he was very shrewd, and many were they who went to him for advice and assistance. He was always interested in the cause of education and served a number of years on the school board of South Woodbury Township. He was a member of the Lutheran Church, Independent Order of Odd Fellows and Grange He was one who was always ready to assist in any cause which was for the good of the community, and was especially good to the poor

"The funeral, which was one of the largest held in the community for some time, was held in the Burger Church at Salemville, conducted by Rev

M. S Sharp of Martinsburg, and Rev D T. Detwiler of New Enterprise.
Interment in the Burger Cemetery."

      Children (4):

[C416] + Gertrude Salome[5], *b* Sept. 23, 1876
[C417] + Grace[5], *b* 1878
[C418] + Oscar Luther[5], *b* 1881.
[C419] + Simon Clarence[5], *b* 1885

      [C107] MARGARET EVALINE[4] BRUMBAUGH ([C24] Samuel David[3], [C5] Daniel[2], Johann Jacob[1]) *b* Jan. 3, 1838, May 21, 1860, *m John G. Felmlee, b* Dec 10, 1833, at State Line, Franklin Co, Pa, farmer; Dem ; member Pres. Ch.; *Margaret[4] d* May 30, 1871, and was buried at Greencastle, Franklin Co, Pa. John *m* (2) *Henrietta Stewart*, address, Perulack, Juniata Co., Pa.

      Children by 1st m (5), surname Felmlee.

i   Nicholas W.[5], *b* Aug 10, 1862; *d* May 31, 1864.
ii Samuel T.[5], M D , *b* March 30, 1864, at Bakersville, Washington Co., Md ; June 19, 1890, at Chicago *m Lillian Wright, b* Nov 21, 1871, at Louisville, Ky ; dau *Richard* and *Sarah (Waltz) Wright;* physician; Dem , Protestant; graduated Rush Med Col (M.D.) 1891, memb Chicago Med Soc , Prof Splanchnology Harvey Med. Col , Chicago (Reg) , residence, 1645 Garfield Boul , Chicago, Ill.

      Children (2) ·
      (1) Evaline[6], *b* Aug. 5, 1891.
      (2) Raymond Leslie[6], *b* Nov 2, 1896.

iii Eliza R [5], *b* May 12, 1866; *d* Jan , 1890; *m Robert Woodside.*
iv George W.[5], *b* July 25, 1868, *m Jeannette Pierce;* St. Louis, Mo.
v Eva Belle[5], *b* April 4, 1871 , *d* June 25, 1871.

      [C108] JOHN NICHOLAS[4] BRUMBAUGH ([C24] Samuel David[3], same ancestry as [C107]) *b* May 22, 1840, on the old homestead farm north of Hagerstown, Washington Co, Md , where his bro, [C111] *Philip Napoleon Brumbaugh,* lives , Feb. 8, 1866, *m Elizabeth J. Lewis,* b Jan 4, 1843, one mile from Hagerstown, Md ; dau *Anthony Wayne* and *Sarah (Newcomer) Lewis*—Anthony s of *William Lewis*, a Captain under Gen. George Washington and a namesake of "Mad" Anthony Wayne. John was educated in public schools and Hagerstown Acad.; at marriage they settled on present farm of 170 a, which he later purchased with 30 a additional, making a valuable farm of 200 a near Hagerstown, elected Sheriff upon the

Dem. ticket in 1891; 1897 nominated for Co Comr, but was defeated with entire party ticket, 1903 elected Judge of Orphans' Court for a term of four years; has been school trustee and a director of the Hagerstown and Greencastle Turnpike Co.

He was taken sick during the Summer of 1908 and recovered after a long illness. Dec 3, 1909, he became sick with pneumonia and died at his home, Middleburg, Md, Dec 10, 1909—"one of the most widely known men in Washington County"

"J. Nicholas Brumbaugh, a former sheriff and judge of the orphans' court, and one of the best known residents of Washington Co, Md, died at 10·15 o'clock yesterday morning at his home in Middleburg of pneumonia, after a brief illness dating from last Friday. His death produced a shock throughout the county

"Mr Brumbaugh was a type of the sturdy, industrious and influential farmer and citizen   He had a ready smile and a charitable heart and was widely known and esteemed for the combination of virtue and qualities that won him friends everywhere   He was faithful in the performance of his duties as a public official and a man of honest convictions and integrity   His death will be greatly mourned in the county and wherever he was known." *

Children (11)

[C281] + John Kissecker[5], b Nov 23, 1867
[C282] + Samuel David[5], b May 23, 1868.
[C283] + Rose Eliza[5], b Dec 26, 1870
[C284] + Anthony Wayne[5], b Sept 20, 1872
[C285]   Adam Kissecker[5], b March 27, 1874; 1901 *m Annie Young, b 1874*
[C286]   Robert Newcomer[5], b Nov 25, 1875, unm; huckster, Los Angeles, Cal.
[C287]   Nicholas Roy[5], b Aug. 20, 1877; d Aug, 1890.
[C288] + Edward Clarence[5], b April 13, 1879
[C289] + Mary Lucile[5], b April 13, 1881
[C290]   Bessie Lewis[5], b Sept. 29, 1882, d y.
[C291]   Augustine Mason[5], b March 4, 1885; d Nov., 1888.

[C109] SUSAN ISABELLA[4] BRUMBAUGH ([C24] Samuel David[3], same ancestry as [C107]), *m William Preston Bentz*; residence, near Funkstown, Md.

*From the Chambersburg (Pa) *Public Opinion* of Friday, Dec 10, 1909

Son, surname Bentz:

1 Clay Brumbaugh[5].

    Children (3):

(1) Clay Preston[6]

(2) Susan Harnish[6].

(3) Katherine Isabella[6].

[C111] PHILIP NAPOLEON[4] BRUMBAUGH* ([C24] Samuel David[3], same ancestry as [C107]) *b* Sept. 18, 1847, on the old Md. homestead farm, where he resides. Aug 15, 1872, *m Alice Martin, b* Oct 25, 1854, dau *David Long* and *Mary Louise (Spickler) Martin*—latter was dau of [C20] *Elizabeth[3] Brumbaugh* (Daniel[2], Johann Jacob[1]), educated in common schools of Washington Co., Md , 4 yrs. in Cumb Valley Institute, and graduated Poughkeepsie (N Y.) Bus Col , he was general merchant in Middleburg, Franklin Co , Pa , 8 yrs , and in same occupation at Waynesboro, Pa , 1888-1896, he then returned to the old homestead farm and acquired the adjoining 80 a As noted (p. 141, and Pl. 50), the mansion has been remodeled, but was erected in 1746, and is supposed to be the oldest house in Washington Co., Md. In Waynesboro, Pa , he served as a member of the town council, both himself and his wife are members Ref. Ch., he is Dem ; Royal Arch Mason, etc , address Hagerstown, Md , R. R. No 6, or Greencastle, Pa , Box 118.

    Children (11)

[C332]   Edith Martin[5], *b* July 11, 1873, *d* Aug 22, 1873

[C333]   Edna Evelyn[5], *b* July 9, 1874; *d* June 27, 1892.

[C334] + Grace Geraldine[5], *b* Nov 11, 1876.

[C335] + Jessie Josephine[5], *b* Nov 24, 1878; *d* Feb 25, 1905.

[C336]   Philip Napoleon[5], *b* Dec 6, 1880, *d* Nov. 7, 1903

[C337] + Florence Irene[5], *b* Feb 8, 1883

[C338]   Alice Martin[5], *b* April 1, 1885; *d* July 16, 1885.

[C339]   Allen Nicholas[5], *b* June 1, 1888; *d* July 4, 1892.

[C340]   Thomas Bloom[5], *b* March 31, 1891, *d* April 20, 1891.

[C341]   Edwin Strickler[5], *b* May 7, 1892, *d* Aug. 28, 1892.

[C342]   Alexander Neill Long[5], *b* Jan 1, 1895, at home.

[C117] EMELINE[4] BRUMBAUGH ([C30] Elias David[3], [C6] David[2], Johann Jacob[1]) *b* Aug 28, 1843, *m Webster Hartle, b* Sept 20, 1844; s *John H.* and *Barbara Hartle* Webster and Emeline[4] are members Ref. Ch., and reside on a farm near State Line, Franklin Co., Pa.

*His full name is Philip Napoleon Stine Brumbaugh, but the "Stine" is unused. Notes are taken from History of Washington Co , Md —Williams, Vol II, p. 1077.

Children (7), *surname Hartle*

i   Elias Brumbaugh[5] Hartle, *b* March 29, 1869, near Hagerstown, Md.; 1898 *m* *Nettie Kieffer*, *b* Nov 29, 1874, dau *Cyrus* and *Missouri Kieffer* of Highfield, Md   Elias[5] attended public schools of Franklin Co., Pa., and of Washington Co, Md , academy at Buckhannan, W Va , in 1889, graduated from Mercersburg College 1892; received degree of LL.B from Univ of W. Va 1897, attorney-at-law since 1889—firm name "Hartle & Wolfinger," Hagerstown, Md.; Police Justice; Secy Bar Assn 1905, was defeated for State's Atty. of Washington Co, Md , by 43 votes in 1907, member Ref. Ch , and of various secret organizations

      Children (5), *surname Hartle*

    (1) Eveline Brumbaugh[6], *b* Nov. 24, 1898

    (2) Calvert Kieffer[6], *b* June 1, 1900.

    (3) Mable Loraine[6], *b* May 3, 1903

    (4) Mary Vivian[6].

    (5) John Webster[6], *b* Nov 17, 1908.

ii   S— Clyde[5], *m Elva Pensinger*, merchant, State Line, Pa

iii Stanley W.[5], *m Nellie Barnhart*, farmer, near State Line, Pa.

iv Charles L [5]; unm, merchant, State Line, Pa.

v   Leila E.[5] , res. State Line, Pa.

vi John W [5]; *d* y.

vii Gertrude V.[5] ; *d* y.

[C118]MARGARET PERMELIA[4] BRUMBAUGH ([C43] Andrew[3], [C7] Henry[2], Johann Jacob[1]) *b* June 17, 1847, *m William Martin* (as his first wife) , s *David Long* and *Mary Louise (Spickler) Martin*, latter dau *Thomas* and [C20] *Elizabeth[3] (Brumbaugh) Spickler*, they lived at State Line, Franklin Co , Pa ; she *d* 1878   For William's second wife see [C149] *Susan Maria[4] Brumbaugh*, *b* Dec 5, 1848, dau [C31] *Nathan Henry[3] Brumbaugh*. (No children reported)

[C119] UPTON S—[4] BRUMBAUGH ([C43] Andrew[3], same ancestry as [C118]) *b* April 1, 1849, on a farm north of Hagerstown, Md ; educated in public schools, Cumberland Valley Institute, Dickinson College, graduating in class of 1870, teacher public schools of Washington Co , Md , 1867-'81; since engaged in mercantile pursuits—at present is traveling salesman for agricultural implements, in 1887 moved from Hagerstown to Baltimore, Md ; residence, 1535 Park Avenue, that city   Feb 17, 1875, *m Katharine Rosanna Stake*, *b* Jan 4, 1851, at Williamsport, Washington Co , Md , dau *Andrew*

Kershner and *Adaline Susan (Oster) Stake.* He is Dem, member Epis Ch, and furnished considerable information and assistance during the early investigations connected with this work.

Children (3):

[C433]   Minnie Claire⁵, *b* Feb. 17, 1876; unm.

[C434] + Susan Stake⁵, *b* Jan 9, 1881

[C435]   Andrew Kyle⁵, *b* Dec. 29, 1883, unm, student Lehigh Univ.

[C123] PHILIP D⁴ BRUMBAUGH ([C11] Jacob³ (?), [C2] Jacob², Johann Jacob¹); *m Jane Mateer,* lived in "Lancaster (?) Co, Pa," and also near Hagerstown (?), Md, according to an old letter written by the son, Dr. Andrew M. Brumbaugh [C389]

Children (6)

[C389] + Andrew M⁵, M D, *b* 1831 (?).

[C390]   Jane⁵; *m Richard Childers,* (3 ch).

[C391]   Mateer⁵, *d*

[C392]   Francis A⁵, *d*

[C393]   Joseph S.⁵, *d*; (ch· Elizabeth⁶, Dorotha⁶, Ida M.⁶).

[C394]   Rosannah M.⁵, *d*

[C134] SAMUEL⁴ BRUMBAUGH ([C17] Jacob S—³, [C5] John², Johann Jacob¹) *b* Dec 27, 1824, in Morrison's Cove, Bedford Co, Pa. Nov, 1892, he lived at Avilla, Noble Co, Ind, and had a family—all daughters No further information obtained

[C135] JACOB⁴ BRUMBAUGH ([C17] Jacob S—³, same ancestry as [C134]) *b* Aug 1, 1834 (?), in Richland Co, O.; *d* Sept. 7, 1866

Children (2)

[C452] George⁵.

[C453] Jacob⁵.

[C146] DAVID⁴ BRUMBAUGH ([C31] Nathan Henry³, [C6] David², Johann Jacob¹) *b* Nov 29, 1841, in Washington Co, Md; Feb 22, 1872, *m Dorothy Osbaugh* at Mercersburg, Franklin Co, Pa.; *b* Jan 28, 1851, at Greencastle, same county, dau *John* and *Katherin (Koser) Osbaugh.* David⁴ lives a retired life on the 140-acre farm owned by his father, [C31] Nathan Henry³, and the same is actively farmed by his son-in-law, William Kriner. Dorothy is member of Ref Ch of Greencastle. Address Greencastle, Franklin Co., Pa.

Children (2):
[C248]   Infant, *b* Dec 23, 1872; *d* Jan 4, 1873
[C249] + Catharine⁵, *b* Dec 23, 1881.

[C148] EVELINE MARIA⁴ BRUMBAUGH ([C31] Nathan Henry³, same ancestry as [C146]) *b* May 8, 1846, *m Daniel Snively,* s *Andrew Snively.* He farmed near Greencastle, Franklin Co , Pa , for a few years, then moved to a farm near Lanark, Carroll Co , Ill , and there *d* about 1897 Eveline⁴ moved to Rockford, Winnebago Co , Ill , and lives at 207 Oakwood Avenue (9 ch.)

[C149] SUSAN MARIA⁴ BRUMBAUGH ([C31] Nathan Henry³, same ancestry as [C146]) *b* Dec 5, 1848. *m William Martin* (as his second wife), s *David Long Martin* and *Mary Louisa (Spickler) Martin;* the latter was a dau of *Martin Spickler, b* June 18, 1800, and [C20] ELIZABETH (BRUMBAUGH) SPICKLER. William Martin's first wife was [C118] MARGARET PERMELIA⁴ BRUMBAUGH Address Mason & Dixon, Franklin Co , Pa.
    One son, surname Martin.
  i Harry, cattle dealer.

[C151] WILLIAM⁴ BRUMBAUGH ([C31] Nathan Henry³, same ancestry as [C146]) *b* June 13, 1853. He served as Deputy Sheriff at Vesper, Kans., under [C282] *Samuel David Brumbaugh,* and is reported to be at Lincoln, Kans.

[C152] EMMA⁴ BRUMBAUGH ([C31] Nathan Henry³, same ancestry as [C146]) *b* Dec. 12, 1854; *m Franklin Binkley,* and they live upon their own farm near State Line, Franklin Co , Pa , members U B Ch ; address Mason & Dixon, Pa
    Children (2), *surname Binkley*
  i D——, unm; at home
  ii Daughter, *m David Eshleman,* live on his father's farm near Greencastle, Franklin Co , Pa. (6 ch.)

[C157] WILLIAM GREENBERRY⁴ BRUMBAUGH ([C46] George³, [C7] Henry², Johann Jacob¹) *b* March, 1844, in Washington Co , Md., June, 1867, *m Ann Eliza McKnight, b* 1839 in Adams Co , O He served as Corp , Co. E, 64th O V I —"Sherman Brigade"—during the Civil War; Commander McLaughlin Post, G. A R , Mansfield, O., 1886, Repn., proprietor of repair shop; address 126 E. 2d St., Mansfield, O.

One son reported
[C447] Harry Lawrence⁵, *b* Nov , 1868

[C159] JOHN HENRY⁴ BRUMBAUGH ([C46] George³, same ancestry as [C157]) *b* 1848, *m* *Phoebe Murphy*, carriage manufacturer and machinist; last address Lexington, Nebr
    Children (2):
[C456] Ora⁵.
[C457] Daisy⁵.

[C161] CHARLES S⁴ BRUMBAUGH ([C46] George³, same ancestry as [C157]) *b* 1852; *m* (1) *Rebecca Croft*, *m* (2) *Blanche Ludwig*; last information is that he was a policeman in Mansfield, O

[C162] ANDREW WESLEY⁴ BRUMBAUGH ([C46] George³, same ancestry as [C157]) *b* 1855, *m* *Minerva Blosston*, said to have been a conductor on Erie R R , with address Dayton, O.

[C165] EVELINE⁴ ("EVA") BRUMBAUGH ([C13] David³, [C2] Jacob², Johann Jacob¹) *m* (1) *Peter* (or *Joseph*) *Binkley*, a carpenter. She *m* (2) *Henry Shelito*.
    Children by 1st m (3), surname Binkley·
  i Infant, *d.*
  ii David Independence⁵; an extensive dealer in cattle; *m* *Margaret Stine*, residence, State Line, Franklin Co , Pa (No issue.)
  iii Laura⁵, *m* *Rigdon Risner*, they live in Ill. and have two sons.

[C168] HIRAM EMRICH⁴ BRUMBAUGH ([C13] David³, [C2] Jacob², Johann Jacob¹), *m* (1) his cousin [C36] ANN MARIA³ BRUMBAUGH, *b* Dec. 26, 1824 ([C6] David², Johann Jacob¹), Ann Maria³ *d* about 1866 Hiram Emrich⁴ *m* (2) *Isabel Sites*. They lived near State Line, Franklin Co , Pa.
    Children by 1st m (2).
[C426] Hulker Jerome⁵, widower, butcher, residence, Philadelphia, Pa   (No issue.)
[C427] Howard⁵, unm, mail carrier; resides with his mother-in-law near State Line, Pa
    Children by 2d m (3)·
[C428] Howard Winfield Scott⁵; *m*; *d*
[C429] Mason Jerome⁵.
[C430] Mary⁵

[C169] JEROME DAVID⁴ BRUMBAUGH ([C13] David³, [E2] Jacob², Johann Jacob¹) *b* 1833 near Hagerstown, Md   He was a member of the Maryland Legislature from Washington Co.   He moved to Marysville, Marshall Co, Kans, and in 1858 there *m Elizabeth Waterson, b* 1839 near Hagerstown, Md ; dau *Thomas W. and Caroline (Hall) Waterson.* Elizabeth *d* Dec. 13, 1878, at Marysville, Kans, and Jerome *d* March 1, 1878, both buried at Marysville.

He served in Kansas as County Commissioner, County Attorney, Probate Judge, Member last Territorial Legislature, Member Legislature 1864 and 1876, Attorney General of Kansas Jan, 1865, to Jan., 1867

"The last House of Representatives of the Territorial Legislature contained seven members who were among the delegates to the Wyandotte Convention + + +. Three of its members subsequently became Attorney General of the State, and I give them in the order of their election Simpson, Guthrie and Brumbaugh " *

· "During the Senate of 1865-'66, the executive officers were Governor S. J. Crawford; Lieutenant-Governor James McGrew, Secretary of State R A Barker, and J. R. Swallow, Treasurer Wm. Spriggs; Supt of Pub Inst. I. T. Goodnow; Attorney General J. D. Brumbaugh " ᵇ

"The first commission on the Price raid claims was appointed by act of legislature approved Feb 11, 1865 (Session Laws, 1865, p 124), and consisted of the Secretary of State, Adjutant General and Attorney General, who were R. A. Barker, T. J Anderson, and J. D Brumbaugh This commission audited and allowed Price raid claims to the amount of $342,145 99," etc ᶜ

BRUMBAUGH, JOHN M, Concordia, Kans, Commissioner of Fisheries, 1889-1892 ᵈ See [E1965] +.

Protographic portraits of Hon J. D. Brumbaugh and of Thomas W Waterson of Marysville, Kans, were presented by the latter to the Kansas Historical Society ᵉ

"DEATH OF JUDGE BRUMBAUGH.ᶠ

"The people of this city were startled yesterday morning by the announcement of the death of Judge Brumbaugh. While many knew of his illness, few besides his physicians and relatives knew of his dangerous condition   His

ᵃ*Kans. Hist Collections, Vols I and II*, 1875-'80, pp 239 and 240.
ᵇ*Kans Hist Collection, Vol IX*, 1905-06, p 364
ᶜ*Ibid*, p 411.
ᵈ*Kans. Hist Collections, Vol. IX*, 1905-'06, p. 522.—*Report*, p. 639.
ᵉ*Ibid, Vol III*, 1881-84, p 55.
ᶠNewspaper clipping preserved by Elizabeth (Waterson) Brumbaugh, mother of [C426]
+ Alberta Jessie⁵ (Brumbaugh) Day, and furnished by the latter.

gentle spirit took its flight to a better world at one o'clock. His sickness, disease of the heart, was painful, but near the end he went to sleep like a little child.

Jerome D. Brumbaugh was forty-five years old, a native of Maryland. He came to Marysville in 1858, and has been identified with its interests ever since. He has been honored by the people with many offices, and in each faithfully dischargd his duty   In the county he has held the positions of Probate Judge, County Attorney, Commissioner and Representative, and honorably discharged the duties of Attorney General of the State one term   His was a pacific spirit, and he was conservative in politics

Few men have done so much for the material interests of Kansas   He was a hard-working, conscientious lawyer, a public-spirited citizen, a faithful friend, and a generous opponent. His place will not be filled in Marysville   About the old law office there will always remain a vacancy, and in the memory of the people of this city and county his memory will long be cherished "

> *One child·*

[C426] + Alberta Jessie[5], *b* Dec 21, 1871

[C172] MARY CATHERINE[4] BRUMBAUGH ([C33] Jacob Benjamin[3], [C6] David[2], Johann Jacob[1]) *b* Nov 10, 1856, *m Hamilton Hartman Shrader*, *b* Oct 12, 1847, s *William* and *Lydia (Myers) Shrader*, member Ref Ch ; address Greencastle, Franklin Co , Pa , R R 4

> *Children* (3), *surname Shrader.*

i Lillian Blanche[5], *b* July 17, 1879
ii Jacob Brumbaugh[5], *b* March 5, 1882
iii Samuel Leroy[5], *b* Aug 5, 1883

[C173] SNIVELY STRICKLER[4] BRUMBAUGH ([C33] Jacob Benjamin[3], same ancestry as [C172]) *b* Dec. 28, 1858, at Middleburg, Franklin Co , Pa.; Nov. 20, 1882, *m Ella Elizabeth Wolford*, dau *Erskine* and *Jane (Ronley) Wolford*, both from Schoharie Co , N. Y., he was educated in public schools, Welsh Run Academy, Chambersburg, Pa ; member Ref Ch of Upton, Pa., and M E Ch. of Rockford, Ill   They live at 807 North Church St., in Rockford, Ill , where he is engaged in the real estate business and she has been cashier of Forest City Natl. Bk. since 1903   Snively Strickler moved to Rockford March 15, 1881, and superintended a large bolt works for seven years , became assistant postmaster for four years, he then operated a large laundry for a number of years   (No issue)

[C174] IDA LOUISA[4] BRUMBAUGH ([C33] Jacob Benjamin[3], same

ancestry as [C172]) *b* July 10, 1860, *m* DAVID R[4] LOGAN [C32-v] They lived in State Line, Franklin Co , Pa , for several years after m , bought the home farm of 160 acres and lived there six years, in 1907 sold the farm to *John Edward Hoke* (who *m* ELIZA JANE[4] BRUMBAUGH [C177]. Ida[4] is a member Ref. Ch   (No issue)

[C175] ELIAS GUILFORD[4] BRUMBAUGH ([C33] Jacob Benjamin[3], same ancestry as [C172]) *b* Nov 27, 1862, Sept 15, 1902, *m Ella Light*, dau *Jacob* and *Sarah Light*.   Ella graduated from the Shippensburg (Pa) State Normal School, and successfully taught three or four years in the public schools of Pa before her marriage   At Lemasters, Pa , they were both members of the Ref Ch , but they are members of the West State St M. E Ch of Rockford, Ill., where he is supt of a laundry, residence, 1820 West State St. (No issue)

[C176] ANNA EVA[4] BRUMBAUGH ([C33] Jacob Benjamin[3], same ancestry as [C172]) *b* Jan. 16, 1864; *m Thomas McCullough* of Lemasters, Pa., farmer, Anna *d* April, 1897
>   *One son*
>   i   Howard Brumbaugh[5] McCullough

[C177] ELIZA JANE[4] BRUMBAUGH ([C33] Jacob Benjamin[3], [C6] David[2], Johann Jacob[1]) *b* Dec 25, 1867, near State Line, Franklin Co., Pa ; Dec. 17, 1889, *m John Edward Hoke, b* Dec. 18, 1865, in Antrim Twp , Franklin Co , Pa , *s Benjamin* and *Elizabeth (Statler) Hoke;* farmer ; common school education, family are members Ref Ch , of which for over 13 years he has been an official, address Greencastle, Franklin Co., Pa , R. R 1.
>   *Children* (3), *surname Hoke*
>   i   Mary Florence[5], *b* 1891.
>   ii   Jacob Leroy[5], *b* 1893
>   iii Rebecca Elizabeth Ruth[5], *b* 1898.

[C180] JOHN HENRY[4] BRUMBAUGH ([C47] Calvin[3], [C7] Henry[2], Johann Jacob[1]) *b* April 1, 1851, July 20, 1870, *m Annie Foster Little* They lived at 609 18th St , Moline, Rock Island Co , Ill , about 1900, where he was a practical horseshoer   (Further facts unobtainable.)
>   *Children* (3)
[C461] Arthur Ross[5]; residence, 1003 Hamilton St , Racine, Wis
[C462] George Little[5], residence, Moline, Ill
[C463] Vera Corriline[5], *m* ―― *Lundirg*, residence, 1726 12th Ave , Moline, Ill.

[C181] ELI HARRISON[4] BRUMBAUGH, M D , D D. ([C47] Calvin[3], same ancestry as [C180]) *b* 1853 at Millersburg, Holmes Co., O.; Jan. 11, 1877, *m Caroline Eleanor Reddish* at Memphis, Mo , *b* 1857; dau *J. B* and *Sarah Newell (Asbury) Reddish.*

The "Conference Biographical Album of Eminent Men in Methodism (North West Indiana Conference, 1898)" contains the following biography:

"Rev. E. H Brumbaugh, S T B , M D , D D , is a native of Ohio. At an early age he removed with his parents to Iowa, where he resided with his parents on the farm until he was fourteen years of age, at which time he left home to complete his education   He studied medicine and received the degree of M D from the College of Physicians and Surgeons, Keokuk, Iowa.   Dr. Brumbaugh practised medicine ten years.

Being impressed that he ought to preach the gospel, he received license to preach and a recommendation to the travelling connection from the Unionville (Mo) Quarterly Conference, and was admitted to the Missouri Conference in 1882   At the request of the people of Unionville, he was sent to them as their pastor

At this time he took a three years' course in Garrett Biblical Institute at Evanston, Ill , and during the time of his attendance at the Institute Dr. Brumbaugh served as pastor of Central Avenue Church   He was president of his class at Garrett and was chosen by the faculty as one of the commencement speakers when he was graduated with the degree of Bachelor of Sacred Theology.   He has served as president of the Alumni of Garrett.

Dr Brumbaugh's first appointment after graduation was to First Church, St. Joseph, Mo , the most important charge in the Missouri Conference   He took rank at once as one of the foremost preachers of Methodism in his State   His discourses on the great moral questions of the day gave him a wide reputation.   Many of his discourses, some of which were on our public schools and their foes, have been published in book form, and have been circulated in nearly every State of the Union.

During his pastorate in St. Joseph the church was strengthened with the addition of 452 members, and was built up in many ways

In March, 1893, Dr Brumbaugh was transferred to the Kansas Conference and stationed at Atchison.   His pastorate there was characterized with a spirit of indomitable energy, intense loyalty to the church and unswerving opposition to all forms of evil   Dr Brumbaugh was five years in Atchison   At the end of the fourth year, he was appointed to the District, but at the request of the church in Atchison, Bishop McCabe changed the appointment from District work to the pastorate

In 1891 Soule College of Dodge City, Kans., gave him the degree of D D.

September, 1897, Dr Brumbaugh was transferred to the Northwest Indiana Conference and stationed at Crawfordsville. Here his usual success attends his labors.

Dr. Brumbaugh is a very eloquent and forceful speaker, and as a lecturer, as well as preacher, has won an enviable reputation He has more demands for lectures and addresses than he can meet. He has attracted marked attention with his pen, and is a paid writer for the Methodist Press "

Dr. Eli Harrison[4] Brumbaugh d Jan 19, 1902, at Chicago, Ill, after an operation for gall stone. His wife lives at Memphis, Scotland Co, Mo, and furnished the above biography

July 10, 1891, from St. Joseph, Mo, he wrote: "How soon do you expect to get out your Brumbaugh History? I am anxious to get hold of it!"

"He is a trained speaker, a man who has something to say and knows how to say it"—*Evanston (Ill) Index*

Children (5).

[C466] + Enol Vane[5], b Nov 17, 1877
[C467]   Maleta Boone[5], b April 20. 1879; d July 31, 1879
[C468] + Mable C.[5], b Jan 29, 1881
[C469] + Louise[5], b June 7, 1884
[C470]   Florence[5], b March 12, 1892

[C186] EMMA JANE[5] BRUMBAUGH ([C51] Alexander[4], [C9] Joseph[3], [C2] Jacob[2], Johann Jacob[1]) b March 17, 1864, at Valparaiso, Ind, Dec. 2, 1884, m *Frank Warren Hutchinson* of Beattie, Kans. Emma[5] was educated in the public schools of Sibley, Ill, and the residence is given as Marysville, Marshall Co, Kans. (No ch reported)

[C200] JOHN FRANKLIN[5] BRUMBAUGH ([C68] Samuel David[4], [C21] Daniel[3], [C5] Daniel[2], Johann Jacob[1]) b Nov. 12, 1854; m *Sarah M Campbell* of Darke Co, O ; farmer, d Sept 10, 1898, and was buried in the Abbottsville Cemetery of that county

Children (2):

[C507] Maude Elizabeth[6].
[C508] John Walter[6], d at age 2.

[C201] DANIEL HARMON[5] BRUMBAUGH ([C68] Samuel David[4], same ancestry as [C200]) b Oct. 11, 1856; m *Ella Bender* of Darke Co., O., farmer; address Arcanum, O.

Children (6):

[C524] Grace P.[6]

[C525] Pearl[6].
[C526] Bessie E.[6]
[C527] Elizabeth[6]
[C528] William W [6]
[C529] Ruba Belle[6].

[C202] VIRGINIA BELL[5] BRUMBAUGH ([C68] Samuel David[4],
same ancestry as [C200]) *b* Dec. 21, 1859, *m John W Stephens;* farmer, address Greenville, Darke Co., O
> *Children* (3), *surname Stephens*
> i   William Roscoe[6]
> ii Samuel Clifton[6].
> iii Bert Victoria[6].

[C203] CLEMENT LAIRD[5] BRUMBAUGH ([C68] Samuel David[4],
same ancestry as [C200]) *b* at Greenville, Darke Co , O , Feb 28, 1863, his
father dying when he was but five years old; he was reared upon the farm,
attended the public schools, worked upon the farm during the summers and
taught the district school during winters, graduated in 1887 from the National Normal University, Lebanon, O ; attended Scientific and Classical courses
in the Ohio Wesleyan University 1891-'93, graduated from Harvard Univ
(B A.) 1894 He founded and conducted the Van Buren Academy 1887-'91;
was Professor of History and Literature in Prep Dept of Howard Univ 1894-
'95; was Supt. Greenville (O.) public schools 1895-1900; Member Ohio Leg
1900-'04, was admitted to the Ohio Bar in 1900, and is actively engaged in the
practice of law in Columbus, O , where he is Deputy Supt of Insurance for
Ohio; Dem , member K P and also of M E. Ch., address Insurance Dept. of
Ohio, Columbus, O   Oct. 25, 1911, he *m Elizabeth Griswold Martin.* dau
Henry and *Mary (Griswold) Martin,* educated at Amherst, Mass.

[C204] WILLIAM DAVID[5] BRUMBAUGH* ([C68] Samuel David[4],
same ancestry as [C200]) *b* Aug 1, 1866. Sept 17, 1885, *m Carrie Elmyra
Ridenour* He attended the public schools of Darke Co , O , the Greenville
High School; graduated from the Natl Normal Univ , Lebanon, O (B.S.),
and later took the B A and Civil Engineering courses at the same institution He began teaching in the district schools at age sixteen, and taught for
seven winter sessions He was elected Co. Surveyor of Darke Co. in 1890, and
served six years and eight months, was City Engineer of Greenville, O , for
eleven years: was admitted to the practice of law at the January (1904) term

---
*Assisted materially in securing family data.

of the Ohio Supreme Court, was candidate for Probate Judge on the Dem.
ticket in 1908, but failed to secure the primary nomination, was candidate for
Mayor of Greenville on the Dem. ticket (1909); address Greenville, Darke
Co., O

   Children (3).

[C543] Laird R[6]
[C544] William David, Jr[6]
[C545] Nina Elizabeth[6]

[C207] ARTHUR ST CLAIR[5] BRUMBAUGH M D. ([C76] David
Stuckey[4], [C28] Simeon K—[3], [C6] David[2], Johann Jacob[1]) b Aug 23, 1879,
at Roaring Spring, Blair Co, Pa., attended public schools of Roaring Spring,
Pa.; graduated from the High School 1893, attended Altoona High School
1894-'95, Penna. College, Gettysburg, Pa, 1895-'99, graduated Classical
Course (A B), A M. conferred 1902, Med. Dept Univ. of Pa, gradu-
ated 1902 (M D.), attended Summer Semester 1905, Univ. of Strasburg,
Germany, began the practice of medicine (Reg) at 1405 10th St, Altoona,
Pa.; Pathologist to Altoona Hospital; June 25, 1912, m *Mary Louise Dunn*,
b Jan. 17, 1890, dau. *James Moore* and *Mary (Lafferty) Dunn.*

[C208] MAUDE EDNA[5] BRUMBAUGH ([C76] David Stuckey[4], same
ancestry as [C207]) b June 27, 1882, graduated from the Millersville (Pa)
State Normal School, Class 1902, and since then has been successfully teaching at Roaring Spring, Pa; asst principal of its High School during '08 and
'09; address Roaring Spring, Blair Co, Pa

[C209] SARAH BARBARA[5] BRUMBAUGH ([C76] David Stuckey[4],
same ancestry as [C207]) b Aug 27, 1883, graduated with first honors from
Roaring Spring High School ([C208] Maude Edna[5] received second honors);
graduated from Millersville State Normal School 1902 with her sister Maude[5];
taught several years, graduated from Penna College (A B, Class '07) in the
same class with her brother, [C210] Roland Edward[5]; elected principal of
Holly Beach (N J) High School, and has since continued in that position.

[C210] ROLAND EDWARD[5] BRUMBAUGH ([C76] David Stuckey[4],
same ancestry as [C207]) b Nov 9, 1885, graduated from High School,
Roaring Spring, Pa., taught one term in public schools, completed the classical course at Penna. College, Class 1907 (A B); asst. prof Mathematics
Lake Forest College, Ill, one year, began the study of law and was in charge
of athletics at Penna College 1908-'09, June, 1909, received the appointment
of Lieut. in U. S Navy, and is stationed at the Port Royal (S C) training
school.

[C211] RUTH MARGARETTA[5] BRUMBAUGH ([C76] David Stuckey[4], same ancestry as [C207]) b Oct 11, 1893; graduated from Roaring Spring High School, being salutatarian Class 1908, student in classical course at Irving College, Mechanicsburg, Pa.

[C249] CATHARINE[5] BRUMBAUGH ([C146] David[4], [C31] Nathan Henry[3], [C6] David[2], Johann Jacob[1]) b Dec 23, 1881; Dec 15, 1908, m William Kriner, b Sept 9, 1886, at Williamson, Franklin Co , Pa.; s Andrew B. and Alice Myers Kriner. They live on the Brumbaugh homestead farm, and are both members G. B B Ch , address Greencastle, Franklin Co , Pa. (No issue.)

[C281] JOHN KISSECKER[5] BRUMBAUGH ([C108] John Nicholas[4], [C24] Samuel David[3]. [C5] Daniel[2], Johann Jacob[1]) b Nov 23, 1866, 1889 m Emma Gordon, b 1868, address Hagerstown, Md.
   One child:
[C610] Prudence[6], b 1890

[C282] SAMUEL DAVID[5] BRUMBAUGH ([C108] John Nicholas[4], same ancestry as [C281]) b May 23, 1868. Sept 8, 1898, at Salina, Saline Co , Kans., m Susan Marshall, b Oct 17, 1872, at Texas City, Saline Co , Ill.; dau William and Phoebe (Walker) Marshall   He attended public schools of Washington Co., Md.; Academy at Hagerstown, Md., graduated from Northern Ind Bus. Col at Valparaiso, Ind , in 1885, moved to Lincoln Co , Kans , in 1888; elected Sheriff Lincoln Co. Nov., 1902; reelected Nov , 1904, served 4 years, is engaged in extensive grain and live stock business at Vesper, Lincoln Co., Kans   (No issue)

[C283] ROSE ELIZA[5] BRUMBAUGH ([C108] John Nicholas[4], same ancestry as [C281]) b Dec 26, 1870; 1889 m Harvey Swisher, b 1866; address Vesper, Lincoln Co , Kans.
   One daughter.
   i Vesta Grace[6] Swisher, b 1891.

[C284] ANTHONY WAYNE[5] BRUMBAUGH ([C108] John Nicholas[4], same ancestry as [C281]) b Sept 20, 1872, 1892 m Lillian Chaney, b 1875, address Vesper, Lincoln Co , Kans.
   One son
[C620] Anthony Wayne, Jr [6], b 1903

[C288] EDWARD CLARENCE[5] BRUMBAUGH ([C108] John Nich-

olas[4], same ancestry as [C281]) *b* April 13, 1879; 1900 *m* *Rhoda May Summers*, *b* 1892, resides near State Line, Franklin Co , Pa.

   One son:

[C630] Gale Summers[6], *b* 1901.

[C289] MARY LUCILE[5] BRUMBAUGH ([C108] John Nicholas[4], same ancestry as [C281]) *b* April 13, 1881; 1902 *m* *Joseph Stine*, *b* 1880, residence, near Shadygrove, Franklin Co , Pa

   One son.

   i Robert Wesley[6] Stine, *b* 1903

[C320] JOHN FURRY[5] BRUMBAUGH ([C97] Jacob Snyder[4], [C16] David[3]. [C4] John[2], Johann Jacob[1]) *b* March 16, 1850, near New Enterprise, Bedford Co , Pa , 1872 *m* *Margaret Imler*, *b* April 30, 1854, at Everett, Bedford Co , Pa ; dau *Solomon* and *Mary (Otto) Imler*, farms part of the parental homestead, on which there are thirty, bearing fruit trees over 100 years old; Repn.; member G B B Ch , address New Enterprise, Pa

   Children (7) ·

[C500]   George Ransom[6], *b* May 11, 1873, *d* April 30, 1887
[C501] + Horace Atlee[6], *b* Oct. 10, 1874
[C502] + Charles Leonard[6], *b* March 17, 1877.
[C503] + Mary Lystra[6], *b* Jan. 14, 1881
[C504] + Roscoe Conkling[6], *b* Nov 7, 1883.
[C505]   Warren[6], *b* Aug 1, 1889; *d* Aug 11, 1889.
[C506] + Floy[6], *b* Sept 18, 1895, *d* Feb 13, 1910

[C321] CAROLINE POTE[5] BRUMBAUGH ([C97] Jacob Snyder[4], same male ancestry as [C320]) *b* Dec 16, 1852, *m* *Robert C. McNamara*, *b* at Newry, Blair Co , Pa His parents died while he was a baby, he was put in the Blair Co. Alms House, and adopted by Samuel Weeking of New Enterprise, Pa , was a school teacher, Justice of the Peace, was admitted to the Bedford Co (Pa) Bar, and served two terms as Dist. Atty ; served two terms in the Pa. State Legislature, was Captain of National Guard of Pa —Major 5th Regt. Natl Guard, Pa , in Spanish-American War., residence, Bedford, Pa ; Caroline[5] *d* June 19, 1878

   Children (2), surname *McNamara*

   i Mertie[6], *m* *Frank King;* Salemville, Bedford Co., Pa
   ii Elsie[6], adopted by [C97] Jacob Snyder[4] Brumbaugh after Caroline's death.

[C323] ALISON POTE[5] BRUMBAUGH ([C97] Jacob Snyder[4], same

male ancestry as [C320]) *b* Feb 14, 1856, near New Enterprise, Bedford Co, Pa.; Jan 29, 1879, *m* *Elizabeth Guyer*, *b* March 18, 1862, at New Enterprise, Pa ; dau *Adam* and *Elizabeth (Snyder) Guyer*, Dem , member G B B Ch ; plumber; address New Enterprise, Pa

Children (6) ·

[C516] Robert Edwin⁶, *b* Oct 17, 1881, Jan 18, 1906, *m* *Flora Cassiday*
[C517] Mary Irene⁶, *b* Jan 8, 1884
[C518] Olive⁶, *b* Nov. 17, 1887.
[C519] Ada⁶, *b* Feb. 7, 1891
[C520] Bertha⁶, *b* Nov. 14, 1894
[C521] Pearl⁶, *b* Dec 26, 1898

[C324] JACOB POTE⁵ BRUMBAUGH ([C97] Jacob Snyder⁴, same male ancestry as [C320]) *b* March 7, 1858, in South Woodbury Twp, Bedford Co, Pa.; June 29, 1884, *m* *Delilah Potter*, *b* June 16, 1858, in South Woodbury Twp.; he was educated in public schools of Bedford Co., farmed 1885 to Spring of 1907, when the family moved to Lancaster, Pa, and there engaged in general mercantile business and also was hotel proprietor: the family recently returned to New Enterprise, Pa, where he is farming; has served as P M. of New Enterprise, Pa ; member G B B. Ch

Children (5):

[C537] Elda Pote⁶, *b* Jan. 21, 1884.
[C538] Susan Frances⁶, *b* April 29, 1886
[C539] Walter Wood⁶, *b* July 7, 1888
[C540] Bruce Graham⁶, *b* April 30, 1890
[C541] Edith Pote⁶, *b* Nov. 26, 1894.

[C325] MARY JANE POTE⁵ BRUMBAUGH ([C97] Jacob Snyder⁴, same male ancestry as [C320]) *b* Aug 7, 1860, at New Enterprise, Bedford Co, Pa.; *m* *John Albert Good*, *b* Aug 7, 1860, at New Enterprise, Pa He is a salesman at Altoona, Blair Co, Pa , recently lived on the Eve (Brumbaugh) Snowberger farm near New Enterprise, Pa , member G B. B. Ch ; Repn.

Children (3), *surname Good.*

i Carrie Eva⁶, *b* May 16, 1880, *d* June 12, 1889.
ii Robert Pote⁶, *b* April 6, 1886
iii Allen Langdon⁶, *b* March 11, 1895

[C327] DAVID POTE⁵ BRUMBAUGH ([C97] Jacob Snyder⁴, same male ancestry as [C320]) *b* Jan. 10, 1865, at New Enterprise, Bedford Co, Pa.; Jan 17, 1887, *m* *Martha Isadora Eberly*, *b* June 19, 1866, at Waterside,

Bedford Co , Pa., dau *John* and *Matilda (Enyeart) Eberly*, salesman , Dem , member G B B. Ch ; residence, 2924 5th Ave., Altoona, Blair Co , Pa
Children (2):

[C547] John Albert[6], *b* Nov. 22, 1888.

[C548] Jacob Quinter[6], *b* Dec 15, 1890.

[C328] MARTIN POTE[5] BRUMBAUGH ([C97] Jacob Snyder[4], same male ancestry as [C320]) *b* April 12, 1867, at New Enterprise, Bedford Co , Pa ; July 15, 1896, *m Sadie A— Wilt, b* April 4, 1872; dau Rev *Joseph W.* and *Amanda (Wagner) Wilt*, of Altoona, Blair Co , Pa , where they lately resided He conducts a general merchandise store; attended public schools of Bedford Co , Pa , and Zeth Business College; actively interested in church and Sunday school work , is chorister, etc., Proh ; member G. B B Ch.; address 1102 Second Ave , Juniata, Pa.
Children (2):

[C550] Zula Bernice[6], *b* Oct. 30, 1897.

[C551] Elva Pauline[6], *b* Aug 19, 1901.

[C329] DANIEL STRALEY[5] BRUMBAUGH ([C97] Jacob Snyder[4], same ancestry as [C320]) *b* at New Enterprise, Bedford Co , Pa , Oct 1, 1870 , *m Elizabeth King Stiffler, b* Oct. 24, 1869, at Woodbury, Bedford Co , Pa.; dau *Nathaniel* and *Nancy (King) Stiffler*, and sister to *Carrie (Stiffler) Brumbaugh*, w of [C330] *Franklin Straley[5] Brumbaugh Daniel[5]* worked on his father's farm until he was twenty-two, and then moved to Altoona, Pa., where for twelve years he worked as street car conductor; 1904 became dispatcher for Altoona and Logan Valley Street Ry Co., and continues in that position, memb G B B Ch ; 1897 was elected from the 12th Ward to Altoona Council, and reelected in 1908 for two years, residence, 3018 Maple Ave., Altoona, Blair Co , Pa., has furnished extensive information for this volume.
Children (2):

[C553] Orville Chalmers[6], *b* June 1, 1888

[C554] Fannie Viola[6], *b* Oct 29, 1889

[C330] FRANKLIN STRALEY[5] BRUMBAUGH ([C97] Jacob Snyder[4], same ancestry as [C320]) *b* March 2, 1872, March 19, 1893, *m Carrie King Stiffler, b* at New Enterprise, Bedford Co , Pa , Oct. 14, 1871. sister of *Elizabeth (Stiffler) Brumbaugh* (See [C329]) Franklin[5] is member G B B Ch , Dem. , and farms the homestead near New Enterprise, Pa.

Children (2).

[C556] Lena May[6], *b* May 12, 1896.

[C557] Nathaniel Russell[6], *b* Dec 9, 1905

[C334] GRACE GERALDINE[5] BRUMBAUGH ([C111] Philip Napoleon[4], [C24] Samuel David[3], [C5] Daniel[2], Johann Jacob[1]) *b* Nov. 11, 1876, graduated from Prot. Epis. Hosp., Phila, and for a number of years has been an active graduate nurse in Baltimore, Md

[C335] JESSIE JOSEPHINE[5] BRUMBAUGH ([C111] Philip Napoleon[4], same ancestry as [C334]) *b* Nov 24, 1878, she graduated as a trained nurse from Md Gen Hosp, Baltimore, Md, and *d* Feb. 25, 1905.

[C337] FLORENCE IRENE[5] BRUMBAUGH ([C111] Philip Napoleon[4], same ancestry as [C334]) *b* Feb. 8, 1883, graduated as trained nurse from Moses Taylor Hosp, Scranton, Pa, Nov. 10, 1910, *m Frank Raymond Crow, M D*, and they live at Uniontown, Pa.

[C366] CYRUS EDWARD[5] BRUMBAUGH ([C100] John Snyder[4], [C16] David[3], [C4] John[2], Johann Jacob[1]) *b* June 12, 1858; Nov 16, 1879. *m Hannah Burger*, *b* Sept 3, 1861, dau *Samuel M* and [C3-(9)] *Catharine[3] (Furry) Burger*; latter dau of Eld *Leonard* and [C3-i] *Hannah[4] (Brown) Furry*, the latter especially well known throughout Morrison's Cove; members G. B B Ch., residence, New Enterprise, Bedford Co., Pa.

    Children (6)·

[C560] Carrie May[6], *b* May 31, 1883; *m Elmer Snyder*

[C562] Herman[6], *b* July 31, 1891, *d* Sept 14, 1900.

[C563] Catherin Maud[6], *b* Feb. 28, 1894.

[C564] Annie F.[6], *b* March 10, 1900

[C561] Laura Blanch[6], *b* May 1, 1888.

[C565] Ella Fay[6], *b* March 7, 1905

[C367] DAVID IRVIN[5] BRUMBAUGH ([C100] John Snyder[4], same ancestry as [C366]) *b* Jan 12, 1861, at New Enterprise, Bedford Co, Pa.. Jan 16, 1887, *m Elizabeth Charlotte Arnold*, *b* at Ashland, O., Dec. 28, 1866; dau *Richard* and *Sallie (Flickinger) Arnold*, bookkeeper in the National Bank of Denison, Denison, Grayson Co, Texas.

    Children (3):

[C567] Marie Josephine[6], *b* Jan 3, 1888

[C568] Richard Irvin[6], *b* July 16, 1890.

[C569] John Marshall[6], *b* Oct. 3, 1897.

[C368] CHARLES OBER[5] BRUMBAUGH ([C100] John Snyder[4], same ancestry as [C366]) *b* March 25, 1863, at New Enterprise, Bedford Co., Pa.; attended public schools of his county; worked upon his father's farm until 1884, then at the carpenter trade one year, was postmaster at New Enterprise 1903-'07, has since conducted a general merchandise store together with extensive auctioneering, also served as Collector of Taxes for nine years, address New Enterprise, Pa. Sept. 13, 1885, *m Annie Ebersole* of Salemville, Bedford Co, Pa, *b* July 16, 1865, dau *Daniel C* and *Regina (Specht) Ebersole*, also sister of *Lydia Catharine Ebersole*, who *m* [C501] *Horace Atlee*[6] *Brumbaugh.*

   Children (3) ·
[C572] Howard[6], *b* Sept. 16, 1887.
[C573] Ruth[6], *b* March 10, 1897.
[C574] May[6], *b* Aug 24, 1901, *d* Sept 6, 1908

[C369] HARRY OBER[5] BRUMBAUGH ([C100] John Snyder[4], same ancestry as [C366]) *b* at New Enterprise, Bedford Co, Pa, Oct. 16, 1866, educated in the public schools of New Enterprise; has been engaged in retail clothing business since 1888, 1893 *m Edith Dimmer*, *b* June 4, 1874, dau *Frank* and *Thresa Ohmennes Dimmer* of Luxemberg, and also of Baden, Germany; address 2210 Warren St, Toledo, O. (No issue)

[C370] NANNIE MAY[5] BRUMBAUGH ([C100] John Snyder[4], same ancestry as [C366]) *b* March 25, 1869, at New Enterprise, Bedford Co , Pa., Oct. 7, 1881, *m Charles William Lacy.* Nannie was educated in Bedford Co. (Pa) public schools, and one year in Denison (Texas) High School; in 1886 united with G B B Ch ; they live at Tishomingo, Johnston Co , Okla.

   One child
i   William Brumbaugh[6] Lacy, *b* April 17, 1893

[C371] WILLIAM OBER[5] BRUMBAUGH ([C100] John Snyder[4], same ancestry as [C366]) *b* March 19, 1872, at New Enterprise, Bedford Co , Pa.; educated in the public schools of New Enterprise and in Stayer's Bus. Col.; July 11, 1897, *m Emma Sophia Foreman,*[*] *b* in the same county March 19, 1872, dau *George Frederick* and *Anna Eliza Foreman*, works in the Juniata shops of P. R R , res. 120 Cherry Ave , Altoona, Blair Co , Pa

   One daughter
[C581] Mildred Dorothey[6], *b* June 7, 1898

---

[*]*No. 372 in Steele's Genealogy*—Welfley, 1909, p 79.

[C372] JOHN SHANNON⁵ BRUMBAUGH ([C100] John Snyder⁴, same ancestry as [C366]) b Feb 18, 1875, at New Enterprise, Bedford Co, Pa.; m Carrie Virginia Willis, b 1876 at Ridgely, Md., dau Caleb Todd and Rebecca Willis. He farmed for a number of years in South Woodbury Twp, Bedford Co, Pa, devoting considerable time to raising, buying and selling fine horses Owing to impaired health, he quit farming and moved to New Enterprise, where for several years he was a butcher; served as Assessor, Supervisor, Director of the Poor 1861-'64, Co. Comr 1872-'75   The present address of the family is 1508 French St, Wilmington, Del, in which city he is in employ of a railroad

Children (2).

[C585] William Irvin⁶, b 1900
[C586] Elva May⁶, b 1903.

[C386] LAWRENCE McKINSTRY⁵ BRUMBAUGH ([C84] George⁴, [C42] Otho³, [C7] Henry², Johann Jacob¹) b at Eaton, Preble Co, O., Dec 22, 1867; April 28, 1897, m (1) Cora E Wentz, from whom he was divorced Feb 5, 1907, June 10, 1907, m (2) Lenore Hodges, b Feb. 19, 1877, at Monroe, Sevier Co, Utah; dau John and Anna (Jordan) Hodges   He graduated from Eaton (O) High School in 1887, and attended the Ohio Col of Dental Surgery, but left one year before graduation   He has practiced dentistry in Cincinnati, Chicago, St Louis, Cleveland and Salt Lake City, Utah, address in the latter city is 260 S. Main St   (No issue.)

[C387] VIRGIL VICTOR⁵ BRUMBAUGH* ([C89] George⁴,•same ancestry as [C386]) b Aug 18, 1874, on a farm near Eaton, Preble Co, O, since 1888 has lived in Eaton   He graduated from its High School, taught in the public schools for six years thereafter, studied law under Judge James A Gilmore, and in the Law Dept of Ohio Northern Univ.; was admitted to practice by the Supreme Court of Ohio, was elected Probate Judge of Preble Co., O., on the Dem ticket, and served one term, refusing nomination for a second term, is actively practicing law in Eaton, is unmarried.

[C388] ZENOBIA ERNESTINE⁵ BRUMBAUGH ([C89] George⁴, same ancestry as [C386]) b Dec 19, 1876, graduated from Eaton (O) High School; taught six years in Eaton schools, attended Chicago Univ. and art schools in Chicago, Cleveland, and New York, has a certificate from N Y. School of Art (4 years)   She has charge of Art Dept of Fifth Dist. Ag

---

*Both himself and his father George [C89] have furnished considerable information concerning the descendants of Otho³ [C42].

School, Wetumpka, Ala., and spends her vacations at Eaton, O., where for
several years she has served as Secy of Brumbaugh-Rinehart Reunion Association, and has materially assisted in securing facts for this publication

[C389] ANDREW M.⁵ BRUMBAUGH, M.D ([C123] Philip D⁴,
[C11] Jacob³ (?), [C2] Jacob², Johann Jacob¹) b 1831 (?) in Butler Co,
Pa , m Sarah F Blake, b in Galia Co, O   Andrew⁵ practiced medicine at
Dahlgren, Hamilton Co, Ill, "before the Civil War," but all medical records
accessible omit any reference to the college of his graduation; he d June 29,
1908, "aged about 78", his w is reported to survive him at Dahlgren, Ill
    Children (4)·
[C411] Conna L—⁶; m Theodore Cotes, and lives at Dahlgren, Ill. Children:
    Bessie M.⁷; Andrew⁷; and Elmer⁷.
[C412] Vermadel⁶; m Lewis Kuykendal   Children   Merrel F ⁷, Normal⁷,
    Herman⁷.
[C413] Jennie⁶, m Dr L. C Morgan; res Dahlgren, Ill.   (3 ch.)
[C414] Francis⁶; (3 sons).

[C397] IRA MILEY⁵ BRUMBAUGH ([C102] David Snyder⁴, [C16]
David³, [C4] John², Johann Jacob¹) b Dec. 1, 1866, at New Enterprise, Bedford Co, Pa ; educated in public and select schools, Millersville State Normal
School, and Eastman Business College; recently a ranch owner and stock
dealer at Trinidad, Colo ; now stock inspector of B A. I at Kansas City, Mo ,-
ad. Hotel Brunswick, 11th and Broadway, unm.

[C399] SAMUEL LONGENECKER⁵ BRUMBAUGH ([C102] David
Snyder⁴, same ancestry as [C397]) b Dec 8, 1869, at New Enterprise, Bedford Co, Pa , attended public and select schools, graduated from Eastman
Bus Col 1891; for a number of years was with Bell Tel. Co of Phila, Pa ,
1905 became pres. and gen mgr. Juniata Hydro-Electric Co, which successfully erected and maintains a large electric plant across the Juniata River
at Warrior Ridge, Huntingdon Co, Pa ; 1910 became interested in the development of real estate in Pittsburg, and is secy. and treas R E Imp Co. of
Pittsburg, Pa ; unm; Repn., memb. G. B. B Ch.; ad. Eastwood Farms, Pittsburg, Pa.

[C400] MARY EFFIE⁵ BRUMBAUGH ([C102] David Snyder⁴, same
ancestry as [C397]) b March 10, 1875, educated in the public schools of Bedford Co, Pa, and attended several terms at Millersville State Normal School,
unm; address 419 N. 32d St., Philadelphia, Pa.

[C401] CHARLOTTE AMANDA⁵ BRUMBAUGH ([C102] David Snyder⁴, same ancestry as [C397]) b Sept. 25, 1877, attended public and select schools in Bedford Co, Pa, and Perkiomen Seminary, unm; address 419 N 32d St, Philadelphia, Pa.

[C416] GERTRUDE SALOME⁵ BRUMBAUGH ([C105] Simon Snyder⁴, [C16] David³, [C4] John², Johann Jacob¹) b Sept 23, 1876, educated in public schools of Bedford Co, Pa, and Irving College, from which she graduated June, 1898; taught in public schools; m Charles Wilson Gensinore, M D, b April 24, 1875, at Birmingham, Huntingdon Co, Pa.; s William C and Mary Esther (Harding) Gensinore. He was educated in public schools, Univ. of Buffalo, and Balto Univ Sch of Med, graduating (M.D) from latter April, 1878. He served 7 yrs. with Sheridan Troop of Tyrone, N G. Pa, and 11 mos in Span.-Amer. War—chief musician Squadron of Pa Cav Since Dec., 1898, he has been engaged in the general practice of medicine at New Enterprise, Bedford Co, Pa

One child.

i Helen Gensinore⁶, b Nov 1, 1901, d Jan. 21, 1906

[C417] GRACE⁵ BRUMBAUGH ([C105] Simon Snyder⁴, same ancestry as [C416]) b 1878, m Rollin Wintrode Lynn, res. Altoona, Pa. (No ch)

[C418] OSCAR LUTHER⁵ BRUMBAUGH ([C105] Simon Snyder⁴, same ancestry as [C416]) b 1881, completed the business course at Jun. Col., recently m —— Plummer of Altoona, Pa, and lives upon the home farm.

[C419] SIMON CLARENCE⁵ BRUMBAUGH, M D ([C105] Simon Snyder⁴, same ancestry as [C416]) b 1885; completed the Normal Eng course at Jun Col, graduated M D (1910) from Jeff. Med Col, ad New Enterprise, Bedford Co., Pa.

[C422] ROBERT NEVIN⁵ BRUMBAUGH ([C92] Levi⁴, [C42] Otho³, [C7] Henry², Johann Jacob¹) b Feb. 16, 1878, at Miamisburg, Montgomery Co., O.; Nov 28, 1900, at Dayton O, m Rose Wagner, dau Samuel and Mary Ellen (Beckel) Wagner He is a graduate of State High School, Dayton, O ; spent three years in the Academic and Law Depts of Ohio State University; is atty-at-law, has served as Secy Board of Fire Commissioners of Dayton, 1901-'02; Clerk Board of Public Safety, Dayton, 1903-'06 Address, 1009 Grand Ave., Dayton, O.

Children (3):

[C511] Mary Ellen⁶, b Sept 10, 1901.

[C512] Phyllis Louise[6], *b* March 6, 1904
[C513] Nathan Kingsbury[6], *b* March 2, 1906

[C426] ALBERTA JESSIE[5] BRUMBAUGH ([C169] Jerome David[4], [C13] David[3], [C2] Jacob[2], Johann Jacob[1]) *b* Dec 2, 1871, at Marysville, Marshall Co, Kansas; Jan 6, 1896, at Kansas City, Mo, *m* *Fred Almonte Day*, *b* May 9, 1871, at Butler, Bates Co, Mo . s *Ira Almonte* and *Mary Annis (Wagner) Day*. Alberta was educated in the public schools of Marysville, Kans, Bethany College, Topeka, Kans —graduate School of Elocution, Episcopalian, residence, 119 16th St, Lexington, Mo

> *Children* (3), *surname Day*
> i Harry A.[6], *b* Sept. 6, 1898.
> ii Belle B.[6], *b* Oct. 13, 1900
> iii Alberta E.[6], *b* Nov. 20, 1905.

[C434] SUSAN STAKE[5] BRUMBAUGH ([C119] Upton S—[4], [C43] Andrew[3], [C7] Henry[2], Johann Jacob[1]) *b* Jan 9, 1881, Jan 1, 1904, *m* *Maurice Chapman Thompson*, farmer, address, Hollywood, St. Mary's Co, Md.

> *Children* (3), *surname Thompson:*
> i Maurice Chapman[6], *b* Sept 21, 1904.
> ii Mary Katharine[6], *b* Oct. 23, 1905
> iii Elizabeth Claire[6], *b* March 4, 1907.

[C447] HARRY LAWRENCE[5] BRUMBAUGH ([C157] William Greenberry[4], [C46] George[3], [C7] Henry[2], Johann Jacob[1]) *b* November, 1868; *m* *Nellie Brott*, he is reported as recently yardmaster for S F. R. R. at Wellington, Kans One son Floyd[6].

[C466] ENOL VANE[5] BRUMBAUGH ([181] Eli Harrison[4], [C47] Calvin[3], [C7] Henry[2], Johann Jacob[1]) *b* Nov 17, 1877, at Memphis, Scotland Co, Mo ; attended St Joseph (Mo) High Sch ; graduated from Baker Univ. (B A) 1897, Wabash College (M A) 1900 Taught school at Pardee, Kans., 1898, Whiteside, Ind, 1899, Professor of Chemistry Upper Iowa Univ 1900-'04, principal of High School Marshalltown, Ia, 1905-'07, Independence, Ia, 1908, Aberdeen, S Dak, 1909, member Amer. Chem. Soc.; Chair Section Secondary and Normal Schools Iowa State Teachers' Assn. 1908, attending Milwaukee Med. Col., as well as teaching biology therein; ad 228 13th St., Milwaukee, Wis.   •

[C468] MABLE C [5] BRUMBAUGH ([181] Eli Harrison[4], same

ancestry as [C466]) *b* Jan 29, 1881,' at Memphis, Scotland Co , Mo ; Dec 25, 1903, *m Clarence Benjamin Werts*, D D S , *b* at Sunbeam, Mercer Co , Ill , Feb 14, 1870 , *s George W* and *Mary Elizabeth (Decker) Werts*   He attended Aledo Academy, Hedding College, and graduated (D D S) from Western Dental College, Kansas City, Mo , in 1899   Mable is teaching in public schools of Ladoga, Montgomery Co . Ind , which is their home address. (No issue)

[C469] LOUISE⁵ BRUMBAUGH ([C181] Eli Harrison⁴, same ancestry as [C466]) *b* in Memphis, Mo , June 7, 1883, educated in public schools of St. Joseph, Mo , Atchison, Kans., Crawfordsville, Ind , Quincy, Ill , Oklahoma City, Okla , Upper Iowa Univ , Iowa State Normal School, Valparaiso Univ (1907-'08)   These various places in a general way represent the various charges held by her late father [C171] *Eli Harrison⁴ Brumbaugh*   Since 1902 Louise⁵ has been teaching in the public schools of Iowa, and of Moline, Ill , residing in the latter place at 2024 Sixth Avenue.

[C501] HORACE ATLEE⁶ BRUMBAUGH ([C320] John Furry⁵, [C97] Jacob Snyder⁴, [C15] David³, [C4] John², Johann Jacob¹) *b* Oct 10, 1874, at New Enterprise, Bedford Co , Pa , 1883 *m Lydia Catharine Ebersole, b* Sept , 1871, also at New Enterprise, Pa ; dau *Daniel C* and *Regina (Specht) Ebersole*, and sister of *Annie Ebersole*, who *m* [C368] *Charles Ober⁵ Brumbaugh*, he was educated in the public schools and at Juniata College, from which he graduated (B.E , 1901) in the Normal English course, and later there pursued some special work; he carried mail for five years; taught in the public schools 1897-'99 and 1901—, was principal of Juniata (Pa) public schools, and in 1911 is principal of the Taylor Twp High Sch , Blair Co , Pa   He published a volume of poems, "Life in Verse"; another, "Life in Song—Vol I," and some miscellaneous poems, which have been well received by the public   He is a member of G. B B Ch ; Repn ; address, Roaring Spring, Blair Co., Pa.   He has materially assisted the compiler

SUNNY SIDE OF LIFE.

The wintry winds are cold and chill,
    The bare trees weep and shiver,
And restless willows sway their boughs
    Above the frozen river.

And as I watch the fading sun
    That scarcely warms the meadows,

I seek to find some sunny soul
   To brighten gathering shadows.

But as the last beam fades away,
   And I am at the heather,
There joy and home are radiant beams
   Amid the wintry weather.

H. A. B.

LIFE'S STORY BOOK

Years make the chapters,
  As we grow old,
Days make the pages,
  As deeds are told,
Hours will paragraph
  The kindness shown,
Minute, a sentence,
  Is the seed sown,
Second, a fragment,
  Like a swift brook;
Perhaps, keeps unmarred
  Life's story book

—H Atlee Brumbaugh

THE FLOWERS OF JUNE.

Oh, how can my spirit of mortal be sad
When the flowers of June are making it glad?

I long for the fragrance of roses in June
And for smiles and blushes when nature's in tune.
Then away to the woods, where wild flowers grow,
To hear the birds singing just all that they know.

I'll speak and I'll sing of the queen of the year,
For no other month is so fragrant or dear.

—H. Atlee Brumbaugh.

BRUMBAUGH SONG
(Tune, "America.")

Our German fathers came.
And brought our famous name,
    The name we love
Name that we praise so well,
Fame from our fathers fell,
Greater than man can tell,
    Inscribed above.

May we united be
In great Eternity,
    And world below,
Brave in the forests wild,
Where lived the savage child,
Our fathers, strong and mild,
    Joined hearts we know.

Our Father, good and great,
Is caring for our fate,
    As those of yore
Long may our voices raise
In gladness and in praise
A song in tuneful lays,
    From shore to shore
        —*Horace Atlee⁶ Brumbaugh.*

Children (3):
[C700] Mabel Alice⁷, *b* Oct. 1, 1894.
[C701] Daniel Grant⁷, *b* Aug 15, 1897, *d* June 1, 1899
[C702] Harold Clay⁷, *b* Aug 28, 1901.

[C502] CHARLES LEONARD⁶ BRUMBAUGH ([C320] John Furry⁵, same ancestry as [C501]) *b* at New Enterprise, Bedford Co, Pa, March 17, 1877, educated in Blair Co. (Pa) public schools and Bedford Classical Academy; Millersville State Normal School, graduating 1898 (M E), Harvard University summer sessions   He began teaching in public schools at 16, principal New Enterprise and Riddlesburg (Bedford Co.) public schools, asst. prin and supt. of Hollidaysburg (Blair Co, Pa) public schools, was

secy. Western Pa. Audubon Soc . pres and mgr Burroughs Club of Amer ,
1901; spl dep Game Piotector (Pa) 1905   Has published "Songs of the
Alleghenies," "Papers on Nat Hist of Pa ," "Fugitive Poems and Stories";
editor on staff of *Pittsburg Post*, residence, Tioga and Pitt Sts , Wilkinsburg,
Pa.   June 12, 1902, *m Mabel (Brenneman) Buck*

   One child

[C704] Seth Buck⁷, *b* June 20, 1906

   [C503] MARY LYSTRA⁶ BRUMBAUGH ([C320] John Furry⁵, same
ancestry as [C501]) *b* Jan 14, 1881; graduated from Normal English Course
of Juniata College in Class of 1902 (B E).   Mary *m William Ragan Cromwell, b* June 2, 1883, at Salem, Oregon; s *William Jesse* and *Sarah Elizabeth
(Bridges) Cromwell*   William was educated in the Los Angeles public and
high schools, and in the Occidental College; in 1903 he entered the service of
the Home Telephone and Telegiaph Co , and since January, 1907, has been
manager of the Directory Department of the company; residence, 511 North
Wellington St , Los Angeles, Cal

   [C504] ROSCOE CONKLING⁶ BRUMBAUGH ([C320] John Furry⁵,
same ancestry as [C501] *b* Nov. 7, 1883, *m Sarah Summers*   He was educated in the common schools of Blair Co , Pa , and graduated from Juniata
College in Class of 1901, is engaged upon newspaper and magazine work,
circulation mgr *Suburban Life*, ad. care John Furry Brumbaugh, New Enterprise, Pa.

   [C506] FLOY⁶ BRUMBAUGH ([C320] John Furry⁵, same ancestry as
[C501]) *b* Sept 18, 1895; *d* Feb 13, 1910, from pneumonia and disease of
the heart, and was interred in the cemetery at New Enterprise, Bedford Co ,
Pa   She was greatly interested in music, in which she showed marked ability;
was organist in her school, and also took an active part in its literary work.

SECTION D

GERMANNA, VA., AND MELCHIOR BRUMBACH, JOHN BRUMBACH (BROMBACH) OF LANCASTER CO., PA., [D1] JOHAN MELCHIOR BROMBACH, AND [D2] "THE WIDOW BRUMBACH" AND THEIR DESCENDANTS.

Within this chapter are gathered interesting findings resulting from extended research, which, upon the first consideration, were disassociated, but which are becoming more and more closely identified It is probable that the future will make clear at least most of the mysterious points involved, as the finding of the Bible records of [D3] Henry[2] Brumbach established the proper spelling of his family name, and the certainty that the Brumback descendants belong to the "Brumbach Families."

GERMANNA—GERMANTOWN, VA., AND MELCHIOR BRUMBACH.

The reader will look in vain upon current maps for these ancient settlements, and almost in vain in historical literature for descriptions of them; yet, in "1721 it [Germanna] marked the farthest westward advance of civilization in Va." Germanna appears upon the Va. map of Fry & Jefferson, 1751 (a copy of which is in Library of Congress); upon the Reid, 1796, map used in Heads of Families, First Census of the U S, 1790, and in one other map. It was the German colony of Gov Spottswood in Stafford Co ; was founded by direct importation in 1714 of iron workers from Nassau-Siegen, Westphalia, Germany, and it is of special interest to Brumbach families because we there find Milcard—Milchert—Melchior Brumbach (various forms in which the English recorder wrote the names) taking part in the first iron blast furnace operation in America

ORDER OF THE VA EXECUTIVE COUNCIL, APRIL 28, 1714 *

This is apparently the first Va record of the German colonists (German Reformed) who settled Germanna in 1714:

"The Governor acquainting the Council that Sundry Germans to the number of forty-two men, women and children who were invited hither by Baron de Graffenreid are now arrived[b] + + + "The Governor therefore proposed to settle them above the falls of Rappahannock River to serve as a

---

* Va Mag of Hist and Biog, Vol 13, p 362 et seq ; Vol 11, p 231, etc, the interested reader should see the full references, also Genealogy of the Kemper Family by Willis M Kemper, who has also furnished some new material for this chapter

[b]—— sailed to Va in the spring of 1714—conclusively that these colonists came directly from Germany"

Barrier to the Inhabitants of that part of the Country against the Incursions of the Indians," etc.

This settlement was at once made a fort by order of the Council; its inhabitants, in view of their exposed position and their inability to raise crops, were exempted from "publick Levies of the Government", and they were designated as "Rangers" and thus given general hunting privileges.

AFFIDAVITS OF MILCARD—MILCHERT [MELCHIOR] BRUMBACH AND OTHERS.

Twelve Germanna colonists made affidavits in June, 1724, for the purpose of obtaining 1800 acres of land, as shown by the Spottsylvania Co (Va.) records* Germanna was first in Stafford Co, later Prince William, and in Fauquier about 1720.

"At a Court held per adjournment from yesterday the 2d day of June, 1724, for Spotsylvania County "

"*Milcard Brumbach* in order to prove his right to take up land according to the Royal Charter, made oath that he came into this country to dwell in the month of April, 1714, and that he brought with him *Elizabeth* his wife, and that this is the first time of proving their said importation, whereupon certificates is ordered to be granted them of right to take up one hundred acres of land."

The names of these colonists were*

"John Spellman [Spillman] and Mary his wife,

Hamon Fitshback [Herman Fishback] and Kathrina his wife,

John Huffman [John Henry Huffman] and Kathrina his wife,

Joseph Guntz [Coons] and Kathrina his wife and his son John Annilis,

John Fitshback [Fishback] and Agnes his wife,

Jacob Rickart [Rector] and Elizabeth his wife and son John,

"*Milchert [Melchior] Brumbach*, the same order for himself and his wife Elizabeth."

Dillman Weaver and Ann Weaver his mother,

Lekewin [Likewise ?] Peter Hitt and Elizabeth his wife."

These certificates were not issued until May 30th, 1729

A true copy   Teste:

Jan. 10, 1906   T. A HARRIS, Clerk."

John Broil, and Frederick Cobbler and his wife Barbara also on the same day make similar oaths.

*Will Book A, pp. 3-4
*The quotations above given are from Va Mag of Hist and Biog, Vol 13, pp 367-373, wherein the further statement is made that the original English writing clerk made evident grave errors in the German spelling of the names

"The original German forms of the surname of the 1714 colonists are Holzklau, Kemper, Martin, Spielman, Fischbach, Hoffman, Kuntz, Richter, *Brumbach,* Weber, Weide."

"The history of Germanna is of importance because the colonists of 1714 were the first organized body of Germans who came as permanent settlers to Va., and were the pioneers of that sturdy element which has done so much to develop the western part of the State. Germanna was the first county seat of Spotsylvania in 1722 and continued as such until 1732 It was originally in old Essex County, but is in the eastern portion of present Orange Co., on

ADDENDA AND ERRATA

Upon page 246, following "The names of these colonists were,"b there should be added the names of the first three to file affidavits, thus completing the twelve colonists

"Jacob Holxrow [Holtzclaw] and Margaret, his wife, and sons John and Henry (200 acres)

John Camper [Kemper] and Alice Kathrina, his wife (100 acres)

Johannes [John Joseph] Martin and Maria Kathrina, his wife, (100 acres) "

The Westover Manuscripts, "Progress to the Mines," partly reproduced in History of Orange Co , Va., Scott, p 87, et seq , contain the interesting description of Col Byrd's visit to Col Spotswood and Germanna in 1732

Journals of House of Burgesses, 1712-1726, edited by H. R. McIlwaine, Va State Librarian, p xvii, contains especially interesting references to Germanna.

Page 605, [E1230], read Mark Floiy.[7]
Page 606, [E656-1], read Miriam Kern.[7]

"The original German forms of the surname of the 1714 colonists are: Holzklau, Kemper, Martin, Spielman, Fischbach, Hoffman, Kuntz, Richter, *Brumbach*, Weber, Weide "

"The history of Germanna is of importance because the colonists of 1714 were the first organized body of Germans who came as permanent settlers to Va., and were the pioneers of that sturdy element which has done so much to develop the western part of the State. Germanna was the first county seat of Spotsylvania in 1722 and continued as such until 1732. It was originally in old Essex County, but is in the eastern portion of present Orange Co , on the south bank of the Rapidan, about thirty miles above Fredericksburg For at least seven years Germanna was an armed fort on the extreme western frontier of Va. as it then existed "[a]

"These Germans were invited over, some years ago, by the Baron de Graffenreed, who has her Majesty's Letter to ye Governor of Virginia to furnish them Land upon their arrival. They are generally such as have been employed in their own country as miners, ' etc.[b]

"The first organized community in the new county [Spotsylvania] consisted of twelve German families from the old principality of Nassau-Siegen [Westphalia], Germany, who came to Va in the month of April, 1714[c] + + They were skilled workers in iron, and built for Gov Spotswood a blast furnace about 10 miles n w of Fredericksburg, which, according to his testimony, was the first in North America"[d] + "Thus the great iron and steel industries of the U. S had their genesis in the forest of Spotsylvania Co., Va ," etc [e]

"The Assembly failing to take action on this measure, Spotswood himself some four years later, or in 1714, inaugurated the iron industry at Germanna, on the Rappahannock River, with German Protestant workmen, who came over with Baron de Graffenreidt "[a*] + "for improvem't of the Iron Mines lately discovered in this Country, which upon Tryal have been found to be extraordinary rich and good."[a*]

July 21st, 1714 + + "I continue, all resolv'd, to settle out our Tributary Indians as a guard to ye Frontiers, and in order to supply that part, w'ch was to have been covered by the Tuscaruros, I have placed here a number

---

[a] Va Hist Mag , Vol 13, p 363
[b] Letters of Gov Spotswood, Vol 2, p 70
Vol. XI, pp 231-233, Gen of Kemper Family, pp 5-53
[c] Hinke Jour of Pres. Hist. Soc , 11, 1-3, Phila., Pa ; Va Mag. of Hist. and Biog,
"It will be almost like hunting for a needle in a haystack, as there are 6 or 8 Reformed churches in the neighborhood of Siegen, where Brumbach family have come from; so far as I know, not another member of the colony came from Muesen "—Letter from Willis M. Kemper to compiler, Feb 16 1911
[d] Va Mag. of Hist and Biog , 12, p 342
[e] Same reference, and also Slaughter, History of St Mark's Parish, p. 5.
[a*] Spotswood Letters, Vol. 1, pp 20, 21

of Prodestant Germans, built them a Fort, and finish'd it with 2 pieces of Cannon and some Ammunition, which will awe the Straggling partys of Northern Indians, and be a good Barrier for all that part of the Country   These Germans were invited over, some years ago. by the Baron de Graffenreed, who has her Majesty's Letter to ye Governor of Virginia to furnish them with Land upon their arrival.   They are generally such as have been employed in their own country as Miners, and say they are satisfyed there are divers kinds of minerals in those upper parts of the County where they are settled, and even a good appearance of Silver Oar, but that 'tis impossible for any man to know whether those Mines will turn to account without digging some depth in the Earth, a liberty I shall not give them until I receive an Answer to what I represented to your Lo'ps concerning y'r Ascertaining her Maj't's Share, which I hope by y'r Lo'p's interposition be speedily signifyed" + +*

"A settlement of German Protestants was also effected, under the auspices of the Governor, on the Rapidan river, which was called after the name of his residence, Germanna " [b]

"In the county of Spotsylvania, Spotswood had about the year 1716, founded on a horseshoe peninsula of four hundred acres on the Rapidan, the little town of Germanna, so called after the Germans, sent over by Queen Anne, and settled in that quarter, and at this place he resided after his retirement   A church was built there mainly at his expense.   Possessing an extensive tract of forty-five thousand acres of land, which abounded in iron ore, he engaged largely in connection with Robert Cary of England, and others in Virginia, in the iron manufacture "[c] + +

"As to the other Settlement, named Germanna, there are about forty Germans, Men, Women and Children, who, having quitted their native Country upon the invitation of Herr Graffenreidt, and being grievously disappointed by the failure to perform his Engagement to them, and they arriving also here just at a time when the Tuscaruro Indians departed from the Treaty they had made with this Government to settle upon its Northern Frontiers, I did, both in Compassion to those poor strangers, and in regard to the safety of the Country, place them together upon a piece of land, several Miles without the Inhabitants, where I built them Habitations and subsisted them until they were able, by their own Labour, to provide for themselves, and I presume I may, without a Crime or Misdemeanor, endeavour to put them in an honest way of paying their Just Debts "[d] + +

"The earliest description of Germanna that has been found is in the

*Spotswood Letters, Vol II, pp 70, 71
[b]Spotswood Letters, Vol I, X
[c]Same, Vol I, XIII
[d]Spotswood Letters, Vol II, p 96

diary of John Fountain.[*] He + + visited the settlement on Nov 20 and 21, 1715. He says "About 5 P M we crossed a bridge that was made by the Germans, and about 6 we arrived at the German settlement. We went immediately to the minister's house, we found nothing to eat, but lived upon our small provisions, and lay upon good straw Our beds not being very easy, as soon as it was day we got up It rained hard, notwithstanding we walked about the town, which is palisaded with stakes stuck in the ground, and laid close the one to the other, and of substance to bear out.a musket shot. There are but nine families, and they have nine houses built all in a line, and before every house, about twenty feet distant from it, they have many sheds built for their hogs and hens, so that hog styes and houses make a street. The place that is paled in is a pentagon very regularly laid out, and in the very center there is a block house made with five sides which answer to the five sides of the great inclosure, there are loop holes through it, from which you may see all the inside of the inclosure This was intended for a retreat for the people, in case they were not able to defend the palisades if attacked by the Indians. They make use of this block house for divine service They go to prayers constantly once a day and have two sermons on Sunday. We went to hear them perform their service, which was done in their own language, which we did not understand, but they seemed very devout, and sang the Psalms very well.

This town or settlement lies upon the Rappahannock River, thirty miles above the falls, and thirty miles from any inhabitants The Germans live very miserably. We would tarry here some time, but for want of provisions we are obliged to go. We got from the minister[b] a bit of smoked beef and cabbage, which was very ordinary. We made a collection between us three, of about thirty shillings, for the minister, and about twelve of the clock we took our leave, and set out to return."

HUGH JONES' DESCRIPTION OF GERMANNA, 1724.

"Beyond Col Spottswood's Furnace above the Falls of the Rappahannock River, within View of the vast Mountains, he had founded a Town called Germanna, from some Germans sent over thither by Queen Anne, who are now removed up farther Here he has Servants and Workmen of most handycraft Trades; and he is building a Church, Court-House and Dwelling-House for himself; and with his Servants and Negroes he has cleared Plantations about it, purposing great Encouragement for People to come and settle in that uninhabited Part of the World, lately divided into a County

---

[*]Memoirs of a Huguenot Family, p 267, and Kemper Genealogy, pp 19-20
[b]Henry Hager, the first German Ref pastor in the U. S

Beyond this are seated the Colony of Germans or Palatines, with Allowance of good Quantities of rich Land, at easy or no Rates, who thrive very well, and live happily, and entertain generously."[*]

MORAVIAN DIARIES.

"The Great Fork of the Rippehannng [Rappahannock][b]

It is situated about twenty-six miles from the Upper Germans towards the 'Potomik' Three German families live there," etc.[c]

"Extract from the Diary of Bros. Joseph [Spangenberg] and Matthew Rentz Through Md. and Va July and Aug., 1748.

"On July 30th, they came, towards evening, to the Licken Run [Licking Run] or Germantown, where they lodged with an old friend by the name of *Holzklau*. The little village is settled with Reformed miners from Nassau-Siegen. They live very quietly together and are nice people."[d]

At another place we find. "We spoke with each other about Bethlehem"— 400 miles distant through the forest

"These colonists remained at Germanna until the year 1721, when they acquired lands in the Northern Neck and removed about twenty miles northward from Germanna, locating in old Stafford Co. That section of Stafford fell into Prince William in 1730, and later (1759) into present Fauquier Co. Their new home, called Germantown, was on Licking Run about eight miles south of present Warrenton, Va. Midland Station, on the Southern Railroad, is near this ancient settlement, which, in 1721 marked the farthest westward advance of civilization in Virginia. The importance of the preceding Council Order and the Court Orders relating to the colonists of 1714, consists in the fact that these documents settle every doubt which has been raised with reference to the time when and place from which they came. The Court Orders also furnish for the first time positive evidence with reference to the names of all the persons who composed this."[e]

"But where is Germanna?[a*] Or, rather, where was it? For this famous town of Gov. Spottswood—the first German settlement in Va ; the first county

---

[*]The Present State of Virginia, Hugh Jones, London, 1724, p. 59

[b]Va. Mag. of Hist and Biog, Vol II, p 231—Gottschalk's Travels—1748 "The colonists came from Muesen and Siegen, situated in the principality of Nassau—Siegen, which is now a part of the Prussian province of Westphalia Muesen has been an important iron center since the year 1300," etc

[c]Same, p. 229 "This settlement was composed of German Lutherans, the second colony to locate at or near Germanna came in 1717, 20 families and about 80 persons Rev John Caspar Stoever was their first pastor "

[d]Same, pp. 235 and 241.

[e]Va. Mag. of Hist and Biog, Vol. XIII, p. 368

[a*]Kemper Genealogy, pp. 18-19.

"Thirty Thousand Names of Immigrants," Rupp (reprint), pp 460-461, also contains data concerning "Germanna "

town of Spottsylvania Co., where St. George's Parish was organized, where the first iron furnace in America was built, and the first pig iron made as Spottswood claims; the place from which the famous expedition of 'the Knights of the Golden Horseshoe' started; where the first Ger. Ref. Cong in the U S was organized, its first pastor settled, and its first services held—*is no more.* It is now only a ford in the river. Take your map of Va., and in the extreme northeastern corner of what is now Orange Co., on a remarkable horseshoe peninsula of about 400 acres, with the Rapidan to the north, west, and east of it, was the site of this famous town   Gov. Spottswood had a very large tract of land here, he had discovered iron on this tract, he brought these Germans over to work this body of ore, he built a furnace near the tract, the ruins of which have lately been discovered, crumbling to dust, and overgrown with vegetation; the Governor built himself a handsome residence on this tract, to which he retired in 1723, after he ceased to be Governor."

"With the Reformed colonists Haeger left Germanna in 1721 and settled at Germantown, Fauquier Co. + + Occasionally ministers from Pennsylvania visited the congregation." [a]

DEED FROM CHILDREN OF "MILCARD BRUMBACK", JULY 23, 1746

July 23, 1746, Stephen Huntzenbiller, Jacob Newswanger and Christopher Wingle of Frederick Co., Va., conveyed for natural love and affection *"which we bear to our beloved brother and sister Henry Otterback and Agnes Otterback his wife"* 100 acres lying in Prince William Co., Va., *"in the Germantown,"* it being part of the land taken up by John Fishback, Jacob Holtzclaw and John Henry Hoffman, by grand patent and by them conveyed by a lease for 99 years yet to come, to *Milcard Brumbach,* and by him conveyed to the grantors, the said lease to Brumbach being recorded in Stafford Co., Va. This land adjoins that of Elizabeth Rictor and John Fishback

The above appears in the deed book of Prince William Co., [b] and in the same records also appears a deed of Feb. 21, 1738, by which Just Hite conveyed to *Jacob Niswanger,* in consideration of 5 sh., 400 a. granted to Hite by patent June 12, 1734, lying "on ye west side of 'Shenando River' [Shenandoah] bounded by North Branch of Crooked Run, to Walnut which divides this and Peter Stephen's land [c]

Further, on Feb. 22, 1738, at a court held for Orange Co., Va., "on the

[a] Va. Mag. of Hist. and Biog., Vol 12, p 75.
[b] Abstract made by Willis M Kemper, Esq Cincinnati, O., in his researches for Genealogy of the Kemper Family   Stafford Co records were destroyed during the Civil War
[c] Information kindly furnished by Prof Wm J Hinke, Auburn, N. Y., who, together with Mr Chas E Kemper, Washington D C, searched the records of Orange, Culpepper and Prince William counties, and both of whom have published data in Va Magazine, and elsewhere, on this locality

petition of Just Hite and others for clearing road from Hyte's mill to Ashby's bent, its ordered that Lewis Stephen and *Jacob Niswanger* lay of ye same, make report of their proceedings to ye next court."

"Pursuant to the within order we, the subscribers, have lay'd of the road from Just Hite Mill to the foard that leads to Ashby's bent, viz., from the Mill south about half a mile, from thence southeast to Caseys foard. Witness our hands the 22nd of March, 1738.

· LEWIS STEPHENS,

JACOB NISEWANGER."

MARRIAGE OF MARIA GERTRAUDT BRUMBACH, JUNE 5, 1738,[a]
AND THE REV. STOEVERS

The baptismal and marriage records of Rev John Caspar Stoever (Notes and Queries, Egle, 1896, p. 83) contain this important family record.

"June 5, 1738, *John Jacob Neuschwanger* and *Maria Gertraudt Brumbach*, Opaken (Opequon)."

Opequon[b] is an old hamlet with a P O and a creek, in Frederick Co, Va., N.E. of Winchester (the northernmost Co. of the State, and S W. of Hagerstown, Md) Frederick Co, Va, was formed from Orange Co. in 1738 In this connection it is interesting to note that none of the Brumbacks about Opequon can throw any light upon the life or even existence of these earlier Brumbachs or their marriages

The above marriage was made by Rev. John Casper Stoever, Jr. "This man probably organized more churches than any one else, not even excepting Muhlenberg himself."[c] "He also traveled beyond the Susquehanna in a S W. direction, penetrating almost to the center of Va, via the Shenandoah Valley, stopping in Md. on the way, preaching to the scattered Lutherans and baptizing their children '''[c] He was the first Lutheran minister ordained in the colonies; was pastor in the Tulpehocken region (Pa) 1733, after his father went to Va, to 1779, and ministered to the people of all religious beliefs The considerable interval occurring before and after the entry of the Brumbach-Neuschwanger marriage seems to justify the conclusion that he then traveled to the Opequon, Va, region to see his father, Rev. John Caspar Stoever, Sr. (Note that this learned and precise German minister spells the name Brumbach, as Henry[3] [D3] also wrote it.) The lives and activities of the celebrated Stoevers are extensively given in Transactions of The Pennsylvania-German

---

[a] Reference found and furnished by M A Gruber, 932 O N W, Washington, D C, who has prepared a card index to the Stoever baptisms and marriages

[b] Shenandoah Valley Pioneers and Their Descendants—Frederick Co, Va, Cartmell, pp 165-169, contains interesting facts concerning this old settlement

[c] Proceedings Pennsylvania—German Society, Vol XX, pp 82 and 86

Society, Vol. XX, pp 82-89, 128-141, and the will of the elder is reproduced upon pp 135 to 141—registered in Will Book F, pp 96 and 126, etc., Philadelphia, Pa   Said will is signed, "John Caspar Stoever, Minister of the Dutch Lutheran Church in Virginia," and is of exceptional interest. In it he writes: "Now unto *my well beloved son John Caspar Stoever, minister of Conestoken*, unto thee and Michael Schmidt do I give, etc "

"On Sept. 11, 1728, there arrived in Philadelphia Johann Caspar Stoever, Sr., Missionaire, and Johann Caspar Stoever, S S Theo. Stud. The latter remained in Pa and was instrumental in founding many Lutheran churches. The former went to Madison County, Va , in 1733 + +." (Va. Hist. Mag., Vol. XI, p 241.)

"The German colony on Robinson river, west of the present town of Madison, prospered under the kind government of Sir Alexander Spotswood. The colonists were laborious and pious people. In 1735 they founded a congregation with Rev. *Johann Caspar Stoever* [Sr.] as parson, who also took charge of the church at Germanna, upon Rev. [Gerhard] Henkel's acceptance of a call to the congregation near the Yadkin River in N. C." (History of the German Element in Va , Schurecht, 1898, Vol I, p. 74)

"Maria Gertraudt Brumbach," "Agnes Otterback" and the wives of Stephen Huntzenbiller and Christopher Wingle were undoubtedly sisters, and daughters of Melchior Brumbach, deceased. and the three sisters were apparently giving their interest to the other sister in the absence of male heir.

It is evident from the affidavit of June 2, 1724, by "Milcard [Melchior] Brumbach" that upon landing in 1714 there were no children, as, under the early Va. laws, an additional allowance of fifty acres was granted for each child. Mr. Willis M. Kemper reports that the records of Prince William Co., Va., are incomplete, owing to destruction during the Civil War, and that the existing records and those of Fauquier Co. show no further trace of Milcard or Melchior Brumbach.

Heads of Families—Va , 1782, Frederick Co., gives· "David Nisewanger 5 whites," "John Nisewanger 6 whites" and "Colo John Nisewanger 7 whites and 1 black." John Neuschwanger who, on June 5, 1738, m Maria Gertraudt Brumbach of Opequon, was probably the ancestor of the above persons, but no extensive efforts have been made to verify the supposition

The names Huntzenbiller, Wingle and Otterback do not appear in the above mentioned "Heads of Families," or in the Stoever baptisms and marriages

Children (at least 4):
Daughter; *m Stephen Huntzenbiller.*
Maria Gertraudt; *m John Jacob Neuschwanger*

Daughter, *m Christopher Wingle*
Agnes; *m Henry Otterback.*

EXTRACT FROM THE KEMPER GENEALOGY

"12 *Anna Juliana Kemper* (John George—Germanna, Va., settler—Johann) *b* Musen 30 Dec., 1708, bap 6 Jan, 1709, *d* in Pa., *m* —— *Broomback*

Issue:

41 1　*Daughter, b* 1736, *m (Jacob ?) Hicstand*
　　　and others ?—at least 2 sons.
　　　Abraham
　　　Samuel—both *m* and were living in Fairfield Co., O , in 1813—nothing
　　　　known since " '

JOHANN KEMBER *b* Musen, Nassau-Siegen (Westphalia), Germany,
about 1635 (o s.)

John Henry Kemper (John George, Johann) *b* Musen, March 23, 1696
(o. s.), *d* Lititz, Pa , April 3, 1769 (n s); *m* about 1728, in Holland, *Catharine Reichen,* dau. *Daniel Reichen*　Came on *Nancy* (Rotterdam), Sept 20,
1738,' settled in Lititz, Earl Twp , on Conestoga River," Lancaster Co., Pa

Mr. Kemper further says· ' The spelling on p. 59, Kemper Genealogy, is
the way I copied it from a letter dated 1814, written by Abraham Hiestand of
Fairfield Co , O., to my great-grandfather, James Kemper　The latter was
85 years old when I copied it, and I could not be certain whether the spelling
was Brumbach or Broomback—it was one or the other "

EXTRACT FROM THE HIESTAND GENEALOGY.ᶜ

"(1)　*Jacob¹ Hiestand* came from Pa. to Shenandoah Co , Va., in 18th
century, 'married a *Mrs. Brombach,* a German lady, who first came to America in her 14th year.'　Jacob *d* through a canoe upsetting in the Shenandoah
River—date unknown　(Family in 1804 moved from Shenandoah Co., Va , to
near where Baltimore, Fairfield Co , O , was later built)

　　　Children discovered (7), *surname Hiestand*

　2　Jacob².
　3　John², (Rev), *b* in Shenandoah Co., Va , before 1800; *m Barbara
　　　Strickler* (10 ch)
　4　Abraham², (Rev), Washington Co , Ind —*m* 3 times.
　5　Joseph², (Rev.).

─────────

ᵃGenealogy of the Kemper Family, p 59
ᵇThirty Thousand Names—Rupp, p 124
ᶜFrom *Hiestand Manuscript,* kindly loaned by Mr W H H Turner, Hustead, O

6   Elizabeth[2], *m Jacob Stouder*
7   Maria[2], *m Jacob Bixler.*   .
8   Samuel[2], J. P of Fairfield Co , O —later Bishop U. B Church.

The Hiestands lived in Page Co , Va ,* and another dau , Barbara, *m* ——— *Boyer*, the latter fact will be of interest to the Pa. Boyers, Brumbaughs, etc [E18, 68, 69], etc.

There is a will, dated 1765, of *Jacob Hiestand*, recorded in 1769 in Montgomery Co , Pa.—probably that of the father of Jacob, who *m* Mrs. Brombach [Eli

---

*See "Heistand's Corner" [A1], p 76. See also [D9], p. 275.

LANCASTER CO., PA., FAMILY RECORDS OF UNASSIGNED BRUM-BAUGHS, AND JOHN BRUMBACH

SAMUEL BRUMBAUGH [?] m *Rosanna Kauffman*, daughter of *David Kauffman* and viu *Sophia³ Keller* (Carl Andrew², Johann Peter¹).

Pennsylvania Genealogies, Egle, 1896, pp 344-345, contains a record of the above marriage in the families of "Keller of Lancaster," unfortunately without dates of birth, and nowhere in Pa. has the compiler been able to find any identification of this "Samuel Brumbaugh," or of the David Kauffman Query: Are these descendants of Michael Kauffman,* the early Va Mennonite minister, who received the patent for 400 a —"Michael Coffman of Lancaster County, Province of Pennsylvania," etc ? Samuel [D17], s of Henry² Brumbach [D3], probably married in Lancaster Co., Pa., and the presumptive evidence strongly indicates that the Widow Brumbach¹ [D2] came from that county.

Children (5):

i   Wilhelmina; m *Spencer Barrett*
ii Mary; m *John Thomas* (Elvin and William).
iii Samuel.
iv Emma, m *George J Bolton* (5 ch).
v   Jennie.

JOHN BRUMBACH (BROMBACH) [?], b LANCASTER CO., PA —
Although possibly irrelevant, these records are here introduced, in connection with the various facts leading to Lancaster Co., Pa., in the hope that further facts may be discovered, and that the position of this John Brumbach in the "Brumbach Families" may be fully determined

JOHN BRUMBACH (BROMBACH), of Lancaster Co., Pa., m *Magdalena* ———, he d 1760   His widow m (2) *Stephen Hornberger*

The Census of 1790 enumerates Stephen Hornberger's family in Hempfield Twp., Lancaster Co., Pa., as 2 white males over 16 and 4 females

AGREEMENT BETWEEN MICHAEL STREBLE AND JOHN BROMBACH.—FEB. 28, 1757.*

Michael Strebel
    and   *An Article or Agreement, Anno 1757, Feb. 28th.*
John Brombach

We the subscribers declare that we have mutually made an Agreement as follows, to wit, that I Michael Streble, a weaver by trade, have sold to *John Brombach*, a smith by trade, my improvement, for the sum of ninety pounds

---

*See pages 257, 265.

current Pennsylvania money, and John Brombach is to pay in money to Michael Streble the sum of 35 pounds before the next May court, and the second part he is to pay in one year from next autumn, that is to say 15 pounds in the year 1758, and the remaining parts to be paid in sums of 10 pounds annually until the whole is paid; and he is to give the housewife a gratuity of one doubloon at 1 pound and 6 shillings, and by this agreement Michael Streble promises to give together with the place whatever is nailed fast, and the stove in the (sitting) 100m, and the plow, and the small and large clevis, together with the farm-scales, and Michael Streble shall have the privilege of remaining on the place until the May court, and he is to look after affairs of *John Brombach* and to take charge thereof and to guard him from injury as much as he can, and I, Michael Streble, reserve for myself two acres of land so that I can build a house upon it, if I should not find a location that pleases me elsewhere, that I can dwell in it as long as I live, and after [I and] my wife are deceased it is to be the property of John Brombach, but it is to be located on one side and not in the middle of the land, and Michael Streble further makes the following condition, that Adam Heinrich is to remain in possession for four years of the 4 acres of land on which the cottaeg stands, he having moved to this land on the 2d of August, 1756 The above are acknowledged with our own signatures.

JOSEPH LANG,   MICHAEL STREBEL,
ADAM HEINRICH,   JOHANNES BROMBACH

I, John Brombach, herewith declare that after Michael Strebel on March 5, 1757, has given me additional written security, the aforesaid remains unchanged in so far as concerns the two acres of land for a house for himself and his wife, so long as they or either of them shall live, for their residence but for no other persons, and all that is aforesaid remains as we agreed, this I testify with my own signature   Done at Lancaster, March 5, 1757

JOHANNES BROMBACH *

Witness.

Henry Kemper,
Joseph Long

Lancaster County, ss   Before me the subscriber, one of the Justices of the Peace in and for the county aforesaid, personally appeared John Long who upon his solemn affirmation according to law did declare that he is well acquainted with the handwriting of his brother Joseph Long one of the sub-

---

*Translated from the German record by the late Dr Jos H Dubbs of Franklin and Marshall College

scribing witnesses to the within and above instrument of writing, etc., etc.

Signed with hand and seal, Sept 1, 1796.

JOHN HUBER.   [Seal]

Recorded Sept. 2, 1796   George Ross, Recorder   Record Book YY, p. 164, Lancaster, Pa

"LANCASTER COUNTY, PA , 1760 TO 1763"—Page 9.

"At an Orphans Court held at Lancaster for the County of Lancaster the first Tuesday of December, 1760, before Emanuel Carpenter Esquire and his Companions Judges, etc. Caspar Biuner Administrator etc. of *John Brumbough* decd produced to the Court the Acct of their Administration on the Estate of the said deceased whence their appears to be a Ballance in his hands of £112-11-10 which after deducting 12/ their Expences at this Court is reduced to the sum of £111-10-10 is distributed as follows

112-11-10

12- 0"

"Caspar Biuner Admr. of John Brumbaugh deceased produced to the Court the Account of the Admn on the Est. of the deceased passed Before the Deputy Reg whereby their appears to be a Ballance in the hands of the said Admr of 112-11-10 which account is allowed and approved of and the said Admr is allowed the further sum of £20-0-0 paid by him to Ulrich Strable for two Bonds of the decd which with the sum of 12/ their Expences at this Court Reduces the Ballance to the sum of £91-19-10 which is ordered to be paid and distributed as follows vis

To Stephen Hornberger and *Magdalene* his Wife late Wid of decd, £30-13-3¼
To *Magdalene Brombaugh* only dau of the decd,   61- 6-6¾

£91-19-10

Philip Schriner is apptd Guardian over the Person and Est of Magdalena Brombaugh an Orph & Minor Dau of John Brombaugh decd during her minority *

"Stephen Hornberger and Magdalene his wife late Magdalena Brombaugh and Caspar Briner Admr of the est of John Biumbaugh bal £31-1-4

To Stephen Hornberger and Magdalena his wife widow of decd £10-3-1½
Magdalena the Daughter £20-6-2¹ ."ᵇ

"Magdalena wife of Stephen Hornberger and Caspar Briner admr John

*Same, 1760-1763, p 17
ᵇSame, p 40

Brumbaugh John owned 50 acres for which propr Warrant but no survey and less one child an infant then about 2 yıs—share £20-60-2½'"[a]

"Magdalena daughter of John and Magdalena Brumbach Feb 23rd 1759, Bap'd March 25, 1759, by Rev. William Stoy"[b]

Issue from 1st m (2), surname Brumbach or Brombach:
Magdalena, *b* Feb. 23, 1759.
Infant.

JOHAN MELCHIOR BROMBACH [D1] AND HIS DESCENDANTS

[D1] JOHAN MELCHIOR BROMBACH arrived in Philadelphia, Pa , on the ship *Halifax*, Capt Thomas Coatam, September 22, 1752, from Rotterdam, and last from Cowes.

Immigrant List of the Ship Halifax—September 22, 1752.
In Philadelphia Friday the 22d September 1752
Present Edward Shippen Esquire

The Foreigners whose names are underwritten Imported ın the Shıp *Halifax* Captn. Thomas Coatam from Rotterdam and last from Cowes in England took this day the usual Qualifications to the Government   No 145

[D1] *Johan Melchior Brombach*
John Conrod Blecher
Johann Gorg Kuntz
Christophel Witmer
Philip Engel
Nickolas ✕ Kohler
Friederik ✕ Eberhart
Michael ✕ Springer
Martin Decker
Johan Gorg Kreybach ?
Joh Johannes Griese ?
Joannes Josephus Roth
Davit ✕ Sasmanhausen
Jacob Roth on bond (sick)
Hans Feltz

Henry ✕ Meyer
Hans Jacob Serber Zimmerman
Peter Duweiler (?)
Leonhart Weidman (?)
Heinrich Maag
Caspar ✕ Wincker
Henrich Mercki (?)
Friederich Horsch
Hendrık Frey (sik on board)
Willhelm Haussaman (?)
Johannes ✕ Rudolph
Friedrich Kammer (?)
Lorentz ✕ Durr
Hans Jacob Mulli (Muller ?)
Fılıpi Hirdt (?)

✕ ın above means "His mark"

[a] Same, p 12
[b] Penna —German Society—Baptismal Records of the First Reformed Church at Lan- . See also Vol IV, p 275, Trinity Lutheran Ch Records—same record

Anthony × Zinck

Christian T Groz

Hans George × Doctor

Johanes × Paulus

George × Paulus

Christian × Herman

Johann Jacob Bersey

Johann Lüdwig Bersey

Jacob (?)

J Jacob × Bruker

Philip × Hoffman

Bartholomae × Evar

Joas Imschiedt (?)

Peter Reeb

Hans Michael × Geyer

Friederich × Flekstein

Hans Michel Hammer

Hans Philip Elter

Jacob Muller

Conrad Muller

  (?)

  (?)

Jacob Muller

Johannes Surber

Jacob (?) Surber

Heinrich Zolli

Henry Kuntz

Ulrich Kreyser (?)

Hans Heinrich Weiss (?)

Hans Conrad × Wird

Hans Jacob Rummen

Hans Caspei Schladter (?)

Johannes × Meyer

Johannes × Jordan

  (?)

Jacob Klein

× in above means "His mark"

The testimony of the early Moravian diaries and the known migration and close intercourse between the settlement of Germantown, Bethlehem, and Lititz in Lancaster Co., Pa., and those German settlements of Germanna and Germantown in Va. seem to indicate a probable relation between the *Brumbach— Broomback* who m *Anna Julian Kemper,* and the *Melchior Brumbach* of Germanna, who "came into this country to dwell in the month of April, 1714," and that he brought with him Elizabeth his wife" The compiler's study of the problems involved also leads to the theory that there is a further relation between the foregoing and [D1] *Johan Melchior Brombach* who landed at Philadelphia September 22, 1752, and the [D2] *Widow Brumbach* (or *Brombach),* whom we find in Page Co., Va, about 1760—recently from Pa. The former seemingly died in Pa, but the searches thus far possible amongst the records of Eastern Pa. have failed to throw further light upon the time and place of the death of [D1]. He *may* be the long-sought husband of the "Widow Brumbach"; and the latter has been assigned [D2], but is given as the head of the American ancestry of Section D, in the following pages

The "Marriage and Baptismal Records of the Rev. John Waldschmidt, a Minister of the Reformed Church who served the Congregations of Cocalico, Seltenreich, Weissachenland and Muddy Creek in Lancaster Co., Pa." contain:

"*Brumbach, Margaretta,* daughter of *Melchior* and *Christian Conrad,* son of *Lenhard Conrad,* married March 6, 1770, at Riehmstown in Andrew Reihm's House." [a]

The Conrads lived in Tulpehocken Twp., Berks Co., Pa , and the Marriage Records of the Rev. John Casper Stoever, Jr , show that Christian Conrad was *b* June 19, 1745, and baptized July 6, 1746. [b]

---

[a]Translated and furnished by Luther R Kelker, Custodian of Public Records, Pa
[b]Pa Arch , 6th Series, Vol IV, p 211

THE WIDOW[1] BRUMBACH [D2] AND HER DESCENDANTS.[*]

"About A. D. 1760 a German woman, a widow Brumbach, first name unknown, with her 5 children settled on the South Branch of the Shenandoah River above Bixley's Ferry and three or four miles north from Luray, in what is Page County, Virginia The family had then recently come from Germany and probably landed in Pennsylvania and passed through the Tulpehocken region, that State, without a long stay, into the Luray Valley, Va. The children were four daughters and one son—Henry. Two of the daughters were Elizabeth and Mary, but the names of the others are unknown."[a]

"A large majority of our first immigrants were from Pennsylvania, composed of native Germans or German extraction. There were, however, a number directly from Germany, several from Md and N. J., and a few from N. Y. These immigrants brought with them the religion, habits and customs of their ancestors. They were composed generally of three religious sects, viz.: Lutherans, Menonists and Calvinists, with a few Tunkers. They generally settled in neighborhoods pretty much together.

"The territory now composing the County of Page, Powell's fort, and the Woodstock valley, between the West Fort mountain and North mountain, extending from the neighborhood of Stephensburg for a considerable distance into the county of Rockingham, was almost exclusively settled by Germans. They were very tenacious in the preservation of their language, religion, customs and habits. In what is now Page County they were almost exclusively of the Menonist persuasion, but few Lutherans or Calvinists settled among them."[b]

SUSANNA BRUMBACH and JOHANNES OEHRLE, (JOHN EARLY). [*Is this D6?*].

April 10, 1753 Susanna Brumbach *m Johannes Oehrle, b* Jan 9, 1824; *s Thomas and Margaret Fensterle Oehrle*. John Early left Jesingen Kircheim, Anderteck, Wurtemberg, arriving at Phila in the ship "Brothers" Aug. 24, 1750. He immediately proceeded to Londonderry Twp, Lebanon Co, then

---

[*]Much of the original investigation for the Va portion of this work (comprising about 90 typewritten pages) was carefully made by the late Judge Jefferson[5] Brumback [D291], who spent several summers in that State making personal investigations He died June 22, 1907, and evidenced the greatest interest, approval and co-operation in the work of the compiler The "Tulpehocken" statement is important, and the recently discovered Mennonite records showing a probability that the husband of the "Widow[1] Brumbach" [D2] will yet be identified

The late Judge Jefferson[5] Brumback and Judge Orville Sanford[6] Brumback [D263], Toledo, O, closely worked together in the effort to gather authentic family records, and, since the death of the former, the latter has been constant in his co-operation to further the success of this work

[b]History of the Valley of Va—Saml. Kercheval, Woodstock, Va, 1850, pp. 50-51.

Lancaster, Pa Before Jan , 1752, he had become a resident of Reading, Berks Co , Pa Jan 6, 1752, at a congregational meeting, he was elected one of a committee to superintend the erection of a church for the newly organized congregation. His name also appears in the first list of contributors toward its maintenance. Between Oct 22 and Nov. 12, 1754, Susanna d according to the records of Trinity Ch . "The wf of John Early Johannes Oehrle, Reformist " Some time during the following winter Mr Early settled on the banks of the Swatara, then Derry Twp , Lancaster Co , Pa.[*]

Mr. M A Gruber, Washington, D C , furnishes these references concerning Susanna's marriage, etc Penna German, Vol X, p. 74, Notes and Queries, Egle, 3d Ser , Vol II, p 176, same ref., An Vol 1897, p. 49, and An. Vol. 1899, p 96, also Notes and Queries, 3d Ser , Egle, p 232

Rev. J W. Early, Reading, Pa , author of Lutheran Ministers of Berks Co , Pa., also furnished information.

> John Early Mch 11, 1756, m (2) *Mary* or *Christina Regina Sichele*
>> Son by 1st m
> i Christian, *b* Jan 13, 1754, May 24, 1779, m *Elizabeth Hillinger*, he *d* Aug 23, 1803. There were 13 ch , widely scattered Rev. J. W Early, Reading, Pa , is a son by the 2d m

Hermanus Emanuel[1] Brumbach [G1], *b* 1751 and *d* 1803 at Amityville, Berks Co., Pa , is of a later generation, though living in the same general locality. The children of Gerhard[1] Brumbach [A1] were *b* between 1716 and 1735 The Susanna,[b] as per tombstone inscription, *b* 1758 and *d* Dec 6, 1840, m William Posey. For various reasons this Susanna cannot be a dau of Gerhard[1] [A1]. The deed from descendants of Melchior Brumbach, July 23, 1746,[c] seems to exclude her from this family. There is a possibility that Susanna may have been a dau. of the Widow Brumbach, and, because there seems no better place these facts are here introduced

> *Children* (5, [D6] *and* [D7] *vacant*).

[D3] + Henry[2], *b* Feb 4, 1739, *d* 1799.
[D4] Elizabeth[2].
[D5] Mary[2].

[D3] HENRY[2] BRUMBACH ([D2] Widow[1] Brumbach), *b* Feb. 4, 1739; Sept. 18, 1761, m (1) *Ann Kauffman*, orphan dau *Martin Kauffman*, then late of Frederick Co , Va , deceased. Ann *d* Sept. 22, 1778. April 17, 1779, Henry[2] m *Anna Strickler*.

---

[*]Additional facts are contained in History of Berks Co , Pa , Montgomery, 1909, pp 443-444, from which the above facts are taken
[b]See p 88
[c]See p 251

PATENT FOR 400 ACRES TO MICHAEL COFFMAN—JUNE 15, 1754— "SPRING FARM."

The Right Honourable Thomas Lord Fairfax, Baron of Cameron in that part of Great Britain called Scotland, Proprietor of the Northern Neck of Virginia, To all to whom this present writing shall come sends Greeting Know Yee That for good causes for and in consideration of the Composition to me paid and for the annual rent hereinafter reserved, I have given, granted and confirmed and by these presents for me my heirs and assigns do give, grant and confirm unto *Michael Coffman* of Augusta County a certain tract of waste and ungranted land in said County which was surveyed for him in behalf of and for the Orphans of Martin Coffman, deceased, and bounded as by a survey made by Mr John Baylis as follows: Beginning at a large white oak on a hill on the north side of dry run, then N 80° E 340 poles to three pines on a levell, then S 10° E 189 poles to three pines standing triangular in a meadow, then S 85° W 340 poles to a large pine by dead one on a hill side, then N 10° W 189 poles to the beginning containing 400 acres together, with all rights, members and appurtenances thereunto belonging Royal Mines Excepted and a full third part of all Lead, Copper, Tinn, Coals Iron Mines & Iron Ore that shall be found thereon   To Have and to hold the said 400 acres of Land, together with all rights, profits and benefits to the same belonging or in any wise appertaining, except before excepted, to him, the said Michael Coffman, his heirs and assigns forever, he, the said Michael Coffman his heirs and assigns, therefor yielding and paying to me, my heirs or assigns, or to my certain attorney or attorneys, agent or agents, or to the certain attorney or attornies of my heirs or assigns, proprietors of the said Northern Neck, Yearly and every Year on the feast day of St. Michael the Archangel the fee rent of one shilling sterling money for every fifty acres of land hereby granted, and so proportionably for a greater or lesser quantity, Provided that if the said Michael Coffman, his heirs or assignees, shall not pay the said reserved annual rent as aforesaid so that the same or any part thereof shall be behind or unpaid by the space of two whole years after the same shall become due if Legally Demanded that then it shall and may be lawful for me, my heirs or assigns, Proprietors as aforesaid, my or their certain attorney or attorneys, Agent or Agents, into the above granted premises to re-enter and hold the same so as if this grant had never passed.   Given at my office in the County of Fairfax within my said proprietary under my hand & seal   Dated the 15th day of June in the 27th year of his Majesty, King George the Second reign, A. D., 1754.

Fairfax

Michael Coffman in behalf of Martin Coffman orphan his deed for 400 acres of land in Augusta County.

Land Office, Richmond, Va.

I hereby certify that the foregoing is a true copy from the records of this office. Witness my hand and seal of Office this 23d day of September, 1889

[Seal]   W. R. GAINES,
                                           Register of Land Office.

The patent of Lord Fairfax of June 15, 1754, shows that the 400 acres was conveyed to *Michael Coffman* for the orphans of *Martin Coffman,* without naming them. There is recorded in the County Clerk's office of Frederick County, Virginia, at Winchester in Volume 10 of Deeds, p. 193, a deed from *Michael Coffman of Lancaster County, Province of Pennsylvania,* and late of the County of Augusta, in the Colony of Virginia, to *Henry Brombach* and *Ann,* his wife, late *Ann Coffman,* daughter and orphan of *Martin Coffman,* deceased, of Frederick County, Virginia. This deed is a lease and release dated April 1, 1765, and conveys the 400 acres* covered by the patent from Lord Fairfax of June 15, 1754. It is signed by Michael Coffman in German and attested by Samuel Newman and Thomas Wood and one whose German signature is illegible. The record of the deed in giving Henry's signature is written indistinctly, as are most early English transcripts, and the name of Frederick County reads 'Friederich ' " [b] (Especial attention is directed to the autographic Bible Record of [D3] "Henrich Brumbach.")

"Henry[2] Brumbach [D3] died testate in 1799 in Rockingham County, Virginia (that County was established in 1778), and by his will, probated there, devised the 400 acre Spring Farm tract to his sons [D8] John[3] and [D12] David[3], and to his son [D10] Henry[3] another tract of 206 acres. By deed dated May 12, 1805, Book P, p. 338, at Woodstock, Virginia. 'Ann Broombach,' the widow of 'Henry Broombach,' of Rockingham County, Virginia, in consideration of 150 pounds, released her right of dower in the tracts devised by Henry Brumbach to his sons John[3], David[3] and Henry[3]. The lands were then in Shenandoah County, established in 1772, under name of Dunmore, last name being changed to Shenandoah in 1777. Page County was cut off from Shenandoah in 1831."[c]

---

*Now known as the "Spring Farm," containing a large spring which runs both a grist and a saw mill

[b]Judge Jefferson[2] Brumback's investigations

[c]Record made by the late Judge Jefferson[4] Brumback [D231]   .

FURTHER RECORDS OF [D3] "HENRY BRUMBACH," AND OF THE EARLY MENNONITE SETTLEMENTS OF VIRGINIA.

Letter from Dr. John W. Wayland.

"Harrisonburg, Va., Jan. 2, 1912.

"X X X I have just come from the clerk's office (Harrisonburg, Rockingham Co., Va), and submit the following facts:

April 7, 1806, John[3] [D8], Henry[3] [D10], and David[3] Brumback [D12], made a deed to their younger brother, Jacob[3] Brumback [D16], which is recorded in Burnt Records Deed Book No. 0000, pp. 427, 428. From this deed it appears that Henry[2] Brumback [D3], deceased, made his last will and testament May 14, 1792, which was duly admitted to record in Rockingham County; that he willed among other things a tract of land each, in Shenandoah County, to his sons John, Henry, and David; also to his widow, Nancy* Brumback, the whole of his plantation in the County of Rockingham, called and known by the name of 'New Glasgow,' until his son Jacob Brumback [D16] should be 21. Other conditions are mentioned.

It also appears that New Glasgow comprised 124 acres, but as yet I have not been able to locate it

Henry signed in German (in 1806)   This was Henry, Jr. [D10]   ·

It is quite possible that the land referred to as being in Shenandoah County is now in Page County.

It is also possible—probable—that Henry Brumback, Sr [D3], was a Mennonite, for 4 miles west of Harrisonburg would put him right in a Mennonite settlement; but I find no Mennonite minister by that name in Rockingham. Write Bishop L J Heatwole, Dale Enterprise, Rockingham Co., Va , who can likely help you regarding the Mennonite relations

I could not find Henry Brumback's will—many of our records were burned in 1864. But there are other records regarding the Brumbacks. As yet I have not found the sale to Daniel Smith X X X

With kindest regards, I remain

Yours very truly,

JOHN W. WAYLAND."

Letter from Bishop Lewis James Heatwole [b]

"Dale Enterprise, Rockingham Co , Va , Jan. 11, 1912.

"X X X The Ruffners of our county were among the first pioneer Men-

---

*Often used interchangeably with Anna   See [D3] Bible Record
[b]Lewis James Heatwole, b Dec. 4, 1852, ordained bishop in Mennonite Ch May 2, 1892, in Middle District of Va Conference   His letter and that of Dr John W Wayland, preceding, throw important light upon the problem of the identity of the "Widow Brumbach"

nonites who formed the greater part of the Massanutten colony in the page Valley of the Shenandoah river from 1727 to 1735—and at all events had reached this point from Lancaster Co , Pa , coming by way of the Susquehanna River, Chesapeake Bay, and the Potomac River and across the Blue Ridge through Swift Run Gap by the Spottswood route of 1716.

The records in my possession show that at least the Ruffners, Stricklers, Stovers and Kauffmans were Mennonites, and that Michael Kauffman, Jacob Strickler, Henry Brumbach [D3] and probably Peter 'Ruffner with John Rhodes were Mennonite preachers.

The first court of Rockingham County was held April 17, 1778, at the house of Daniel Smith, two miles north of what is now Harrisonburg. His father, John Smith, had come from England as an officer in the French and Indian War, but his wife appears to have been a German woman. It was Daniel, a son of Daniel Smith, who later became the distinguished Judge Smith of our county, and his portrait now occupies a prominent place in the County Court House at Harrisonburg to-day   It was this same Judge Smith who came into possession of the Brumbach farm as the following records show· [See D9—p. 275]

"Deed Book No. 1 Records of Rockingham County Va." Page 73

Daniel Smith, on 17th day of April, 1806, buys of Henry Brumbach [D3] through Jacob Brumbach administrator of the will of Henry Brumbach a plantation known as the "New Glass" farm for $1500, not including the part reserved by said will for the benefit of Nancy Brumback the widow of Henry Brumback during her life time, and containing 90 acres—witnessed and signed by Hugh Boyd and [D12] David Brumback. [See "Anna" in Bible Record]

"Deed Book No. 4. Records of Rockingham County"—Page 268.

In year 1817 (day and year not legible) the heirs of Henry Brumback sell to Daniel Smith and William Cravens 47 acres of "New Glass" farm as the dowry of Nancy "Broomback."

The signatures to this deed are· Samuel Kauffman, Abraham Miller, David Ruffner (signed in German), David Brumback [D12], Samuel Stover, Samuel Miller, Samuel Brumback [D17], Christian Brumback [D19], Tobias Brumback [D21], Jacob Brumbach [D16].

According to the phraseology of this deed, which is very wordy and lengthy, the inference is to be drawn that besides the five sons there were also five daughters in the family. Of these Barbara [D7] was the wife of Samuel Kauffman, Elizabeth [D11] the wife of Abram Miller, Ann [D9] the wife of

David Ruffner, Susanna [D13] the wife of Samuel Stover, and Mary [D15] the wife of Samuel Miller

In making a search through the County Records again, with the assistance of the clerk in charge, it develops that all the names signed to the deed of the Henry Brumback heirs to Daniel Smith gave affidavit and signed the deed at Lancaster, Fairfield Co , Ohio, April 27th, 1817

I am not sure, but the evidence is almost conclusive that almost all the descendants of the "Massanutten" colony on the Shenandoah River, 1727 to 1735, at a later period settled in the part of Rockingham County, this State, occupied by the Brumbacks—hence the evidence that the wives of the Brumback sons were of the Kauffmans, Stricklers, Millers and Stovers of the same generation—as were also the husbands of the Henry Brumback daughters.

Have made a fruitless effort to find the will of Henry Brumback, but it is evident that it was recorded here and lost with many others during the period of the Civil War.

As to the said Samuel Brumbaugh* being identified with the [D17] Samuel whom you say was born Dec. 17, 1786, cannot be established here further than that he was of the same generation with the Virginia Brumbacks

Trusting that the above data may answer the purpose for which you intend it, and wishing you much success in your efforts to bring forward a reliable register of the Brumbaugh family, and that in return it may meet with an extended patronage from a generous public, I beg to remain

Humbly but sincerely,

L. J. HEATWOLE."

THE EARLY MENNONITE CONFERENCE OF VIRGINIA

The recently discovered fact that Henry Brumbaugh [D3] was a minister in the Mennonite colony in the Shenandoah valley, together with a number of others in the second generation closely connected with the ancestors of various families, and the uncertainty surrounding the principals in the statement, "About A. D. 1760 a German woman, a widow Brumbach, first name unknown, with her 5 children, settled on the South Branch of the Shenandoah River," from Pa , etc., requires a close search of the early Mennonite records of Va. and Pa.

"Up until this time (1800) all ministers and deacons residing in Va. appear to have been ordained in Pa , and it seems that all matters of organization and oversight were vested in the Lancaster Co. (Pa) conference; in

---

*A search of the Fairfield Co (O) records has not yet been possible since the discovery of these facts

short, the church in Va was regarded but as the southern arm extending from the central or parent body of Mennonites in America." "Minister's visits from Pa. were frequent, etc."

The above quotation and the following statements and quotations are from a 14-page pamphlet, "A History of the Mennonite Conference of Virginia and Its Work, etc."—Mennonite Pub. House, Scottdale, Pa., 1910[*]:

The establishment of the Massanutten colony on the Shenandoah River in 1727, and the petition of Michael Kauffman and 7 others in 1733 asking the protection of acting Governor Gooch of Va. "in their rights as landholders in the settlement then known as 'Massanuting' [now] in Page Co , Va "[b]

Michael Kauffman "so far as known is the first Mennonite who preached in Va." His remains lie in the cemetery at Lindale Ch., near Edom, Rockingham Co., Va.—b June 21, 1714; d Dec 21, 1788. "Adam Miller, the founder of the first German settlement in the Shenandoah Valley " Adam Miller and his comrades are said to have come from Lancaster Co., Pa. [See Wayland, p. 40.]

"Mention is made of another Mennonite minister in connection with this colony by the name of Jacob Strickler, who in the year 1731 is said to have established his home near the site where the town of Luray is located " (Henry[2] Brumbach [D3] m (1) Anna Kauffman Sept. 18, 1761; m (2) Anna Strickler April 17, 1779—were these daughters of above?)

"In the year 1754 a strong colony of Mennonites located on the North Fork of the Shenandoah River near what is Woodstock These people, it would appear, came here from Pa by way of the Cumberland Valley across the Md. border to Va Two ministers by the name of Stauffer and Graybill preached regularly here, while, still later, mention is made by Saml Kercheval, p. 91, "The History of the Valley, of a Mennonite minister, John Rhodes [See D10—Marcus Grove m (1) his dau, and Christian Grove m (1) a Rhodes], who in the latter part of August, 1766, with 4 members of his family—wife and 3 sons—were killed by the Indians and their home burnt to ashes. His daughter Elizabeth, carrying her baby sister in her arms, escaped to the barn and later by flight through a field of tall hemp to the river, which she crossed in safety. This awful tragedy took place on the Shenandoah River [later] in Page Co , some miles below Luray. The circumstances of the daughter's escape, and the burning of the buildings by the Indians was witnessed by the Stauffer family, who lived on the opposite side of the river."

[*]Kindly given the compiler by Bishop Lewis J Heatwole, member of the Committee of 3 preparing the pamphlet
[b]Palmer's Calendar of State Papers, Vol I. pp 219-229, as quoted by Dr John W Wayland in "The German Element in Shenandoah Valley," pp 35-56, wherein will be found much of especial interest concerning the early settlement of these localities

The Bible records of [D3] Henry² Brumbach and [D10] Henry³ Brumbach, herewith reproduced, were carefully intensified and translated by Prof Michael Alvin Gruber of Washington, Pa (after all this section was in type), and he is positive that the original records are " Brombach." This strengthens the supposition of relationship between [D1] Johan Melchior Brombach and [D2] the " Widow¹ Brombach ", but no attempt has been made to change the printed " Widow¹ Brumbach," so as to conform to the latest translations Brombach and Brumbach are frequently used interchangeably, as found in the foreign records and noted in the beginning of this publication

BIBLE RECORD OF [D3] HENRY² BRUMBACH, KEPT BY HIS SON [D10] HENRY³ TO THE BIRTH OF [D18] DANIEL³, b JANUARY, 1789 *

Henry Brumbach was born 1739, the 4th day of February.

On the 18th day of September, 1761, I, Henry Brumbach, and Anna Kauffmann entered into wedlock.

The 17th of August, 1762, a young daughter was born to us named Barbara, her sign is in the Cancer.

The 9th day of September, 1764, a young boy was born to us named Johannes, his sign is in the Fishes.

The 11th of November, 1766, a young daughter was born to us named Anna, her sign is in the Fishes.

The 5th of March, 1769, a young son was born to us, named Henry, his sign is the Waterbearer

The 19th of August, 1771, a young daughter was born to us named Elizabeth, her sign is the Archer

The 12th of March, 1774, a young son was born to us named David, his sign is the Fishes.

The 3rd of July, 1776, a young daughter was born to us named Susan, her sign is the Waterbearer.

The 22nd of September, 1778, my wife died.

The 17th of April, 1779, I, Henry Brumbach, and Anna Strickler entered into wedlock.

The 11th of February, 1780, a young son was born to us named Joseph, his sign is the Taurus.

---

*The Bible Records of [D3] Henry³ Brumbach and [D10] Henry³ Brumbach are reproduced through the kindness of [F256] Joseph Martin⁴ Brumback, Luray, Page Co, Va, R R 1 He has added an historical and genealogical treasure to this work, and especial thanks are extended to himself and to his sister [D259] Frances Elizabeth⁴ Brumback, who joined him in the search for records

The 19th of December, 1782, a young daughter was born to us named Maria, her sign is the Fishes.

The 2nd of January, 1785, a young son was born to us named Jacob, his sign is the Ram

The 17th of December, 1786, a young son was born to us named Samuel.

1789 is the year, January, a young son was born to us named Daniel.

Children by 1st m (7).

[D 7] + Barbara[3], *b* Aug 17, 1762.
[D 8] + John[3], *b* Sept 9, 1764.
[D 9] + Anna[3], *b* Nov. 11, 1766.
[D10] + Henry[3], *b* March 5, 1769; *d* 1846.
[D11] + Elizabeth[3], *b* Aug 19, 1771; *d* March 6, 1862.
[D12] + David[3], *b* March 12, 1774
[D13] + Susanna[3], *b* July 3, 1776.

Children by 2d m (8):

[D14]   Joseph[3], *b* Feb. 11, 1780.
[D15] + Maria[3], *b* Dec 19, 1782 '
[D16] + Jacob[3], *b* Jan. 2, 1785.
[D17]   Samuel[3], *b* Dec 17, 1786.
[D18]   Daniel[3], *b* January, 1789
[D19]   Christian[3].
[D20]   Matthew[3].
[D21]   Tobias[3].

[D7] BARBARA[3] BRUMBACH ([D3] Henry[2], [D2] Widow[1] Brumbach), *b* Aug. 17, 1762, *m Samuel Kauffman*   As an heir of Henry Brumbach he signed a deed' in 1817 to land in Rockingham Co., Va.

[D8] JOHN[3] BRUMBACH—"Brumback" ([D3] Henry[2], [D2] Widow[1] Brumbach), *b* near Luray, Va , Sept. 9, 1764; until about 40 years old he was a man of means, with his farm and mills thereon (both grist mill and saw mill) run by water power. About that age he engaged in handling produce and transporting it to the seaboard, or points east of his home   He appears to have been something of a speculator, met with reverses, and some time prior to 1819 his property was sold by the sheriff

John[3] [D8] is reported to be the one who changed the spelling of the family name to "Brumback," and it has so continued in his family line.

March 27, 1787, John[3] *m Elizabeth Rothgeb* (or *"Roadcap"*), dau *George*

_____
*Page 267

and *Magdalena (Beidler*—or *Piedler) Rothgeb*, who moved to Ohio from Va in 1819. Elizabeth was *b* Oct. 28, 1766; *d* April 18, 1858, at Van Burenton, Licking Co., O.

"Elizabeth was a woman of great force of character, and one of the women who with only a limited education, are thoroughly good, true and heroic. After her husband's failure in Virginia she emigrated to Ohio with her seven children (1818), the youngest, John, being only about 10 years old, remembers walking behind the wagon on the long journey. They located in or near Licking County, Ohio, where the husband and father followed them later. He never accomplished a revival of his fortune after coming to Ohio Upon the death of the first wife of his son John (youngest), 1835, he and his wife went to live with him until they died at great age." *

JACOB ROTHGEB—ROADCAP; "REDEMPTIONER"

Jacob Rothgeb (name in English in many early documents, including patent of September 15, 1749, hereinafter mentioned, being spelled Roadcap) settled in the Valley of Virginia some time before 1749. According to tradition among some of his Virginia descendants, he and a young woman, his fellow passenger across the Atlantic, served *Joseph Strickler* for seven years in consideration of Strickler having paid for their passage to America, he having in some way become entitled to their labor for that term for such payment

During the reign of Frederick the Great, and between 1740 and 1760, many thousand German emigrants landed at Philadelphia, Pennsylvania, a number going to the valley of Virginia Many of these emigrants were from the Palatinate on the Rhine Some of these emigrants had money.

"Others again who had not the means of paying their passage across the Atlantic were, on their arrival at Philadelphia, exposed at public auction to serve for a series of years to pay their passage Those thus disposed of were termed Redemptioners, or Palatine servants. The Palatine Redemptioners were usually sold at ten pounds, for from three to five years Of this class many became men of wealth and influence in their day, and their descendants are among the first in society, as to intelligence, wealth and respectability "[b]

A Colonial law of Virginia of March 16, 1642 (1 Henning's Statutes at Large, page 257), provides·

"Such servants as shall be imported having no indentures or covenants, either men or women, if they be above twenty years old, to serve four years;

*According to the late [D231] Jefferson' Brumback
[b]Rupp's History of Berks and Lebanon Counties, page 93 Rupp's History of Dauphin, Cumberland, Franklin, Bedford, Adams and Perry Counties, page 9

if they shall be above twelve and under twenty to serve five years, and if under twelve to serve Seaven years."

Other Colonial laws of Virginia on this subject are the following:

Act of March 18, A D. 1657.

"An act concerning servants and slaves," Oct.———1705

Probably Jacob Rothgeb and the young woman became bound in Pennsylvania to serve Strickler for paying their passage across the Atlantic. They may, however, have been bound to him under indentures as apprentices, or been compelled to serve him under the Virginia law, because they were not indentured when brought into the Colony

After their service to Strickler ended they married and had one son, *George*. After the death of this wife Jacob Rothgeb married a widow *Good* (first name unknown), and had by her one child, *Peter*.

Lord Fairfax, by patent dated Sept 15, 1749, conveyed to Jacob Rothgeb under the name of *Jacob Roadcap* 400 acres of land on Mill Run, a few miles from Luray, Page County, Va   Jacob Rothgeb must have died before 1770, as in that year his sons George and Peter, under the name of Roadcap, partitioned the 400 acres by deeds.   Sometimes his descendants used the name Rothgeb and sometimes it was written Rotgeb.   The name, however written, must have been pronounced so that Lord Fairfax and other Englishmen understood it to be Roadcap and so wrote it.

George Rothgeb [3] had three wives.   His first wife was a *Biedler* or *Piedler* (first name probably Magdalena), and he had by her the following children: Isaac, Abram or Abraham, Jacob and *Elizabeth*, latter born Oct. 28, 1766.

The second wife of George Rothgeb [3] was a *Graybill* or *Greybill* (first name unknown), and by her he had the following children: David, Barbara, George and Christian (twins), their mother dying in childbed soon after their birth.

There was a son named Daniel, the issue of the first or second wife, who died very young.

The third wife of George Rothgeb [3] was *Barbara Bear*, and he had by her the following children· Samuel, Joseph, John, Michael, Reuben, Henry, Anna, born January 20, 1874, Esther, Mary, and another girl who died when a very young baby, and probably without a name   Henry Rothgeb died when a very young man, about or before the time his father died.

Sixteen children of George Rothgeb [3] survived him for a number of years, the date of his death being unknown

THE FIRST CENSUS OF THE UNITED STATES—VIRGINIA.

Heads of Families—Va , 1785, for Fairfax Co., p. 85, enumerates *"John Bromback"* as having a family of "9 white souls, 1 dwelling and 3 other buildings."

Page 66 of the same census, in 1784, for Shenandoah Co., Va , mentions *"George Roodcap* 14 whites, 0 blacks," and the same in 1785 13 whites, 1 dwelling and 2 other buildings—also in same year and county Isaac Roodcap as having 2 whites, 1 dwelling and 1 other building

Page 104 of the same census, in 1785, for Shenandoah Co., states that *Isaac Roadcap* had a family of 2 white souls and 1 dwelling, and that *Peter Roadcap* had a family of 6 white souls, 1 dwelling and 1 other building. They were neighbors of *Peter, Mary, Benjamin* and *David Rufner.* [See p 275, &c.]

John[3] Brumbach [D8] m Elizabeth Rotgeb March 27, 1787. Henrich[2] Brumbach [D3] had 10 ch. in 1785, and his autographic Bible Record also precludes any supposition that his name could be "Johannes Henrich Brumbach" [E1] who landed at Germantown, Pa , Sept. 30, 1754. The latter is known to have settled in the Conecocheague district of Md and thence to have moved to Pa , with his family of 6 whites, including himself.

BIBLE RECORD OF [D8] JOHN[3] BRUMBACH.

"John Brumbach was born 9th day of September, 1764.

27 of March 1787 I was married to Elizabeth Rotgeb. She was born 28 of October 1766

On the 3rd day of June 1790 a young daughter is born to us, and her sign is in the Fishes, her name is Christiana.

The 2nd day of August, 1792 a young daughter is born to us, her name is Barbara, and her sign is the Fishes.

15th day of November 1794 a young daughter is born to us, her name is Anna and her sign is the Virgin.

22d day of February 1797 a young son is born to us, his name is David, his sign is Steinboch (capricorn).

14th day of August 1799 a young son is born to us, his name is Joseph, his sign is the Waterman

11th day of March 1802 a son is born to us, his sign is the Twins, his name is Henry.

3d of February 1808 a young son is born to us, his sign is in the Widder (the Ram), his name is John."

Children (7) ·

[D24] + Christiana[4], b June 3, 1790; m *Samuel Moore.*

[D25]   Barbara⁴, b Aug 2, 1792, m Daniel Hanson
[D26]   Anna⁴, b Nov 15, 1794, d y.
]D27]   + David⁴, b Feb. 22, 1797.
]D28]   Joseph⁴, b Aug. 14, 1799, m "Polly" Parr.
]D29]   + Henry⁴, b March 11, 1802; m Lizzie Pitzer.
[D30]   + John⁴, b Feb. 3, 1808, d June 24, 1899

   [D9] ANN³ BRUMBACH ([D3] Henry², [D2] Widow¹ Brumbach),
b Nov 11, 1766 (?); m David Ruffner, "b 1767 on his father's (Joseph) farm
on the Hawksbill creek, near Luray, and there lived until 1796, the year of his
removal to Kanawha"* "Before he was 23 years of age he was appointed
justice of the peace for Shenandoah Co, Va, no small honor in those days of
intelligent and high-toned magistrates This was the beginning of his magis-
terial career, which with but little intermission continued to the day of his
death, 53 years later"*
   "For about forty years his big brain and muscular arm led in a multitude
of important enterprises, both economic and moral. His mind was characterized by originality and activity, his energy seemed tireless, and his philanthropy
and public spirit, especially in the latter half of his Kanawha life, seemed to
dominate even his private interests"*
   "When David died, Rev. Stuart Robinson, his pastor, wrote: 'Colonel
Ruffner was one of our first settlers, and by general acknowledgment has been
our most useful citizen' He represented Kanawha in the Va. Legislature in
1799, 1801 and 1802, 1804 and 1811 The Kanawha saltworks and the first
coal mines, the chief industries of this district, were established by this energetic German-Virginian. Col Ruffner died Feb. 1, 1843 "ᵇ
   Dr. John W. Wayland kindly searched the wills and deeds of Rockingham
Coᶜ and the result verifies the statement that "Henry Brumbach, a Mennonite
preacher," is [D3] and that he lived in a Mennonite community, where also
lived the Ruffners. These discoveries may lead to important findings concerning the identity of the "Widow Brumbach [D2]."
   Peter Ruffner came to America "from the German border of Switzerland
in 1732, whilst still a young man." He m Mary Steinman of Lancaster Co.,
Pa., and they settled upon a tract given by his father-in-law in Frederick, later
Shenandoah, now Page Co, Va There were 6 ch., of which Joseph was the
oldest, b 1740.   1764 Joseph m Ann Hiestand, dau Henry, and they had 8 ch.

─────────
*W Va. Hist Mag, Vol I, No 4, pp 46-54—See also Nos 2 and 3, same vol, and
German Element of the Shenandoah Valley, Wayland, 1907, p 270
ᵇHistory of the German Element in Va—Schuricht, Vol II, p 23
ᶜSee Dr. Wayland's letter in [D3], a few pages forward His publishers, Ruebush-
Elkins Co, Dayton, Va, announce the issue about Nov, 1912, of a History of Rockingham
Co., Va, by John W Wayland, Ph D

One of the latter discovered "Ruffner's Cave" on their property about 1795, and the name was later changed to "Luray Cave." Joseph's oldest son David, *b* 1767, *m Ann Brumbach*—the early Ruffners and Brumbachs were Mennonites. (Extracted from W. Va. Hist. Mag , Vol I, to which interested persons are referred for further details See also [D10] and [D11]).

Heads of Families, Va., 1784, Shenandoah Co , gives the following "Ruffner" enumerations   List of Alexr Hite, p. 65, gives Benjamin 8 white souls Page 66 mentions Emanuel 4 white souls, Peter 9, Reuben 6   For the same county the list of enumerations in 1785, p. 104, by Edwin Young is: Peter 10, Mary 3, Benjamin 7, Joseph 10. For the same county the list of Richd. Branham for 1785, p 105, mentions Reuben as having a family of 5 white souls, 1 dwelling and 2 other buildings.

"In 1789 he [David Ruffner] was married to *Ann Brumbach*, daughter of *Henry Brumbach*,[*] a Mennonite preacher who owned and lived upon the beautiful farm four miles west of Harrisonburg, Rockingham county, which afterward became the property and residence of the eminent Judge Daniel Smith This was a happy marriage. The sweet face, deep blue eyes, and gentle temper of the wife softened the sterner and developed the more amiable qualities of the husband, forming as harmonious a combination as was possible between man and wife. She ultimately became the well-known and greatly beloved 'Mother Ruffner' of Kanawha salines, and lived to a great age " [b]

"Most of the Brumbacks are farmers, industrious, honest, and prosperous. * * * Most of them were Old School Baptists until Eld. Burnam introduced and organized Sunday Schools amongst us * * * Most of the Brumbacks (O S B.) have gone with the 'New Departure or Burnam Division.' "—Lucy Gertrude (Lanck) Brumback [see D104].

> *Children (4), surname Ruffner:*
> i   Henry[4], *b* in Shenandoah Co., Va.
> ii Ann[4], *b* in Shenandoah Co , Va , *m Richard E. Putney.*
> iii Susan[4], *b* in Shenandoah Co., Va.; *m Moses Fuqua*
> iv Lewis[4], *b* Oct. 1, 1797, "the first child born in Charleston, W. Va."

[D10] HENRY[3] BRUMBACH ([D3] Henry[2], [D2] Widow[1] Brumbach), *b* March 5, 1769, May 27, 1794, near Luray, Shenandoah Co (now Page), Va., *m Mary Graff (Grove)*, *b* Oct , 1772, dau *Marcus* and *Mary Grove* —latter was the 2d w, and is reported to have come from Pa , but her identity is yet undetermined. Henry[3] was a farmer, Primitive or Old School Baptist,

---

[*]See letter from Dr. John W Wayland under [D3], p. 266
[b]W Va Hist Mag, Vol I, No 4, pp 46-54

and lived on the Shenandoah River about 3 mi. W. of Luray. His d occurred in 1846, and that of his w on March 7, 1860; both were buried in the family graveyard on the farm.

GROVE FAMILIES IN VIRGINIA.*

Heads of Families, Records of the State (Va.) Enumerations, 1782 to 1785—First Census, 1790 Series, p 64, gives· *"Marks Grove"* as the head of a family of "10 whites" in Shenandoah Co., and in the same locality and reference, p 66, *Christian Grove* as having a family of "11 whites"—no "blacks" in either family. Same locality, same reference, p. 105, also appears *Christian Grove* as having a family of "12 white souls, 1 dwelling, 1 other building."

Marcus Grove[b] m (1) —— *Rhodes*, dau *John Rhodes*, who, with some of his family, was killed by the Indians in 1765 After the d of his 1st w. Marcus went to Pa., and there met *Mary Grove*, whom he afterward married. The identity of this Mary is yet to be determined.

    Children by 1st m (2)[c]·

  i David; m and lived near the old home

  ii Barbara, b 1767; m *Christian Bumgardner*, b 1766 and d 1855; s John, who is said to have come from near Basel, Switzerland.

      Children (4):

      (1) David, b 1790, d 1870; m *Virginia* ——.

      (2) Joseph, b 1797; d 1892; m *Nancy Stover.*

      (3) Mary, b 1799, d 1864; m *Abraham Stover.*

      (4) Elizabeth, b 1802; d 1828; m *Thomas Crawford.*

    Children by 2d m (more than 6):

  iii-v Martin, Samuel, and John—all moved to Ohio.

  vi Mary, b Oct , 1772, m [D10] + *Henry*[3] *Brumback*

  vii Nancy, m *James Bumgardner.*

Christian Grove m (1) —— *Rhodes;* (2) —— *Musselman.*

    Children (at least 7):

  i Christian, farmer; Baptist; b and d near Luray, Va.; m *Mary Gochenour.*

Owing to repeated intermarriages between the Brumbacks and Groves, these details are given, partly through the help of [D224] Laura Ann (Brumback) Grove and her husband, John William Grove, Luray, Va , and of Lucy Gertrude (Lanck) Brumback [D104]

[b]It is thought that Marcus and Christian Grove were brothers. See p 269 for details concerning Indian depredations

[c]Information furnished by Ira C. Bumgardner, b June, 1837; m *Susan V. Long*, ad. Luray, Va , R R 1, son Joseph, b 1797

Children (10):

(1) Barbara, *m Marshall Yowell*

(2) Anna; *m Benjamin Coffman.*

(3) Joseph, *m Catharine Ponn.*
    Children:
    (a) Benjamin F, *d, m* [D105] + *Martha Washington Brumbach.*
    (b) Mary Susan; *m Frank Yowell*, Newark, O.
    (c) John C, Luray, Va, R. F. D. 4.

(4) Rebecca, *m Daniel Hite.*

(5) Jacob, *m Rebecca Lionberger*, La Crosse, Ill.

(6) Elizabeth, *d* age 18.

(7) Emanuel, *b* Sept 12, 1812; *d* Jan. 29, 1890, *m* **[D42]** + *Frances[4] Brumback, b* Jan. 30, 1814.

(8) Catharine, *m* (1) [D36] + *Samuel[4] Brumback*; (2) *Daniel Grove*

(9) Isaac, *m Elizabeth Price.*

(10) Noah; *m Isabella Kiblinger.*

ii Samuel, *m Mary Lionberger.*
    Children (3):
    (1) John, *b* Feb 15, 1810, *m* [D41] + *Mary[4] Brumback, b* Aug 12, 1812
    (2) Nancy, *b* Nov. 5, 1814, *m* [D39] + *Jacob[4] Brumback, b* 1809.
    (3) Mary, *b* Jan 9, 1823, *m* [D43] + *Henry[4] Brumback, b* Nov 4, 1816

iii David; unm

iv Susan, *m Jacob Gochenour*

v Catharine.

vi Eve.

vii Peter, *m Catharine Frank* (3 dau and 2 s)

BIBLE RECORD OF [D10] HENRY[3] BRUMBACH ("BROMBACH")[a]

Anno 1794 The 27 May I, Henrich Brumbach, and Maria Graff were married and entered into matrimony in october the ——— she was born in the year 1772 [D10]

---

[a]The photographic reproduction of the original, latter kindly furnished by [D256] Joseph Martin[4] Brumback, was carefully intensified and translated by Prof Michael Alvin Gruber, Washington, D C The latter also carefully translated the [D3] record, after the former translation had been put into type.

Anno 1795 The 29 october there was born to us a young son, his name is Johannes, his constellation is Taurus (der Stier), the ruling planet is Mercury. [D32].

Anno 1797 The 23 March there was born to us a young daughter, her name is Sussana, her constellation is Aquarius (der Wasserman), the ruling planet is Saturn [D33].

Anno 1798 The 19 December there was born to us a daughter, her name is anna (Anna), her constellation is Taurus (der stir), the ruling planet is Jupiter. [D34].

Anno 1800 The 15 May there was born to us a young daughter, her name is barbra (Barbara), her constellation is Aquarius, the ruling planet for the year was the Sun. [D35]

Anno 1802 The 22 July there was born to us a young son, his name is samuel (Samuel), his constellation is Taurus (der Stur), the ruling planet for the year was Mercury. [D36].

Anno 1804 December The 26 there was born to us a young son, his name is Daniel, his constellation is Scorpio, the ruling planet for the year was Saturn. [D37].

Anno 1807 Abrill (April) The 19 there was born to us a young daughter, her name is Eelisabet (Elizabeth), her constellation is Virgo (die iunfrau—for Jungfrau). [D38]

Anno 1809 abrill (April) The 6 there was born to us a young son, his name is Jacob, his constellation is Capricorn (steinbock—the final " k " being obliterated on the photographic copy) [D39].

Anno 1810 october The 4 there was born to us a young son, his name is Joseph, his constellation is Sagittarius (der schutz). [D40]

Anno 1812 august the 20 there was born to us a young daughter, her name is Maria, her constellation is Aquarius. [D41].

Anno 1814 Jenner (January) the 30 there was born to us a young daughter, her name is frene (pronounced as if spelled *Frainay*), her constellation is Gemini (die Zwiling—for Zwilling). [D42]

Children of [D10] Henry[3] and Mary (12):

[D32] + John[4], b Oct. 29, 1795; d Jan. 12, 1877.
[D33] + Susannah[4], b March 23, 1797, d Aug., 1890.
[D34] + Anna[4], b Dec. 19, 1798
[D35] + Barbara[4], b May 15, 1800.
[D36] + Samuel[4], b July 22, 1802
[D37]   Daniel[4], b Dec. 26, 1804
[D38] + Elizabeth[4], b April 19, 1807

[D39] + Jacob⁴, *b* 1809; *d* Jan , 1853
[D40] + Joseph⁴, *b* Oct 4, 1810, *d* Feb. 19, 1874.
[D41] + Mary⁴, *b* Aug 12, 1812, *d* Oct. 2, 1894
[D42] + Frances⁴, *b* Jan. 30, 1814; *d* June 20, 1880.
[D43] + Henry⁴, *b* Nov. 4, 1816; *d* Sept. 13, 1895.

[D11] ELIZABETH³ BRUMBACH ([D3] Henry², [D2] Widow¹ Brumbach), *b* Aug 19, 1771, *m Abraham Miller* of Pa. July 5, 1791, according to the marriage records of Shenandoah Co , Va ; ceremony performed by Rev Paul Hinkle, and her name is therein spelled "Elizabeth Brombach " ᵃ

April 27, 1817, at Lancaster, Fairfield Co , O , as an heir of the late Henry² Brumbach [D3] Mr. Miller signed a deed to land in Rockingham Co , Va ᵇ He *d* in Licking Co , O , Sept 3, 1831, and Elizabeth *d* March 6, 1862

A search amongst the histories of Fairfield Co , O., brought to light several interesting quotations, which are herewith reproduced ᶜ

"*David Miller*, deceased, Walnut Twp ; was born in Rockingham county, Va , Feb. 2, 1803, the eldest son of *Abraham* and *Elizabeth (Brumbach) Miller*. David came with his parents to Ohio in the spring of 1805 He was educated in Walnut Twp , and assisted his father in clearing the farm, until his marriage. Dec 9, 1828, to *Frances D , dau of Jacob Guile*, a former well-known resident of Berne Twp Mrs Miller was born in this county Sept. 11, 1810. After marriage they continued to reside on the home place. Upon his father's death, 1831, he took sole charge of the place. His mother resided with him In 1833 he built a nice residence The barn built by his father is still in use; it was built in 1820 Mr. and Mrs. Miller were parents of one daughter and eleven sons, eight sons and the daughter still living, all residents of this Co Elizabeth, the wife of John Eversole; three sons still at home, Jacob K., an ex-grain buyer, of Millersport; Josiah C and Benjamin F. on the home place. Mr. Miller was grandfather to 30 children and great-grandfather to 4. They were members of the United Brethren Church He was a successful farmer, owning at his death 260 acres—the home place and 110 acres elsewhere in the Co. He died Dec 3, 1882, in his 80th year."

"*Henry Miller*, farmer, Walnut Twp [Fairfield Co , O.]; son of *Abraham* and *Elizabeth (Brumbach) Miller*. He was born in Walnut Twp Nov 12, 1805. Abraham Miller, born in Pa , removed to Va , where he was married and came with his wife and five children to O in the spring of 1805, settling in this township, on the place owned by David Miller, which is still owned by his heirs.

ᵃShenandoah Co , Va , marriage records, kindly furnished by Mr Luther R Kelker, Custodian of the Public Records, Harrisburg, Pa
  ᵇSee letter from Bishop Lewis James Heatwole, pp 266-268
  ᶜHistory of Fairfield and Perry Counties, O , Graham, Chicago, 1883, p 881

Abraham entered a half section of land and improved it   He raised a family of nine children, two living. Barbara, widow of Joseph Berry, a resident of Iowa, and Henry Miller.   Abraham Miller was Justice of the Peace for a number of years   He was a member of the Mennonite Church   He died Sept. 3, 1831; his widow March 6, 1862, in her ninety-first year.   Henry Miller completed his education and helped in clearing the home place.   In 1826 his father gave him a one-fourth section of land.   This he improved   He built a hewed log house, where his present residence stands.   In 1839 he was married to *Rachel Ann Biddell*, who was born in this county   To that marriage have been born eight children, four of whom are living   Mrs. Miller died about 1861. Mr Miller now owns 500 acres.   He never desired office, but accepted that of township treasurer one year.   In 1862 Mr Miller was married to *Mary Shane*, who was born in Walnut Twp.   They are the parents of three children; one living, Alma Jane, residing with her father   Mrs Miller died in 1872   Mr. Miller is a member of the Baptist Church   He owns 160 acres of land, which he cleared.   He is a self-made man "[a]

[D12] DAVID[3] BRUMBACH ([D3] Henry[2], [D2] Widow[1] Brumbach), b Aug. 19, 1771; Sept 23, 1800, in Shenandoah Co, Va, was *m* to *Rebecca Ruffner* by Rev. J. Koontz, and in the records the name appears "David Brumbaugh "[b]

April 27, 1817, as an heir to the late [D3] Henry[2] Brumbach, the heirs then living near Lancaster, Fairfield Co, O, he signed a deed to land in Shenandoah Co, Va.,[c] and a search of the histories available in the Library of Congress discloses the following interesting statements:

"David Brumback came [to Liberty Twp, Fairfield Co, O] in 1803 or 1804, and settled half a mile south of the present town of Baltimore, near Walnut Creek bridge, on the west side of the present pike   The farm is owned by Emanuel Rinch.   Mr Brumback afterwards settled on Poplar Creek, where his son lives   Martin Brumback [D49], the son, has the most extensive vineyard in the county."[d]

"Our old pioneer, David Brumback, was the undertaker in our township. He buried, or rather made all the coffins when I was a small boy.   I remember

[a]Same references, p 332
[b]Memorial Record of Licking Co, O, 1894, pp 344-345
Shenandoah Co, Va, marriage records, kindly furnished by Mr Luther R Kelker, Custodian of Public Records, Harrisburg, Pa -
[c]See pp. 266-268
[d]A Complete History of Fairfield County, Ohio, by Hervey Scott, Columbus, O, 1877, p 183
A similar reference is found in Pioneers of Fairfield Co, O —Wiseman, Columbus, 1901, p. 106

once I went with my grandfather to a funeral at Showley's, and as screws were scarce in those primitive times, nails were used to fasten down the lid of the coffin, and I heard my grandfather tell my mother this. 'Barbi, wenn ich sterbe, will ich nicht mit dem Hanmer zugenagelt sein' ('Barbara, when I die, I will not have my coffin nailed with a hammer')." [a]

"Cabinet makers were undertakers—he cut down a dry walnut tree, split it into puncheons, and with ax and adz dressed them down sufficient to make a rude coffin."

Children (6), the first B b in Va.:

[D44] + Isaac[4]; m Hannah "Bury" (Beery ?).
[D45]   Nancy[4], m George Yerkle (1 s)
[D46] + Benjamin[4]; m Catharine "Hanze"
[D47]   Mary[4], d; unm
[D48]   Phoebe[4], d, m Jacob Snider, Basil, O. (2 ch)
[D49]   Martin[4], d; unm.

[D13] SUSANNA[3] BRUMBACH ([D3] Henry[2], [D2] Widow[1] Brumbach), b July 3, 1776, m Samuel Stover. As an heir of Henry[2] Brumbach [D3], he signed a deed[b] April 27, 1817, to land in Rockingham Co, Va, and was then living near Lancaster, Fairfield Co., O

[D15] MARIA, or MARY[3], BRUMBACH ([D3] Henry[2], [D2] Widow[1] Brumbach), b Dec 19, 1782; m Samuel Miller. April 27, 1817, at Lancaster, Fairfield Co, O, as an heir of Henry Brumbach, he signed a deed[b] to land in Rockingham Co, Va

[D16] JACOB[3] BRUMBACH ([D3] Henry[2], [D2] Widow[1] Brumbach), b Jan 2, 1785, acted as administrator of the will of Henry Brumbach, and April 17, 1806, transferred 90 acres of land in Rockingham Co, Va [c] (Deed Book 1, p 73.) The wills and their records in that county are reported as destroyed.

[D24] CHRISTIANA[4] BRUMBACH ([D8] John[3], [D3] Henry[2], [D2] Widow[1] Brumbach), b June 3, 1790, Sept. 15, 1807, was married to Samuel Moore in Shenandoah Co., Va., by Rev. J. Koontz.[d]

---

[a]Same reference, p 188   Recollections of Henry Leonard
[b]See pages 266-268
[c]See pages 266-268.
[d]The late Judge Jefferson[5] Brumback [D231] discovered that Christiana[4] was b June 3, 1790, and m ——— Moore   Mr Luther R Kelker, Custodian of Public Records (Pa), supplied the Shenandoah Co (Va) Marriage Records [See D11], and the latter were furnished to him by L B Altaffer, Ph D, Cleveland, O, thus illustrating how piece by piece this record has been built together and verified from original sources   The latter are also being consulted by Dr John W Wayland for his announced book on Rockingham Co, Va

[D27] DAVID⁴ BRUMBACK ([D8] John³, same ancestry as [D24]), *b* Feb 22, 1797; *d* suddenly in a hay field Aug 1, 1833, and was buried at Johnstown, Licking Co., O.; farmer.   He wrote his name Brumback, and July 25, 1822, *m Frutilda Bearnes, b* March 2, 1805; dau *George* and *Catharine (Sigler) Bearnes* of Hog Run, Licking Co., O   Frutilda *d* July 3, 1891, aged 86, and was interred in the family vault at Van Wert, O .

Frutilda (Bearnes) Brumback was thus left a widow at age 28, with a family of six small children, four girls and two boys, the eldest ten years old, and the two boys only six and four years old respectively.   They inherited from the husband and father forty acres of wild land with a cabin upon it, near Johnstown, O.   Only a small portion of this land was cleared, and the problem of subsistence was one of the most serious character for the widow to meet.   She showed herself equal to the occasion, and by strict economy and wise management succeeded in bringing up her family to mature age, with the exception of the elder boy George⁵ [D94], who died at the age of nineteen.

The struggle for a living in those early pioneer days in Ohio was most strenuous, and many were the times when the family subsisted for days on cornmeal and potatoes   Although the good mother Frutilda had only a limited education, she realized the desirability of educating her children, and assisted them to get the common school education afforded in those days   She also trained her girls in all that goes to make good wives and mothers, so that they all married well and reared children who have been a credit to their ancestry   The boy, [D95] John Sanford⁵, who handed down the family name, although starting with such limited advantages, became "a man among ten thousand," with a career so successful that it is set forth at length elsewhere in this publication.

  Children (6):
[D91] + Melinda⁵, *b* July 23, 1823, *d* July 4, 1889.
[D92] + Nancy⁵, *b* Sept 4, 1824; *d* April 22, 1882.
[D93] + Elizabeth⁵, *b* Nov. 4, 1825; *d* Sept 13, 1889.
[D94]   George⁵, *b* July 28, 1827, *d* April 8, 1846; unm.
[D95] + John Sanford⁵, *b* March 4, 1829, *d* Dec. 11, 1897.
[D96] + Catharine⁵, *b* Feb 1, 1833, *d* June 19, 1901.

  [D29] HENRY⁴ BRUMBACH ([D8] John³, same ancestry as [D24]), *b* March 11, 1802; *m Lizzie Pitzer.*

  [D30] JOHN⁴ BRUMBACK ([D8] John³, same ancestry as [D24]), *b* Feb. 3, 1808, on the ancestral farm in Shenandoah Co. (later Page), Va.; in 1819 his mother, brother [D29] Henry⁴, and himself went to Licking Co., O.,

where they rented a tract of land   The father, [D8] John³, joined his family three years later and rented a blacksmith shop, in which father and son worked until the latter was twenty years old. May 8, 1828, [D30] John⁴ *m* (1) *Rebecca Davis, b* April 20, 1809, and *d* July 4, 1835; dau *Samuel* and *Mary Davis.*

After marriage he settled on the farm of his father-in-law, 5 miles south of Newark, O., and in three years purchased the same, paying $8 per acre for it. For several years he conducted a small blacksmith shop upon the farm, also attending to the farming   Owing to a trouble with his shoulder, he abandoned blacksmithing and thereafter gave his entire time to tilling the soil and to stock raising. He gradually acquired 570 acres of excellent land.

"In educational affairs Mr. Brumback has always maintained a deep interest. Having had no advantages in his youth, he has always been especially desirous that his children should have the best opportunities for gaining a practical education   They have amply repaid his efforts in their behalf, as they are well educated men and women, who are highly respected in their several communities   For seven years he was Comr of Licking Co., and for one term served as J P. While not a member of any denomination, he is in sympathy with the work of the churches, and was a liberal contributor to the support of the gospel " [1]

Aug 28, 1837, John⁴ *m* (2) *Sarah Ann Essex, b* Dec. 28, 1814, and *d* Nov. 19, 1868; dau *Isaac* and *Anna Smoke Essex.*

Sept 24, 1873, John⁴ *m* (3) *Priscilla (Essex) Parkinson,* widow of *William Parkinson,* and sister of his 2d w   Priscilla *d* Aug or Sept., 1893 (no ch). John⁴ *d* June 24, 1899, having retained his exceptional mental and physical activity until his death

     Children by 1st m (3) :

[D231] + Jefferson⁵, *b* Feb. 7, 1829 , *d* June 22, 1907.

[D232] + Mary Ann⁵, *b* July 18, 1831 , *d* Jan 10, 1879.

[D233] + Jeremiah⁵, *b* Sept. 16, 1833

     Children by 2d m (8)

[D234] + Amanda⁵, *b* July 1, 1838 , *d* July 10, 1884.

[D235] + Henry⁵, *b* March 28, 1840.

[D236] + Elizabeth⁵, *b* May 28, 1842

[D237] + Artemisia⁵, *b* June 17, 1844

[D238] + Rebecca⁵, *b* March 29, 1847; unm

[D239] + Marietta⁵, M.D., *b* June 19, 1849

---

[1] Memorial Record of Licking Co , O , 1894, pp 341-345

, [D240] + Elma[5], b Oct. 16, 1851; d Jan 3, 1869
[D241] + Newton N [5], M D , b March 10, 1854.

[D32] JOHN[4] BRUMBACK ([D10] Henry[3], [D3] Henry[2], [D2] Widow[1] Brumbach), b Oct. 29, 1795; d Jan 12, 1877 (81 y. 12d.); Dec. 26, 1822, m Elizabeth Thomas, b Oct. 17, 1804, dau Richard Thomas of New-market, Shenandoah Co , Va , they lived on a farm 8 miles south of Luray, Page Co., Va , now occupied by [D104] Edward Trenton[5] Brumback. John[4] never identified himself with any church; farmer, Dem , d Jan. 12, 1877, and his w. d Dec. 23. 1893 , both buried in the family burying ground.

"March, 1822, an account of what I gave my son John for a beginning

To one sorrel mare at	$100 00
To one saddle at	15 00
To one shovel plough at	1.25
To one desk at	20.00
To iron ware at	7.20
To one writing desk at	4.00
To one bucket at	.50
To one cow at	12.00
To two sows at	9.00
To one feather bed at	20.00
To an old bellows and anvill	12.00
To an old wagon at	30.00
	$230.95

HENRICH BRUMBACH "

Children (9) ·

[D 97] + Richard Thomas[5], b Feb 5, 1825.
[D 98] + David Hershberger[5], M.D., b April 28, 1827.
[D 99] + Henry Franklin[5], b June 5, 1829
[D100] + Mary Elizabeth[5], b Feb 1, 1832 - --
[D101] + Ann Eliza[5], b April 16, 1834.
[D102] + Frances Amanda[5], b May 1, 1837.
[D103] + John Benton[5], M.D , b Nov. 20, 1839.
[D104] + Edward Trenton[5], b April 8, 1842
[D105] + Martha Washington[5], b Dec. 25, 1847.

[D33] SUSANNAH[4] BRUMBACK ([D10] Henry[3], same ancestry as

[D32]), *b* March 23, 1797; *d* Aug 13, 1890 (93-4-10), baptized 1825, on her
18th birthday *m* (1) *David Hershberger*; the entire family are members Old
Sch Bap Ch. Susannah[4] *m* (2) *John R Burner.* She was confined to the
house during 5 years prior to her death, and to her bed 6 months, and amongst
her last words were. "I am only waiting for my appointed time to come; I am
ready and willing to go at any moment the summons comes" Mary Ann
(Burner) Huffman "unremittingly" cared for her in the last illness

    Children from 1st m (6), *surname Hershberger*
- i   Henry Pendleton[5]; ii Mary Ann[5], iii Barbara Ellen[5], iv Andrew
     Jackson[5].
- v   Elizabeth Ann[5], *b* May 4, 1825, *d* July 22, 1852; Dec. 16, 1841, *m*
     Daniel Beaver (Luray, Va., 7 ch).
- vi John David Silas[5]
    Children from 2d m (2), *surname Burner:*
- vii Jacob Franklin[5].
- viii Frances Virginia[5].

[D34] ANNA[4] BRUMBACK ([D10] Henry[3], same ancestry as [D32]),
b Dec. 19, 1798; Aug 10, 1820, *m Christian* or *Christopher Keyser*, a Baptist
minister; lived and *d* in Page Co, Va.

    Children (9), *surname Keyser* ·
- i   Mary Catharine[5], ii Elizabeth Ann[5]; iii Sarah Ann[5]; iv John Ander-
     son[5], v Rebecca[5]; vi Abigail Caroline[5], vii Henry Marcellus[5]; viii
     Emily[5]; ix Pamilia Margaret[5].

[D35] BARBARA[4] BRUMBACK ([D10] Henry[3], same ancestry as
[D32]), *b* May 15, 1800, Dec. 27, 1822, *m William Follis Wood;* lived in
Page Co., Va, and later moved to Mo.

    Children (8), *surname Wood.*
- i   Sarah Ann[5]; ii Benjamin Franklin[5]; iii Mary Elizabeth[5]; iv Susannah
     Nancy[5]; v Frances[5]; vi William Henry[5]; vii Elizabeth Ann[5]; viii
     Jacob Follis[5].

[D36] SAMUEL[4] BRUMBACK ([D10] Henry[3], same ancestry as
[D32]), *b* July 22, 1802, near Luray, Page Co, Va., 1824 *m Catharine Grove,*
dau *Christian* and *Mary (Gochenour) Grove,* and bro of *Emanuel Grove*, who
m [D42] + *Frances*[4] *Brumback* [See D10—"Grove Families in Va."]

    Samuel[4] was a farmer; Dem., member Prim. Bap. Ch.; address, Luray, Va.,
R. R.

Children (7):

[D158] + William Henry[5], *b* 1834, *d* 1906.
[D159]   Mary Susan[5]; *m Richard Deal.*
[D160]   Isaac Newton[5], killed in Brandy Station fight, 1863.
[D161]   Barbara Ann[5].
[D162]   Joseph Christian[5], *m Barbara Rothgeb.*
[D163]   James K Polk[5]; *m Ella Bunn.*
[D164]   George M Dallas[5], *m Luzett Strickler*

[D38] ELIZABETH[4] BRUMBACK ([D10] Henry[3], same ancestry as [D32]), *b* April 19, 1807; April 12, 1826, *m Isaac Stover;* they lived and *d* in Page Co, Va

Children (10), *surname Stover:*

· i Samuel Henry[5], ii Daniel[5]; iii Mary Jane[5]; iv Joseph Franklin[5]; v Ann Eliza[5]; vi John William[5]; vii Frances Rebecca[5]; viii David Stickley[5]; ix Martha Ellen[5]; x Charles[5].

[D39] JACOB[4] BRUMBACK ([D10] Henry[3], same ancestry as [D32]), *b* near Luray, Va, in 1809, Feb 2, 1835, *m Nancy Grove, b* Nov. 5, 1814, in the same locality, dau *Samuel* and *Mary (Lionberger) Grove.* [See D10—"Grove Families in Va"] In the autumn of 1835 they moved near to Carthage, Hancock Co., Ill., accompanied by her father and his family, using wagons, and were six weeks on the way. He actively farmed until his *d* Jan, 1853; his w. *d* April 28, 1905.

Children (8):

[D217]   Joseph Samuel[5], *b* 1836, *d* 1845
[D218] + Thomas Benton[5], *b* March 4, 1838; *d* April 18, 1894.
[D219] + Henry Pendleton[5], *b* March 14, 1840, *d* June 27, 1900
[D220] + Mary Ellen[5], *b* June 4, 1842.
[D221]   Susan Frances[5], *b* 1844; *d* 1853
[D222] + Emily Elizabeth[5], *b* July 31, 1846
[D223]   John William[5], *b* 1849, *d* Oct. 23, 1860.
[D224] + Laura Ann[5], *b* Feb. 12, 1851.

[D40] JOSEPH[4] BRUMBACK ([D10] Henry[3], same ancestry as [D32]), *b* in Page Co, Va, Oct. 4, 1810, *m Christena Huffman,* of Hawkeville, same county, *b* Oct. 2, 1816, Oct, 1843, moved to Frederick Co., Va, where he purchased the "Dr. Carr farm" of 240 acres and other lands; Dem.; Bap., *d* Feb. 19, 1874, at Fawcett Gap, Va.

"The Brumback Family"

"The handsome estate adjoining the Pitman home, owned by this family, justifies a brief mention + + +. The family belongs to the Colonial settlers, but their first settlement was in old Frederick County, now Page   Joseph Brumback + + made his home where his son Jacob [D243] now lives, being the old Carr homestead   There he reared his family and spent a long and useful life. He was Justice of the Peace for several terms. + + + Dr. Isaac Milton[5] Brumback [D246], living in the same neighborhood ('on the Cedar Creek Grade,' p. 482), is well known   He has one son, a physician, and also several (other) children."[a]

"The Glebe, often called the Glade, was a celebrated tract of land lying on the west side of the old Cartmell and Froman roads   One part of it is owned by Mr. *Andrew Brumback*. This tract occasioned much trouble   When the first Vestry was formed in Frederick Co., a certain survey was designated as the Glebe land, to be known as the property of the Established Church (Episcopal). All revenues to be for the use of the vestry towards the 'living of the Minister.' In 1754 Nathaniel Carr obtained a grant from Fairfax, and located where the old Pitman property is now seen. Later on he built a house where *Jacob Brumback* now lives. Carr's grant lapped over the Glebe   He and the vestry compromised, Carr paying a nominal rent, and was the virtual owner.   He sold a portion of his grant and included part of the Glebe to Peter Gilham in 1777. At this time the vestry was so demoralized by changed conditions in their church, brought about by the war then in progress, that the tenants were forgotten; and the Glebe was regarded for many years as the property of the Gilham estate. Titles to the Glebe were disputed for many years.   Col. Carr, as he was called, retained over 1,200 acres of land at a cost of one dollar per acre   Several well-known homesteads were founded from this tract."[b]

Children (10) ·

[D242]   Mary Ann E.[5], *b* July 4, 1838, *d* Feb. 4, 1879; *m Joseph Snapp*
[D243] + Jacob Henry Francis[5], *b* Nov. 22, 1839.
[D244] + Joseph Benton[5], *b* Nov. 22, 1842.
[D245]   James Dallas[5], *b* Nov 10, 1844; *d* Sept. 8, 1868, unm.
[D246] + Isaac Milton[5], M D, *b* Sept. 27, 1846
[D247]   Andrew Jackson[5], *b* Oct 20, 1849; *m Henrietta Newell.*
[D248]   Franklin Pierce[5], *b* March 13, 1853; *m Kate Hershey* (2 s *d* y).

[D41] MARY[4] BRUMBACK ([D10] Henry[3], same ancestry as [D32]),

---

[b]Shenandoah Valley Pioneers and Their Descendants—Cartmell, pp. 115, 292, 482 and 493

b Aug. 12, 1812, *d* Oct 2, 1894; April 26, 1832, *m John Grove, b* Feb 15, 1810; *d* Sept. 13, 1886; s *Samuel* and *Mary (Lionberger) Grove* [See D10— "Grove Families in Va "]

"My daughter Polly was married on the 26th April, 1832. An account of what I gave her for a beginning in the world.

	To two feather beds 1 French bed stead	$45 00
	To two cows and one heifer	30.00
	To one Bureau at	12 00
	To one walnut chest at	5 00
	To one saddle at	18 00
	To one mare at	60.00
	To one washing tub & one butter churn	3 25
	To two buckets at	1 00
	To one iron kettle & other ware	13 06¼
	To one sheep at	7.00
	To one set of ladles	2.00
1836	To one hundred Dollars	100.00
		$296 31¼
Dec. 22nd,1839	To ten Dollars paid in cash	10.00
		$306.31¼
Aug. 28th,1841	To one hundred and seventy-five dollars by Emanuel Grove	175 00
		$481.31¼
	To amt property purchased at my sale 2d Sept. 1843	39.19
		$520 50¼

Mr. Grove was a farmer, and the family lived near Luray, now Page Co., Virginia.

    Children (12), *surname Grove·*

i   Samuel Henry[5], *d*; *m Eliza Grove.*

ii   Andrew Jackson[5], *d* y.

iii   John Pendleton[5], *b* Oct 9, 1835, *m Lucy Rebecca Varner, b* Mch 6, 1842; dau *Ambrose Booten* and *Frances Eleanor Varner* He is v. p. Valley Natl. Bank, Luray, Va.

Children (8)

(1)   Elenor Mary[6], *b* Mch. 13, 1865.

(2)   Frank Green, *b* June 29, 1866.

(3)   Annie Eliza*, *b* June 29, 1868

(4)   William Ambrose, *b* Oct 21, 1872.

(5)   John Gill, *b* July 23, 1876

(6)   Clark, *b* May 1, 1880.

(7)   Burnam, *b* May 1, 1880.

(8)   Pearl Lillian, *b* Jan 21, 1883

iv   Joseph Martin, *b* Mch 23, 1837; Aug. 25, 1869, *m Martha Broy*; ad Dun Loring, Va.

v   David Franklin[5], *b* June 6, 1838; *d*, *m Mary Susan Varner*, *b* May 26, 1845; dau *Joseph* and *Mary (Huffman) Varner*.

Son: (1) David Charles[6], *b* Cooper Co., Mo., June 26, 1865; *m Alice Grey Limberger*, *b* Sept 9, 1865; dau *Samuel J.* and *Susan (Huffman) Limberger;* contractor and builder, ad., Otterville, Mo (2 ch.)

vi   Mary Frances, *b* Oct 15, 1839, *d* Sept 18, 1892; unm.

vii   Jacob Benton, *b* Aug 6, 1842; *d* Aug 12, 1870; unm.

viii   Sarah Jane, *b* June 16, 1844, unm.

ix   Susan Isabella, *b* 1845; unm

x   Martha Ann, *b* June 20, 1847, *d* Aug. 20, 1875, *m Benjamin Grayson; d* (1 dau).

xi   Emma Victoria, *b* Oct 20, 1850; *m John W Spitler*, *b* 1849; *d* 1897.

xii   Ida Marcellus, *b* Jan 19, 1851; *d* Mch. 26, 1886, *m David Spitler*, *b* 1847; bro. of John W. Spitler.

[D42] FRANCES[4] BRUMBACK ([D10] Henry[3], [D3] Henry[2], [D2] Widow[1] Brumbach), *b* Jan 30, 1814; March 7, 1833, *m Emanuel Grove*, *b* Sept. 12, 1812, s *Christian* and *Mary (Gochenour) Grove*. [See D10—"Grove Families in Va"] Mr. Grove was a merchant, Dem.; and lived at Luray, Va., where himself and w were members of the Primitive Bap Ch. Frances[4] *d* June 20, 1880, and her husband *d* Jan 20, 1890

"My daughter Frances was married on the 7th March, 1833. An account of what I gave her for a beginning in this world.

To two cows and one heifer	$27.00
To two feather beds 1 French bedstead	45.00

_____

*Miss Annie Eliza Grove, Luray, Va, has furnished many facts, and searched various cemeteries, etc, for accurate records

	To one gray mare at		85.00
	To one walnut chest		5.00
	To one Bureau at		12.00
	To one washing tub		2 00
	To two buckets at		1 00
	To one saddle at		16 00
	To one set of ladles at		2.00
	To one Large Iron kettle		6 00
	To six window chairs at		8 00
	To six sheep at		7.00
Aug., 1835	To fifty dollars cash		50.00
Feb., 1836	To note on B Blackford	$36.12½	
Aug., 1836	To thirteen dollars cash	13.87½	
		———	50.00
			$316.00
Aug. 28, 1841	To one hundred and seventy-five dollars		175.00
			———
			$491.00
	To amt purchased at my sale		
	2d September 1842		24.75
	To Iron ware		5.37½
			———
			$521.12½

HENRICH BRUMBACH "

These accounts were written by Henry[3] [D10] in German, values being in £, s. and d.; and also in English, the latter being in $ and c. They are somewhat similar for each child, and Emanuel Grove seems to have made the final entries in the later accounts.

Children (11), *surname Grove:*

i   Mary Jane[5], *b* July 30, 1834; *m James R. Campbell.*

ii   Ann Eliza[5], *b* June 30, 1836; *d* Aug., 1888; Oct., 1854, *m* [D98] + *David Hershberger Brumbach, M D.*

iii Susan Catharine[5], *b* May 26, 1838; *d* May 20, 1911; *m James R O'Neal.*

iv   Sarah Frances[5], *b* June 27, 1840, *d* Dec. 26, 1897; *m Joseph F. Stover.* [See D105.]

v   Elizabeth Ann[5], *b* July 18, 1842; *d* Feb. 26, 1910; Nov., 1870, *m George K. Fitch.*

vi   John William⁵, *b* Dec. 16, 1844; Nov., 1869, *m* (1) *Eliza Jane Koontz*, who *d* 1874   Ch. (1): Minnie Ella⁶, *m Hunter Oliver Brubaker*, Washington, D. C.; (2) William Wallace⁶, *d y.*; 1874 he *m* (2) [D224] + *Laura Ann⁵ Brumback* (4 ch)

vii   Martha Ellen⁵, unm.

viii   Charles Henry⁵, unm.

ix   Virginia Edwena⁵, *b* Aug. 16, 1851; Feb., 1875, *m John W. Ellison.*

x   Flora Lee⁵, unm.

xi   Frank Wilburn⁵, M.D., *b* Nov. 12, 1855; Sept. 12, 1882, *m Mary Hershberger*, dau *Emanuel* and *Catherine Hershberger.*

[D43] HENRY⁴ BRUMBACK ([D10] Henry³, [D3] Henry², [D2] Widow¹ Brumbach), *b* Nov. 4, 1816, 3½ miles north of Luray, now Page Co, Va.; Feb. 4, 1841, *m Mary Grove*, *b* Jan 9, 1823; dau *Samuel* and *Mary (Lionberger) Grove* [See D10—"Grove Families in Va."], farmer, Dem ; member Old School Baptist Ch.; Mary *d* Oct 13, 1881, and Henry⁴ *d* Sept. 12, 1895; both buried upon the old home farm.

     Children (10) :

[D252]   Samuel Henry⁵, *b* Aug 19, 1843; *d* Nov. 13, 1851.

[D253]   Andrew Jackson⁵, *b* April 15, 1845; *d* Feb. 2, 1897; *m Florence Grubbs* (no ch).

[D254]   John William⁵, *b* March 27, 1847, *d* Aug. 5, 1868; unm.

[D255]   Mary Susan⁵, *b* June 19, 1849; *d* Jan. 15, 1868, unm

[D256]   + Joseph Martin⁵, *b* Oct. 4, 1851; unm.

[D257]   + Charles Daniel⁵, *b* March 1, 1854.

[D258]   Martha Ellen⁵, *b* May 27, 1856, *d* Sept 1, 1897; unm

[D259]   Frances Elizabeth⁵, *b* March 4, 1858; unm.

[D260]   Emma Florence⁵, *b* April 10, 1860, *d* Oct. 9, 1864.

[D261]   Infant, *b* Oct. 24, 1862; *d* June 5, 1863.

[D44] ISAAC⁴ BRUMBACH ([D12] David³, [D3] Henry², [D2] Widow¹ Brumbach), *b* in Va ; *m Hannah "Bury."*

     One son reported:

[D107] Adam⁵; lived in "Pleasant Plain, Huntington Co., Ind." (no P. O.)

[D46] BENJAMIN⁴ BRUMBACH ([D12] David³, [D2] Henry², [D2] Widow¹ Brumbach), *m Catharine "Hanze"* He was living in February, 1892, with his step-daughter, Mrs. E. J. Emfield, at Basil, Fairfield Co., O., and then said his grandparents and great-grandparents came from Germany, but that he could not recall their names and had no records.

[D91] MELINDA[5] BRUMBACK ([D27] David[4], [D8] John[3], [D3] Henry[2], [D2] Widow[1] Brumbach), *b* July 23, 1823; *d* July 4, 1889; Aug. 9, 1840, *m Orrin Bigelow;* they lived in Pierceton, Ind.

Children (2), *surname Bigelow:*

i   Lorenzo[6], *b* Aug. 15, 1841; *d* Dec. 10, 1910; unm.

ii Russell[6], *b* Aug. 29, 1844; Nov. 16, 1865, *m Hannah C. Turner;* res. of entire family, Van Wert, O.

   Children (2), *surname Bigelow:*

   (1) Frank E.[7], *b* Jan. 20, 1867; June 28, 1894, *m Josephine E. Klotz.*

   (2) Charles L.[7], *b* Sept. 16, 1872; May 28, 1894, *m Jennie D. Halliwill.*

[D92] NANCY[5] BRUMBACK ([D27] David[4], same ancestry as [D91]), *b* Sept. 4, 1824; *d* April 22, 1882; Dec. 4, 1842, *m* (1) *George S. Pennell, d* April 29, 1851; Jan. 4, 1855, she *m* (2) Dr. *H. N. Coomer;* lived in Ashley, O.

Children by 1st m (2), *surname Pennell:*

i   Spencer[6], *b* Dec. 9, 1844; *d* May 10, 1873; unm.

ii Frutilda[6], *b* Dec. 2, 1849; *d* Oct. 27, 1909; Nov. 11, 1873, *m Robert Harroun.*

   Children (3), *surname Harroun:*

   (1) Harry[7], *b* Aug. 23, 1875.

   (2) Wyley[7], *b* June 17, 1877.

   (3) Frank[7], *b* Sept. 20, 1881.

Son by 2nd m, surname Coomer:

iii Harry[6], *b* March 14, 1865; *m Lizzie Trindle.*

[D93] ELIZABETH[5] BRUMBACK ([D27] David[4], same ancestry as [D91]), *b* Nov. 4, 1825; *d* Sept. 13, 1889; Aug. 17, 1843, at Johnstown, O., *m William Bateman Belknap, b* Feb. 2, 1819; *d* May 11, 1903; s *Forest* and *Sarah (Bateman) Belknap;* lived in Ashley, O.

Children (4), *surname Belknap:*

i   Oressa V.[6], *b* April 21, 1846; *d* March 30, 1865; unm.

ii David G.[6], *b* May 3, 1849; *d* April 22, 1889; *m Minerva Atcheson, b* Oct. 2, 1853; dau *Windsor* and *Maria (Kiser) Atcheson;* lived in Columbus, O.

   Children (6), *surname Belknap:*

   (1) Maud Helen[7], *b* Nov. 14, 1875; *m William S. Harley;* resides Columbus, O.

   (2) Windsor[7], *b* Aug. 21, 1877; *d* Oct. 13, 1889.

   (3) William David[7], *b* Sept. 22, 1879; May 19, 1901, *m Elizabeth C. Forrester;* resides Columbus, O.

(4) Charles Rigby[7], *b* Feb 23, 1882.

(5) Claud Ewing[7], *b* Feb 15, 1885.

(6) Sherman[7], *b* Aug 5, 1887, *d* May 5, 1889.

[D95] JOHN SANFORD[5] BRUMBACK ([D27] David[4], same ancestry as [D91]), *b* March 4, 1829; *d* Dec 11, 1897, and was buried in the family vault built by himself at Van Wert, Van Wert Co, O   He was a remarkable man. Having been brought up by a widowed mother under the most trying circumstances, he was trained to a life of frugality and taught from childhood how to battle with the world. Being compelled from boyhood to depend upon himself and to labor for those he loved, he was one of those strong, self-reliant, generous men who win the affection of those who know them and make the world better for their having lived.

John Sanford early showed such self-reliance, sagacity and good judgment that at ten years of age he plowed the fields, and at fourteen attended to all the family's financial affairs   At eighteen, with only fifty dollars' capital, he succeeded in obtaining credit sufficient to open a country store in Ashley, O. In this he was so successful that at the end of five years he had accumulated two or three thousand dollars, with an income to justify his getting married.

May 26, 1852, at Ashley, Delaware Co., O, he *m Ellen Perlena Purmort*, *b* Aug 10, 1832, at Jay, N Y, and a school teacher at the former place; dau of *Minor* and *Perlena Nettleton*   Her father was s of *Joshua* and *Eunice (Walworth) Purmort*, Joshua Purmort being a descendant of New England ancestors of that name, and his w Eunice Walworth being a descendant of the old New England Walworth family.[a]

The Purmort Genealogy gives the following reference to her life:[b]

"Ellen Purmort, born at Jay, N Y., August 10, 1832. She was the oldest child of Minor No. 45 and Perlena Nettleton, his wife. She went with them to Kempville, Canada, when eight years old, and later to Berlin, Delaware County, Ohio, in the summer of 1847   She taught a term or two of school at Berlin, and became noted as the little teacher who could manage the rude, rough boys. Upon the death of her mother in 1850 the care and responsibility of the large family fell upon her young shoulders, which burden she kindly and successfully assumed for two years. As the oldest in the large family of children, she had passed through all the trials and burdens of her parents in their losses and removals and sad experiences, yet she kept a happy heart and was her father's helper in those heavy years. On May 27, 1852, at

[a]The Walworths of America, pp 60, 73   By Clarence A Walworth   Published by Weed-Parsons Co, Albany, 1897
[b]Purmort Genealogy, pp 89, 117   By Chas H Purmort, D D. Published by The Homestead Company, Des Moines, Iowa, 1907

Ashley, Delaware County, Ohio, she was married to John Sanford Brumback, a merchant at Ashley. Owing to poor health of her husband, they moved on a farm on the Old State Road north of Worthington, Ohio, where they lived for two years They then moved to Casey, Clark County, Illinois, where Mr. Brumback again engaged in mercantile business and succeeded very well In the spring of 1852 they moved to Van Wert, Ohio, a new and undeveloped country at that time, and there they made their home and have lived ever since. Mr. Brumback was a shrewd, thrifty business man, and became at Van Wert a man of influence and wealth Beginning as a poor boy, he made his way up the ladder to a noted financial success "

The loving and sacrificing nature of Mrs. Brumback and her husband was well shown when her parents died shortly after her marriage, and they took into their own home her five young brothers and sisters, for whom she and her good husband made a home and brought up two of them as their own children to lives of usefulness. What this meant in the early days when the wife of a household did most of her own work can hardly be appreciated in these days of labor-saving appliances and small families.

When her husband moved to the farm, he employed two and sometimes three or four farm hands to help him on the farm Mrs Brumback did most of the housework and had a hired girl to help her only part of the time She tells how she would bake six loaves of bread a day for the large family of seven and hired help, and that they would eat a whole sheep in three or four days.

About this time her eldest son, Orville, was born, so that the young wife's life was not an easy one, but she was happy and uncomplaining, and her untiring efforts to help her husband doubtless brought the good health that now rewards her with a happy old age.

One of those unselfish, self-sacrificing characters who think of others more than of themselves, she was a loving, faithful mother, and an unfailing inspiration and helpmate to her good husband until his death. It was her wise counsel and frugality that enabled him to accumulate his ample fortune. The fact is that few men who start in life without a fortune ever succeed in acquiring one unless they have wives to help them who are willing to work and economize Certainly none do when the fortune comes through safe business methods without speculation Mr and Mrs J. S. Brumback were a happy, congenial pair, and the world helped them because they helped themselves—by living sober, prudent, industrious lives They lived as a husband and wife should— she as an unfailing inspiration and helpmate to the husband, and he a loving, tender husband to the wife.

In 1858 he removed to Casey, Clark Co , Ill , where he again embarked in a country store business with such success that when in the spring of 1862 he

moved his family to Van Wert, O., he brought with him $5,000 in gold which
he and his good wife had accumulated by careful economy.

Van Wert County was then a new and thinly settled country. Mr Brumback embarked in the dry goods business, and used such good judgment and
so won the confidence of the people and made such wise investments, that he
gradually increased his fortune until in 1884 he sold out his dry goods business
and became president of the Van Wert National Bank

As a banker Mr. Brumback was careful, conservative and withal progressive. He became well known all over Northwestern Ohio, and became one of
the leading citizens of that section He helped create and finance many enterprises of great value to the people, notably the Cincinnati, Jackson & Macki-
naw Railway (now part of the Big Four system), which he undertook when it
seemed Ohio was about to lose this valuable adjunct to its prosperity. He
never was identified with a failure, and so when he took hold the people knew
it would be a success, and gave it the hearty assistance it so greatly needed.
Mr. Brumback was prominent in many other large enterprises in Northwestern
Ohio, such as The Central Manufacturers' Insurance Company, and a Toledo
Street Railway Company, which he likewise started on the road of prosperity
when collapse was imminent to the great loss and damage of large numbers of
people.

Space forbids further details of Mr. Brumback's large and active business
career. It is sufficient to say that seldom has any man ever carried on a more
upright business career, and no man ever more enjoyed the entire confidence
of the people.

In his later years Mr. Brumback's generous heart, always seeking to do
good for his fellowmen, prompted him to found a public library for his native
town. It was before Mr Carnegie had entered upon his library career, and
the idea of building and donating a public library building was not so common
then as now Mr. Brumback, after consulting with the members of his family
and being encouraged by them, had plans prepared for a fine library building
to be located in a particularly beautiful park in Van Wert; but when the plans
were about perfected he was taken seriously sick and shortly died Finding he would not be able to carry out his library plans, he called his son Orville[6], a lawyer in Toledo, to his home in Van Wert, and there after fully dis-
cussing the project with the members of his family, his will was drawn, providing for a library that would forever be a monument to the Brumback name

But even in so important a matter as this the loving, sympathetic, self-
sacrificing heart of the man was shown by the fact that he ordered his will so
drawn that any one of the heirs could defeat the project if not willing to join
in the expense.

Another feature of the will is the unique idea, undoubtedly original with Mr. Brumback, of *having the library benefits extended to the whole county,* so that the country folks as well as the town folks could reap the benefits This idea has been carried out with the greatest success, and the Brumback Library has the proud distinction of being the first County Library ever inaugurated. At this date (December, 1910) the library has fifteen sub-stations, located in different parts of Van Wert County, bringing the books within walking distance of all the farmers' homes A small salary is paid to each person having charge of a sub-station, and books are delivered at each station in traveling boxes, which contain 125 books each. They start at Station No 1, and in turn are sent to each of the other stations before being returned to the Central Library. The school teachers over the county, some fifty in number, are also supplied with books for their pupils, and annually circulate a large number of instructive books among the children. The interest taken by the country people and benefits they derive are shown by the great number of books drawn from the sub-stations.

The terms of the will under which the Brumback Library was built are of such interest that it is given in full:

LAST WILL OF [D95] JOHN SANFORD[5] BRUMBACK.

In the name of the Benevolent Father of all, I, J S. Brumback, of Van Wert, Ohio, being of sound mind and disposing memory, do make and publish this my last Will and Testament.

It is my will and I do give and devise and bequeath all my property, both real and personal, as follows ·

Item 1. I do give, devise and bequeath all my property, both real and personal and mixed, to my dear wife, Ellen P. Brumback, so long as she may live, she to have and enjoy all the income from the same so long as she may live.   If it becomes necessary for her comfort and best welfare to use any part of the principal it is my will that she may do so in so far as it may be absolutely necessary for her personal comfort and best welfare

The foregoing bequest and devise to my said beloved wife to be in lieu of her dower estate in my property

It is my further will and devise that my said wife leave the management and control of all my said property to my living children (a majority controlling), so long as they profitably manage the same.

Item 2. I do give, devise and bequeath to my dear children, Orville S. Brumback, David L. Brumback, Estelle B. Reed, and Saida M. Brumback, *per stirpes,* all my property, both real, personal and mixed, in fee simple and

absolutely, subject, however, to the life estate of my dear wife, Ellen P Brumback, and conditions thereof as contained in Item I.

Any notes that I hold against any of my said children by way of advancement to them to be taken out of his or her respective share (without interest)

Item 3 Feeling a great regard for my fellow townsmen of Van Wert, Ohio, and affection for the said city, in which I have spent so many happy years of my life, I have long contemplated a gift to them of a Library Building as a token of my affection and regard . In that behalf I have had plans prepared for such a building, but owing to the condition of my health have not been permitted to enter upon its construction It is my will and desire that my said dear wife and children expend sufficient of my estate willed to them in Items 1 and 2 to carry out my wishes known to them by the erection and gift of a library building, something after the plans and designs I have had prepared for that purpose; Provided and this item is upon the express condition, that my said wife and children can make arrangements satisfactory to them with the said City of Van Wert, or *if they desire and think best, with Van Wert County,* for a location for said building and the maintenance of the library to be placed therein.

Item 4. It is my will that my said dear wife and children, or so many of them as may desire to qualify, act as executors of my estate, without giving bond or having any appraisement thereof. I know they will not fail to carry out my wishes herein stated, whether sufficiently stated in law or not. .

In witness whereof, I, the said J. S. Brumback, have hereunto set my name and do declare and publish this instrument as my last will at Van Wert, Ohio, this the 29th day of March, A D 1897.

J. S. BRUMBACK   [Seal]

When, after Mr Brumback's death (Dec. 11, 1897) the heirs came to arrange a contract with the County of Van Wert for the maintenance of the library after it was started, it was found there was no law in Ohio under which a contract could be executed. This afforded an excellent pretext for the heirs or any one of them to have declined to go further, but they all inherited a good deal of the Brumback loyalty, and so set about it to get a law enacted to give the County Commissioners power to act. Orville S.[6] Brumback prepared a bill to introduce in the Legislature, and, with the assistance of prominent men all over the State, the Van Wert people succeeded in having it enacted into a law as follows:

A BILL

To supplement Section 891 of the Revised Statutes of Ohio, so as to provide for the acceptance of Bequests, Donations, and Gifts for Public Libraries, and to Equip and Maintain the same

Section 1 Be it enacted by the General Assembly of the State of Ohio, that Section 891, of the Revised Statutes of Ohio, be supplemented so as to read as follows·

Section 891 (a) The Commissioners may receive a bequest, donation, or gift of a building, or property wherewith to construct a building for a County Public Library in the county-seat of the county, and may enter into an agreement on behalf of the county to provide and maintain a Public Library therein Any county accepting such bequest, donation or gift shall be bound to faithfully carry out the agreement so made to provide and maintain such Library

Section 2 The Commissioners of any such county are hereby authorized, at the March or June session each year, to levy a tax of not exceeding one mill on each dollar of taxable property of such county, and the fund derived from such levy shall constitute a special fund to be known as Library Fund, and shall be used for no purpose other than is contemplated in this section

Section 3 This act shall take effect and be in force from and after its passage —(Sec 93, Ohio Laws, 355)

The next step was to accomplish an agreement with the County Commissioners that would forever insure the maintenance of the library upon a broad basis and provide ample funds for carrying it on in a way to enable it to accomplish all that such a library ought to accomplish. How the negotiations were carried on to this end, and the terms of the contract as finally agreed to, is best told by *The Van Wert Republican*, in its issue of Thursday, July 28, 1898:

THE BRUMBACK'S MEMORIAL LIBRARY

Offered the People of Van Wert County. Conditions Upon Which This Great Gift Is Made

"For several months, those who have the welfare of Van Wert County people at heart, have been anxiously inquiring what was being done toward accepting the late J S Brumback's magnificent gift to the county of a fine library building Owing to the absence of Hon. O S Brumback in the West, the matter was delayed somewhat, and nothing was done until his return The heirs have now submitted to the citizens of Van Wert County a contract, and, upon the signing of which, they are prepared to proceed to erect and furnish a Public Library building that any county in the State may feel proud of, costing upward of $50,000 to be presented to the county of Van Wert free of all incumbrances The heirs of the late J S Brumback, desiring that his liberal gift should be of a personal benefit to every person in the county, have wisely determined to offer it to the entire county The only condition they make is that first, the representatives of the people of the county and the Board of County Commissioners enter into an agreement to care for the building after they have received it The town council of Van Wert is asked to enter into the contract, inasmuch as they control in part, the proposed site, the Second Ward park Let it be distinctly understood that the town of Van Wert has never had the offer of this magnificent gift, does not now, and we fear never will, only in common with the county The heirs have concluded to offer it to 30,000 people and not limit its benefits to 8,000 The Van Wert Library Association is ready to donate its little library of nearly 2,000 volumes as well as other properties as a starter for a good county library We understand if the offer is accepted and the building erected, that local librarians will be appointed in every district in the county and that the rules and regulations will be made such that the people living in the remotest part of the county may borrow just as many books to read at their homes as those living nearest the building

The progressive farmers of our county have already, at their meetings, expressed their readiness to accept so generous a gift, and are willing to pay their mite to maintain the building Copy of the contract given below has been presented the Ladies' Library Association, the Board of County Commissioners, and the Common Council of Van Wert There is no reason whatever why any member of these bodies should hesitate to sign the contract on behalf of the people We fear this may be the last opportunity to accept or reject, and if they fail to sign the contract Van Wert county people may forever lose the privilege of receiving a gift, which if accepted, will be greatly appreciated not only by the present genera-

tion, but thousands yet to be, will express their gratitude for so great an inheritance   We look for prompt action to be taken in the matter, and it is a settled fact that all who bend their efforts to secure such a gift for Van Wert county will be forever considered as bene-factors of the people of our county.

———

Van Wert, Ohio, July 16, 1898

To the Ladies' Library Association the Board of County Commissioners of Van Wert County, Ohio, and the Common Council of The City of Van Wert, Ohio

LADIES AND GENTLEMEN:—

To carry out the will of the late J S Brumback, we hand you herewith a copy of an agreement we have prepared providing for the construction of a Library Building in the Second Ward Park of Van Wert. Ohio, and for the maintenance therein of a free public library for the benefit of the citizens of Van Wert County, Ohio

We have endeavored by the terms of the contract to insure the success of the library when the building is erected in accordance with the designs which Mr Brumback had prepared for it.

We request that your respective bodies give the matter your early consideration and advise us if the terms meet your approval

We believe such a library will prove so great a success that other counties in the State will in a few years acquire like institutions

Assuring you of our desire to facilitate the project in every reasonable way, we remain, sincerely yours,

> ELLEN P BRUMBACK,
> ORVILLE S BRUMBACK,
> DAVID L BRUMBACK,
> ESTELLE B REED,
> SAIDA M BAUMBACK

———

AGREEMENT.

WHEREAS, The will of the late J S Brumback provides as follows

"Feeling a great regard for my fellow townsmen of Van Wert, Ohio, and affection for the said city, in which I have spent so many happy years of my life, I have long con-templated a gift to them of a library building as a token of my affection and regard   In that behalf I have had plans prepared for such a building, but owing to the condition of my health have not been permitted to enter upon its construction   It is my will and desire that my said dear wife and children expend sufficient of my estate willed to them in items one and two to carry out my wishes known to them, by the erection and gift of a library building, something after the plans and designs I have had prepared for that purpose, provided and this item is upon the express condition that my said wife and children can make arrangements satisfactory to them with the said city of Van Wert, and if they desire and think best, with Van Wert County, for a location for said building and the maintenance of the Library to be placed therein "

AND WHEREAS The heirs of the estate of the said J S Brumback are unanimous in their desire to fully carry out his wishes as expressed in his will,

AND WHEREAS, A free public library would be of inestimable benefit to the people of Van Wert County, Ohio, and afford to them, their children, and descendants most valuable privi-leges and educational advantages,

Now, therefore, For the purpose of carrying out the will of the said J S Brumback, to establish a free public library for the people of Van Wert County, Ohio, and to provide for the proper equipment and maintenance thereof,

It is agreed by and between Ellen P Brumback, Orville S Brumback, David L Brum-back, Estelle B Reed, and Saida M Brumback, heirs of the said J S Brumback, parties of the first part, and H H Ludwig, Peter Knittle and H G Schumm, County Commissioners of Van Wert County, Ohio, and their successors in office, parties of the second part, and the Ladies' Library Association of Van Wert, Ohio, party of the third part, and The Village of Van Wert, Ohio, party of the fourth part, as follows, to-wit

The parties of the first part do covenant and agree that they will with all reasonable despatch build and construct a stone library building in the Second Ward Park of The Village of Van Wert, Ohio, in first-class condition, substantially as shown in the drawings which the said J S Brumback had made therefor in his lifetime, and will furnish the same with the necessary furniture and heating apparatus, ready for use for the library to be placed therein, as hereinafter provided

And the parties of the first part further agree to turn over and donate on behalf of the said J. S Brumback's estate said library building, so built and constructed, to the County of Van Wert, Ohio, free of all encumbrances or charges thereon, to be held by said county and used for library and educational purposes only

In consideration of the receipt of the said library building and the donation thereof as aforesaid to the County of Van Wert, Ohio,

The parties of the second part do covenant and agree for themselves and their successors in office that the said Van Wert County will forever maintain and operate in said building a free public library for the benefit of the citizens of the whole county And in that behalf do promise and agree that the Commissioners of said Van Wert County will each year at their March or June session levy a tax as the Board of Trustees of said library may designate not exceeding one-half a mill upon each dollar of taxable property of said Van Wert County, to form a library fund with which to so maintain and operate said library Said library fund so to be raised by said tax shall constitute a special fund in the hands of the Treasurer of Van Wert County, Ohio, to be drawn upon only by the Board of Trustees of said library as hereinafter provided

Said parties of the second part further covenant and agree that the said parties of the first part shall have full right and authority to enter upon the said Second Ward Park in The Village of Van Wert, and there construct said building in compliance with the plans and directions of the architect thereof with the right to occupy, grade, improve and embellish said park as may be directed by the architect of said building

The parties of the third part (a duly incorporated association under the laws of the State of Ohio), in consideration of the construction and donation of said library building by the parties of the first part, do covenant and agree that they will turn over and donate to the free public library to be placed in said building all the books, furniture, money or other personal property of said association, to be and become the property of the said County Library

And the party of the fourth part (a duly incorporated Village, and County Seat of Van Wert County, Ohio), in consideration of the construction and donation of the said library building by the parties of the first part, does covenant and agree that the said parties of the first part shall have full permission to enter upon the said Second Ward Park in The Village of Van Wert, Ohio, and there to construct said building, and to occupy, grade, improve and embellish said park as may be directed by the architect of said building

It is further mutually covenanted and agreed by and between all the parties hereto that the said County Library herein provided for shall be called the "Brumback Library" It shall be managed and controlled by a non-partisan board of seven trustees, who shall be appointed for a term of three years, and until their successors are duly appointed, as follows, to-wit Two to be appointed by the parties of the first part or their descendants Three to be appointed by the parties of the second part or their successors, and two to be appointed by the party of the third part

Provided, that the first appointees shall hold office from the first day of February, 1899, as follows, to-wit

One of those to be appointed by the parties of the first part to hold office for one year, and one for three years One of those to be appointed by the parties of the second part or their successors to hold office for one year, one for two years and one for three years One of those to be appointed by the party of the third part to hold office for one year, and one for two years

In case the parties of the first part or the parties of the third part shall fail for a period of ninety days to make their respective appointments of Trustees from time to time, then the Common Council of the party of the fourth part shall make such appointments

The said trustees shall duly qualify by taking an oath of office to faithfully fulfill all the duties of their positions to the best of their knowledge and ability during their respective terms of office They shall organize by the election of a President, Vice-President and Secretary, who shall hold their offices for one year and until their successors are elected Said officers shall be elected by ballot at the first regular meeting of the Board after the first day of February in each year A majority of the whole Board being required to elect

The President of the said Board of Trustee shall be President of the library, and it shall be his duty as such to preside at all meetings of the Board, appoint all standing committees, and otherwise act as the executive head of the Board of Trustees and perform such other duties as usually pertain to the office

The Vice-President, in the absence of the President, shall perform his duties, and In case

of death, removal or resignation shall perform the duties of the President until a President is elected to serve for the unexpired time

The Secretary shall keep accurate minutes of the proceedings of the Board of Trustees, together with accurate accounts of all receipts and expenditures of money for and on behalf of the library He shall pay over to the County Treasurer of Van Wert County, each months, for the benefit of the Library Fund, all monies received by the library, and shall take and keep on file for six years vouchers for all monies expended He shall render a complete and accurate financial statement of the library as shown by his books to the parties of the second part on or before the end of each fiscal year, to-wit The first day of February in each year, and perform such other duties as usually pertain to the office

All warrants on the County Treasurer of Van Wert County for payment of monies out of the special Library Fund shall only be issued upon an aye and nay vote of the Board of Trustees entered upon the minutes and signed by the President of the Board and countersigned by the Secretary Four Trustees shall constitute a quorum of the Board, but no appropriation shall be made or indebtedness incurred to an amount exceeding $100, without the concurring vote of a majority of all members of the Board

The Board of Trustees shall employ a Librarian and other necessary persons to properly keep and carry on said Library and Library Building, and shall fix their reasonable compensation. The term of office of all regular employes shall expire on the first day of March of each year, and they shall be subject to removal at any time at the pleasure of the Board of Trustees

The Board of Trustees shall prescribe such further rules and regulations for the direction and operation of the Library as they may deem advisable

IN EVIDENCE WHEREOF witness the signatures of each and every of the parties hereto at Van Wert, Ohio, this 16th day of July, A D 1898

ELLEN P BRUMBACK,
ORVILLE S BRUMBACK,
DAVID L BRUMBACK,
ESTELLE B REED,
SAIDA M BRUMBACK

The proposition was duly accepted as stated by the *Van Wert Bulletin* in its issue of August 1, 1898, as follows:

GIFT ACCEPTED

The Brumback Library Building Will Be Erected—The County Commissioners Give Unanimous Consent for Its Maintenance

At the office of the Van Wert County Commissioners, on Saturday last, one of the most important meetings ever held in this county assembled and its acts have passed into history The proceedings will adorn a bright page They are an honor to those who took part in them They secure to this county an educational distinction possessed by few in the State and by no other county in the prosperous northwest At the same time, they give to all, old and young, in town and country, benefits which are an auxiliary to and in harmony and sympathy with our peerless public school system

The County Commissioners, by this act, have honored themselves, have made a record to which they can point with pride in all time to come, and which will grow in popularity as the years roll on, by saying "Yes"—every man of the same opinion—to the proposition of the heirs of the late John Sanford Brumback, to carry out a stipulation of the will of their father, which provides for the gift to Van Wert County of a public library building, of magnificent proportions, fully furnished and equipped for the purpose for which it is intended—the home of a free public library It is the most valuable gift ever bestowed upon the citizens of Van Wert County, and will remain for all time a monument to the generosity of the donor, an embellishment to our magnificent parks, a lasting benefit to every citizen of the county,

The following account of the cornerstone laying appeared in the *Toledo Daily Blade* Tuesday, July 18, 1899:

THE BRUMBACK MEMORIAL

Laying of the Cornerstone at Van Wert To-Day —Beginning of the Beautiful Building for
the Brumback Memorial County Library

[Special Telegram to The Blade]

VAN WERT, O , July 18 —The cornerstone of the Brumback Memorial County Library, a
building that will cost $50,000, donated to the county of Van Wert by the late J S Brum-
back, president of the Van Wert National Bank, was laid to-day in Second Ward Park,
Van Wert The ceremonies were conducted under the auspices of the Grand Lodge of Ohio,
F. & A M , Grand Master Nelson Williams acting as master of ceremonies

The event was made a county affair in every particular Every fraternal organization
in the county was well represented A grand parade of lodges and citizens, headed by
several bands, marched and counter-marched through the principal streets of the city It
was a grand spectacle, showing in a measure the appreciation of Van Wert County citizens
for a gift that any county in this rich country of ours might well feel proud of The
exercises consisted of several selections by Heistand's band, prayer by Rev J A Gordon;
oration by Rev A J Fish, selections by Venedocia Club, address by Hon O S Brumback
of Toledo, proclamation by the Grand Marshal, prayer by the Grand Chaplain, presentation of a silver trowel to the Past Grand Master, invocation by the Worshipful Master,
Masonic ceremonies, lowering of the stone, laying of the same, and an oration by Grand
Master Nelson Williams The ceremonies and exercises throughout were impressive and
grand

One of the provisions of this magnificent gift was that it was to be maintained by the
county and every citizen in the county was to share equally of its benefits A general law
was passed by the last legislature authorizing county commissioners to accept similar gifts
and empowering them to enter into a contract for the maintenance of the same by levying a
small tax on all the taxable property of the county

The Brumback library will be one of the finest buildings for library purposes possessed
by an American city No town in this great State of Ohio can equal it It is erected
throughout of the most costly and lasting material, and is a lasting monument to its donor
and a grand memorial to the liberality and faithfulness of his heirs, who so nobly carry out
his wishes The ceremonies held in the city of Van Wert to-day will long be remembered
by all who participated

The address of Hon O S Brumback, of Toledo, was as follows

"Ladies and Gentlemen, Friends of Van Wert County:—There are occasions in the
affairs of men, of nations and of communities which mark epochs in their history To-day
marks an epoch in the history of Van Wert County Fifty years ago this county was a
primeval wilderness, inundated by water that had no sufficient outlet This beautiful park
was formerly a swamp from the overflow of the neighboring stream, and even here where
we now stand I have, in my boyhood days, fished in summer waters, and in winter skated
on unyielding ice

"It has only been by years of tireless toil and unremitting industry that Van Wert
County has been redeemed from swamp and beast and forest. until it has become the
garden spot of Ohio When the genial summer sun kisses her loamy soil and the 'tears of
Nature' fall upon her fertile fields—

'Every clod feels a stir of might,
   An instinct within it that reaches and towers,
And, groping blindly above it for light,
   Climbs to a soul in grass and flowers '

"With such a metamorphose to accomplish in the face of nature, with all the privations
consequent upon such work, it is little wonder the mass of the people have had but scanty
opportunity for higher education The schoolhouses which dot the township, and the church
spires towering amid the groves and meadows, all give proof that the people of Van Wert
County have been awake to the need of early education tempered with righteousness But
it is reserved for to-day to inaugurate an era of the broadest education and the widest
culture for all the people

"In laying the cornerstone of this library we are taking steps to place the knowledge and
wisdom of all the ages within the reach of the humblest citizen and his children

"Edward Everett said 'It is our common schools which give the key of knowledge to

the mass of the people   Our common schools are important in the same way as the common air, the common rain, the common sunshine, invaluable for their commonness'

"Carrying forward these beautiful analogies, we may well add, it is our public libraries that form the repositories of knowledge, ready for the application of the key of knowledge Our public libraries are important in the same way as the public parks, the public high-ways, the public government, invaluable for their publicity

"The common school system can only afford a preparatory education for the youth of our land   To utilize and make the most of that education is the work of a lifetime after leaving the public schools.   And here is where the public library opens wide its doors to freely offer its treasures of learning

"When Abraham Lincoln was a poor country boy yearning for that higher education by which alone he could aspire to lead his fellowmen, his opportunities for acquiring knowledge were so limited, it is almost miraculous he persevered in his purpose until he became the savior of his country, the emancipator of a race

"Alas, how many minds equally bright have become discouraged under such conditions and given up a higher education through lack of opportunity!

"That the people of this country are willing to tax themselves for the growth and maintenance of a library speaks volumes for their intelligence.   It shows they realize that just in proportion to the advantages offered will Van Wert County afford a desirable place to live, and every acre of land and every piece of property thereby proportionately increased in value   It shows they realize that success in life comes not from accident, but from intelli-gent action based on the wisdom and experience of those who have lived before

"The public library gathers the books in which are stored this wealth of human knowl-edge, and there the people of every occupation, creed and profession can go to learn the best method to accomplish the best results   It is not too much to say that under the inspira-tion of such a work, under the inspiration of such an institution, generation after generation will reap boundless benefit from the Brumback library

"He whose name it bears was himself an example of what the poor country boy can accomplish by high aspirations and intelligent, faithful industry   He himself realized what it was to be debarred from the higher education through lack of opportunity, and in the liberality of his generous heart, with true philanthropy, he willed that Van Wert County boys and girls—the sons and daughters of his old friends and associates, should have oppor-tunity second to none in the land   When that is accomplished, John Sanford Brumback will not have lived in vain

"And when in the future under the beneficent example of Van Wert County other counties in Ohio, yea, the counties of other States, shall have followed in our footsteps and laid cornerstones of *county libraries*, to Van Wert County will belong the meed of praise as leader in a glorious work.   Though young in years, she will be among the foremost in achievement

"And when in the widening brotherhood of man, every one shall feel he is his brother's keeper; when each shall know that all he is or can be he owes his fellowmen, and in return stands charged with a debt of gratitude only to be repaid by the happiness he secures for others, when all society realizes that by higher education, a better, nobler, broader civiliza-tion can be attained, in which the happiness of each is best secured by the happiness of all, then will come 'peace on earth, good will to men'   Then the era upon which we are now entering of humanity for humanity will have accomplished its full fruition, and the corner-stones of public libraries will not have been laid in vain

> "And each shall care for other,
> And each to each shall bend,
> To the poor a noble brother,
> To the good an equal friend"

It took a year and a half to build and complete the library, and on New Year's Day, 1901, it was ready to be dedicated.   The following is the program of the exercises:

DEDICATORY EXERCISES OF THE BRUMBACK LIBRARY

Presiding Officer. .. . . Rev Jas A Gordon
Director of Music . Wm H Hiestand
Music by Moebus' Orchestra and Hiestands Band

Music—"National Hymn" . . . . Geo W Warren
CHORUS AND ORCHESTRA
Invocation . Rev J H Fitzwater, D D
Music—"Inflammatus" . . . . Rossini
SOLO AND CHORUS
Address . . . . Rev P P Pope, D D
Music—Solo .. . . Chas W Clark, Chicago
Address of Presentation Hon O S Brumback, Toledo
Address of Acceptance on Behalf of Board of Trustees. .. ... Judge H C Glenn
Music—"Columbia" . . . . Dozitta
CHORUS AND ORCHESTRA
Dedicatory Prayer . .. . Rev I D Worman
Music—Solo .. . .Chas W. Clark
Address .. . . .. Hon C B Galbreath, Columbus
Ohio State Librarian and President National Association of Librarians
Music—"America" ... . .Orchestra, Chorus and Audience
Benediction . . . . Rev D B Koenig
A reception will be held at the Library Building immediately following, also in the evening Weather permitting, Hiestand's Band will give an open air concert

A full account of the dedicatory exercises was given in the *Van Wert Bulletin,* issue of January 3, 1901, from which we print the opening paragraphs, the Presentation Address and Address of Acceptance, as follows:

THE BRUMBACK LIBRARY.
Dedicated Tuesday, January 1, 1901

An appreciative audience of grateful people filled every foot of space in the large auditorium of the First M E Church, New Year's afternoon, to participate in the exercises attendant on the dedication of the Brumback County Library Building—the grandest gift ever bestowed upon the people of this county Long before two o'clock, the time announced the exercises would commence, standing room was at a premium As we looked over the sea of faces it was indeed a delight to notice not only the splendid representation of the citizens of Van Wert, but also among the throng in large numbers the citizens of the various townships of our county, for the library belongs to them as much as to the citizens of the town It was a day upon which the boy of the farm and the boy of the city alike cherished their fondest hopes of having equal rights and privileges to enter the portals of a storehouse of knowledge far grander and superior in every way than had the most ambitious ever expected to enter

Turn where you will from the Norman Conquest, along the whole course of English history, and you will find the source of strength of the English-speaking race lies largely in their love of books, and so the habits of mind and of morals engendered in the citizens of our county by their great love for the noblest and the best were never better demonstrated than by their presence from every section of our county at the dedicatory exercises They all realize that books are the strength of individuals and nations

All the time the Brumback Library has been in course of construction the interest of the people has increased, until to-day the splendid building bequeathed to the county through the generosity of John Sanford Brumback is the pride of all, and as we review it all it is no wonder that strangers from other States in the throng Tuesday afternoon and evening wished that they, too, lived in this town and county to enjoy in the fullest measure the benefits to be derived from such an institution

The Rev James A Gordon, pastor of the First Presbyterian Church, presided over the exercises, and the splendid musical portion of the program was under the direction of W H Hiestand, who conducted a mixed chorus, accompanied by Moebus' Orchestra Hiestand's Band played during the reception in the building in the evening A very pleasing feature

of the afternoon exercises was the two solos rendered by Mr Charles W Clark, a Van Wert boy, who has delighted audiences at home and abroad He is always welcomed home, but never more cordially than this time, when he voluntarily came home to help our people sing the songs of joy upon receiving such a handsome present on the dawn of the twentieth century

Rev. Gordon, in his introductory remarks, spoke as follows

"LADIES AND GENTLEMEN —I do not believe that in all the world there will be a celebration of the new year, or the new century, more significant and typical of the spirit of progress that marks the age than we are having here to-day Here where a hundred years ago was an unbroken wilderness, the home of savages and wild beasts, we dedicate to-day a temple of civilization and knowledge, noble in the spirit that prompted it, classic in its architectural beauty, and complete in all its appointments As one who has been interested in the library from its inception and who participated in the cornerstone laying, I rejoice in this proud day for the people of Van Wert County I have the honor to introduce the exercises of this afternoon We have a rich and varied program and while it is somewhat lengthy, this is an event which will never occur again, and I am sure you will all give patient attention to the speakers "

Presentation Address by Hon O S Brumback, of Toledo

The following splendid address of presentation of the building by Hon O S Brumback, of Toledo, the eldest son of the generous donor, needs no word of commendation Words are inadequate to express the gratitude of our people and their feeling as they listened to the revelations herein contained

"LADIES AND GENTLEMEN —Men may come and men may go, but their thoughts inscribed in books live after them Books afford the true transmigration of souls, since in them the minds of men live on long after their bodies have returned to dust A library is a mausoleum of the souls of great men and women who have lived on earth, and the open doors of a public library are a standing invitation to enter and become acquainted with them He who accepts the invitation should tread lightly and with awe, for there the learning of the ages awaits his call The scintillating wit, the flights of eloquence, and the rhythmic pathos of the human race there surround him, and there the hopes and fears, the sorrows and joys, the failures and successes of mankind for centuries are portrayed to him who reads

"The pleasure, the satisfaction, the profit, that books afford cannot be overstated Do you desire to ponder over the glorious achievements of men? Gibbon, Macauley, Bancroft and all the rest will detail with faithful accuracy the history of the past Do you desire to revel in imaginary scenes of human life? Dickens, Scott, Thackeray, Cooper and hundreds of others will lead you through scenes and bring you face to face with characters, so true to life that you forget it is all a fiction of the brain Do you desire to wander through Elysian fields where poesy lulls the senses into sweet content? Then Shakespeare, Byron, Tennyson, Bryant, Longfellow, or other of the hundred bards will carry you away on the wings of ecstasy, until with Wordsworth you feel—

> "'For ever something is or seems,
> That touches us with mystic gleams,
> Like glimpses of forgotten dreams'

"Long days become as hours, and dull hours fly unnoticed, when rapture thrills the heart, and the weary brain forgets its tribulations in the entrancement of a good author

"Assembled as we are to-day, to dedicate a temple to literature, the mind spontaneously recurs to all that books are to man

"After printing was invented, books at first were to be found only in the convents of mediæval times, ponderous in size and crude in form Learning was then confined to the priesthood, few among the people could read, and inability to write, even among the nobility, caused the use of a signet seal.

"From the convents, books gradually spread into the hands of the people, until at the time of the Colonial Period in America most families had one or more books, commonly a Bible with a few others Books being so precious, favored was he who had access to a few volumes, and happy was the one who had a small library at his command Because of the scarcity and value of books, no one was able to acquire a library of much magnitude, and from the very necessity of the situation, following the Colonial Period came the Institutional Period, from about 1638 to 1731, when libraries were to be found in Harvard, Princeton, Yale and other early colleges

"In 1731 began a Co-operative Period, in which men and families clubbed together in cities and villages to form libraries of their own This lasted until 1854, when the Free Public Library Period was inaugurated by Boston opening a library free to all who sought admission From Boston they have spread over the country, until to-day nearly every city of note in the United States, and many villages as well, have their free public libraries to promote education and intellectual growth

"The remarkable spread of knowledge in the United States is directly ascribable to these public libraries, acting in conjunction with the public schools The wonder of Europe is the amazing progress of the United States, accomplished by enterprise, inventive genius and intellectual superiority And yet these are but the product of our schools and libraries, sending forth inventors, poets, authors, statesmen, jurists and divines

"A boy of humble parentage comes out of our public schools, he applies himself assiduously to master the books at hand, and lo! a Lincoln, a Blaine, a Beecher, a Morse, or an Edison lives to elevate and glorify the race

"Or perhaps a boy after leaving the public school goes to work at a bench, in a factory, or upon a farm, or enters upon a business career, with a library at hand and wise use of his time he grows in knowledge, his wisdom sheds its light upon his fellowmen, and his fraternal spirit warms all with whom he comes in contact Honest, faithful and true to all the duties of life, he may remain a quiet, unobtrusive citizen, content to fill a humble sphere in life But 'tis such as these make up American citizenship. 'Tis such as these that form the anchor and stay of American institutions

"John Sherman wrote to a young friend· 'Learn to love your books, for there is pleasure, friendship and instruction in books'

"The public library instills a love for books by creating a taste for reading, and a taste for reading is a taste of Paradise Happy indeed is he who can say from his heart

> "My books are friends, whose cheerful greeting
> Delight my heart with each new meeting;
> With them I take the greatest pleasure,
> Enjoy their wit in fullest measure
> Whene'er I feel the need, or yearning,
> For knowledge, wisdom, counsel, learning,
> I steal away to quiet nooks
> To interview my faithful books " *

"Every citizen—even the humblest—can enter the public library with a sense of ownership, for it is maintained by his own contribution with that of others He feels that he is at home and entitled to share the privileges which surround him The people of a community animated by such a spirit soon become a reading community, and a reading community soon becomes an educated community.

"In 1890 some of the prominent ladies of Van Wert, realizing the great good to be derived from a library free to all who would aid in the enterprise, incorporated The Van Wert Library Association Without books or money, except such as they could hope to secure from donations, the prospect of success was anything but flattering But nothing daunted, the ladies entered vigorously upon the work They canvassed the town for subscriptions and gave entertainments in aid of the project until a nucleus of a circulating library was formed Any person who contributed $3 00 each year was permitted to share in the use of the library So heartily were they encouraged in the work, and so enthusiastic and persevering were they in their efforts, that at the end of the first year they had a collection of 600 books, placed in charge of a lady librarian in a general reading room rented by the association for library purposes The annual dues paid by the patrons of the library were only sufficient to pay the running expenses, leaving but scant means to add new books. Notwithstanding many and varied discouragements, the ladies persevered in their good work until the library became so generally appreciated that in 1896 the Common Council of Van Wert voted a tax of three-tenths of a mill in aid of the Library; realizing about $575 annually for that purpose This served to pay running expenses, and, together with the money realized from the dues of patrons, furnished a small income upon which the library could be maintained

"The field for the work was, however, so much larger than the means wherewith to accomplish it, and the future was so dependent upon constant and unremitting effort, that

---

*Original with the speaker

the ladies, although justly proud of what had been accomplished, might well feel apprehensive for the future when their personal efforts should cease. A like library established some years before had finally gone into bankruptcy, and it was only too apparent that this also might fail if not placed upon a firm and enduring foundation

"It was at this stage that the will of John Sanford Brumback was made public, providing for the gift to the people of Van Wert County of a splendid building in which to forever maintain a free public library, by the following clause in the will

"'It is my will and desire that my said dear wife and children expend sufficient of my estate willed to them in items one and two to carry out my wishes known to them by the erection and gift of a library building, somewhat after the plans and designs I have prepared for that purpose, Provided and this item is upon the express condition that my said wife and children can make arrangements satisfactory to them with the City of Van Wert, or if they desire and think best, with Van Wert County, for a location for said building and the maintenance of the library to be placed therein'

"Before going to what has been accomplished under this provision, let us take a cursory view of the life of the man who made possible the firm establishment of a public library in Van Wert County to bless present and future generations

"John Sanford Brumback was born on a farm in Licking County, Ohio, on the 4th day of March, 1829 His father descended from an old Virginia family of German extraction, the progenitor of which had emigrated to America in early Colonial days His mother's name was Frutilda Bearnes, her parents having emigrated to Ohio from Pennsylvania at an early day From her he inherited many of his sterling qualities of mind and heart

"When he was four years old his father died, leaving his mother a legacy of six young children and forty acres of undeveloped land, having a log house upon it With nothing to rear and educate her four girls and two boys except what could be produced from the soil of this wild land, his mother, like others of that day, no whit discouraged, set bravely to work to eke out a precarious livelihood In a few years she was called upon to mourn her eldest son. No other course remained but for herself and four daughters to make their own living, aided only by John's efforts Unable to spare her only boy from his work except in the winter season, John's early education consisted of the crude instruction received in a country school during the few winters he was privileged to attend school at all He was quick to learn and acquired even in this short time the rudiments of an education that added to and rounded out by a lifetime of close observation and keen perception made him a man of general information and broad intelligence

"Had J. S. Brumback received a liberal education, such as most boys receive now days, there is no station in life his natural ability, industrious habits and moral worth would not have eminently fitted him to fill

"As illustrative of his self-reliance and capability, even in early life, I often have heard his mother tell how she entrusted him at the age of ten years to drive to market the farm produce the family had to sell, which he disposed of with rare judgment for one of his years. He was as good a horse trader at fifteen as David Harum himself His mother used to say she never knew what horse John would bring home It was sufficient for her that he rarely, if ever, got the worst of a bargain He laughingly told me that he never got beaten in a horse trade but once, and that was when he traded a horse for a cow—and the cow died

"The commercial instinct thus early aroused, he left the farm and entered the grocery business at the early age of seventeen The only capital he had was $50 his mother had saved up, which she willingly entrusted to him On this he went to Cincinnati, and so won the confidence of wholesale dealers by his frank and manly bearing that they trusted him to enough goods to open up a small country store It is needless to say that from this small beginning his after success and fortune was attained Attained by honorable, upright dealing It was never said of J S Brumback that he was otherwise than perfectly fair, honest and just in every business transaction

"No man ever acquired wealth and position in a community without arousing the jealousy of some less fortunate. And yet, although J S Brumback did business in Van Wert for over 35 years, first in the dry goods business and then as a banker, never was he accused of making a dollar dishonestly. He was shrewd, far-seeing, and expected every man to fulfill his contracts, but unjust or oppressive—never

"His heart was as tender as a child's; his sympathy went out to the needy and distressed And many in Van Wert County will bear me witness that when J S Brumback had it in his power to profit greatly by their misfortunes, he did not do so, but instead helped them out of trouble at no small cost of time and effort to himself

"His judgment was so wise and perception so unerring that his opinion was constantly sought by people in all walks of life No one appealed to him in vain for assistance in a righteous cause, whether it was alms to the poor, aid to his relations, encouragement to the down-hearted, succor to the unfortunate, or a donation for the public good, he always gave freely when merit demanded In short, in the words of Shakespeare·

"'His life was gentle, and the elements
So mixed in him, that nature might stand up
And say to all the world—*this is a man'*

"Such a man, with such a heart full of philanthropy, could not die without remembering his fellowmen, if it could be accomplished in justice to his own family, toward whom he recognized his first duty So when he came to draw his will, he did not conceal what he had in mind and secretly consult a lawyer, but openly, as he had lived, he called his family around him and freely expressed his thoughts He said he had long felt like doing something for Van Wert, and that he knew of no way in which so much good could come to his old friends and associates and their children as through a public library He said

"'I would like to firmly establish for them such an institution, if you are all willing If any of you feel I ought not to do so, I will dismiss it from my thoughts'

"It is sufficient to say that in the discussion which followed the vote was unanimous But even then, when I was drawing his will, he said

"'I want you to draw it so as to make it entirely optional If hereafter any of my heirs should not be satisfied to carry out my wish, I want it so that it will not be obligatory'

"And so the will was drawn, and under it the magnificent steel and stone fireproof building has been constructed for the Brumback Library, on the condition made by the heirs that it be forever maintained by Van Wert County under that name, in honor of the donor

"The unanimity with which the heirs have carried out the wish expressed in the will bears testimony to the affection and veneration felt for the husband and father What a glorious life to live, and be thus remembered! Had J S Brumback spent his life in a sordid pursuit of wealth, he could have accumulated a much larger fortune Instead, he wisely chose to make good use of his money as he went along Liberal, but modest in his mode of life, he educated his children and aided them to become established in life, and when he passed away they could not but feel that they in turn owed him a debt of gratitude that never could be repaid

"'Gratitude is the fairest blossom which springs from the soul, and the heart of man knoweth none more fragrant'

"One thing to be especially noted in the will is the provision for *a County Library* The suggestion was a noble conception, full of great possibilities Up to the date of this will, no thought apparently was ever directed to the establishment of a county library

"The population of our cities and towns are less in need of the advantages of a free public library than the rural communities, since books in the centres of population are readily accessible and pass from hand to hand by loan and exchange Not so in the country, where people are widely separated and books are not so plentiful on the family shelves

"There is a great yearning among the youth of the country districts for more of the opportunities and pleasures that go to make up life in the twentieth century, causing a great drift to the cities and towns, to the detriment doubtless of the national welfare If the farms are to be kept populated, rural life must be made attractive, and opportunity there afforded to enjoy the pleasures of literature and enter the world of knowledge

The statistics of our insane asylums show a remarkably large percentage of patients from the rural districts This has been ascribed to the monotony of life on the farm, without mental vicissitude and relaxation There can be little doubt that with good books circulating through the country districts affording mental recreation, there will be fewer inmates of asylums from the farm.

"When it was first proposed to make the Brumback Library a county institution, many looked askance and could hardly believe it practicable Some of the residents in different parts of the county have thought such a library could be of but little or no advantage to them. They little realized how books are now being circulated in our great cities many miles from the central library, and there is no reason why they cannot be had almost as freely in distant parts of the county as in the county seat itself The only need is the books themselves, and they will surely be acquired in a few years in sufficient number to supply the whole county Under a sub-station or branch library system, books are delivered in any number at stations in distant localities, there to be called for and returned when read

Ready means for their transfer is afforded in this day of constant communication and rapid transit facilities

"Of course, the inauguration of a County Library was not accomplished without much effort and many discouragements When I drew a bill to be presented to the Ohio Legislature, to permit the County Commissioners to bind the County to maintain a library by taxation, I believed its passage could only be secured by the most strenuous efforts When, however, the farmers of Van Wert County assembled in their Granges, and after full discussion declared almost unanimously in favor of such a library, I knew their voice must be heeded and their intelligence receive the reward of success By the assistance of leading citizens, both in town and county, the bill became a law, and later the County Commissioners took the necessary action under the law to execute a tripartite agreement with the Ladies' Library Association and the heirs of J S Brumback

"By the terms of that contract the Ladies' Library Association turned over to the Brumback Library all the books—some 1,600 in number—belonging to the Association, the County agreed to forever maintain the library by the levy of an annual tax upon all the taxable property of the county, and the Brumback heirs agreed to construct, and furnish complete and ready for use, a stone building in one of the parks of the City of Van Wert, the county seat of the county, wherein the library might have a home, and its influence be extended in ever-widening circles

"How well the heirs have much more than fulfilled the terms of the contract let the splendid building and furnishings—substantial, commodious and beautiful in every detail—speak It is sufficient to say that no expense has been spared to make it the best From the solid stone walls three feet thick to the steel truss tile-covered roofs, stability and grace have been sought Upon entering the arched portal and obtaining a view of the commodious rooms, lofty arched ceilings, Mosaic floors, marble mantel and wainscoting, polished oak woodwork and furniture, with space for 40,000 books and more—it certainly must be said that Van Wert County is indeed fortunate in having had J S Brumback live within its borders

"Believing the ladies would exercise a most beneficent influence in the management and work of the Brumback Library, and to keep it out of political broils as much as possible, the tripartite agreement provides that the library shall be managed by a non-partisan board of seven trustees, three to be appointed by the County Commissioners, two by the Ladies' Library Association, and two by the Brumback heirs. Their term of office is for three years, and in case any appointment is not made by the parties designated, the City Council of Van Wert is to make the appointment

"It will thus be seen that the governing board of the library is selected by various interests, and the best qualified persons for such a work will, in all probability, be secured

"The income of the library under the tax levy now produces nearly $5,000 per annum Twice this sum could well be utilized Under the new decennial valuation of property, this amount will be substantially increased Only lack of means will prevent the library from at once entering upon its full usefulness To fill the demands of the whole county under the sub-station or branch library system a large library is necessary, and the fear is that in the beginning the supply will not be equal to the demand If the people, however, will be tolerant, a few years ought to suffice to accumulate an extensive and valuable collection of books, embracing all departments of literature

"When the people once realize how much good is to be had from the few cents collected from each for the library, it is believed a strong sentiment will grow up to increase the levy until a sum can be had adequate to meet all demands It is certainly better that people should tax themselves for libraries and schools, rather than for almshouses, jails and other asylums of misery

"As the first to inaugurate a County Library, Van Wert County owes it to herself and the world to see that it is made a complete success I doubt not that with such an example other counties in Ohio will soon take up the work, and the system extend to other States, until the results accomplished will be tremendous

"The prominence Van Wert County will receive as the pioneer in such a work cannot but be a proud distinction, and of the greatest benefit to all her people Since the law was enacted for the benefit of the Brumback Library of Van Wert County, Cincinnati has already taken up the cue, and procured the enactment of a law extending the field of her library work to all of Hamilton County Toledo and other localities are considering the same action

"The demands of the time are for greater literary advantages and fuller opportunities to learn all the wonders of science and the achievements of the past

"Give the people full opportunity for mental culture and free access to the world of books, they will not be slow to wander with Proctor into the realms of space, to learn the wondrous stories of suns that glow, and systems that circle there, or go with La Place to other worlds to hear how ages since the rock-ribbed hills and ancient sea were but a fiery cloud, a morning mist of creation. They will quickly understand how Cuvier finds a bone and builds the mammoth to which it belongs, and reads the hoary rocks which tell of primeval seas and towering forests. With Carlyle they will pass through the terrible scenes of the French Revolution, and from John Stuart Mill soon learn the true relation of economy and thrift to supply and demand. Who can doubt that wisdom, good judgment and wise action must result from such instruction?

"Prosperity and success have ever attended upon intelligence. And so it is that the elevation and advancement of the whole race to the higher planes of social development and fraternal brotherhood is along the road of a wider dissemination of knowledge. Nor is the field of human effort by any means exhausted. Indeed, it is scarcely curtailed. Vast fields of learning yet unexplored, and heights of intellectual attainment beyond belief, await those who attempt them.

"Great problems yet remain to be solved, the greatest indeed that have ever confronted mankind. The true relation of capital and labor, the proper union of diversified interests, the economical administration of public affairs, in short, all the great questions that will arise as population increases and the human race strives to attain the greatest good to the greatest number, must be determined, and determined rightly. In these great controversies, destined to test the stability of human institutions, the wisdom drawn from the whole past experience of man can alone lead the race aright.

"The people of the great Middle West have in the past been chiefly occupied in developing their material resources. The time is come when they are to devote more attention to literary and scientific pursuits. That intellectual giants will be forthcoming cannot be doubted, and they will be the product of just such institutions as the Brumback Library.

"The libraries of a community are the foster-mothers of intellectual prominence. Many of the foremost statesmen, historians, poets and orators of America have been Massachusetts men—the product of a State that boasts the great libraries of Cambridge and Boston, and where nearly every village has a public library. Bancroft and Prescott, and Motley and Parkman, and Fiske, as historians, Bryant and Longfellow, and Lowell and Holmes and Emerson, and Whittier, as poets, Winthrop and Choate, and Everett and Sumner, and Wendell Phillips, as orators, have brought imperishable fame to themselves and the Old Bay State. Ohio has already taken rank as the mother of Presidents. Her sons are yet to attain still higher pinnacles of success, and surprise the world with their versatile genius.

"In opening a library designed to aid in these great accomplishments, we are starting upon its career an educational institution whose silent but wholesome influence will reach through all the future. When we think of the character the Brumback Library will mould, the pleasure it will give, and the knowledge it will spread, we cannot but realize this is indeed a momentous occasion. As said by Senator Hoar of Massachusetts

"'The opening of a library is an event of the highest importance in any community. It is one of the institutions which tend to build up and adorn the local life. There is no city so great and renowned that it does not wear its library as the chief jewel of its crown. There is no town so humble that a good library will not raise it to distinction and honor. However excellent may be their schools, however admirable the training that the children get at home, the community where there is no good library is but half educated.'

"What considerate man can weigh the dollars it will cost to maintain this library against the immortal minds it will train? One youth kept from a dissolute and vicious life by the charms of literature supplied from its shelves will more than repay the expense of years. God has implanted his Divine essence in the mind of man to be trained and educated for good citizenship on earth and immortality hereafter. This library, engaged in broadening and ennobling the mind of man, is kindling a flame 'Which will shine not merely when every artificial beam is extinguished, but when the affrighted sun has fled away from the heavens'

"To-day we enter upon a new century. To-day mankind all over the world is contemplating the past and standing tip-toe to peer into the future. Surpassing day, transcendent day. All living millions will never see its like again.

"Upon this Natal day of the twentieth century, while loving congratulations are echoing around the globe, on behalf of John Sanford Brumback, now gone beyond the stars, but whose spirit hovers near, on behalf of his wife and children, who have striven as best they knew to carry out the will of him they loved, I now here present to the Trustees of the

Brumback Library, acting on behalf of all the people, this building, wherein it hath been covenanted to forever maintain a free public library

"And may every man, woman and child in Van Wert County reap the benefit to be obtained by delving into the mysteries upon its shelves, and their descendants in turn drink deep at the 'Pierian Spring'"

Address of Acceptance by Judge Glenn

The address of acceptance by Judge H C Glenn was as follows:

"Mr President —With uncovered head I make my most gracious bow to Mrs Brumback and her family While I address them I also address the ladies and gentlemen present

"I have never received a summons to duty which I obeyed with such supreme pleasure as the present one, of accepting from this family, in the name of the Trustees of the Library and in behalf of the citizens of Van Wert County, yonder well-proportioned and exquisitely finished and furnished library building

"This little library, or what used to be a little library, but which has grown to be one of considerable proportion, has a warm place in my memory

"I remember so well the time when and by whom was first conceived the plan by which it was hoped to provide for the people of Van Wert a free public library I also well remember the dozen true and philanthropic women who organized themselves into a society to materialize this conception and to promote this plan The plan succeeded, but would not have done so but for the liberality of the people of the city.

"I have always thought that the fate of the enterprise was determined, and success became assured at our own home An entertainment had been arranged by the ladies for the benefit of the library fund The same one just spoken of by Mr Gordon Everybody was invited and nearly everybody came The children came with their pennies and nickles and dimes, the grown people came bringing their quarters, their halves and their dollars, but the acme of success was reached when it was ascertained that Mrs Marsh had sent her check for a generous sum and that Mr J S Brumback had brought his check for $50

"It is also my good pleasure to know something of the history of this library building Aside from his own family, Mrs Glenn and I were the first persons to whom Mr Brumback communicated his purpose of erecting a library building, and of donating the same to the public It was not his original idea to make this a post-mortem gift When we talked with him he had a hope that he might so far recover his health as to be physically able to erect the building himself and with his own hand turn it over to the public This idea had progressed so far that he had plans prepared by an architect, which I understand to be the same plans, in the main, after which the building has been constructed—changed and added to only so far as modern architects' experience and good taste, convenience and utility suggested. His hope of recovery was only a hope He informed us that he had talked the matter over with his family, who heartily acquiesced, so that whether he recovered or not the library was a fixed fact, unless conditions should exist rendering the same impracticable

"My friend, Mr Brumback, in his presentation address, referred to one matter which I wish to emphasize as a matter of justice to the living It is this This building has not been erected in pursuance of any mandatory provisions of Mr Brumback's will There is no such provision in his will Every reference to the library is in form of a request or wish on the testator's part I am satisfied, however, that there would have been such mandatory provision had he not been entirely satisfied that the same were unnecessary Any objections, or rather failure to concur on the part of Mrs Brumback, his direct legatee, or of any one of his sons or daughters, his ultimate legatees, would have defeated the enterprise

"This does not detract from Mr Brumback's generosity or our obligations of gratitude to him, but extends the circle of our beneficiaries and creates new objects of gratitude This is both refreshing and commendable, in an age when the chief end of heirs and legatees often seems to be, to have and to hold the ancestral estate, and often results in strife among themselves as to which shall obtain the lion's share In this family the only strife seems to have been, if there was any, as to which should be the most liberal and liberal in carrying out the ancestral wish

"Having said this much, there remains but little more for me to say or do than to proclaim, in the presence of this vast audience, in behalf of the Trustees of this library, and in behalf of the citizens of the county, whose servants they are, that yonder great storehouse of knowledge is accepted for the uses and purposes for which it has been presented And knowing the trustees as I do, and knowing the sentiment and temper of the people, and full of confidence in the future, I do feel perfectly safe in promising that the same shall never be perverted from the use intended Being so massive and substantially built, I do not see

why the end of the century, the threshhold of which we are just passing, should not see this building still standing and the stream of knowledge, education and morality then, as now, flowing from it in all directions, lighting up the dark places of this community as the great luminary of the day shall then, as now, send out its rays in every direction, illuminating the dark corners of the Universe of God

"Again allow me to say that the benefits flowing from this magnificent library building and its contents will not be confined to the present age nor will gratitude cease with the present generation After the last survivor of this vast audience shall have been gathered to the fathers, hundreds and thousands of grateful men, women and children, deciphering the Inscription engraved with mallet and chisel over yon grand entrance will roll the name 'Brumback' as a sweet sound under their tongues, and on their lips sweet gratitude will lovingly and lastingly linger "

The following is a summary of the acquisition, and a full description, of the Library, as printed in the *Van Wert Republican* December 27, 1900:

THE BRUMBACK LIBRARY
Description of the New Building

ITS FINE ARCHITECTURE

No pen can describe the many words of gratitude heard expressed on every hand by the citizens of Van Wert, and the county in general, since they heard the good news of the provisions made in the will of the late John Sanford Brumback, former president of the Van Wert National Bank, and long ere the building was completed many of the people of this State, as well as other States, also rejoice with us in our good fortune, as will be seen by extracts taken from State papers pertaining to the gift

When the seal of the envelope containing the last will and testament of the late John Sanford Brumback was broken, Peabody's sentence, "Education—a debt due from the present to future generations," proved to be the main theme, and by reason thereof our town and county received on the dawn of the twentieth century a handsome gift to build and furnish which has cost the Brumback estate nearly $50,000

Well may Van Wert feel proud of the day John Sanford Brumback sought a home in her midst, and particularly so as he has provided that his great aim in life—of working for the higher interest of Van Wert County people and mankind in general—should continue through his directions and provisions after he had crossed the silent river of death

Mr Brumback took great interest in the little city library, established a few years ago through the efforts of a few noble women He also did much toward making the city's handsome little parks what they now are The fine grove of trees in Second Ward Park were planted by him, so it is no wonder he selected this beautiful spot as the site on which should stand one of the most lasting monuments that a Van Werter could possibly erect

It has also been very gratifying to our people to see his children, viz Mrs J P. Reed, Jr, Mrs. E I Antrim, D L Brumback, president of the Van Wert National Bank, and Hon O S Brumback, now a prominent attorney in Toledo, all working so faithfully and unitedly carrying out the desires of their noble father, devoting much time to see that the building should be a perfect one in every particular and worthy of the memory of one who truly loved his fellowmen Such zeal and devotion merits the highest praise, by their deeds they have not only proven themselves truly heirs of a noble man, but also have erected for themselves a monument, which time cannot efface With them we can right here very properly speak of Mr John P. Reed, who has had the supervision of nearly everything in connection with the building He has worked early and late, and it is due in a measure to his ability and unceasing efforts that next Tuesday Van Wert County will be presented with one of the most handsome and most perfect structures ever erected in Ohio

Space will not permit us to mention the many difficulties and discouragements the heirs had to contend with while endeavoring to carry out the wishes of their father First, there was no authority on the statute book authorizing the Board of Commissioners to accept of the gift, great as it was This difficulty, however, was soon removed, through the efforts and solicitations of the heirs, a general law was passed authorizing County Commissioners to receive on behalf of the public such a bequest and to make suitable provisions for keeping it up Thus it will be seen that the Brumback heirs have opened the way to have a county library building in every county in the State of Ohio

The plans for the building were made by David L. Stine, Toledo's popular architect It is a handsome structure as well as a durable one, view it from any point you will, and is strictly fireproof The cornerstone of the building was laid with appropriate ceremonies in the summer of 1899, under the auspices of the Masonic Order, Grand Master Williams of Ohio being master of ceremonies

The entire material used in the building and the work of constructing same are the very best that money and skill can produce The grounds surrounding the building have been terraced, the finished grade stands about eighteen inches above the level of Main street, and the floor of the library four feet higher Upward of 10,000 wagon loads of dirt were used in the construction of terrace and grade The exterior walls are of blue Bedford stone, rock faced We cannot enter into details as to the perfect system of drainage made surrounding the building prior to the construction of the foundation All footings for foundation walls and pieces are of concrete laid in courses of eight inches each, and each course was allowed to stand two days before subsequent course was laid The boundary walls of the foundation from top of concrete footings to level are constructed in first-class rubble work and stones used are of uniform size (18 x 24 inches) and from six to eight inches thick On the top course of rubble walls have been placed large cut stones of even thickness Upward from these large foundation stones have been laid Bedford rock-faced stones laid in alternate courses of stones four and ten inches thick The base or "plinth" course around the entire building is hammer dressed, the basement windows and sills being of the same dressed material The exterior in general is rock faced with small margin draught cut on all outer vertical corners All stones rest on natural bed, the larger courses in base projecting beyond the building line about four inches The size of the entire building is 60 x 70 feet, with an elevation of two stories

All the beams, channels, angles, T's and plates throughout the building are of American manufactured steel uniform in quality, and in the entire construction of the building upward of seventy-five tons of steel were used, all of which was subjected to a severe test, the beams being subjected to a tensile strength of from 60,000 to 69,000 pounds per square inch In the construction of the roof the greatest care was taken, the roof sections, the valley rafters and trusses being of steel with two-inch purlins for fastening wood as sheathing, the same being notched pine planks, not over six-inch face running up and down roof, on which are securely fastened the terra cotta or Spanish tiles These tiles are of the very best material made, three-fourths of an inch thick, and the total weight of tile on roof is upward of 50,000 pounds

By referring to the picture it will be seen that the building has two towers, the western tower being square, rising to a height of nearly forty feet from grade; the east tower is round, and larger in every way, its extreme height being forty-five feet, this gives the structure an imposing appearance, like that of a castle The building stands in the center of the park, and the main entrance is about 127 feet from the north curb line of Main street

Without further description of the exterior, reader, follow us in, and we will endeavor to give you a pen picture of the interior We approach the main entrance of the building over a fine cement walk, nine feet wide As we near the building we are much impressed with the elaborately carved portico

We ascend the eight steps in the entrance platform which brings us immediately under the carved portico The stone in the rough was put in place for the carver and the mouldings and capital carved The work is fine, and the longer you look at the carvings in the portico, the more you become impressed with the fact that a master hand handled the chisel Notice the five columns on each side The height of entrance is twelve feet We enter very handsomely carved heavy oak-panelled doors, and are now in the vestibule, which is 12 x 6½ feet. We first notice the handsome floor beneath our feet The vestibule has a very attractive marble tile floor of a Grecian design In the center there is a geometrical figure and the "Lamp of Knowledge," with Grecian torches and wreath Even the vestibule is inlaid in French and Italian marble wainscoted in white Italian marble eight feet high Just over the inner doors we notice in white plaster cast an open book, surrounded by a wreath

In the center hangs a very handsome hall lantern, of a green tint, made especially for the building The ceiling is painted pink and tinted into a cream in the center We now pass through the two inner vestibule doors which are also of richly carved oak with plate glass the full length Now we are within the library proper

To say it is magnificent does not express it, words are inadequate to do the building justice, and it is indeed hard to know just where to begin to describe the array of costly things The reading room is 61 x 23½ The floor is marble of a Mosaic design, with a large geometrical figure in the center, and the entire reading room is laid with tile in small

pieces not quite half an inch square—there is estimated to be in the entire flooring over 400,000 pieces   The foundation of the floor, which is fireproof hollow tile and concrete, rests on steel beams   It took seven expert Italians from Chicago four weeks' time to lay the tile

The vaulted ceiling, which is twenty-five feet high, has ninety rosettes of unique design, also very attractive borders and mouldings and nearly two hundred plaster panels cast singly In staff, placed in position and wired to angle fasteners, the whole cemented together with plaster Paris   The fine arches have ninety handsome rosettes, from the center of each protrudes an electric bulb, and when they are all lighted they present a handsome sight   They look like so many diamonds, and the light shows the ornamentations in a manner that is fascinating

Below a heavy moulding on the sidewalls are fifty-eight lights, each of eight candlepower The reading room, as well as the reference room, is wainscoted three and one-half feet high, with white Italian or Cararra marble   Between the reading room and the stack room are two imposing columns, 36 inches in circumference, finished in Florentine onyx   Next we would call your attention to the delivery counter, on each side of which are two very handsome settees, each five feet long, the seats, backs and ends being upholstered in a rich green corduroy   At the extreme ends of the settees are two doors or gates, through which access is gained to the stack room, these are handsomely carved out of solid oak, the wreath pattern on center panel being found wherever there is wreath ornamentation on the various things in the building, including floors, furniture, etc   The lighting fixtures throughout the building are made of a special design of heavy cast brass, and are combination fixtures for both electric lights and gas   We step in the direction of the northeast corner of the reading room and find hanging on the wall a large, rich oil painting of the noble donor of the edifice, Hon John Sanford Brumback   If we could but take a glimpse into the veiled and mysterious future, at times, even for centuries yet to come, we would see many a young man standing almost on the same spot as we now stand and here we could see them not only admiring the kind and noble features of Mr Brumback, but also wishing that they could express their gratification to him or his heirs for providing so generously not only for their comforts, but even their children's children   Thousands yet to be will rise up within the bounds of Van Wert County and call him "blessed," as the gift will increase in value as time rolls on

Near us we now notice a card catalogue case, which is in the extreme northeast corner of the reading room, it has a capacity for 72,000 cards.

Next we would call attention to the handsome marble mantle and fireplace   Notice the large marble shelf and the columns on either side   It stands seven and one-half feet high The fireplace is faced with red French marble   The grate and trimmings are of brass   In the fireplace are imitation logs, which will be heated with gas so as to have the appearance of burning timber   Notice the unique solid brass trimmings and the old-fashioned andirons
-    In the panel just below the marble mantel shelf is a solid bronze tablet with the following

1829   IN MEMORY OF   1897

JOHN SANFORD BRUMBACK,

Who Bequeathed to the People
of Van Wert County
this Building
In which to forever maintain
a free Public Library

The reading room is furnished with four large solid oak tables, similar in design to those used in the Chicago Library, the ends being panelled   The chairs are also solid oak, with convenient arms so that one sitting close to a table can raise up and get out of his seat without moving his chair   A fine rack for newspapers and a solid oak periodical rack are also a part of the furniture in the reading room, and all movable furniture has rubber tips, so as to prevent making noise when moving same on the floor

In the west tower is a reference room   The floor of this room is also laid in marble Mosaic tile   In the center as we enter we notice a solid oak table and chairs of the same design as those in the reading room, in front of us is an oak bookcase containing reference books

In the eastern tower is a room designed for the children   This has Georgia pine floor, being almost round, having a radius of 19½ feet   This room is furnished similar to the

other rooms mentioned excepting that it has a round table In time this will be filled with books expressly for the children In the second story of this tower is the Trustees' room, which is also neatly furnished We reach the Trustees' room by flights of steel winding stairs From here one can have a splendid view of Fountain Park and the Central School campus

Before we enter the stack room let us again take another look at the handsome ceiling, which is of pure white, as well as the moulded frieze and panels The sidewall to the ceiling moulding is of cream, the colors and scroll work blending admirably

The stack room is 27½ x 33 feet The floor is of Georgia pine, laid on fireproof concrete, edged grain strips being three inches wide, perfectly matched and hand smoothed The floor was coated twice with filler and finished with Johnson s wax in mahogany color The room is tinted in green and shaded to a cream ceiling Here also the colors blend perfectly. There are six stacks, twelve feet long, two feet thick and seven and one-fourth feet high, made of enameled steel, with adjustable shelves, the whole being olive green color with brass trimmings There is space in the stack room for additional stacks, but the six now in will be sufficient for some time to come Over the stack room is another room designed to be used when the present stack room becomes too limited for the library

On the east side of the stack room is a Librarian's room, with a suitable desk Here also we found a fine switchboard with twenty-four switches to operate the many electric lights in the various parts of the building

On the west side of the stack room is a marble stairway leading to the side door and the basement On our right as we descend the stairs is a toilet room, fitted up with the very best in that line, this floor as well as the hallway also being laid in marble Mosaic tile Space will not permit us to enter into minute description of the basement, which has cemented floors and is partitioned with fireproof hollow tile into suitable rooms for storage, etc

"THE PIONEER COUNTY LIBRARY"

The prominence attained by the Brumback Library as "The Pioneer County Library" is well shown in a Washington Communication printed in the *Cincinnati Commercial Tribune* (daily) under date of January 20, 1912, as follows·

WASHINGTON, Jan 19—Ohio has the ideal public county library system of the United States, according to an announcement of the United States bureau of education

The announcement which gives an interesting description of the Ohio plan, says

"Every inhabitant of the United States, no matter how far from the centers of population, will have practically as good library facilities as are now enjoyed by the average city dweller if plans for the establishment of a new type of book-distributing agency work out according to the anticipation of the United States commissioner of education, Dr P P Claxton, who is personally interested in their development As the rural population of the United States numbers about 55 per cent of the total population, the new library plan may have the effect of doubling the effectiveness of libraries and of raising the standard of culture in this country to a corresponding degree

"The county library plan has already been put into successful operation in Van Wert county, O, where a main depository and fifteen branches are maintained at an expenditure of between $6,000 and $7,000 a year, this sum being raised by levying a half-mill county tax The same appropriation also covered the cost last year of placing eighty-nine additional branch libraries in the public schools Fourteen counties in Wisconsin are now enjoying similar facilities

"Dr Claxton went on to say that his advocacy of the county library was based on his personal observation of the Brumback library of Van Wert county, O, which is at present one of the few institutions of this kind in the country * * *

"The heirs of the late John Sanford Brumback spent $50,000 on the building With the money realized from a county tax levy, some 3,000 books were purchased in 1899, and these, together with 1,600 others turned over by the merger of an existing library, formed the nucleus of the present collection

"The library building erected by the Brumback estate was turned over to the county in 1901 It is a beautiful structure in the Gothic-Romanesque style of architecture, built of Bedford blue sandstone, with a tile and marble interior, fireproofed throughout The book stacks have a capacity of 25,000 volumes With the handsome park in which it is located the Brumback library has become one of the show places of Van Wert.

"This is the central depository for the county's system of branch libraries and school libraries The branches are in charge of librarians who are paid $50 a year and are made responsible for the safe keeping of the books sent them Rural merchants and postmasters

are generally selected to conduct the branch libraries, as their establishments are most centrally located and most frequently visited

"BOOKS FOR LOCAL READERS

"The collections of books in their charge range from 100 to 150, although if this is not a sufficient number, additional volumes will be sent on request Four times a year, or oftener, the branch librarian boxes up the books for which he is responsible and returns them to the central depository, receiving at once another collection

"The books thus forwarded are not the arbitrary hit-or-miss selection of the head librarian, but conform to the desires of the local readers, as ascertained at the branch itself Before any books are sent out the branch librarian receives a list of the titles in every available traveling collection Each title is accompanied with a note explaining the character and contents of the books listed

The users of the branch library then discuss these lists, and the box of books which contains the greatest number of works that interests the greatest number of readers is the box called for If the contents of no one box prove interesting to the neighborhood the main library will make up a special selection upon request In this way the rural book lover can obtain practically any work he desires for which there is an appreciable call

"The kind of books read by the country people of Van Wert county are of an unusually high character. One representative box contains 100 works, dealing with such varied subjects as philosophy, religion, sociology, language, science, the useful and fine arts, literature, travel, biography, history and fiction Books for young people comprise about one-fourth the entire list * * *

"A most valuable feature of the Brumback library's work is the establishment of loan collections for use in schools These school libraries will be sent to any teacher who asks for them, the selection being made by the teacher or by the librarian, as the borrower prefers. Although this school library department is only about four years old, it has grown so rapidly that to-day all but about 40 of the 125 country school teachers in Van Wert county make use of its facilities

"INSTRUCTIVE BOOKS POPULAR.

"The selections which teachers may draw out for school use are as large as desired Usually as many books are taken as there are children in the rooms These school sets are exchanged sometimes twice a month, but usually once a term, the interval being fixed by the teacher

"In this way books dealing with history, geography and biography have been made popular subjects of reading among the school children of Van Wert county Nature studies and easy scientific books are also in demand, while fairy tales, myths and legends provide the children with an enjoyable introduction to literature

"Occasionally members of school boards object to the introduction of library sets into the schools, on the ground that the children should give all their time to textbooks and the study of the three R's However, it is the experience of a number of teachers that this supplementary reading has resulted in better schoolroom discipline and an increased interest in such subjects as geography and United States history

"The work of the school library department of the Brumback library is now broadening in an unexpected direction, for the parents of school children are coming more and more to borrow from these loan collections, as well as from the formally constituted branch libraries Thus Van Wert county provides that the whole world of books is brought to the very doorsteps of the remotest farmstead in its borders by a clearing house system of libraries which Commissioner Claxton wishes to see in equally successful operation throughout the United States."

Ellen Perlena (Purmort) Brumback is a member of the M. E. Ch. and lives at Van Wert, O., now in her 80th year. She preserves much of the beauty that distinguished her in younger years, and has a clear recollection of her eventful life.

Children (4):

[D263] + Orville Sanford⁶, *b* Dec. 2, 1855.
[D264] + David La Doyt⁶, *b* July 30, 1861.
[D265] + Estella⁶, *b* April 14, 1863.
[D266] + Saida May⁶, *b* Dec. 24, 1870.

[D96] CATHARINE⁵ BRUMBACK, ([D27] David⁴, same ancestry as
[D91]) *b* Feb 1, 1833; *d* June 19, 1901; June 4, 1854, at Ashley, O., *m Levi
Meredith*, *b* July 25, 1829, *d* March 10, 1895, s *Jesse Meredith*, lived in Van
Wert, O

> *Son, surname Meredith*
> i Bion Le Vaughn⁶, *b* July 30, 1857, *d* April 30, 1893, Oct. 6, 1880,
>   *m Daisy Upham*, *b* Feb 28, 1861; *d* April 16, 1902, lived in Van
>   Wert, O
> *One daughter.*
> (1) Catharine⁷, *b* Aug 19, 1881, March 7, 1904, *m Frank E. Harter*,
>   Norwalk, O

[D97] RICHARD THOMAS⁵ BRUMBACK ([D32] John⁴, [D10]
Henry³, [D3] Henry², [D2] Widow¹ Brumbach) *b* Feb. 5, 1825, *m* (1) *Elizabeth Keyser*, dau Col. *Andrew Keyser* of Page Co , Va , who *d* Feb., 1904,
Richard⁵ *m* (2) *Susan (Keyser) Rothgeb*, widow of *Abraham Rothgeb* and
dau of *William Keyser*, ad Rileyville, Page Co., Va., R R.

"The father and Thomas William live in their lovely home near Rileyville, which commands a charming view of the historic Shenandoah River
Richard is a Regular, or Burnam Baptist; will be 87 on Feb. 4, and is remarkable for one of his age."

> *Children by 1st m* (5).

[D267] + John A⁶, *b* Jan. 21, 1850.
[D268] + Henry⁶, *d* age 2½ yrs
[D269] + Emma P⁶, *b* Sept 9, 1852
[D270] + Mary E.⁶, *b* Aug 15, 1854
[D271] + Frank C.⁶, *b* March 13, 1858.

> *Child by 2d m*

[D272]   Thomas William⁶, unm., at home.

[D98] DAVID HERSHBERGER BRUMBACK, M D. ([D32] John⁴,
same ancestry as [D97]) *b* April 28, 1827, in Page Co., Va ; Oct 4, 1854,
m Ann Eliza⁵ Grove, *b* June 30, 1836, and *d* Aug., 1888; dau *Emanuel* and
Frances⁴ (Brumbach) Grove [D42-11] and sister to *John William⁵ Grove*

[D42-vi], who *m Laura Ann⁵ Brumback* (D224], as his 2d w. [See D10—
"Grove Families in Va."] Dr. Brumback was educated in the Academy at
Luray, Va., attended Jeff. Med Coll. Sept., 1858, to Dec, 1859, then went to
Va. Med. Coll, where he graduated (M. D, March, 1860). In Va. he owned
and lived upon the farm adjoining that of [D103] John Benton⁵ Brumback,
M. D. He served as coroner for Page Co

Soon after graduation he moved to Manchester, Tenn, where at first he
farmed, and later became actively interested in the Manchester Manufacturing
Co. (makers of hard wood farming implements) His son-in-law, Thomas
Benton Clark, is sec and treas. of the company and Dr Brumback recently
moved to McMinnville, Warren Co, Tenn.

Children (4)

[D275]   John Ashby⁶, *b* June 18, 1862, *d* July 2, 1862
[D276] + Carrie Lee⁶, *b* May 27, 1864
[D277]   Mary Blanche⁶, *b* March 6, 1866, *d* Sept, 1888
[D278]   Charles Edward⁶, *b* Nov 3, 1868, *d* May, 1869.

[D99] HENRY FRANKLIN⁵ BRUMBACK ([D32] John⁴, same an-
cestry as [D97]) *b* June 5, 1829, *m* (1) *Nannie* ———, moved West in 1853,
1871 *m* (2) *Mrs* ——— *Dewey*, lives in Hamburg, Fremont Co, Iowa.

Reported issue by 2d m (1 dau)·

[D279] Martha W ⁶, *b* 1873, *d*; *m* ——— *Rowe* (1 ch).

[D100] MARY ELIZABETH⁵ BRUMBACK ([D32] John⁴, same an-
cestry as [D97]) *b* Feb. 1, 1832, June 10, 1847, *m Martin Biedler* of Page
Co., Va., *b* Feb. 11, 1821: *d* June 6, 1890, *s Ulrich* and *Barbara* (*Varner*)
Biedler; Mary⁵ survives him; ad. Stanley, Page Co, Va.

Children (7), *surname Biedler*

  i Edward⁶, *b* May 24, 1856, Nov, 1883, *m Ida V Zirkle,* of New Mar-
    ket, Va.
 ii Lizzie B.⁶, *b* Aug 8, 1861, Nov 10, 1881, *m Walter Smith,* of New
    Windsor, Md.

    Children (2), *surname Smith·*

    (1) Claude V.⁷, *b* Aug, 1885
    (2) Ruth Anna⁷, *b* Jan. 28, 1889.

iii H. Walter⁰, *b* Dec. 24, 1865
 iv Mattie V.⁶, *b* March 1, 1868, Feb 27, 1889, *m Wm F Jones,* of N Y.
  v Lester L ⁶, *b* June 13, 1871
 vi Mary I ⁶, *b* Jan 26, 1874
vii Annie May⁶, *b* Sept 3, 1877; *m* [D289]+ *Edward Gibson⁶ Brumback,
    M. D.*

[D101] ANN ELIZA⁵ BRUMBACK ([D32] John⁴, same ancestry as [D97]) *b* April 16, 1834; Feb. 14, 1859, *m James B. Hudson*, widower, since *d*, ad. Luray, Page Co, Va.

    Children (3), *surname Hudson*

  i John Russell⁶, *b* Dec. 7, 1859, *d* June 12, 1863.

  ii James E.⁶, *b* Oct. 20, 1868; *d* Oct 25, 1868

  iii Edmonia M.⁶, *b* Oct 16. 1874; *d* 1885 (typhoid fever), member and organist of New Sch Bap Ch.

[D102] FRANCES AMANDA⁵ BRUMBACK ([D32] John⁴, same ancestry as [D97]) *b* May 1, 1837; *m Judah Forrer*, of Page Co., Va, who *d* 1875.

    Children (3), *surname Forrer*

  i Frank⁶, *m* and lives near Luray, Va. (8 ch alive)

  ii Catharine⁶, *m Samuel Walton*, atty, Luray, Va. (2 ch.) · Miriam⁷ and Lynn⁷.

[D103] JOHN BENTON⁵ BRUMBACK, M. D ([D32] John⁴, same ancestry as [D97]) *b* Nov. 20, 1839, graduated from Med. Coll of Va (M D, 1861), and continues in the practice of his profession (Reg), living four miles north of Luray, Va, member Bap Ch. At Luray, Va., on April 30, 1861, he was *m* by Eld. John W Watson to *Virginia Grayson*, dau Eld. *Frank* and *Elizabeth (Coffman) Grayson* Ad. Luray, Va., R. R. No. 1

    Children (11)

[D283] + Mary Lizzie⁶, *b* Aug. 10, 1862, *d* Aug 25, 1895.

[D284] + Minnie⁶, *b* 1864; *d* March 2, 1888.

[D285] + Emma Gertrude⁶, *b* March 5, 1866.

[D286] + Annie Grayson⁶, *b* March 7, 1868.

[D287] + John Franklin⁶, *b* May 7, 1870

[D288] + Kate⁶, *b* Aug 6, 1871

[D289] + Edward Gibson⁶, M. D, *b* March 6, 1874.

[D290]   Estelle⁶, *b* April 21, 1877; *d* July 27, 1892.

[D291] + Roscoe Conklyn⁶, *b* July 12, 1878; *d* Dec. 31, 1907.

[D292] + Robley Dunghson⁶, *b* Jan. 19, 1880

[D293]   Margaret⁶, *b* July 27, 1885, *m* [D426 + *Vernon M.⁷ Brumback*.

[D104] EDWARD TRENTON⁵ BRUMBACK ([D32] John⁴, same ancestry as [D97]) *b* April 8, 1842, Nov 21, 1872, *m Lucy Gertrude Lauck*, *b* Dec. 4, 1849, dau of the late Eld *William Cunningham* and *Eliza Jane (Sowers) Lauck*. The latter was dau of *James Sowers*, who served as Col in

the War of 1812, and the former (Wm) was s of *Peter Lauck*, who served as
Capt in the same war   Edward⁵ was educated in the pub. schs , bought and
lives on the farm eight miles from Luray; is pres. Farmers and Merchants
Bank of Stanley. His wife was also educated in the pub. schs. and at Wesleyan Female Institute, Staunton, Va.   She has shown much interest and
assisted in gathering information for this publication   The family are members of the Primitive or Old Sch Bap Ch ; ad " Mountain Home," Stanley,
Page Co , Va , R F. D. 2

    Children (9) ·

[D295] + John William⁶, *b* Dec 14, 1873
[D296]   Harry Lee⁶, *b* Sept. 29, 1875 , *d* March 11, 1879.
[D297] + Theodore Lauck⁶, *b* Oct. 17, 1877.
[D298]   Frank Edward⁶, *b* Oct. 3, 1879 , *d* Jan. 3, 1887.
[D299] + Mary Eliza⁶, *b* Sept 16, 1881
[D300]   Mattie Elizabeth⁶, *b* Dec 8, 1883 ; *d* Dec. 10, 1886 (diphtheria).
[D301]   Charles Correll⁶, *b* March 1, 1886 , *b* March 8, 1893 (pneumonia).
[D302] + Emily Gertrude⁶, *b* Dec 13, 1887.
[D303]   Adelia May⁶, *b* March 16, 1892 , unm., at home

    [D105] MARTHA WASHINGTON⁵ BRUMBACK ([D32] John⁴, same
ancestry as [D97]) *b* Dec. 25, 1847 , Nov 9, 1875, m (1) *Benjamin F. Grove*,
who *d* Feb 27, 1881 (tuberculosis) ; s *Joseph* and *Catharine Grove* [see D10—
" Grove Families in Va "]   Dec. 12, 1889, Martha⁵ *m* (2) *David E. Almond*,
s *Mann* and *Barbara Almond* of Luray, Va.. they lived 3 miles south of Luray,
in Hawksbill Valley, Page Co , Va. (One ch d y) Martha⁵ recently *m* (3)
John W Stover, bro of *Joseph F. Stover* [see D42-iv] ; res. 3 miles s. of
Luray, Va One ch by 2d *m* , *d*

    [D158] WILLIAM HENRY⁵ BRUMBACK ([D36] Samuel⁴, [D10]
Henry³, [D3] Henry², [D2] Widow¹ Brumbach) *b* 1834 near Luray, Page
Co , Va., 1859 *m Mary Susan Huffman*, *b* at Luray, 1837 , dau *Joseph* and
Mary Susan (*Hershberger*) *Huffman*   William⁵ *d* at Middletown, Frederick
Co , Va , 1906, and his w *d* at the same place in 1907 ; farmer , Dem , memb.
Prim Bap Ch.

    Children (11) :

[D325]   Elizabeth E.⁶, *b* 1860.
[D326]   Joseph S ⁶, *b* 1862 , *m Lizzie Hershburger*.
[D327]   Susan⁶, *b* 1864 ; *d* 1869
[D328]   J William⁶, *b* 1866 , *m Bessie Burner*.
[D329]   Edwin⁶, *b* 1868 , *d* 1877.

[D330]   Henry W⁶, *b* 1870, *m Annie Huffman.*
[D331]   Frank H.⁶, *b* 1872, *m Mary Gander.*
[D332]   Herbert V⁶, *b* 1874, *m Dora Harmer.*
[D333]   + Charles Irvin⁶, *b* 1876, *m Daisy R. Hite*
[D334]   Ella M.⁶, *b* 1878; *d* 1907
[D335]   Robert E⁶, *b* 1880.

[D218] THOMAS BENTON⁵ BRUMBACK ([D39] Jacob⁴, [D10] Henry³, [D3] Henry², [D2] Widow¹ Brumbach) *b* March 4, 1838, at Plymouth, Hancock Co, Ill, and *d* there April 18, 1894, farmer, Dem., baptist. He *m* in 1861 *Abigail Daniels Southwick, b* April 24, 1835, at Minden, Mass.; dau *Berruc* and *Mary (Fowler) Southwick.*

    Children (5):
[D350]   + Arthur Henry⁶, *b* March 31, 1862.
[D351]   Mary⁶, *b* 1864; *d* 1866
[D352]   Lewis Lee⁶, *b* 1866, *d* 1871.
[D353]   Infant, *b* and *d* 1868
[D354]   Jacob, *b* 1870, *d* 1871.

[D219] HENRY PENDLETON⁵ BRUMBACK ([D39] Jacob⁴, same ancestry as [D218]) *b* March 14, 1840, at Plymouth, Hancock Co, Ill, *d* at the same place June 27, 1900   He was a farmer, Dem, and member Primitive Bap. Ch   Sept. 23, 1861, he *m Susan Kendall, b* June 2, 1841, near Plymouth, Ill, dau *Henry* and *Isabel (Lionberger) Kendall*   Susan *d* April 21, 1911, and was buried at Providence Cem., near Plymouth, Ill.

    Children (3)·
[D355]   Emma Ella⁶, *b* Aug. 13, 1862; *m* [D257]+ *Charles Daniel Brumback.*
. [D356]   + David Benton⁶, *b* April 26, 1865, *m Susan R McAfee.*
[D357]   + Jennie Laura⁶, *b* March 26, 1868, *m Wentworth Lee Irwin, M.D.*

[D220] MARY ELLEN⁵ BRUMBACK ([D39] Jacob⁴, same ancestry as [D218]) *b* June 4, 1842, *m* Sept. 14, 1862, *Bolivar Roland Cannon,* farmer, lives in Hancock Co., Ill

    Children (7), *surname Cannon*
  i   Walter E., *b* Jan. 31, 1864
  ii   Emma L., *b* Dec 12, 1867, *m Dr D. W Owens.*
  iii   Nannie Lulu, *b* Aug 6, 1869; *d.*
  iv   Ella A, *b* March 11, 1871, *m D. M. Johnson.*
  v   Abbie E., *b* Sept 24, 1872; *m J. C. Fleming.*

vi   Vernie L., *b* Jan. 18, 1875, *m J. C. Botts.*

vii Ruth Edna, *b* May 24, 1879, *m Asa Hamilton*

[D222] EMILY ELIZABETH[5] BRUMBACK ([D39] Jacob[4], same ancestry as [D218]), *b* July 31, 1846; *m John Wiatt Lewis.* Emily is reported to be living in Corder, Lafayette Co , Mo., and the children to be in Okla.; no replies.

Children (6), surname Lewis:

Nancy[6], Laura, Henry, Neal, Benton, Elizabeth.

[D224] LAURA ANN[5] BRUMBACK ([D39] Jacob[4], same ancestry as [D218]) *b* Feb 12, 1851, near Carthage, Hancock Co., Ill.; April 20, 1880, *m John William[5] Grove* [D42-vi] *b* at Luray, Page Co., Va., Dec. 16, 1844, as his 2d w [a] Mr. Grove is s *Emanuel* and *Frances[4]* (*Brumback*) *Grove* [D42]. [See also D98 and D10—" Grove Families in Va "] Mr Grove and his bro. Charles Henry[5] [D42-viii] conduct a general merchandise store, " Grove & Bro.," at Luray, Va The former, his wife, and s *Capt. Arthur Ashby[6] Grove*, have shown much interest in securing facts for this publication.

Children (4), surname Grove:

i   Arthur Ashby[6], *b* April 5, 1883.

ii   Jessamine Lee[6], *b* Nov. 25, 1887.

iii Harold Elton[6], *b* Feb. 1, 1889.

iv   Julia Anita[6], *b* July 6, 1892.

[D231] JEFFERSON[5] BRUMBACK ([D30] John[4], [D8] John[3], [D3] Henry[2], [D2] Widow[1] Brumbach) *b* in Licking Co., O , Feb. 7, 1829, being the oldest of eleven children he grew up as a country farm lad, attending the public schools until he entered Denison University (O), graduating in 1852, read law in the office of Lucius Case at Newark, O , and upon admission to the bar in 1854 he began the practice of his profession in the same place.

Oct. 18, 1859, Jefferson[5] *m Catharine Fullerton,* *b* Oct. 29, 1834, in Licking Co., O. , *d* Jan. 31, 1880; dau *Franklin* and *Elizabeth Fullerton.*

In 1862 he actively assisted in raising the 95th O. Vol. Inf. and became its Maj. (19 Aug , 1862) , its Lt Col. (19 Aug., 1863) , Brig. Gen. of Vols (13 March, 1865) " for gallant and meritorious service during the war "; served with that regiment until mustered out, Aug. 14, 1865. Member G.A R. and Loyal Legion, Kans. Commandery.[b]

" At the battle of Richmond, Ky , Aug 30, 1862, he was badly wounded

---

[a]Children by 1st m are given under [D42-vi] p 292.

[b]Hist. Reg. & Dic. U S A from Org Sept. 29, 1789, to March 2, 1903—Francis B. Heitman, 1903 2 vols.

and taken prisoner, but was soon paroled and exchanged in the spring of 1863, when he engaged again actively in military service. He took part in both captures of Jackson, Miss., in 1863, and his regiment was among the forces that besieged Vicksburg, which was captured July 4, 1863 Much of the year 1864 the regiment had headquarters at Memphis, Tenn., and was engaged in the battles of Guntown and Tupelo Afterward the regiment constituted part of an infantry force, which, under the command of Gen. A J Smith, pursued Gen. Price and his army through Ark. and Mo during their raid north in 1864. The infantry forces to which Col Brumback's regiment was attached then went to Nashville, Tenn., where the regiment was engaged in the two days' battle in Dec, 1864, which resulted in the defeat of Gen Hood's army. The Confederate army under Gen. Hood having been badly disorganized after the defeat and having left that section, the 95th O , with other troops, went to Mobile, Ala There the regiment aided in capturing the forts above the city in the early part of 1865, while Grant and Sherman were delivering the final blows against the armies of Lee and Johnston. When Lee and Johnston surrendered, the 95th O. was in central Ala and in due time was transported to Columbus, O , where it was paid off and disbanded Col. Brumback commanded the regiment much of the time while it was in service, and he and his men endured many of the hardships and trials incident to active warfare.

After quitting the army Col Brumback resumed the practice of law at Newark, O. In 1866 he was elected judge of the court of common pleas for the district, which included Licking Co He filled the office until he resigned in 1869 to settle in Kansas City, Mo , where he practiced his profession until May, 1900, when he retired. He served the city one term as alderman and several terms as city counselor He was (a Repubn) never active as a politician He preferred to be studious and painstaking in his profession, and to deserve respect and confidence for good work as a lawyer.[a]

" As a lawyer he stands among the most eminent in the state and has been interested in numerous cases requiring the utmost skill and ability."   .
" His life has been an honorable and upright one, characterized by the faithful performance of every duty of both public and private life."[b]

Judge Brumback spent considerable time traveling throughout Va gathering data for a history of his immediate family line, and, after the interchange with the compiler of numerous letters and summaries of work, an intended meeting in Washington, D C , was prevented by his sudden death June 22, 1907. The compiler acknowledges his indebtedness for the excellent and careful foundation work done by the late Judge Brumback, which has been incorpor-

[a]Encyclopædia of the History of Mo —Howard L. Conrad, Vol I, p 406
[b]A memorial record of Kansas City and Jackson Co , Mo , 1896, p 650-652

ated into the early part of Section D, but in a greatly enlarged and altered form. After years of search, an excellent photograph of that co-worker was found through the active assistance of another co-worker,[*] and it is reproduced to perpetuate the memory of those strong, kindly, and rugged features His biography has been gathered from the known published articles, as his death occurred before he furnished the facts pertaining to himself and immediate family.

Children (5):

[D362] + Frank Fullerton[6], *b* Oct. 3, 1860.
[D363] + Hermann[6], *b* May 1, 1862.
[D364] John Dixon[6], *b* May 3, 1867; *d* Oct 5, 1867.
[D365] Margaret Sophia[6], *b* May 13, 1868; *d* Aug 9, 1872
[D366] William Arthur[6], *b* Feb 23, 1872.

[D232] MARY ANN[5] BRUMBACK ([D30] John[4], [D8] John[3], [D3] Henry[2], [D2] Widow[1] Brumbach) *b* on the farm in Licking Twp., Licking Co , O., July 18, 1831, educated in the country school, graduated June 22, 1859, from the Granville (O) Female College, taught school for some years, was one of the early advocates of " woman's rights " and an active worker in the Baptist Ch. and S.S ; unm ; *d* Jan. 10, 1879

[D233] JEREMIAH[5] BRUMBACK ([D30] John[4], same ancestry as [D231]) *b* on farm in Licking Twp , Licking Co., O , Sept 16, 1833; educated in the country school on his father's farm, through soph yr in Denison Univ , Granville, O , grad. from Franklin College, Franklin, Ind , in 1856, prof. of math. about 8 yrs in Franklin Coll. , studied law and grad. in same in Indianapolis, Ind ; practiced law in Indianapolis about 2 yrs. and in Boise, Idaho, from 1866 for about 30 yrs ; member Idaho legislature 188–; also lived in McMinnville, Ore.

" Few, if any, of the graduates of Franklin College have possessed better natural talents than Prof. Brumback, and his scholarship was of a high order His mind had a strong and rigorously analytical cast."[b] He is a Dem. , member Bap. Ch., and led a retired life, being with his son, Arthur Marion[6], in Granville, O , until his *d*, Jan. 6, 1912.

Dec. 19, 1856, at Franklin, Johnson Co , Ind., he *m Harriet Maria Graves, b* Dec 10, 1833, at Sunderland, Mass. (No. 1346, Graves Genealogy) , dau *Ashley* and (2) *Jemima* (*Gunn*) *Graves.* Harriet *d* Jan. 21, 1900, at McMinnville, Ore., and was bur. at Boise, Idaho.

---

[*]Hon Orville Sanford Brumback [D263], Toledo, O
[b]History of Franklin College, in which his s Arthur Marion[6] Brumback has also taught for years.

Children (3)

[D367] + Virgil Jefferson⁶, *b* June 15, 1858; unm

[D368]   Mary Ella⁶, *b* June 1, 1867; *d* July 27, 1868

[D369] + Arthur Marion⁶, *b* Dec 7, 1869

[D234] AMANDA⁵ BRUMBACK ([D30] John⁴, same male ancestry
as [D231]) *b* on the farm in Licking Twp , Licking Co , O , July 1, 1831;
educated in the country school, graduated with her sister Mary Ann⁵ on June
22, 1859, from Granville (O) Female College; taught school for a number of
years, an active worker in the Baptist Ch. and S.S., unm , *d* July 10, 1884,
when living with her father at Woodland, near Jacksontown, 5 miles S of
Newark, O.

[D235] HENRY⁵ BRUMBACK ([D30] John⁴, same male ancestry as
[D231]) *b* on the farm in Licking Twp., Licking Co , O , March 28, 1840;
educated in the common school and in Denison Univ , from which he grad. in
1863; read law at Newark, O , and was admitted Dec., 1865, by the Supreme
Court of O. to practice law, in the fall of 1866 he located at Mount Vernon,
Lawrence Co , Mo , and by thorough and exhaustive attention to the practice
of his profession, throughout more than 40 yrs he was a leader in that section
of Mo. and was widely known as an able, energetic and faithful advocate.
While a Dem he has never been a partisan, and has never sought political
preferment. He has always taken an active interest in the upbuilding of his
country, and in his active days was in the forefront of all tending to its progress. He was especially generous and helpful to worthy young men, and especially to those just starting in the practice of law By frugality and industry he acquired a competency, and retired from active practice of law about
1909 and is passing his well earned years of rest at his home in Mt Vernon,
Mo. He there enjoys the esteem of his countrymen, merited through a long,
upright and honorable life in their midst

The excellent photograph and other biographical matters concerning
Henry⁵ [D235], and others in this portion of the publication were furnished
by Mr Charles Leonard Henson, see [D372].

March 14, 1872, Henry⁵ *m* (1) *Sarah Elizabeth de Mary*, *b* Sept. 23,
1837; dau *Solomon Rand* and *Nancy Frost de Mary.* Sarah *d* July 16, 1890,
at Granville, O., and was interred in the Maple Grove Cemetery Sept. 3, 1894,
Henry⁵ *m* (2) *Ella S. Scroggs*, *b* March 26, 1856; dau *William Lee* and *Leah
Caroline Scroggs*

---

*This name is also written Demary.

Children by 1st m (3).

[D370] $+$ Ernest de Mary[6], M D , *b* Nov 5, 1873

[D371]   Nellie Mabel[6], *b* May 28, 1875, *d* Nov. 19, 1884

[D372] $+$ Grace de Mary[6], *b* July 9, 1876.

[D236] ELIZABETH[5] BRUMBACK ([D30] John[4], same male ancestry as [D231]) *b* May 28, 1842, on the home farm in Licking Twp , Licking Co., O.; educated in the country school and graduated June 28, 1864, from Shepherdson College, Granville, O —grad essay, "Who Shall be Crowned?"

Aug. 16, 1864, *m Thomas W. Powell, D D., b* Sept. 12, 1836 at Chesterville, O.; s *Moses* and *Sarah* (*Jones*) *Powell* Mr Powell grad from Denison Univ. (A.B 1863; A M 1866; D D 1890) He also grad (Class '65) from Colgate Theo Sem , Hamilton, N Y He has devoted his life to the ministry of the Baptist Ch. and has published " Half Hours with The Christ," etc. His w has been an efficient helper in her husband's pastorates , res. 3752 Maple Sq Ave., Chicago, Ill.

Children (5), *surname Powell.*

i   Russell Brumback[6], *b* June 28, 1865.

ii Laura Grace[6], *b* March 1, 1868; March 21, 1889 *m Francis L. Fowler,*
    b Aug 16, 1860. One son: (1) Leon Powell[7], *b* Dec. 9, 1889.

iii Ella May[6], *b* April 25, 1870.

iv Chester Hoyt[6], *b* May 11, 1878.

v   Chalmers Lucas[6], *b* Dec. 9, 1879.

[D237] ARTEMISIA[5] BRUMBACK ([D30], same male ancestry as [D231]) *b* June 17, 1844, on the farm in Licking Twp., Licking Co., O ; educated in the common school; grad. June, 1866, from Shepherdson College, Granville, O , being class valedictorian, taught thirteen years, eleven of which were in Young Ladies' Institute (Almira College), Greenville, Ill

Jan. 18, 1879, *m David Webster Winter, b* Nov. 24, 1849 , s *Christopher* and *Margaret* (*Legg*) *Winter*. In 1881 Artemisia[5] and her husband began the study of medicine at Cincinnati Medical College (O), graduating 1883, Aug. 6, 1883, they opened their office in Newark, Licking Co., O , where they practiced medicine until 1896. In the latter year failing health caused Artemisia[6] to retire. She and her husband live upon their fruit farm about 3 miles S. E. of Newark, O., ad. Route 1. (No ch)

[D238] REBECCA[5] BRUMBACK ([D30] John[4], same male ancestry as [D231]) *b* March 29, 1847, on the farm in Licking Twp., Licking Co , O.; common school education and 3 yrs in Shepherdson College, Granville, O., and

also spent some time in the study of medicine; taught school for some years; since the *d* of their father [D30] John[4] in June 1899, the sisters, Rebecca[5] and Marietta[5], have successfully managed the home farm of 178 acres and they together live in the old home; Baptist, unm., ad Thornville, Perry Co, O, R.R No 5.

[D239] MARIETTA[5] BRUMBACK, M D. ([D30] John[4], same male ancestry as [D231]) *b* June 19, 1849, on the home farm in Licking Twp., Licking Co, O.; educated in the common school, graduated June 28, 1876, from the Young Ladies Institute, Granville, O., and also from Homeopathic Hosp Coll, Cleveland, O —M D March 27, 1889, but never sought to practice medicine She cared for her father until his *d* in 1899, and resides with her sister Rebecca[5] upon the home farm, which they jointly manage; member Bap. Ch., unm ; ad. as noted above

[D240] ELMA[5] BRUMBACK ([D30] John[4], same male ancestry as [D231]) *b* Oct 16, 1851; *d* Jan. 3, 1869. "She had an unusual character, was a great reader of standard works, a poet; and a friend alike to the infirm, the aged, and those in all walks of life who came within her circle of influence."

[D241] NEWTON N.[5] BRUMBACK, A M, M D ([D30] John[4], same male ancestry as [D231]) *b* on the home farm in Licking Twp., Licking Co, O., March 10, 1854, spent early years on the farm; attended public school; received A B. from Denison University in 1878, A.M. from same in 1881; M D. from Iowa State University, 1883; practiced medicine Grinnell, Ia., Beatrice, Neb, and Denver, Colo (Hom.), in addition to medicine, also engaged in other lines of business.

·While at Beatrice, Neb, owned much land in Nebraska and Kansas; laid out five additions to the town; built many houses, an electric railway and an electric lighting and power plant, was alderman for six years

While living in Denver, he incorporated the Eden Irrigation and Land Company of Wyoming, securing irrigation water rights from the state for 206,000 acres and segregation rights from U. S. Government, under the Cary Act, for 100,000 acres, and financed the enterprise by placing a bond issue of $700,000 Through this enterprise a large area in Fremont and Sweetwater counties has been settled and developed

In 1907 and 1908 he built and has since owned and operated a scenic railway to the summit of Mt. Manitou, Colo., at an elevation of 9500 feet above sea level This road carries each summer from 40,000 to 50,000 pleasure seeking tourists.

He is a firm believer in variety of occupation, claiming that such diversity of occupation contributes to health and happiness In politics he is Repn.; in religious faith a Baptist, is an ardent advocate of women's suffrage, is a total abstainer, even from tobacco in any form, is 6 feet tall, weighs 200 pounds, has dark brown hair, blue eyes, and fair complexion   Res. 1027 Colorado Ave., Colorado Springs, Colo

April 17, 1883, *m Nettie Talbot*, *b* Feb 17, 1861, dau *Samuel Talbot*, Pres. Denison University, and *Mary Elizabeth (Morse) Talbot*   Nettie Talbot graduated from the Young Ladies' Institute, Granville, O, 1880   (Illustration)

> *Children* (4) :

[D373] + Florence May[6], *b* May 30, 1884.

[D374] + Chester Talbot[6], *b* Nov. 18, 1885.

[D375]   Ella Beatrice[6], *b* Jan. 11, 1888, *d* Aug 10, 1897, at Beatrice, Neb.

[D376]   Lillian Vera[6], *b* Sep. 7, 1890, *d* Aug 4, 1897, at Beatrice, Neb.

[D243] JACOB HENRY FRANCIS[5] BRUMBACK ([D40] Joseph[4], [D10] Henry[3], [D3] Henry[2], [D2] Widow[1] Brumbach) *b* Nov. 22, 1839, at the old homestead near Bixley Ferry, Page Co., Va., farmer, Dem., member Old Sch. Bap Ch ; ad Fawcett's Gap, Frederick Co, Va.

Jan. 2, 1873, Jacob[5] *m* (1) *Amanda Jane Copp*, *b* in Shenandoah Co, Va, near Luray, Va , dau *Jacob* and *Rebecca (Huffman) Copp*   Amanda *d* May 31, 1878 [see D244]

Jacob[5] *m* (2) *Victoria Virginia Huffman*, *b* Jan 28, 1846, near Luray, Va., and *d* Dec 18, 1894; dau *Joseph* and *Mary Ann Huffman*

Jacob[5] on March 10, 1897, *m* (3) *Martha Jane Strichler*, *b* March 10, 1849; dau *David J.* and *Rebecca Strickler*.

> *Children* (5) :

[D377] Joseph Milton[6], *b* Nov. 17, 1873, Strasburg, Va.; *m Amanda Corn-well* (3ch.).

[D378] Hubert Lee[6], *b* July 29, 1875, Fawcett Gap, Va.; *m Mary Rebecca Burner.*

[D379] Mary Julia[6], *b* Nov 1, 1876, Hagerstown, Md , *m Barry O. Hershey* (4 ch)

[D380] Lena Rebecca[6], *b* Oct. 25, 1884, Fawcett Gap, Va., *m Joseph David Huffman* (1 ch).

[D381] Anna Christina[6], *b* April 21, 1888, Fawcett Gap, Va.

[D244] JOSEPH BENTON[5] BRUMBACK ([D40] Joseph[4], same ancestry as [D243]) *b* Nov 22, 1842, at Winchester, Frederick Co, Va.; *d* May

5, 1892, and was buried at Woodstock, Shenandoah Co., Va ; farmer, Dem., Baptist. He *m Julia Kate Copp*, *b* 1851 at Woodstock, dau *Jacob* and *Rebecca (Huffman) Copp* [see D243, 1st w].

     Children (5)

[D382] +   Henry Lee⁶, *b* Dec. 24, 1875

[D383] +   Wade Hampton⁶, *b* April 4, 1877

[D384] +   Franklin Holliday⁶, *b* Dec 7, 1878

[D385] +   Earl Copp⁶, *b* July 17, 1882

[D386] +   Joseph Edward, M D, *b* June 15, 1886.

[D246] ISAAC MILTON⁵ BRUMBACK, M D. ([D40] Joseph⁴, same ancestry as [D243]) *b* Sept. 27, 1846, in Frederick Co., Va, educated in private schools, at 25 began the study of medicine and graduated (M D, 1872) from the Richmond Med Coll., has continued in the general practice of medicine and surgery near his place of birth, and is also interested in farming, Dem

    In 1874 Dr. Brumback *m Euphrasia Ellenor Funkhouser*, *b* Aug. 13, 1855, at Fawcett's Gap, Frederick Co., Va., dau *Joseph Edward* and *Martha Ellenor (Harman) Funkhouser*   Ad. Fawcett's Gap, Frederick Co., Va

     Children (10)

[D387] +   Hunter McGuire⁶, *b* Feb. 12, 1875

[D388]   Martha Christina, *b* Sept 17, 1877; *d* June 9, 1884.

[D389]   Lela Bell⁶, *b* Oct 11, 1879.

[D390]   Ada May⁶, *b* Oct 10, 1880; *m Walker William Johnson.*

[D391]   Maud Evelyn⁶, *b* Jan 16, 1884, *d* Oct. 23, 1911; *m Carl King Wright.*

[D392]   Harman Milton⁶, *b* June 21, 1885

[D393]   Ellen⁶, *b* Jan. 13, 1887, *d* Sept 27, 1887

[D394]   Jessie Amelia⁶ *b* May 29, 1889

[D395]   Joseph Byron⁶, *b* Feb. 23, 1894; *d* April 7, 1900.

[D396]   Mary⁶, *b* March 10, 1899, *d* April 13, 1899

[D256] JOSEPH MARTIN⁵ BRUMBACK ([D43] Henry⁴, [D10] Henry³, [D3] Henry², [D2] Widow¹ Brumbach) *b* Oct. 4, 1851; both himself and his sister [D259] Frances Elizabeth⁵ live together near Luray, Page Co., Va. They are afflicted with cataract, and yet have preserved important original records and sent them to the author with the warmest possible words of commendation, expressing the wish that while they will never be able to see the printed result, others may soon enjoy as complete a publication as it may be possible to produce. Possibly no other single incident in the author's long

years of search and compilation has had such a stimulating effect—it has over-
come much experienced indifference where active co-operation would naturally
be expected, and has settled the questions of spelling of the original name, and
of descent in the Va. families.

Joseph[5] joined the Old Style Baptist Ch. of Big Spring, Page Co, Va.,
in 1887, himself and sister received a large farm from their father, which they
rent to others, both unm.; ad Luray, Va., R.R. No. 1.

[D257] CHARLES DANIEL[5] BRUMBACK ([D43] Henry[4], same ancestry as [D256]) *b* March 1, 1854, Oct, 1881, *m* [D355] *Emma Ella[6]
Brumback, b* Aug 13, 1862, dau [D219] *Henry Pendleton[5]* and *Susan (Kendall) Brumback;* farmer, ad. Plymouth, Hancock Co., Ill, R F D (no ch.)

[D263] ORVILLE SANFORD[6] BRUMBACK, A.M, L L B ([D95]
John Sanford[5], [D27] David[4], [D8] John[3], [D3] Henry[2], [D2] Widow[1]
Brumbach) *b* on a farm in Delaware Co, O, Dec. 2, 1855, attorney-at-law,
Toledo, O, and one of the leaders of the Ohio Bar; was thoroughly educated
for his profession, his father sparing no expense to afford him the advantages
of the best educational institutions Finishing his preparatory work in the
Van Wert schools when but sixteen years of age, he matriculated in the classical
course at Wooster University. At the end of his sophomore year Mr Brumback entered the junior class in Princeton University. Throughout the two
years of his work in that institution he maintained the same high standard
of scholarship that had before characterized him, and won for himself such
recognition in the minds of students and faculty alike, that he was chosen one
of ten, out of a class of one hundred and thirty members, to deliver commencement day orations His graduation at Princeton was in the class of 1877, and
his selection to this honor in his class was the more marked by reason of his
being a western man in an eastern institution, where he had only two years
of collegiate work The Princeton faculty granted him the degree of B.A, and
later conferred upon him the degree of M.A.

In the fall of 1877 he entered the College of Law of the University of
Michigan, and in June, 1879, was graduated with the degree of B L. The
following winter he passed the examination necessary for admission to practice
at the Ohio Bar and located in Toledo In 1880 he had so far progressed in
his profession that he felt the time was ripe to open an office of his own and
" hung out his shingle." Ever since he has made his profession the chief concern of his life, and has been so successful that he is recognized as one of the
foremost lawyers in the Northwest, and is retained in cases of great importance,
especially in corporation litigation.

Mr. Biumback is a member of the First Congregational Church of Toledo, and fraternally, socially and in a business way, is identified with the principal local organizations of Toledo   While a student at Woostei he became a member of the collegiate Greek letter fratei nity, Sigma Chi, and having never lost his interest in the order, has made it the means of keeping in touch with colleges and college men.   He has been honored with the office of Grand Consul in the national body of the Sigma Chi, and at the present time is one of the Grand Trustees of the fiaternity.

In politics, Mr. Brumback has ever been a staunch Republican   In 1885 he became a candidate for Representative from Lucas County in the Ohio Legislature.   It was the year when John Sherman was being opposed by John McLean of the *Cincinnati Enquirer* for the United States Senate, and the fight for the legislature was strenuous thioughout the state   For several years Lucas county had been going Democratic so that it was expected its members in the legislature would continue to be Democratic.   Mr Biumback entei ed into the campaign with his characteristic energy, and when the election returns were counted it was found that he had run far ahead of his ticket and was elected, while the other Republican legislative candidates were defeated.   His election was vital as the Republicans had a majority of only one upon joint ballot with which to elect Senator Sherman, and, if Mr. Brumback had not been elected John McLean would have had one majority   Mr. Sherman's election was of national importance, for it was during this term in the Senate for which he was elected that he secured the passage of the celebiated Sherman Anti-Trust Law   1885 was also the year when the Cincinnati election frauds were perpetrated   Mr Brumback served on the legislative committee to investigate the frauds and thei eby made a state i eputation   He sei ved two years (1885-1886) in the legislature, declined a renomination, and has since many times refused to run for public office, believing it unwise to subordinate his profession to a political career

Oct. 26, 1881, at Indianapolis, Ind , Mr Brumback *m Jennie King Carey, b* Oct 15, 1860, in New York City, dau *Simeon B* (*b* Dec. 22, 1820, *d* Aug. 5, 1902) and *Lydia (King) Carey* (*b* Jan 12, 1837, and living in Indianapolis, Ind.).   Mi Carey was a prominent wholesale merchant of New York, and his ancestry appears in the " Carey Memorials "[a]   In 1873 Mr. and Mrs. Carey moved to Indianapolis, Ind., where he became a prominent citizen and conducted a wholesale hardware business until his *d* in 1902

Mrs. Cai ey is a descendant of piominent New England families, her great grandparents being Adjutant Aaron King, and Hannah Mosely, the daughter of Col. John Mosely, who commanded the 3d Hampshire County regiment of

---

[a]Carey Memorials, Farrell & Co., Cincinnati, O., 1874, p. 215.

the Massachusetts Militia in the Revolution   Aaron King was Adjutant to Col Mosely and, as indicated, married his daughter Hannah.   Col Mosely also commanded a company as Captain in the Crown Point Expedition.   Mrs. Brumback is actively interested in the Natl. Soc. D.A.R., and is a member of " Ursula Wolcott " Chapter of Toledo.

Mr. Brumback's interest in the preparation and publication of this volume has been continuous, substantial financially, and encouraging, and the compiler expresses special appreciation for the same.   Himself and wife occupy the beautiful home at 1603 Madison Ave , Toledo, O , herewith shown, where they dispense a delightful hospitality.   Ad. 432-438 Spitzer Bldg , Toledo, O (Illustrations.)

Children (2)

[D410] + Blanche Carey[7], *b* March 4, 1885.

[D411] + Lydia Ellen[7], *b* Dec. 2, 1888.

[D264] DAVID LA DOYT[6] BRUMBACK ([D95] John Sanford[5], same ancestry as [D263]) *b* in Casey, Ill , July 30, 1861, soon after his birth his parents moved to Van Wert, O , where, except for two years' residence in Toledo, he has since resided   He was carefully educated by his father, who thoroughly believed in higher education, and the success in life attained by all his children has demonstrated the wisdom of those views.   David[6] went from the Van Wert High School to Wooster University which he attended for three years, and then took a business course in Eastman's Business College, Poughkeepsie, N Y.

After leaving college Mr. Brumback chose banking for his life work, and, after serving as cashier of The Farmers Bank at Rockford, O , he accepted the position of teller in the Union Savings Bank of Toledo, O.   Here he obtained a valuable experience in the best city methods of banking, and at the end of two years returned to Van Wert to take the position of cashier in the Van Wert National Bank.   He successfully filled this position for nine years, until the *d* of his father, who was president of the bank, when he was elected to the presidency.

Mr. Brumback is recognized as one of the most sterling, reliable and successful bankers of the Middle West   His judgment and foresight are so unerring that he is constantly consulted on the most important financial matters. His honesty and character are so well known that no man in Northwestern Ohio stands higher in public estimation   It is such men who accomplish the great financial success of the American people, for it is upon them that the safety and stability of our financial system depend.   He is a member of the First Presbyterian Church of Van Wert and a progressive Republican, meaning thereby

that he stands foi Republican principles so long as they are best adapted to the national welfare   He has uniformly declined to run for office, having a field so large for activity in his financial career that the honors and emoluments of office do not suffice to draw him away from his life work

Sept. 4, 1889, he *m Elizabeth Adelia Pinkerton, b* Feb 5, 1863; dau *David Clendenen* and *Elizabeth (Pyle) Pinkerton*, members of an old and prominent family residing in McConnellsville, O   Miss Pinkerton was a highly accomplished lady and the union was a most happy one until the *d* of the devoted wife and mother on Jan. 8, 1910 (interred in the family vault at Van Wert, O.).   Three sturdy sons survive the mother to comfort their father. And in them he takes all the customary pride that the Brumbacks take in those who come to perpetuate the name.   The Van Wert National Bank in Van Wert with D. L. D Brumback as president, Ernest I Antrim, his brother-in-law [D266], as vice-president, and John P. Reed, another brother-in-law [D265], as cashier, comes very near being a Brumback institution.   This with other leading institutions in the thriving little city largely controlled by the gentlemen named, and the Brumback Library, places the Brumback family well in the front in that part of the country   (Illustrations.)

Children (3)

[D412] John Sanford[7], *b* June 4, 1892

[D413] David La Doyt[7], *b* Dec 27, 1893

[D414] William Pinkerton[7], *b* Jan 7, 1896.

[D265] ESTELLA[6] BRUMBACK ([D95] John Sanford[5], same ancestry as [D263]) *b* at Van Wert, O., April 14, 1863, *m* Oct. 26, 1886, at Van Wert, O, *John Perry Reed, Jr*, *b* March 18, 1857, s *John Perry* and *Selinda (Leslie) Reed* of Sharon, Mercer Co, Pa   They reside in Van Wert, O, where Mr. Reed is cashier of the Van Wert National Bank, and a prominent capitalist.

Mrs. Reed and her sister [D266] Saida May[6] (Brumback) Antrim are members of " Isaac Van Wart " Chapter Natl Soc D A R. at Van Wert, O. (Illustration)

Children (3), *surname Reed:*

i Richard Brumback[7], *b* Sept 25, 1891.

ii Orville Sanford[7], *b* Feb 26, 1899

iii Ellen Perlena[7], *b* Sept. 18, 1901.

[D266] SAIDA MAY[6] BRUMBACK ([D95] John Sanford[5], same ancestry as [D263]) *b* Dec 24, 1870   Oct. 17, 1899, at Van Wert, O, *m Ernest Irving Antrim*, s *Francis Titus* and *Ann (Kemp) Antrim* of Germantown, Montgomery Co, O.; graduated, A.B, 1889, from De Pauw; A M. 1890 Bos-

ton Univ., Ph D 1897, Gottingen Univ , Germany   They reside at Van Wert, O , where Mr Antrim is a prominent citizen and V.-P. of Van Wert National Bank   Nov , 1911, he was elected member of Ohio Constitutional Convention to represent Van Wert Co   (Illustration.)

[D267] JOHN A⁶ BRUMBACK ([D97] Richard Thomas⁵, [D32] John⁴, [D10] Henry³, [D3] Henry², [D2] Widow¹ Brumbach) b Jan 21, 1850, m Emma Shirley of Shenandoah Co , Va , memb. Bap. Ch , they live 5 miles from his father's farm; ad Rileyville, Page Co , Va., R.F.D

Children (5)
[D420] Harry⁷, m and lives in New Orleans
[D421] Homer⁷, d
[D422] Virgil, m Mabel Hawkins of Pittsburg, Pa.
[D423] Mary
[D424] Carl

[D269] EMMA P.⁶ BRUMBACK ([D97] Richard Thomas⁵, same ancestry as [D267]) b Sept 9, 1852; Nov 6, 1887, m Eld. Benjamin Lampton of Ky., who d Sept 4, 1890 (tuberculosis), both members Old Sch. Bap Ch , ad. Austin, Tex. (No issue)

[D270] MARY E⁶ BRUMBACK ([D97] Richard Thomas⁵, same ancestry as [D267) b Aug 15, 1854, Dec 16, 1880, m Rev. George William Sedgwick, both members M. E Ch , of which he is a minister , ad. Rileyville, Page Co., Va., R F. D

Children (3), surname Sedgwick ·
i William⁷, d.
ii Bessie⁷, m —— Fulton, Charlestown, W. Va
iii Leona⁷, m Theodore Taylor, Washington, D. C.

[D271] FRANK C.⁶ BRUMBACK ([D97] Richard Thomas⁵, same ancestry as [D267]) b March 13, 1858, m Nannie B. Keyser; dau. Capt Harris and Belzora (Kite) Keyser; miller at Sandy Hook, ad Luray, Va , R R 1.

Children (3):
[D426] + Vernon M ⁷; m [D293] Margaret⁶ Brumback
[D427]   Edna⁷ , m Daniel Heiston, Martinsburg, W Va
[D428]   Lynn.⁷

[D276] CARRIE LEE⁶ BRUMBACK ([D98] David Hershberger⁵, [D32] John⁴, [D10] Henry³, [D3] Henry², [D2] Widow¹ Brumbach) b May

27, 1864, March 10, 1890, *m Thomas Benton Clark*, *b* Nov., 1859, in Van-
buren Co., Tenn , latter is sec. and treas. Manchester Mfg Co., Manchester,
Tenn

[D283] MARY LIZZIE[6] BRUMBACK ([D103] John Benton[5], M D.,
[D32] John[4], [D10] Henry[3], [D3] Henry[2], [D2] Widow[1] Brumbach) *b* near
Luray, Va., Aug. 10, 1862, *b* in S Dak Aug. 25, 1895.   July, 1894, *m Dr.
I. S. Weyand.*

[D284] MINNIE[6] BRUMBACK ([D103] John Benton, M D , same
ancestry as [D283]) *h* 1864, *d* March 2, 1888, *m Rev Jacob E Shenk.*

[D285] EMMA GERTRUDE[6] BRUMBACK ([D103] John Benton,[5]
M.D , same ancestry as [D283]) *b* March 5, 1866; July 15, 1887, *m* (1)
Campbell Haven, 1889 *m* (2) *A. C. Begley*, res. San Antonio, Tex
        Children by 1st m (3), *surname Haven.*
    i Maxwell[7].
    ii Virginia[7].
    iii Joseph[7]
        Children by 2d m (3), *surname Begley:*
    i Abner[7].
    ii Marguerite[7].
    iii Charlotte[7].

[D286] ANNIE GRAYSON[6] BRUMBACK ([D103] John Benton[5],
M.D , same ancestry as [D283]) *b* March 7, 1868, *m William J Houser*, res.
Brownsville, Cameron Co., Tex.
        Children (3), *surname Houser:*
    i Pauline[7].
    ii Harold[7].
    iii Fred[7].

[D287] JOHN FRANKLIN[6] BRUMBACK ([D103] John Benton,
M.D., same ancestry as [D283]) *b* May 7, 1870, April 10, 1894, *m Lizzie
Bowen;* engaged in mercantile business, Knoxville, Tenn.
        Children (6):
[D445] Frank.
[D446] Louise.
[D447] Mildred
[D448] Roscoe Lee.
[D449] Alfred.
[D450] Benton.

[D288] KATE[6] BRUMBACK ([D103] John Benton[5], same ancestry as [D283]) *b* Aug 6, 1871, *m Walter Tansell Oliver;* atty.; res. Fairfax C. H., Va

> *Children* (4), *surname Oliver.*
> i Louis Benton[7].
> ii Walter Tansell, Jr[7].
> iii Robert Windsor[7].
> iv Catherine Grayson[7].

[D289] EDWARD GIBSON[6] BRUMBACK, M D., ([D103] John Benton[5], M D , same ancestry as [D283]) *b* March 6, 1874, upon the homestead farm 4 miles N of Luray, Va , graduated from Med Coll of Va. (MD , 1897) and has since been actively engaged in the practice of his profession (Reg) at " Hope Mills," Page Co., Va (No P O), where both himself and his father live upon large, productive farms within sight of each other.   He is Dem.; member Bap. Ch , ad Luray, Page Co , Va., R. F. D. 4.

March 3, 1898, Dr. Brumback[a] *m Annie May[6] Biedler, b* Sept. 3, 1877, at Marksville, Page Co., Va., dau *Martin* and [D100] *Mary Elizabeth[5] (Brumback) Biedler.*

> *One son.*

[D455] Edward Gibson[7], Jr , *b* May 7, 1899.

[D291] ROSCOE CONKLYN[6] BRUMBACK ([D103] John Benton[5], M.D , same ancestry as [D283]) *b* July 12, 1878, *d* Dec. 31, 1907; Aug , 1903, *m Flora M. Rothgeb,* the latter and her children live near Luray, Va.

> *Children* (2):

[D456] Benton Abraham[7].
[D457] Paul[7].

[D292] ROBLEY DUNGLISON[6] BRUMBACK ([D103] John Benton[5], same ancestry as [D283]) *b* Jan. 19, 1880; educated in Luray, Va., graded schools, and Univ of Va (L L B , 1903), actively engaged in the practice of law in Alexandria, Va , since 1904, member Alexandria City Council; unm ; ad. Brumback & Bent, Mushback Bldg , Alexandria, Va.

[D295] JOHN WILLIAM[6] BRUMBACK ([D104] Edward Trenton[5], [D32] John[4], [D10] Henry[3], [D3] Henry[2], [D2] Widow[1] Brumbach) *b* Dec 14, 1873, Nov. 8, 1899, *m Minnie Brubaker, b* March 22, 1876, at her home in Luray; dau *John* and *Elizabeth Brubaker,* they live upon a farm 1 mile from his father's farm , ad Stanley, Page Co , Va., R. F. D 2.

---

[a]Dr Brumback furnished considerable family data as this work goes to press.

Children (4) ·

[D460] John Oscar⁷, *b* Feb. 5, 1901.

[D461] Lucy Elizabeth⁷, *b* Aug. 30, 1903.

[D462] David Miller⁷, *b* Sept. 25, 1906, *d* July 3, 1908

[D463] Mary Virginia⁷, *b* May 5, 1909

[D297] THEODORE LAUCK⁶ BRUMBACK ([D104] Edward Trenton⁵, same ancestry as [D295]) *b* Oct 17, 1877, Sept 7, 1910, *m Mae Pittman, b* Sept. 7, 1886; dau. *Reden Edgar* and *Sarah Pittman*, who lived near Tarboro, Edgecombe Co., N. C., live upon the home farm; ad. Stanley, Va., R. F. D

[D299] MARY ELIZA⁶ BRUMBACK ([D104] Edward Trenton⁵, same ancestry as [D295]) *b* Sept 6, 1881; June 1, 1904, *m Reuben Nathan Long, b* Oct. 20, 1877, *s Isaac* and *Carrie Long* (latter dau *Philip Long*) ; ad Stanley, Page Co., Va., R F D. 2

    Children (2), *surname Long*

  i Edward Brumback⁷, *b* Aug 5, 1905.

  ii Reuben Harrison⁷, *b* March 6, 1908.

[D302] EMILY GERTRUDE⁶ BRUMBACK ([D104] Edward Trenton⁶, same ancestry as [D295]) *b* Dec 13, 1887; Oct. 18, 1911, *m Elmo David Long, b* Oct 23, 1886; s *Trenton* and *Anna (Shuler) Long*, 2d cousin to above Reuben Nathan Long; ad Luray, Va , R F D. 1.

[D333] CHARLES IRVIN⁶ BRUMBACK ([D158] William Henry⁵, [D36] Samuel⁴, [D10] Henry³, [D3] Henry², [D2] Widow¹ Brumbach) *b* 1876, near Luray, Page Co , Va , *m Daisy R. Hite* at Lebanon Church, Shenandoah Co., Va , *b* 1878 in that county, dau *Nebraska Douglas* and *Elizabeth (Huffman) Hite*. Mr. Brumback is an implement dealer at Stephens City, Frederick Co., Va.

    Children (3).

[D500] Virginia H.⁷, *b* Dec. 8, 1903.

[D501] Fred Irvin⁷, *b* July 15, 1905

[D502] John Daniel⁷, *b* March 21, 1907.

[D350] ARTHUR HENRY⁶ BRUMBACK, M.D. ([D218] Thomas Benton⁵, [D39] Jacob⁴, [D10] Henry³, [D3] Henry², [D2] Widow¹ Brumbach) *b* March 31, 1862, at Plymouth, Hancock Co., Ill.; attended Carthage (Ill.) Coll , 1878-1882, graduated (M D , 1884) from Coll. of Phys. and

Surg., Chicago, adjunct prof gynecology, Coll. Phys. and Surg (Univ of Ill.), gynecologist West Side Hosp.; member consulting staff Cook Co. Hosp , med. director North Amer Union Ins. Assn., member Chicago Phys. Club, of Ill. Med Soc and of Amer Med. Assn. Dr Brumback is Repn., has resided in Hancock Co , Ill , Kansas City, Mo , and for a number of years has been successfully engaged in the regular practice of medicine in Chicago, Ill., res. 1503 Jackson Blvd ; office 100 State St.

Dr. Brumback m (1) *Rose Greenlief Stud, b* at Moberly, Mo ; *d* July 6, 1886, and bur Plymouth, Ill , dau *Abram Stud.* July 17, 1889, m (2) *Sophia Johanna Wiborg, b* April 27, 1860, at Quebec, Canada; dau *Ole Hansen* and *Lorense (Hookenson) Wiborg*

Child by 1st. m
[D525] Benton Lee[7], *b* July 4, 1886, *d* May 14, 1905.
Child by 2d m:
[D526] Marion Abbie[7], *b* Dec 6, 1891; *d* June 11, 1892

[D356] DAVID BENTON[6] BRUMBACK ([D219] Henry Pendleton[5], [D39] Jacob[4], [D10] Henry[3], [D3] Henry[2], [D2] Widow[1] Brumbach) *b* near Plymouth, Ill , April 26, 1865, Oct 6, 1886 m *Susan R. McAfee, b* Jan. 30, 1859, at Emerson, Marion Co., Mo., dau *Samuel B* and *Henrietta (Wyne) McAfee.* David[6] is a farmer, Dem., member Primitive Bap. Ch ; ad Plymouth, Hancock Co , Ill , R. F. D.

One son:
[D580] Henry McAfee[7], *b* Oct. 14, 1891, *d* Sept 24, 1909

[D357] JENNIE LAURA[6] BRUMBACK ([D219] Henry Pendleton[5], same ancestry as [D356]) m *Wentworth Lee Irwin, M.D., b* 1863; graduated in 1898 from Coll. of Phys and Surgs , Chicago, member Amer Med. Assn.; engaged in active practice of his profession (Reg.) at Plymouth, Hancock Co , Ill.

[D362] FRANK FULLERTON[6] BRUMBACK ([D231] Jefferson[5], [D30] John[4], [D8] John[3], [D3] Henry[2], [D2] Widow[1] Brumbach) *b* Oct. 3, 1860, June 11, 1891, m *Louise Upton, b* Jan. 17, 1868; dau *Charles E* and *Louise (Rackett) Upton;* att'y-at-law, 510 New England Bldg , Kansas City, Mo.

One son
[D600] Jefferson Upton[7], *b* June 9, 1892

[D363] HERMANN[6] BRUMBACK ([D231] Jefferson[5], same ancestry

as [D362]) *b* at Newark, Licking Co , O., May 1, 1862; graduated from the High School, Kansas City, Mo , attended Racine College, 1879-1882, and Hobart College, 1882-1883, graduating A B., admitted to the bar at Kansas City, Mo , in 1885, and has since been actively engaged in the practice of law in that city, except when on the bench, was Police Judge, 1901-1902, and Circuit Judge, Jackson Co , Mo , 1904-1911, Repn., member Protestant Episcopal Ch ; ad 813-816 Scarritt Bldg , Kansas City, Mo

June 30, 1891, *m Charlotte Elizabeth Pratt; b* Sept. 27, 1860, dau *Wallace* and *Adaline (Russell) Pratt.*

One son:

[D601] Theodore Beidell[7], *b* Nov 11, 1894.

[D367] VIRGIL JEFFERSON[6] BRUMBACK ([D232] Jeremiah[5], [D30] John[4], [D8] John[3], [D3] Henry[2], [D2] Widow[1] Brumbach) *b* June 15, 1858, educated at Boise, Idaho, and at West Point Mil. Acad., graduating from the latter 2d Lt. June 11, 1881; retired to homestead, ad Santa, Idaho

" Ind. Idaho Cadet M A 1 July '77 (36) ; 2d Lt. 2 Inf. 11 June '81, 1st Lt. 25 Sept. '90; read. 18 May '93."[*]

[D369] ARTHUR MARION[6] BRUMBACK[b] ([D233] Jeremiah[5], same ancestry as [D367]) *b* Dec. 7, 1869, at Boise, Idaho, educated in the Boise pub. schs., Denison Univ (A B., 1892), Univ of Cal (A.M , 1903); principal of Grace Seminary, Centralia, Wash , 1894-96; prof chemistry and physics McMinnville (Oreg.) Col., 1896-1903, and pres of same 1903-1905, prof chemistry Denison Univ. 1905—. Prof Brumback was supt. S.S , McMinnville, Oreg., 1901-1905, and has been clerk of 1st Bap Ch , Granville, O , from 1910, being quite active in religious work. Ad Denison Univ., Granville, Licking Co., O

June 20, 1893, at Clay Center, Kans , he *m Clara Miranda Tuttle, b* Feb 24, 1867, at Urbana, O ; dau *Jonah Baldwin* and *Alma Mary (Peters) Tuttle.*

One daughter.

[D620] Alma Louise[7], b. April 7, 1894.

[D370] ERNEST DE MARY[6] BRUMBACK, M D. ([D235] Henry[5], [D30] John[4], [D8] John[3], [D3] Henry[2], [D2] Widow[1] Brumbach) *b* Nov. 5, 1873, at Mt. Vernon, Lawrence Co., Mo , where he lived until 1888; attended Denison Univ for several years, grad. (M D) Hahn. Med Col. and Hosp. (Phila) 1899, Repn.; Baptist

[*]Hist. Reg. & Dic. U S.A. from Org Sept 29, 1789, to March 2, 1903—Heitman, G.P O 1903 2 vol
[b]His active assistance in securing information is hereby acknowledged

May 10, 1910, *m Jeanne Guelpa* of Vichy, France; dau *Jacques* and *Louise Guelpa*, ad. 347 W. 34th St., New York, N Y.

[D372] GRACE DE MARY[6] BRUMBACK ([D235] Henry[5], same ancestry as [D370]) *b* July 9, 1876, attended public schools at Granville, O., and later Shephardson College, from which she grad. 1899, and later her degree was reconferred by Denison Univ., Granville, O. Thereafter she spent a yr. in special work at Leland Stanford Univ. June 14, 1905, *m Charles Leonard Henson, b* in Stone Co., Mo., Sept. 27, 1877, s *LaFayette* and *Sarah Frances (Melton) Henson.* Mr. Henson attended the pub schs of Galena, Mo., Marionville, Mo.; Marionville Collegiate Institute, graduated (LL B., 1901) from Univ. of Mo. He entered upon the practice of law Oct. 1, 1902, at Mt. Vernon, Mo., under the firm name of Gibbs & Henson; July 1, 1905, entered into law partnership with [D235] Henry[5] Brumback, elected prosecuting atty. for Lawrence Co., Mo., 1911 for a term of two years. Both his wife and himself have materially assisted in gathering information for this work; members Pres. Ch.; res. Mt Vernon, Mo.

> *One son:*
> i Henry Brumback[7] Henson, *b* Sept 15, 1906

[D373] FLORENCE MAY[6] BRUMBACK ([D241] Newton N—.[5] [D30] John[4], [D8] John[3], [D3] Henry[2], [D2] Widow[1] Brumbach) *b* at Grinnell, Ia., May 30, 1884; 1904 graduated from East Denver High School, and in 1909 from Vassar Coll., teacher of biology and botany in High Sch., Waukegan, Ill.; unm. (Illustration.)

[D374] CHESTER TALBOT[6] BRUMBACK ([D241] Newton N—.[5], same ancestry as [D373]) *b* at Beatrice, Neb., Nov. 18, 1885; mechanical and electrical engineer; sec and asst. mgr. Manitou Incline Ry. Co.; ad. Manitou, Colo. (Illustration)

[D382] HENRY LEE[6] BRUMBACK ([D244] Joseph Benton[5], [D40] Joseph[4], [D10] Henry[3], [D3] Henry[2], [D2] Widow[1] Brumbach) *b* Dec. 24, 1875, at Woodstock, Shenandoah Co., Va.; attended common schools of that county, and those of Woodstock, Va., and a yr. at Mercersburg Acad., worked 7 yrs. in a china store, 7 yrs. with Swift & Co. in Phila.; June 1898 became a commission merchant at 2826-26 Dauphin St., Philadelphia, Pa.; res. 2313 Hagert St. Feb 10, 1904, he *m Viola M. Bockins, b* Oct. 18, 1880, dau *Theodore P.* and *Pauline (Vasche) Bockins*

Children (3)

[D633] Mildred Evelyn[7], *b* Feb 27, 1905
[D634] Viola Hazel[7], *b* Jan 1, 1908
[D635] Marion Estella[7], *b* Jan. 24, 1911.

[D383] WADE HAMPTON[6] BRUMBACK ([D244] Joseph Benton[5], same ancestry as [D382]) *b* April 4, 1877, at Woodstock, Shenandoah Co., Va., salesman with his brother [D382]; res Philadelphia, Pa.

[D384] FRANKLIN HOLLIDAY[6] BRUMBACK ([D244] Joseph Benton[5], same ancestry as [D382]) *b* Dec 7, 1878, at Woodstock, Shenandoah Co., Va.; educated in public schools and at Roanoke College, Salem, Va., and graduated in law course at Wash. & Lee Univ (1908), att'y-at-law; Dem; Baptist. He materially assisted by sending family details for this section.

Oct. 24, 1910, Mr. Brumback, at New Market, Va, *m Emma Jane Crim, b* Nov 25, 1883, dau *John William* and *Eliza (Clinedinst) Crim,* ad. Woodstock, Shenandoah Co, Va.

[D385] EARL COPP[6] BRUMBACK ([D244] Joseph Benton[5], same ancestry as [D382]) *b* July 17, 1882, at Woodstock, Va, has been clerking in Philadelphia, Pa, for several yrs.; *m Lucy Clinedinst,* dau *George Milton* and *Anna Bell Clinedinst*

[D386] JOSEPH EDWARD[6] BRUMBACK, M D ([D244] Joseph Benton[5], same ancestry as [D382]) *b* June 15, 1886, unm.; educated in country schools and at Woodstock, Va., grad. (M.D, 1909) Baltimore Med. Coll.; appointed by State of Va asst. surgeon (1910) at Eastern State Hospital, Williamsburg, Va.

[D387] HUNTER McGUIRE[6] BRUMBACK ([D246] Isaac Milton[5], [D40] Joseph[4], [D10] Henry[3], [D3] Henry[2], [D2] Widow[1] Brumbach) *b* Feb. 12, 1875, at Opequon, Frederick Co., Va, attended Winchester High School, Roanoke College, and Univ. Coll. of Med, Richmond, Va, graduating from latter (M.D, 1900), was resident physician at the Retreat for the Sick, Richmond, Va, and has been in active general practice of his profession since graduation   Ad. Opequon, Frederick Co., Va

Nov 25, 1908, Dr. Brumback *m Nellie Ruth Smith, b* 1886 and *d* March 30, 1909, dau *Otis M.* and *Laura (Crabill) Smith.*

[D410] BLANCHE CAREY[7] BRUMBACK ([D263] Orville Sanford[6], [D95] John Sanford[5], [D27] David[4], [D8] John[3], [D3] Henry[2], [D2]

IMMIGRANT LIST, SHIP NEPTUNE, SEPTEMBER 30, 1754

George Meyer

Johson George Decher

Jacob Berdaing

Georg Michael Vitzthum

Georg Michel Loehr

Johannes Henrich Brumbach [1]

Johan Georg Trazel

Joho Adam X X Michael

Matthias Heinet

Johann Peter Decher

Andreas X Bengel

Gottfried Gebhard

Johsones Schumann

Georg Boltz

Johson Henrich Kurchtal

Johann Thomas Biashanta

Georg Jacob Haussman

Josn Carl Hermsdorff

Hans Adam Beckenhaub

Johsnoes Rebh 20

Frederick X Schneider

Georg Hoffman

Johann Bernhard "Meck"

John Adam X Edelman

Johson Niclaus Hauer

Philip Friedrich Wüenger

Hans Adam Bleier
Daniel X Stegner
Johannes X Hoch
Heory X Klein

Johan Paul Gemberling

Hans Nickel Ensminger

Johan Carl Gemberling

Phillip Wilt

V Brucker

Jacob H W Wylard

Fredrich Pries

Augustus Siegfried Eychler

Jacob X Wylard, Jr

Johsooes X Schober

Philippus X Frey

Christian Rieta

Fillib Wild

Georg Hechler

Eberhard Kriechbaum

Philipp Jacob Fösig

Benedict X Forster

Henry X Shafer

Valentine X Dalik

Christoph X Speck

Philip Dietrig

Peter X Ruhel

Coorad X Wagner

Johann Henrich Schneider

J Adam X Angold

J Henry X Schreier

Valentine Clementz

Christian Huch

Johson Christian Weisenbach

Johann Georg Grundloch

Heorich Cappis

Johannes Riedel

Widow[1] Brumbach) *b* in Toledo, O., March 4, 1885, graduated at Miss Smead's Sch. for girls, that city, subsequently from Vassar College, Poughkeepsie, N. Y. Sept. 19, 1906, she *m Lyman Strong Spitzer* of Toledo, O., *b* Feb. 2, 1880; s *Adelbert Lorenzo Spitzer, b* Aug. 15, 1852, and *Sarah (Strong) Spitzer, b* Aug. 13, 1854

Mr. Spitzer graduated at Yale (A B , 1902) ; member of City Council and banker; ad. 2519 Glenwood Ave , Toledo, O.   (Illustration.)

Two daughters, surname Spitzer:

i Lydia Carey[8], *b* Oct. 7, 1909.

ii Luette Ruth[8], *b* Oct 7, 1911.

[D411] LYDIA ELLEN[7] BRUMBACK ([D263] Orville Sanford[6], same ancestry as [D410]) *b* in Toledo, Lucas Co., O., Dec. 2, 1888; also graduated at Miss Smead's Sch and then attended Castle Sch. at Tarrytown-on-the-Hudson.   June 1, 1910, *m Horace Ethan Allen, b* July 12, 1884 , s *Dr. Horace Newton Allen,* ex-U. S. Minister to Korea, and *Fannie Messenger Allen* of Toledo, O , (descendant of Heber Allen, bro. of Ethan Allen, the Revolutionary hero).   (Illustration.)

Mr. Allen graduated from Mass Inst. of Tech (B S , 1908) ; occupation, asst to gen. mgr. Toledo Ry & Light Co., ad. 2040 Robinwood Ave., Toledo, O

[D426] VERNON M.[7] BRUMBACK ([D271] Frank C [6], [D97] Richard Thomas[5], [D32] John[4], [D10] Henry[3], [D3] Henry[2], [D2] Widow[1] Brumbach) *b* ————; *m* [D293] *Margaret Brumback, b* July 27, 1885 ; they live near Luray, Va.

One daughter.

[D650] Janice[8].[a]

---

[a]Numbering and ancestry follow the male line.

OTHER BROMBACH, BROMBACK, BRUMBACK IMMIGRANTS WHO LANDED AT JAMESTOWN, VA , ABOUT 1770

The following families should apparently be considered in connection with Section D, although they are so widely scattered that it has been impossible to gather further information.

The records of the U. S. Pension Bureau contain affidavits, etc , from Peter and Elizabeth (Simpson) Brumback, and letters were received in 1892 from [F28] John James[4] Bromback, and in 1908 from the latter's son [F49] John James[5] Brumback, which contain certain facts herewith presented as the basis for further search by those who may be interested.

Children (14), *parents' names unknown:*

[F2]	+	Peter, *b* 1768, *d* April 6, 1846.
[F3]		Charles.
[F4]		Paul.
[F5]		William
[F6]		John.
[F7]		Willis
[F8]		Martin.
[F9]		Henry.
[F10]		George.
[F11]		Healthy.
[F12]		Ellen
[F13]		Susan
[F14]		Sarah.
[F15]		Elizabeth.

[F2] PETER[2] BRUMBACK (?) *b* 1768, came from Germany about 1770, landed at Jamestown, Va , and became a blacksmith's apprentice.   In 1776 he left the shop and joined Washington's army, serving 6 yrs. and 7 mos. When peace was declared this wounded colonial patriot settled in Fairfax Co , Va., and resumed his trade of blacksmith. Jan 10, 1788, he *m Elizabeth Simpson* of Loudoun Co., Va , and in 1806 the family moved to Garrett Co., Ky. He *d* in that state April 6, 1846, aged 97 yrs , 11 mos   Excepting Peter[2], the entire family were farmers; were members of the Missionary Baptist Ch ; and it is believed all finally lived in Ky   Peter's own family consisted of 6 sons

*Section E Follows Section F.

and five daughters; the sons served in both the Northern and the Southern armies during the Civil War.

MARRIAGE BOND OF PETER BRUMBACK, JAN. 10, 1788

Loudoun County Sc.

Know all men by these presents that we Peter Brumback and George Harman are held and firmly bound unto his Excellency Edmund Randolph Esq Governor of the Commonwealth of Virginia in the full and just sum of Fifty pounds continental to which payment well and truly to be made to the said Edmund Randolph and his successors in trust for the Said Commonwealth we bind ourselves and each of our heirs and administrators jointly and severally firmly by these presents. Sealed with our seals and dates this 10th day of January 1788.

The condition of the above obligation is such that whereas there is a marriage shortly intended to be had and solemnized between the said Peter Brumback and Elizabeth Simpson spinster of Cameron Parish   Now if there shall be no lawful cause to obstruct the said intended marriage then the above obligation to be void else to remain in force and virtue

PETER BRUMBACK   [SEAL]
GEO. HARMAN   [SEAL]

W. BRONAUGH, JR

(Filed by Clerk of Co. Court)

AFFIDAVITS FILED FOR PENSION

" *Elizabeth Brumback* 20 March 1848, under oath says she is 82 years old and was b in Fairfax Co Va.—then *Elizabeth Simpson.* 2 or 3 years after the close of the Revolutionary War she m. *Peter Brumback* [F2] who d. 6 April 1846. Resided in Fairfax Co. Va. when discharged in 1783 until 1806 when we emigrated from Va. to Ky. and settled in Linkin Co.; moved to Garrett Co., and then to Nelson Co., and then to Shelby Co , then to Campbell Co , Ky., then to Boone and here resided 20 odd years—mother of 12 ch. oldest 62 or 63 yrs."

[F2] " *Peter Brumback,* age 80, Boone Co., Ky., under oath says he entered U. S. A., 3d Dragoons for term of during the war in 1779, served 3 yrs in State of Ga. under Col. Elbert, Maj Stark and Capt Wm Lane. Enlisted 3d Reg, Lt. Dragoons under Col. Wm. Washington in 4th Troop commanded by Capt Parsons and discharged at Winchester in Frederick County, Va. Escaped from British by whom he had been taken prisoner he met with Worthington's Reg. in N. C. in Battle of Cowpens, commanded by Col Mar-

gin (?) then at Jefferson C. H., Gen. Green commander at siege of ninety-six, 2d Battle of Camden, and of Eutaw Springs. Prisoner at Sunbury, in battle wounded in thigh by musket ball. Marched through N C., S. C , and Ga. Wounded a second time in left arm."

MEDICAL EXAMINATION OF PETER BRUMBACK

" State of Ky Scott Co s.s

We Robert M Ewing and M A. Feris do certify that by virtue of annexed commission to us directed that we have carefully examined Peter Brownback who seems to have been wounded by a bullet passing through his right thigh and right Hip   Also wounded in the left arm which appears to have been made by a sword or some cutting instrument.   Also in the head by a similar instrument but slight   We are of opinion that at his present age the wounds totally disable him from making a living by manual labor   Given under our hands this 17th of June 1835.

M. A. FERIS,
ROBERT M. EWING."

Farmer, wife old and helpless and 4 ch.—2 sons 9 yrs. and 7 yrs. and 2 das. 14 and 12 (30 June 1820).

4 horses $75, 2 cows and calves $20, 3 sheep $3, old wagon $30, &c, &c, $100.

Peter Brumback pensioned (No. 12,721) June 20, 1839, Ky. Agcy., at $100 a year from June 7, 1832

Children (11—Nos. [F16 to 26])·

[F 26] + George Washington³, *b* July 4, 1810, *d* Aug 17, 1889.

[F26] GEORGE WASHINGTON³ BRUMBACK ([F2] Peter², [F1] ————) *b* July 4, 1810, 1830 *m Elizabeth Vest*, *b* 1810, dau *Hugh* and *Sarah Vest*, they lived in Boone Co , Ky., until about 1889, when the family moved to Owen Co , Ky , where both the parents *d* in 1889.   George³ *d* Aug. 17, 1889; members Missionary Bap. Ch.

Children (10):

[F27]   Abner Legrand⁴.
[F28] + John James⁴, *b* May 21, 1834.
[F29]   Richard⁴.
[F30]   Henry⁴
[F31]   Thomas Hugh⁴.
[F32]   Mary Elizabeth⁴
[F33]   Artemesia⁴.
[F34]   Sarah Washington⁴.
[F35]   Georgiana⁴.

[F28] JOHN JAMES⁴ BRUMBACK ([F26] George Washington³, [F2] Peter², ————) b May 21, 1834, July 14, 1857, at Cincinnati, O , m (1) *Martha Green*, b May 11, 1834; dau *John* and *Martha Green*, Martha d May 12, 1875   John⁴ m (2) *Nancy Littsel*, who d Feb , 1908, he was b in Boone Co , Ky., and lived there 55 yrs ; 1887 moved to Jackson Co , Ky , and d at Gray Hawk Oct 26, 1899   He was a carpenter, squire for 12 yrs ; owned several large mills and did considerable contracting in grading turn-pikes and railroads , later took up farming near Tyner, Jackson Co , Ky ; d at Gray Hawk, Jackson Co., Ky., Oct 26, 1899.

> *Children from 1st m* (4) ·

[F42]   Frances E ⁵, b Sept 11, 1858, m *John Tool.*
[F43]   Georgie Belle⁵, b March 3, 1862; m *Chas. Henderson*
[F44]   Oscar Dolon⁵, b July 25, 1869; m *Fannie Sloan.*
[F45]   Mattie Rahab⁵, b May 8, 1875, m *William Rigg.*

> *Children from 2d m* (9—4 *more ch. reported*):

[F46]   Hallie Marshall⁵, b March 17, 1876; m *Peter Parmer.*
[F47]   Rachel E ⁵, b Dec. 16, 1877 , m *Theresa Howard.*
[F48]   William Thomas⁵, b March 5, 1881.
[F49] + John James⁵, b April 6, 1883
[F50]   Julia E.⁵, b May 12, 1885.
[F51]   Henderson Lee⁵, b June 28, 1888.
[F52]   Patrick Henry⁵, b May 26, 1891; d
[F53]   Artie M.⁵, b Oct. 15, 1893
[F54]   Ruby F.⁵, b Oct. 12, 1897.

[F49] JOHN JAMES⁵ BRUMBACK ([F28] John James⁴, [F26] George Washington³, [F2] Peter², ————) b at Verona, Boone Co., Ky., April 6, 1883; 1904 m *Martha Metcalf*, dau *Butler* and *Malinda Metcalf*, farmer , Dem ; memb Missy. Bap Ch ; ad. Privette, Jackson Co., Ky.

> *Children* (2):

[F80] Foice⁶, b Sept. 2, 1905.
[F81] William Henry⁶, b Jan. 6, 1908.

THE WAY TO THE FOREST OF ARDEN*

No signboards show which road to take
  To reach its ever-peaceful skies;
Each one must his own journey make
  To find where Arden Forest lies.

For who can tell how far to go,
  There is no book from which to learn;
One may stop here or there, and lo!
  It's gates are just beyond the turn.

The path that leads on straight ahead
  May take on farther from the goal,
And this one which so many tread
  May still perplex and vex the soul

What route to take no one can say,
  'Tis found on neither map nor chart,
Only the joyous find the way,
  Only the kind and light of heart
                    BY OSCAR BRUMBAUGH.

*From The Savings Journal, Washington, D C.

CPSIA information can be obtained
at www.ICGtesting.com
Printed in the USA
BVHW040653190620
581365BV00008B/75

9 781297 533952